RESPONDING TO PROSE

RESPONDING TO PROSE

A Reader for Writers

JUDITH FISHMAN

*Queens College of the
City University of New York*

Bobbs-Merrill Educational Publishing

Indianapolis

Copyright © 1983 by The Bobbs-Merrill Company, Inc.
Printed in the United States of America
All rights reserved. No part of this book shall be
reproduced or transmitted in any form or by any means,
electronic or mechanical, including photocopying, recording,
or by any information or retrieval system, without written
permission from the Publisher:

The Bobbs-Merrill Company, Inc.
4300 West 62nd Street
Indianapolis, Indiana 46268

Copyrights and sources of individual selections and quotations are given
in the Acknowledgements, pages 510–17.

First Edition
First Printing 1983
Text Designer: Madelaine Cook
Acquisitions Editor: James B. Smith
Developmental Editor: Diana C. Francoeur
Manuscript Editor: J. M. Matthew

Cover painting: L'Arlesienne (Madame Ginoux)
by Vincent van Gogh, 1888. The Metropolitan
Museum of Art, bequest of Samuel A. Lewisohn,
1951. (51.112.3)

Library of Congress Cataloging in Publication Data

Fishman, Judith.
    Responding to prose.

Bibliography: p.
    Includes index.
    1. College readers.   2. English language—Rhetoric.
I. Title
PE417.F48   1983   808'.0427   82-24330
ISBN 0-672-61569-X

DEDICATION

For My Parents

Contents

Asterisks in this table of contents mark short stories.

	PREFACE	x
	INTRODUCTIONS	
Chapter 1	**Being Active Readers and Writers**	2
	THE PRIVATE VOICE	
Chapter 2	**Writing for Oneself** ♦ **Journals, Diaries, and Notebooks**	18
	Joan Didion, "On Keeping a Notebook"	22
	F. Scott Fitzgerald, from *The Note-Books*	30
	Dorothy Wordsworth, from *The Grasmere Journals*	33
	May Sarton, from *Journal of a Solitude*	38
	Henry David Thoreau, from the *Journals*	42
	Virginia Woolf, from *A Writer's Diary*	48
	Anne Frank, from *The Diary of a Young Girl*	52
	George Orwell, from *War-Time Diary: 1940*	57

THE WRITER'S FORMS

Chapter 3	**"Once Upon a Time"** ♦ **Narrating**	**68**
	Abraham and Isaac	74
	Aesop, "The North Wind and the Sun"	76
	Bullfinch's Mythology, "Echo and Narcissus"	77
	James Thurber, "The Unicorn in the Garden"	80
	Benjamin Franklin, from *Autobiography*	82
	Philip Slater, "A Modern Fable"	83
	Maxine Hong Kingston, "No Name Woman"	85
	Pearl Rowe, "Cookies at Midnight"	88
	*Ernest Hemingway, "Hills Like White Elephants"	92
	Richard Wright, "The Ethics of Living Jim Crow"	97
	*Grace Paley, "Wants"	100
	George Orwell, "A Hanging"	103
Chapter 4	**"How Do You Get to Route 95?"** ♦ **Procedures**	**110**
	Jean John, "The 'How To' of Terrariums"	118
	Sam Long, "How to Sharpen Knives"	120
	Dick Gregory, "Farewell to Food"	123
	*Kate Chopin, "The Story of an Hour"	132
	Alvin and Heidi Toffler, "The Changing American Family"	135
	George Orwell, "Some Thoughts on the Common Toad"	141
	Muriel Rukeyser, "The Process of Writing a Poem"	145
Chapter 5	**"Why Is the Sky Blue?"** ♦ **Cause and Effect**	**153**
	Jean L'Anselme, "Falling Bricks"	161
	Selma Fraiberg, "Why Does the Baby Smile?"	162
	*Tillie Olsen, "I Stand Here Ironing"	166
	Abraham Lincoln, "The Gettysburg Address"	174
	Richard Wright, "My Library Card"	176
	Ellen Willis, "Memoirs of a Non-Prom Queen"	185

viii Contents

	John Holt, "How Teachers Make Children Hate Reading"	188
	Tom Wolfe, "The Sexed-up, Doped-up, Hedonistic Heaven of the Boom-Boom '70s"	199
Chapter 6	**"What's It Like?"** ♦ **Describing**	**210**
	David Bird, "Two Homeless Persons Adrift in Grand Central"	220
	Barbara Meyer, "A Death Gives Life to Fond Memories"	224
	Richard Selzer, "The Masked Marvel's Last Toehold"	227
	Alfred Kazin, "The Kitchen"	232
	N. Scott Momaday, from *The Way to Rainy Mountain*	238
	Joan Didion, "Some Dreamers of the Golden Dream"	243
	*William Faulkner, "A Rose for Emily"	260
Chapter 7	**"A Horse Is a Graminivorous Quadruped"** ♦ **Defining**	**272**
	Leo Rosten, "Bubeleh/Bobeleh"	280
	Suzanne Britt Jordan, "Fun. Oh, Boy. Fun. You Could Die from It"	282
	Russell Baker, "American Fat"	285
	Robin Lakoff, "You Are What You Say"	288
	E. B. White, "Freedom"	295
	Claude Brown, "The Language of Soul"	300
	*Kurt Vonnegut, Jr., "Harrison Bergeron"	307
Chapter 8	**"Okay, So Give Me an Example"** ♦ **Exemplifying**	**315**
	William Safire, "I Led the Pigeons to the Flag"	323
	Susan Page, "All About Pigeons"	327
	Ira Berkow, "Louis Had Style In and Out of the Ring"	338
	David Marcus, "An Older Brother Lets Go"	341
	*Ring Lardner, "Mr. and Mrs. Fix-It"	344
	Russell Baker, "Summer Beyond Wish"	354
	Mary McCarthy, "Names"	357

Chapter 9	"Jack Sprat Could Eat No Fat" ♦ Comparing and Contrasting	368

Don Bauer, "Wartime in Korea"	377
Russell Baker, "School vs. Education"	379
Nora Ephron, "Reunion"	382
Joe McGinniss, "The Village"	390
*Flannery O'Connor, "Everything That Rises Must Converge"	406
Elisabeth Kübler-Ross, "The Fear of Dying"	421
Loren Eiseley, "The Long Loneliness"	426

THE PUBLIC VOICE

Chapter 10	"I Have a Dream" ♦ Argument	438

Art Carey, "The Boston Marathon: Passing of an American Pastime"	445
Ellen Goodman, "Protection from the Prying Camera"	448
Margaret Mead, "Grandparents Have Copped Out"	451
Lewis Thomas, "To Err Is Human"	454
Robert Paul Smith, "Let Your Kids Alone"	458
Jonathan Swift, "A Modest Proposal"	466
George Orwell, "Politics and the English Language"	475
*Edgar Allan Poe, "The Tell-Tale Heart"	489
Toni Morrison, "Cinderella's Stepsisters"	494
Martin Luther King, "I Have a Dream"	497
THEMATIC TABLE OF CONTENTS	504
ACKNOWLEDGMENTS	510
INDEX	519

PREFACE

The principles that underlie *Responding to Prose* can be stated simply:

- Writers read, and readers write.
- Reading is an active, creative activity. So is writing.
- The acts of writing and reading are complementary.

In each chapter, students are encouraged to read *and* to write. They are offered, in Chapter 1, a view of active reading. They are shown one reader responding to a text; they are encouraged to follow suit, to read closely, to become aware of their expectations of a text, and to allow their *own* particular associations to gather round it.

Chapter 2 encourages students to keep a journal of their own experiences, thoughts, ideas, questions; their responses to a text; their own materials for writing. The selections from writers' notebooks demonstrate that writers keep track of their ideas, experiences, their responses to what they read, in journals and diaries. They often move between private and public voices.

Chapters 3 through 9 introduce forms that writers use—narrating, telling how-to-do something or how something happened, searching after causes, anticipating effects, describing, defining, exemplifying, comparing, and contrasting. The forms are seen as acts of mind, what Wittgenstein calls "forms of life"—those acts of perceiving, construing, and sharing that often move between the concrete and the abstract. They allow us to shape what is "out there" with what is "within." Robert Frost says that a poem is "a momentary stay against confusion." Telling a story, describing a scene about us, contrasting one thing with another, can also bring clarity out of a confusing mass of impressions.

In *Responding to Prose*, the forms are separated out so that we can *distinguish* ways of telling stories, describing, contrasting, and so on. But we must remember that these distinctions are not fixed categories; they are, in fact, arbitrary. We must not *isolate* through analysis, but rather invite our students to see how forms merge and meld. We draw on the forms intuitively because they have become habits of mind, patterns of thought. They are syntheses. As experience becomes more complex and subtle, we synthesize these forms as we need them. Wordsworth offers here a reminder and a warning:

> In weakness, we create distinctions, then
> Deem that our puny boundaries are things
> Which we perceive, and not which we have made.
>
> *The Prelude*

The first form we distinguish is narrative, for telling a story is not only one of the oldest forms of discourse but its features are clearly discernible, as the story moves between what William Labov calls the *narrative core* (the story itself, the chronology) and *evaluation* (the interpreting, the attempting to say what the story means). We tell and write stories to create or strengthen social bonds; we want others to know what has "happened" and what those happenings mean to us.

Underlying instructions for a procedure (how to build a terrarium, how to boil an egg), underlying explanations of cause and effect (the causes and effects of the Civil War) is the narrative form: at the center is an event, a chronology of acts to be performed or understood. Describing and defining are two sides of the same coin. When we describe, we particularize; when we define, we generalize. When we exemplify, we move, once more, between the concrete and the general, the abstract, and the evaluative. Comparing and contrasting are fundamental moves of mind that underlie all that we do: we see a tree (the figure) in contrast to the surrounding sky, grass, hedges, sidewalks (the ground).

Argument (Chapter 10) requires us to go public, to persuade an audience to think differently, to act differently. Those who "argue," whether in speech or writing, call upon a variety of forms to convince their audience that they have indeed supported their assertions, have rendered them plausible and acceptable for reasons that are adequately explicit.

The introductions to the chapters begin with everyday situations, so that "forms" are seen first in the context of dailiness and then moved to the reading of prose, both fiction and non-fiction. In each chapter, at least one short story is included, to encourage a range of reading and to demonstrate how modes can merge within a distinctive form of narrative.

The "As You Read" and "As You Write" sections of the introductions invite students to become active readers and writers, paying close attention to the texts they both read and create. Students are asked to move between the jottings, questionings, and observations in their journals to shaped presentations in their public writing.

The selections themselves range from old chestnuts, classic works that often form the core of reading in a composition course, to surprises, contemporary pieces drawn from newspapers and magazines that have not previously been placed in anthologies. Within each chapter, the selections move from shorter to longer and from simpler to more complex form. So that students can enjoy a more extended experience of some writers, a few—George Orwell, Joan Didion, Richard Wright, Russell Baker—are represented more than once. Head-notes to each selection introduce some of the most distinctive features of the writer's work (in many cases the writers speak for themselves about the hows and whys of writing). Where they are significant, details of the writer's life are mentioned; several of the authors, however, do not live prominently in the public domain. Suggestions for further, more extensive, reading are included where appropriate.

At the end of each selection, questions entitled, "How Do You Respond?" ask students to think about what they read, to notice particular features of a text, and to ponder questions about idea and form, subject and strategy. Questions at the ends of chapters, "Focus on Your Reading," and "Focus on Your Writing," ask students to consider features of writing that cut across the particular selections, and then to create their own texts by generating ideas, associations, lists, questions (particularly in their journals); by seeing themselves as readers of their own texts; and by shaping their works to go public. The instructor will find, in these sections, assignments for writing with which to plan a course or two in freshman composition.

The instructor's manual that accompanies this text has a number of distinctive features: a disembedding of the ideas that inform and shape the text; a reader's *response* to the selections within each chapter; suggestions for further reading for both instructor and student; questions for class discussion to encourage close reading and lively conversation about the selections and the student's own writing; and, finally, a philosophical view of reading and writing as richly human and humanizing activities.

Behind every text is a story, how it came to be written. *Responding to Prose* began with an inventive, imaginative editor, James B. Smith, who, throughout, encouraged, supported, and believed in this work. Both he and Diana Francoeur, my knowing project editor, were sympathetic as idea was translated into text. No writer could ask for a more enabling environment.

For her singular role as reader, listener, researcher, I am deeply indebted to Nancy Bobker.

Reviewers—particularly John Clifford of the University of North Carolina, Wilmington; Nancy Sommers of Rutgers University; and Donald McQuade of Queens College—responded to this text with a rigorous criticism that any writer would invite.

Working in a collaborative intellectual community like Queens College over the past decade has resulted in ideas merging and converging; one often forgets where one idea began and whence another sprang. I wish to thank and credit the work of my colleagues—Sandra Schor, Marie Ponsot, Rosemary Deen, Robert Lyons, and, again, Donald McQuade—whose generosity of spirit is remarkable.

There are scholars from a number of fields whose ideas infuse this work: particularly, sociolinguist William Labov and psychologist George Kelly. The works of James Britton, Leo Rockas, and Louise Rosenblatt continue to inspire.

To my daughters Sharon and Lauren who patiently put up with a mother locked away in her study—I give thanks. They, as my students, continually teach me more than they will ever know.

INTRODUCTIONS

CHAPTER 1

Being Active Readers and Writers

Recently, I watched a friend of mine reading a book. He sat holding the book in front of him, and, as his eyes scanned the page, he did a number of things. He wrinkled his nose, he raised his eyebrows, he pursed his lips, he opened and closed his mouth, he pulled occasionally at a tuft of hair, he adjusted his glasses, he wrinkled his forehead. At times he seemed to move his eyes quickly from line to line: at other moments his gaze seemed to stay for a while on a spot on the page. Then he would scribble a note in the margin or glance about, staring for a moment into space. I saw him flip back to pages he had read and flip forward and write a few more lines. I saw him smile a few times. I saw him squint his eyes, as if he were questioning, wondering, speculating.

I call my friend an active reader: he was engaged with his book. He was making meaning of the words on the page. They seemed to be coming alive. The idea that guides this book is simply this: to read is to be involved. "Reading," says the writer E. B. White, "is the work of the alert mind, is demanding, and under ideal conditions produces finally a sort of ecstasy." Think for a moment about a page in a book—this page, for example. Imagine that you have never seen a book before—that you are looking at a page for the very first time. What do you see? Black squiggles on a page? Weird heiroglyphs?

Until you take the book in hand and decode the words, the printed page is meaningless. It is a song unheard—notes and melody floating through the air. A book, in this way, is nothing without a reader. You, the reader, bring it into your life, the life inside your head. And you bring to the book your own life: your ability to read, your history as a reader, your history of the day—your fatigue or energy, your interest or impatience. A student in one of my classes says she has realized that each time she reads is a new experience. When she reads a book now at twenty that she read at fifteen, the reading is a different experience because she is at a different place in her life. Each time she reads she makes it new.

Many readers believe that there are things in a book for them to "get," for them to pull out—main ideas, themes, "the purpose," "the meaning." But each person's reading of the book is different: what I "get" from a book is different from what you "get." Reading is a personal act—an interaction—between you and the page. You bring to the page who you are. What you focus on, what strikes you, what you remember, will be different from what I experience. We experience the world subjectively, for we are subjects.

If you think for a moment about this individual process, you'll see that the idea is a common one. If you are seated on a crowded bus, what you see will be different from what I see, sitting next to you. I notice people: a tired-looking child leaning up against a woman and playing with an umbrella, fingering the spring. You notice the advertisements: you read them, absorbed in the various displays of shampoo and beer and city services. If we were to compare notes afterward, we would confirm for each other that indeed there was a woman and a child, and that there were advertisements, but our interests would have taken us to different places, and our comparing notes would enliven our bus ride. We would learn from each other.

Just as some readers think there is only one way for all to read, some readers believe that whatever they "get" out of a text is okay. If an essay on fireflies reminds them of summers in Pennsylvania, then that is what the book is "about." That is not so. We all have associations when we read—that is one of the pleasures of reading. A story about fireflies *may remind* us of summers in Pennsylvania, but the essay *is* about fireflies. And just as we can verify what we actually saw on the bus, we can verify what is in the book. We may quibble about interpretations, but we must agree on the words that we see. When we look to Tillie Olsen's story, "I Stand Here Ironing," we may discuss different ways of interpreting the story, but we see that there are verifiable facts: an "I" is talking; she is a woman, a mother of four children, one of whom, Emily, worries her. Someone, presumably from Emily's school, has called to ask about her, and the mother wonders about her role as a mother, wonders if Emily's early experiences have been destructive, wonders where she, as mother, may have gone wrong.

How do we read?

We read differently for different occasions. Some of us are like the bus rider who "reads" the world around—advertisements, billboards, street names, cereal boxes. The printed world is absorbing. A child, learning to read, often cannot stop decoding everything she sees. I remember when my own daughter was learning to read, she complained once that her head hurt because she *had* to read *everything*. She was driven, a compulsive reader. Some people read books in this way; they are addicted to reading—novels, mysteries, science fiction—they cannot wait to get their hands on one book and then another. Many of them fly through the books, eager to find out what happens next, caught on a narrative rollercoaster that speeds them right to the last page. We all at times read for information; we need to know something and, at times, we need to know it quickly. A fire breaks out in the kitchen; a never-used fire extinguisher sits in a closet. You pull it out and read the directions to get what you need as quickly as you can get it:

TO OPERATE

1. Swing horn up. Pull pin.
2. Squeeze lever.
3. Direct discharge at base of flame.

You're not interested in pondering these words, in feeling the rhythm of the short phrases, in experiencing pleasure as you read. You read in order to act. At other times, we need to read slowly, painstakingly, to stop and consider, to figure out what a term means. When we read a complex essay in philosophy, we may plod through, we may stop to take notes, we may outline a chapter, we may underline, we may scratch questions in the margin, until we feel satisfied that we have made sense out of the text.

Students who believe that there is only one way to read assume that somehow the words will automatically *impress* themselves on their minds, that they need only sit back and watch, as if they were watching images on a screen. Many of them suppose that good readers all read quickly: they feel handicapped if they read ploddingly. Accomplished readers, however, can read quickly—or they can read slowly. Some readers go after the whole—they want to see where a piece begins and where it ends. They skim. They scan. They take in large chunks. Then, perhaps, they go back after details. They reread, knowing that each time they read, they will discover anew. Others read slowly, focusing on details, forming images in their minds, observing how a piece is built, working their way from its beginning to its end.

If you find reading to be sheer drudgery, then you should ask why and take time to reflect on your attitudes toward reading. In "Writing the Australian Crawl," the poet William Stafford talks about being responsive as a reader, being open, being ready, being willing to interact. He encourages readers to trust their responses. Reading, he says, "is not all your own ideas, and not all the other person's ideas. You toss back and forth against a live backboard. And, particularly, if it is a congenial poem—or friend—you are reading or hearing, you furnish a good half of the life. The travel circuit of an idea or impression is a sequence of reboundings between you and the page."

How can a reader be responsive? Here, we may usefully distinguish between two terms: observation and inference. We *observe* when we pay close attention to what is there, and what we observe must be visible to all. We *infer*, however, when we interpret what we observe, when we draw conclusions based on what is there. In the realm of observation, there will be no disagreement. In the realm of inference or interpretation, there will be some disputes. The word *infer* comes from the Latin *inferre*, which means to carry *in*, to bring *in*. When we infer, we carry our experiences and their meanings into the text. Drawing inferences from what we observe is fundamental to thinking. We get through the world by observing and inferring. If you look out of a window and observe that someone is carrying an umbrella rolled up, you will probably *infer* that it is *not* raining. If you observe someone holding up an open umbrella, you will doubtless infer that it *is* raining.

In certain situations, this distinction becomes especially important. The scientist, for example, must be a particularly keen observer. B. F. Skinner, a behavioral psychologist, observes the minute actions of pigeons. Ray Birdwhistle, a kinesics expert, closely observes hand and facial expressions. The internist who places a stethoscope to your chest is trained to hear—observe—sounds that tell whether or not your lungs are congested. The photographer, the artist, the poet, the surgeon, the musician, the active reader—all must have what Robert Frost calls "passionate attentiveness."

Think for a moment of what you know about detectives, whether from a television series or from reading Ian Fleming or Agatha Christie or Sir Arthur Conan Doyle. The detective is a master of observation. In the following conversation, Sherlock Holmes speaks with a new client, Helen Stone:

> "You have come in by train this morning, I see."
> "You know me, then?"
> "No, but I observe the second half of a return ticket in the palm of your left glove. You must have started early, and yet you had a good drive in a dog-cart, along heavy roads, before you reached the station."
> The lady gave a violent start, and stared in bewilderment at my companion.
> "There is no mystery, my dear madam," he said, smiling. "The left arm of your jacket is spattered with mud in no less than seven places. The marks are perfectly fresh. There is no vehicle save a dog-cart which throws up mud that way, and then only when you sit on the left-hand side of the driver."
>
> "THE SPECKLED BAND"

The woman is startled because Holmes quickly and correctly draws conclusions about her from what he observes; he carries in or puts in meanings; he infers. He notices, he is alert. He repeatedly tells his sidekick, Dr. Watson, "Sharpen your powers of observation." Watson admires Holmes, whose powers of observation, he says, are "rapid deductions, as swift as intuitions, and yet always founded on a logical basis." Between what Holmes sees and what he infers, there is always a thoughtful and reasonable connection.

Although you read differently for different occasions—at times reading for sheer pleasure (at least, I hope so), at other times reading for information, at times reading for both pleasure and learning—whether you are conscious of the processes or not, you move between observation and inference. You also move between your expectations and the satisfaction or disappointment of those expectations. When you open a book or begin a story or start an essay, your expectations are aroused. You begin Russell Baker's essay, "Summer Beyond Wish," for example, and the title intrigues you. It promises something; questions are aroused—why *summer?* Does he have all that he can wish for? Does he have nothing to wish for? If so, why is he satisfied? We move on to the first paragraph:

> A long time ago I lived in a crossroads village of northern Virginia and during its summer enjoyed innocence and never knew boredom, although nothing of consequence happened there.

We see that our hunch is right; we're on the right track: an "I" is talking—we assume that it is Baker—and he tells us that in a particular place—a long time ago—he *enjoyed* innocence and never knew boredom, although nothing of consequence happened there. Why was this place so special, we want to know. Why, if nothing much happened there, was the writer satisfied? We read on to find out about the place and about the speaker. We want to *know*. We are engaged. And as we read, we respond. Here are several notes a reader recorded in reading and responding to Baker's essay:

- The title: intriguing, promises something—or maybe it's exaggeration. Hmmm.
- During the summer? one summer? Why only one?
- He doesn't seem to be exaggerating. (I don't like exaggeration.)
- He recalls the past vividly. He knows about flowers—shares my enthusiasm for such things as the scents of flowers.
- I begin to feel nostalgic for this "lost" simplicity—for this general innocence.
- The writer is a male. His talk about guns—I don't like guns or people who use them.

- This almost unbearable—so close to my own memories.
- Nice "talk"—I enjoy the sound of people's voices in prose: the vividness, directness, immediacy, sense of the individual, the actual.
- I feel here a sense of time passing, sense of fragility of happiness.
- I love bats. He doesn't appreciate the bat enough for me. I wish he'd said more.
- Awkward sentence. I had to read this line twice.
- How sad to be afraid of toads. What odd fears people have.
- Powerful—all the more for being understated and impersonal. Lovely picture of kids sitting up late into the night.
- Conclusion—general sense of quiet pleasure, of something beautiful and lost. I'm glad to have read it.

The reader here has turned writer. He has engaged in a dialogue with Baker: he's talking to himself and he's talking to the writer. He lets us into his likes and dislikes: he likes scents of flowers, he doesn't like guns; he likes bats and toads; he likes lively talk. He appreciates Baker's rendering of the past, of a period of innocence. The expectation aroused by the title is satisfied. He now knows what Baker means, and he's glad he read the piece.

One of the ways to be a responsive reader is to write, yourself—to keep a journal of your own "talks with writers," your own responses to the text. The notes that you take, the responses that you make, become a source of information, of pleasure, of questioning, of speculating—about ideas, about people, about places, about experience. We will talk more about journals in Chapter 2; for now, however, let's look at the act of writing as it relates to reading. Just as many students believe that there is only one right way to read, they also believe that there is only one right way to write. Many of them do not realize that reading is, after all, writing—that a real person wrestled with those words on the page. Many of them seem to believe that words are magically produced on a page, that words somehow spring from the writer's brain—whole—onto the page. But just as reading is an individual activity, so is writing. Each writer writes differently. William Wordsworth, the English poet, was a peripatetic writer—that is, he composed as he walked—and he composed aloud. Here is an account of Wordsworth's walking through his native village, bellowing his forming lines, and frightening the villagers:

> But there was anudder thing as kep' fwoaks off, he hed a terr'ble girt deep voice. I've knoan folks, village lads and lasses, coming ower by t'auld road aboon what runs fra Grasmer to Rydal, flayt a'most to death there by t' Wishing Gate to hear t' girt voice a groanin' and mutterin' and thunderin' of a still evening. And he had a way of standin' quite still by t' rock there in t'path under Rydal, and fwoaks could hear sounds like a wild beast coming frat' rocks, and childer were scared fit to be dead a'most.
>
> REVEREND CANON RAWNSLEY

Afterwards, however, Wordsworth struggled to put his words to paper, and this same diarist tells how Wordsworth locked himself in his study, working and reworking his poems, ignoring or not hearing the call to dinner:

> Mrs. Wordsworth would say, "Ring the bell," but he wouldn't stir, bless ye. "Goa and see what he's doing," she'd say, and we wad goa up to study door and hear him a mumbling and bumming through hit. "Dinner's ready, sir," I'd ca' out, but he'd goa mumbling on like a deaf man, ya see. And sometimes Mrs. Wordsworth 'ud say, "Goa and brek a bottle, or let a dish fall just outside door in passage." Eh dear, that maistly wad bring him out, wad that.

We might remember that when Wordsworth wrote, he didn't have the convenience of a typewriter or a word processor or an automobile. How different his lines might have been had he composed while riding in a car!

No matter how differently writers write, we know that writing is seldom an orderly, systematic activity. Writing does not happen neatly step-by-step. It can be pretty messy, fluid, with a lot of pencil-chewing, hair pulling, throwing away, and scratching out—over long periods of time. We also know writers complain of the hard work, but they talk, as well, of the sheer joy of creating on a page. (See Muriel Rukeyser on the writing of a poem, Chapter 4.)

For the reader engaged in a demanding, involving activity—and for the writer, as well—there is, with hope, *pleasure.*

Pleasure often comes from knowledge, from coming to know, from making meaning. And a fundamental means of knowing is to understand the move between concrete and abstract. By *concrete,* I mean that which is verifiable, that which we experience with our senses, that which we can point to in the world, that which we observe. By *abstract,* I mean, that which we *say* about the concrete, the ideas we have, the generalizations we make, the summaries we form. The concrete is what constitutes the world around us; the abstract is what we think about that world. You may say that a man is cruel: that is a summary statement, a generalization that you draw from examples of what you call his cruelty—his abuse of children, his mistreatment of animals, his carelessness with other's property. The concrete takes shape—as you will see in the succeeding chapters—in examples, in stories that we tell, in our descriptions of what we see, in statistics, in "data." And the abstract takes form in what we make of the observable world, in what we "draw off," or what we drag or pull out (which is what the verb *to abstract* means).

When we write, we continually move between the concrete and the abstract, continually observe or record, trying to make meaning. Throughout this book, you will be asked to respond to what you read by observing closely, by inferring from what you read. And you will be asked to write your own texts; to form what you want to say through story, through example, through description; and to draw out abstractions, to say what you think things mean. You will be asked to respond to what others have written, to wrestle with their ideas, to think about their images—through writing. Writing is a way of being an alert reader. In the following selection, "How Should One Read a Book?" Virginia Woolf suggests, "Perhaps the quickest way to understand the elements of what a novelist is doing is not to read, but to write: to make your own experiment with the dangers and difficulties of words."

> It is simple enough to say that since books have classes—fiction, biography, poetry—we should separate them and take from each what it is right that each should give us. Yet few people ask from books what books can give us. Most commonly we come to books with blurred and divided minds, asking of

fiction that it shall be true, of poetry that it shall be false, of biography that it shall be flattering, of history that it shall enforce our own prejudices. If we could banish all such preconceptions when we read, that would be an admirable beginning. Do not dictate to your author; try to become him. Be his fellow-worker and accomplice. If you hang back, and reserve and criticize at first, you are preventing yourself from getting the fullest possible value from what you read. But if you open your mind as widely as possible, then signs and hints of almost imperceptible fineness, from the twist and turn of the first sentences, will bring you into the presence of a human being unlike any other. Steep yourself in this, acquaint yourself with this, and soon you will find that your author is giving, or attempting to give you, something far more definite. The thirty-two chapters of a novel—if we consider how to read a novel first—are an attempt to make something as formed and controlled as a building: but words are more impalpable than bricks; reading is a longer and more complicated process than seeing. Perhaps the quickest way to understand the elements of what a novelist is doing is not to read, but to write; to make your own experiment with the dangers and difficulties of words. Recall, then, some event that has left a distinct impression on you—how at the corner of the street, perhaps, you passed two people talking. A tree shook; an electric light danced; the tone of the talk was comic, but also tragic; a whole vision, an entire conception, seemed contained in that moment.

But when you attempt to reconstruct it in words, you will find that it breaks into a thousand impressions. Some must be subdued; others emphasized; in the process you will lose, probably, all grasp upon the emotion itself. Then turn from your blurred and littered pages to the opening pages of some great novelist—Defoe, Jane Austen, Hardy. Now you will be better able to appreciate their mastery. It is not merely that we are in the presence of a different person—Defoe, Jane Austen, or Thomas Hardy—but that we are living in a different world. Here, in *Robinson Crusoe*, we are trudging a plain high road; one thing happens after another; the fact and the order of the fact is enough. But if the open air and adventure mean everything to Defoe they mean nothing to Jane Austen. Hers is the drawing-room, and people talking, and by the many mirrors of their talk revealing their characters. And if, when we have accustomed ourselves to the drawing-room and its reflections, we turn to Hardy, we are once more spun around. The moors are round us and the stars are above our heads. The other side of the mind is now exposed—the dark side that comes uppermost in solitude, not the light side that shows in company. Our relations are not towards people, but towards Nature and destiny. Yet different as these worlds are, each is consistent with itself. The maker of each is careful to observe the laws of his own perspective, and however great a strain they may put upon us they will never confuse us, as lesser writers so frequently do, by introducing two different kinds of reality into the same book. Thus to go from one great novelist to another—from Jane Austen to Hardy, from Peacock to Trollope, from Scott to Meredith—is to be wrenched and uprooted; to be thrown this way and then that. To read a novel is a difficult and complex art. You must be capable not only of great finesse of perception, but of great boldness of imagination if you are going to make use of all that the novelist—the great artist—gives you.

AS YOU READ

We all read differently, given our individual experiences, our particular interests and needs, our occasions for reading, and our different speeds of moving our eyes across a page. And yet, even though our experiences may differ, we also stand on common ground as readers. As you read the selections in *Responding to Prose*, I invite you to reflect upon your own reading and writing and to share your experiences with others.

Expectations

Reading is in many ways a guessing game. As soon as we turn to a page, glance at a title, read an opening line, we pick up *clues;* and, as we read, our initial expectations are both denied and satisfied. When reading a mystery-story, we know very well that we're playing a game with the writer; an effective mystery writer will play with our expectations throughout to keep us moving along. Who dunnit? We guess: The butler? The lonely maiden aunt? The judge? We keep playing. Finally, at the end, when we know "who dunnit," we retrace the clues we passed over and say, "Ah, that's right; I overlooked this one and that one," and the whole network of clues may flash before us.

As you read, keep a journal to note the expectations aroused within you. As you meet the first clues—the title and the opening line—record your expectations. What do you think the selection will be about? Who is speaking? Where are they? What tone, what point of view, what form do you expect will follow? As you come to the end, look back over your notes to see how your initial expectations are denied *and* satisfied.

George Orwell's essay in Chapter 3 begins like this:

A HANGING

> It was in Burma, a sodden morning of the rains. A sickly light, like yellow tinfoil, was slanting over the high walls into the jail yard.

What expectations are aroused by Orwell's title, "A HANGING"? Do you have the sense that what will follow is cheerful, light, pleasant? Of course not, and if Orwell is teasing—if he is really talking about, say, a hanging of clothes on a line—then you will no doubt be jolted if you meet a cheerful subject later on. But your expectations that you are to read about a serious matter are reinforced by the brief description of the weather in the first line:

> a *sodden* morning of the *rains*, a *sickly* light.

Expectations are further strengthened when, at the end of the line, you meet the words *jail yard*. You may now be hooked into expecting that a prisoner will be *hanged*.

Orwell sets the stage—where the action will take place, the kind of day it is, the sense of the ominous—all in the title and the first line. You also get a strong whiff of *tone*, how the writer *feels* about the subject. The narrator does not appear to be pleased about what will come: the *sickly light* in that first sentence does not invite you to respond cheerfully. The sickly light is not so much "out there," in the world, as within the perception of the narrator. Therefore, it enters you, as well.

From the first line, we have also some sense of the form to follow:

we anticipate a story about a particular day in a particular place, a particular event, most likely about a particular person. We are not to hear about hangings; we are to hear about one hanging. We anticipate a *story* because of the first word in the first sentence: *It*. It took place on a rainy, yellowish, sickly morning in Burma near or in a jail yard. What is *It?* We want to know. We assume that *it* refers directly back to the title, so that the title itself becomes part of that first sentence: "A hanging (it) was in Burma. . . ."

The opening line invites us to enter a world of a hanging, to discover how the writer approaches the subject and how we are asked to respond.

In conversation, we sense what to expect from the *way* a speaker speaks. A friend, say, tells about the death of a pet. Tone of voice, gestures, choice of words invite us, as listeners, to respond as the teller expects—to be in sympathy with our friend, to share in the loss. So in a work of literature, we enter into a writer's world, where we are invited to share in events and *feelings*.

As you read, imagine yourself talking with the writer, discussing your expectations as you greet the work and puzzling out how those expectations are aroused within you. Notice the words, phrases, images that invite you to anticipate, at the very beginning, the tone, the context, the point of view, the form that will follow.

Associations

When a friend sadly tells of the death of a favorite pet, a collie who had lived with the family for a dozen years, we may not enter into that grief so intensely as the speaker but we, nevertheless, *understand*. For we bring to the conversation our own experiences of death and loss, even if we, ourselves, have had no pets. We are in sympathy, and we respond humanly. We offer up to our friend our own store of memories, experiences, emotions, images. So it is with reading. We bring to a text who we are. As you read, note in your journal those associations that are re-awakened in you, your own past experiences, your sympathies, your questions, and *your* possibilities for writing.

AS YOU WRITE

As you read, think of yourself as a writer—as one who dares to spin off from what you read. Think how you can write a story that you can offer to a friend, as you would tell one in conversation. Record the questions that remain with you—the images, words, phrases, ideas that stay with you—after you close the cover. Note what you like and what you don't. Keep in mind the reader's responses to Russell Baker's essay, "Summer Beyond Wish," pp. 354–356. Try jotting down a running dialogue in response to what you read, keeping track of your observations, expectations, satisfactions, pleasures, disappointments. Record questions raised and answered, personal associations awakened. We interpret as we read. We derive meanings. We evaluate. We value. As you read, make a note of those passages that point up for you what the writer values—the specifics, the details, the concrete images that give body to the writer's assertions, generalizations, and abstractions. You might ask: how does the writer make real for me—*realize*—what he or she is trying to share?

THE PRIVATE VOICE

CHAPTER 2

Writing for Oneself

JOURNALS, DIARIES, NOTEBOOKS

"Why do I keep a notebook?" the writer Joan Didion asks herself. And her answer is simple: "To keep in touch." The words in her notebook record observations she has made of people and places, bits of dialogue she has heard, lists of things she has to do, recipes she didn't want to forget, ideas she has stumbled on. The point of keeping a notebook is not, Didion says, "to have an accurate factual record of what I have been doing or thinking." Rather, it is to remember, to keep hold of things. She wonders why she has recorded a recipe for sauerkraut, and then she remembers:

> It all comes back. Even that recipe for sauerkraut: even that brings it back. I was on Fire Island when I first made that sauerkraut, and it was raining, and we drank a lot of bourbon and ate the sauerkraut and went to bed at ten, and I listened to the rain and felt safe. . . .

Didion's notebook is hers alone. If you were to read it, it would make little sense to you, for each entry is tied to some experience, some event, some thought, of her private world.

Notebooks, journals, and diaries are usually meant to be private.

They are personal storagehouses. For the novelists like Didion or Virginia Woolf or F. Scott Fitzgerald, they can be places where they house "material" that one day they may use in their public writing. Their journals, however, as you will see in this chapter, echo their private voices. The forms they choose—the way they record what happens during a day or make notes that mean something only to them—are theirs alone.

These storagehouses may be called a journal (Thoreau) or diary (Virginia Woolf) or notebook (Didion). To each writer, the purpose of keeping track is different. But in each case, what is written down is a way of holding onto things that rush by in the often tumultuous day-to-day of a life. The word *diary* generally makes us think of a day-to-day account, and indeed there are those who keep track of their lives by recording what happens daily. Famous diarists like Samuel Pepys and Henry Crabb Robinson give accounts of their days that reflect the times in which they lived. Through Pepys's eyes, we get a sense of seventeenth-century England, what it was like to live through a plague that swept the country. Robinson gives us insight into the day-to-day life of a nineteenth-century English gentleman, who dined with the literary giants of his time. He takes us on his walks with the poets Wordsworth and Coleridge through the Lake District in England, into parlors for tea and lively conversation. William Byrd, a Virginia gentleman of the eighteenth century, gives an account of his daily activities—what he ate, whom he met, when he prayed, where he went:

June 22, 1710

I rose at 6 o'clock because it rained in the morning which I thought would hinder my voyage. But when I was up I resolved to go. I ate milk for breakfast and about 8 o'clock got on my horse on the other side of the creek. I neglected to say my prayers before I came out but afterwards I committed my family to God Almighty. About 12 o'clock I got to the ferry, where I heard the Governor was at Green Spring. Just before I came there I changed my clothes and about one o'clock arrived at Green Spring where I found abundance of company. I complimented the Governor who seemed to be a very good man and was very courteous to me and told me I had been recommended to him by several of my friends in England. I met likewise with

> Dr. Cocke, my olde school-fellow. The Governor brought with him a niece, a pretty woman. . . . In the evening I danced a minuet. The mosquitoes bit me extremely. . . .

Often those who are confined—through illness or through imprisonment—hold on through paper and pen, as we see in the famous *Diary of a Young Girl*. Anne Frank, a teenager, turns her diary into one of the extraordinary documents of human courage and growth during one of the most extreme periods of human suffering. Anne's diary was given to her for her birthday and she saw it—as many teenagers do—as a "true friend" to whom she could tell everything. "I hope," she says, "I shall be able to confide in you completely as I have never been able to do in anyone before, and I hope that you will be a great support and comfort to me" (June 12, 1942).

Through their notebooks, writers keep in touch in different ways. Anne Frank's diary is accessible to us, a public audience. Didion's apparently is not: her notes, her bits and pieces of collected dialogue, her observations, must be explained to us through her recollection of events and experiences. How you keep your notebook—whether you write day-by-day or sporadically—is up to you. You should not feel that you *must* write in the notebook every day, nor should you think that you must record only deep, personal feelings. You will note in the following selections that Dorothy Wordsworth and Henry Thoreau are both keen observers of the outer world. Thoreau will spend two pages of a notebook meticulously describing his observations of a woodchuck. Dorothy Wordsworth will describe how the sky looks on a particular evening. Virginia Woolf, while agonizing about her difficulties in writing a novel, uses her journal, as well, to jot down ideas and to work out her difficulties. Fitzgerald's notebook is sketchy, holding descriptions and conversations that he might later use in his novels. May Sarton uses her journal to help her get through a depression, a dark night of the soul. And George Orwell uses his diary to record the catastrophic events around him during the Second World War.

You are invited—as a writer—to keep a notebook, to record what you see about you, the people, the places; to record bits of conversation, as Didion and Fitzgerald do; and to record your thinking—as a reader. You are invited to read actively, through writing, in the following ways:

1. Read a piece straight through and then jot down your *first* impressions of the piece. How does it strike you, personally? Do you identify with what the writer is trying to say? Have you had a similar experience? Similar thoughts? Does the piece call up specific associations? If so, what are they? Record them. Do the experiences the writer presents seem far away, distant? Does the writer present ideas that strike you as inappropriate, wrong-headed? How so?

2. Now go back and reread the piece. Note specifically in your journal where you and the writer meet, where you and the writer part ways. Record your observations.

3. Now read again and notice how the piece is built. How does it begin? How does it end? Do the beginning and ending match up in any way? If so, how? Is the ending an echo of the beginning? Does it repeat a particular idea or a particular image? Record in your notebook as you go: words, phrases, sentences that capture your attention. Try to figure out why they attract you. Is it that personal chords are sounded within you? Is it that the phrase itself is beautifully fashioned? Does the phrasing capture the idea? Does the rhythm of the language catch you? Do you hear the cadences in your ear? Does a metaphor make connections you had not thought of before? Do you know anything now in a way that you didn't before?

As you write, as you keep track in your notebook of your own experience as a reader, trust your own observations, your own judgments. Allow yourself to wrestle with an idea, to talk to the writer, to argue, to debate. Rely on your own powers of reading and rereading, of thinking, and of writing. "To see with one's own eyes," says Albert Einstein, "to feel and judge without succumbing to the suggestive power of the fashion of the day, to be able to express what one has seen and felt in a trim sentence or even in a cunningly wrought word—is not that glorious? Is it not a proper subject for congratulation?" ("Congratulations to a Critic," 1935).

JOAN DIDION

> "Everything you do counts," says Joan Didion (born 1934); "every gesture tells a story and in the moral realm too, everything tells." In her collections of essays, Slouching Towards Bethlehem and The White Album; in her novels, Play It as It Lays, Run River, and The Book of Common Prayer, we are aware of Didion's intense, sometimes anguished, consciousness. At times, as readers, we are painfully aware of her—of her anxieties, tensions, fears; at other times, we are almost unaware of her, for she directs our attention, our energy, outward to the particular part of the world that her prose so vividly evokes. In "On Keeping a Notebook," she lets us into her thinking, her ways of observing, and her need to get it down on paper.

ON KEEPING A NOTEBOOK

" 'That woman Estelle,' " the note reads, "is partly the reason why George Sharp and I are separated today." *Dirty crepe-de-Chine wrapper, hotel bar, Wilmington RR, 9:45 a.m. August Monday morning."* Since the note is in my notebook, it presumably has some meaning to me. I study it for a long while. At first I have only the most general notion of what I was doing on an August Monday morning in the bar of the hotel across from the Pennsylvania Railroad station in Wilmington, Delaware (waiting for a train? missing one? 1960? 1961? why Wilmington?), but I do remember being there. The woman in the dirty crepe-de-Chine wrapper had come down from her room for a beer, and the bartender had heard before the reason why George Sharp and she were separated today. "Sure," he said, and went on mopping the floor. "You told me." At the other end of the bar is a girl. She is talking, pointedly, not to the man beside her but to a cat lying in the triangle of sunlight cast through the open door. She is wearing a plaid silk dress from Peck & Peck, and the hem is coming down.

Here is what it is: the girl has been on the Eastern Shore, and now she is going back to the city, leaving the man beside her, and all she can see ahead are the viscous summer sidewalks and the 3 A.M. long-distance calls that will make her lie awake and then sleep drugged through all the steaming mornings left in August (1960? 1961?). Because she must go directly from the train to lunch in New York, she wishes that she had a safety pin for the hem of the plaid silk dress, and she also wishes that she could forget about the hem and the lunch and stay in the cool bar that smells of disinfectant and malt and make friends with the woman in the crepe-de-Chine wrapper. She is afflicted by a little self-pity, and she wants to compare Estelles. That is what that was all about.

Why did I write it down? In order to remember, of course, but exactly what was it I wanted to remember? How much of it actually happened? Did any of it? Why do I keep a notebook at all? It is easy to deceive oneself on all those scores. The impulse to write things down is a peculiarly compulsive one, inexplicable to those who do not share it, useful only accidentally, only secondarily, in the way that any compulsion tries to justify itself. I suppose that it begins or does not begin in the cradle. Although I have felt compelled to write things down since I was five years old, I doubt that my daughter ever will, for she is a singularly blessed and accepting child, delighted with life exactly as life presents itself to her, unafraid to go to sleep and unafraid to wake up. Keepers of private notebooks are a different breed altogether, lonely and resistant rearrangers of things, anxious malcontents, children afflicted apparently at birth with some presentiment of loss.

My first notebook was a Big Five tablet, given to me by my mother with the sensible suggestion that I stop whining and learn to amuse myself by writing down my thoughts. She returned the tablet to me a few years ago; the first entry is an account of a woman who believed herself freezing to death in the Arctic night, only to find, when day broke, that she had stumbled onto the Sahara Desert, where she would die of the heat before lunch. I have no idea what turn of a five-year-old's mind could have prompted so insistently "ironic" and exotic a story, but it does reveal a certain predilection for the extreme which has dogged me into adult life; perhaps if I were analytically inclined I would find it a truer story than any I might have told about Donald Johnson's birthday party or the day my cousin Brenda put Kitty Litter in the aquarium.

So the point of my keeping a notebook has never been, nor is it now, to have an accurate factual record of what I have been doing or thinking. That would be a different impulse entirely, an instinct for reality which I sometimes envy but do not possess. At no point have I ever been able successfully to keep a diary; my approach to daily life ranges from the grossly negligent to the merely absent, and on those few occasions when I have tried dutifully to record a day's events, boredom has so overcome me that the results are mysterious at best. What is this business about "shopping, typing piece, dinner with E, depressed"? Shopping for what? Typing what piece? Who is E? Was this "E" depressed, or was I depressed? Who cares?

In fact I have abandoned altogether that kind of pointless entry; instead I tell what some would call lies. "That's simply not true," the members of my family frequently tell me when they come up against my memory of a shared event. "The party was *not* for you, the spider was *not* a black widow, *it wasn't that way at all*." Very likely they are right, for not only have I always had trouble distinguishing between what happened and what merely might have happened, but I remain unconvinced that the distinction, for my purposes, matters. The cracked crab that I recall having for lunch the day my father came home from Detroit in 1945 must certainly be embroidery, worked into the day's pattern to lend verisimilitude; I was ten years old and would not now remember the cracked crab. The day's events did not turn on cracked crab. And yet it is precisely that fictitious crab that makes me see the afternoon all over again, a home movie run all too often, the father bearing gifts, the child weeping, an exercise in family love and guilt. Or that is what it was to me. Similarly, perhaps it never did snow that August in Vermont; perhaps there never were flurries in the night wind, and maybe no one else felt the ground hardening and summer already dead even as we pretended to bask in it, but that was how it felt to me, and it might as well have snowed, could have snowed, did snow.

How it felt to me: that is getting closer to the truth about a notebook. I sometimes delude myself about why I keep a notebook, imagine that some thrifty virtue derives from preserving everything observed. See enough and write it down, I tell myself, and then some morning when the world seems drained of wonder, some day when I am only going through the motions of doing what I am supposed to do, which is write—on that bankrupt morning I will simply open my notebook and there it will all be, a forgotten account with accumulated interest, paid passage back to the world out there: dialogue overhead in hotels and elevators and at the hat-check counter in Pavillon (one middle-aged man shows his hat check to another and says, "That's my old football number"); impressions of Bettina Aptheker and Benjamin Sonnenberg and Teddy ("Mr. Acapulco") Stauffer; careful *aperçus* about tennis bums and failed fashion models and Greek shipping heiresses, one of whom taught me a significant lesson (a lesson I could have learned from F. Scott Fitzgerald, but perhaps we all must meet the very rich for ourselves) by asking, when I arrived to interview her in her orchid-filled sitting room on the second day of a paralyzing New York blizzard, whether it was snowing outside.

I imagine, in other words, that the notebook is about other people. But of course it is not. I have no real business with what one stranger said to another at the hat-check counter in Pavillon; in fact I suspect that the line "That's my old football number" touched not my own imagination at all, but merely some memory of something once read, probably "The Eighty-Yard Run." Nor is my concern with a woman in a dirty crepe-de-Chine wrapper in a Wilmington bar. My stake is always, of course, in the unmentioned girl in the plaid silk dress. *Remember what it was to be me*: that is always the point.

It is a difficult point to admit. We are brought up in the ethic that others, any others, all others, are by definition more interesting than ourselves; taught to be diffident, just this side of self-effacing. ("You're the least important person in the room and don't forget it," Jessica Mitford's governess would hiss in her ear on the advent of any social occasion; I copied that into my notebook because it is only recently that I have been able to enter a room without hearing some such phrase in my inner ear.) Only the very young and the very old may recount their dreams at breakfast, dwell upon self, interrupt with memories of beach picnics and favorite Liberty lawn dresses and the rainbow trout in a creek near Colorado Springs. The rest of us are expected, rightly, to affect absorption in other people's favorite dresses, other people's trout.

And so we do. But our notebooks give us away, for however dutifully we record what we see around us, the common denominator of all we see is always, transparently, shamelessly, the implacable "I." We are not talking here about the kind of notebook that is patently for public consumption, a structural conceit for binding together a series of graceful *pensées*; we are talking about something private, about bits of the mind's string too short to use, an indiscriminate and erratic assemblage with meaning only for its maker.

And sometimes even the maker has difficulty with the meaning. There does not seem to be, for example, any point in my knowing for the rest of my life that, during 1964, 720 tons of soot fell on every square mile of New York City, yet there it is in my notebook, labeled "FACT." Nor do I really need to remember that Ambrose Bierce liked to spell Leland Stanford's name "£eland $tanford" or that "smart women almost always wear black in Cuba," a fashion hint without much potential for practical application. And does not the relevance of these notes seem marginal at best?

> In the basement museum of the Inyo County Courthouse in Independence, California, sign pinned to a mandarin coat: "This MANDARIN COAT was often worn by Mrs. Minnie S. Brooks when giving lectures on her TEAPOT COLLECTION."

> Redhead getting out of car in front of Beverly Wilshire Hotel, chinchilla stole, Vuitton bags with tags reading:
> MRS LOU FOX
> HOTEL SAHARA
> VEGAS

Well, perhaps not entirely marginal. As a matter of fact, Mrs. Minnie S. Brooks and her MANDARIN COAT pull me back into my own childhood, for although I never knew Mrs. Brooks and did not visit Inyo county until I was thirty, I grew up in just such a world, in houses cluttered with Indian relics and bits of gold ore and ambergris and the souvenirs my Aunt Mercy Farnsworth brought back from the Orient. It is a long way from that world to Mrs. Lou Fox's world, where we all live now, and is it not just as well to remember that? Might not Mrs. Minnie S. Brooks help me to remember what I am? Might not Mrs. Lou Fox help me to remember what I am not?

But sometimes the point is harder to discern. What exactly did I have in mind when I noted down that it cost the father of someone I know $650 a month to light the place on the Hudson in which he lived before the Crash? What use was I planning to make of this line by Jimmy Hoffa: "I may have my faults, but being wrong ain't one of them"? And although I think it interesting to know where the girls who travel with the Syndicate have their hair done when they find themselves on the West Coast, will I ever make suitable use of it? Might I not be better off just passing it on to John O'Hara? What is a recipe for sauerkraut doing in my notebook? What kind of magpie keeps this notebook? *"He was born the night the* Titanic *went down."* That seems a nice enough line, and I even recall who said it, but is it not really a better line in life than it could ever be in fiction?

But of course that is exactly it: not that I should ever use the line, but that I should remember the woman who said it and the afternoon I heard it. We were on her terrace by the sea, and we were finishing the wine left from lunch, trying to get what sun there was, a California winter sun. The woman whose husband was born the night the *Titanic* went down wanted to rent her house, wanted to go back to her children in Paris. I remember wishing that I could afford the house, which cost $1,000 a month. "Someday you will," she said lazily. "Someday it all comes." There in the sun on her terrace it seemed easy to believe in someday, but later I had a low-grade afternoon hangover and ran over a black snake on the way to the supermarket and was flooded with inexplicable fear when I heard the checkout clerk explaining to the man ahead of me why she was finally divorcing her husband. "He left me no choice," she said over and over as she punched the register. "He has a little seven-month-old baby by her, he left me no choice." I would like to believe that my dread then was for the human condition, but of course it was for me, because I wanted a baby and did not then have one and because I wanted to own the house that cost $1,000 a month to rent and because I had a hangover.

It all comes back. Perhaps it is difficult to see the value in having one's self back in that kind of mood, but I do see it; I think we are well advised to keep on nodding terms with the people we used to be, whether we find them attractive company or not. Otherwise they turn up unannounced and surprise us, come hammering on the mind's door at 4 A.M. of a bad night and demand to know who deserted them, who betrayed them, who is going to make amends. We forget all too soon the things we thought we could never forget. We forget the loves and the betrayals alike, forget what we whispered and what we screamed, forget who we were. I have already lost touch with a couple of people I used to be; one of them, a seventeen-year-old, presents little threat, although it would be of some interest to me to know again what it feels like to sit on a river levee drinking vodka-and-orange juice and listening to Les Paul and Mary Ford and their echoes sing "How High the Moon" on the car radio. (You see I still have the scenes, but I no longer perceive myself among those present, no longer could even improvise the dialogue.) The other one, a twenty-three-year-old, bothers me more. She was always a good deal of trouble, and I suspect she will reappear when I least want to see her, skirts too long, shy to the point of aggravation, always the injured party, full of recriminations and little hurts and stories I do not want to hear again, at once saddening me and angering me with her vulnerability and ignorance, an apparition all the more insistent for being so long banished.

It is a good idea, then, to keep in touch, and I suppose that keeping in touch is what notebooks are all about. And we are all on our own when it comes to keeping those lines open to ourselves: Your notebook will never help me, nor mine you. "*So what's new in the whiskey business?*" What could that possibly mean to you? To me it means a blonde in a Pucci bathing suit sitting with a couple of fat men by the pool at the Beverly Hills Hotel. Another man approaches, and they all regard one another in silence for a while. "So what's new in the whiskey business?" one of the fat men finally says by way of welcome, and the blonde stands up, arches one foot and dips it in the pool, looking all the while at the cabaña where Baby Pignatari is talking on the telephone. That is all there is to that, except that several years later I saw the blonde coming out of Saks Fifth Avenue in New York with her California complexion and a voluminous mink coat. In the harsh wind that day she looked old and irrevocably tired to me, and even the skins in the mink coat were not worked the way they were doing them that year, not the way she would have wanted them done, and there is the point of the story. For a while after that I did not like to look in the mirror, and my eyes would skim the newspapers and pick out only the deaths, the cancer victims, the premature coronaries, the suicides, and I stopped riding the Lexington Avenue IRT because I noticed for the first time that all the strangers I had seen for years—the man with the seeing-eye dog, the spinster who read the classified pages every day, the fat girl who always got off with me at Grand Central—looked older than they once had.

It all comes back. Even that recipe for sauerkraut: even that brings it back. I was on Fire Island when I first made that sauerkraut, and it was raining, and we drank a lot of bourbon and ate the sauerkraut and went to bed at ten, and I listened to the rain and the Atlantic and felt safe. I made the sauerkraut again last night and it did not make me feel any safer, but that is, as they say, another story.

How Do You Respond?

1. Didion writes, "Keepers of private notebooks are a different breed altogether, lonely . . . anxious malcontents . . . ." Do you think this is true? Can you think of any counter examples?

2. Didion admits to a "predilection for the extreme" and says, ". . . I tell lies". Are lies the same as exaggeration? Is she exaggerating even here? Cite examples of exaggeration from this selection.

3. Didion seems to me an edgy, tense writer. What effect do you think she means to have on her reader? Do you think that her style works, that it does what it is meant to do? How?

F. SCOTT FITZGERALD

> Scott Fitzgerald (1896–1940) seemed determined to live out the glamorous, romantic, and poignant fantasies of his own fictional heroes and heroines: sharp, witty, ironic, and close to sentimental, he invented the hedonistic and spendthrift Jazz Age almost single-handed. He gave his readers not mirror-images of their own dreams but those dreams transformed into something of grace, delicacy, pathos, and wit. His intelligence almost saved him, but his heavy smoking and drinking, and the excessive demands that he made on his resources both physical and nervous, exacted their due price, and he died in early middle age. Like James Agee, he had a love-hate relationship with Hollywood; and his notebook is full of good lines from movies that never were but should have been. Among his best-known works are This Side of Paradise, The Beautiful and the Damned, Tender is the Night, *and his masterpiece*, The Great Gatsby.

From *THE NOTE-BOOKS*

- I really loved him, but of course it wore out like a love affair. The fairies have spoiled all that.
- "Just a couple of old drunks, just a couply of ol-l-ld circus clowns."
- "I'm in a hurry."
  "I'm in a hurry—I'm in a hurry."
  "What are you in a hurry about?"
  "I can't explain—I'm in a hurry."
- "This is a tough girl and I'm taking her to a tough place."
- Three hundred a day die in auto accidents in the U.S.A.
- Man looking at aeroplane: "That's one of them new gyropractors."
- Bijou, regarding her cigarette fingers: "Oh, Trevah! Get me the pumice stone."
- His life was a sort of dream, as are most lives with the mainspring left out.
- Suddenly her face resumed that expression which can only come from studying moving picture magazines over and over, and only be described as one long blond wish toward something—a wish that you'd have a wedlock with the youth of Shirley Temple, the earning power of Clark Gable; the love of Clark Gable

Writing for Oneself   31

and the talent of Charles Laughton—and with a bright smile the girl was gone.
- Feel wide awake—no, but at least I feel born, which is more than I did the first time I woke up.
- The cartoon cat licked the cartoon kitten and a girl behind me said, "Isn't that sweet?"
- We can't just let our worlds crash around us like a lot of dropped trays.
- Q. What did he die of? A. He died of jus' dieability.
- "Hello, Sam." When you were a good guest, you knew the names of the servants, the smallest babies, and the oldest aunts. "Is Bonny in?"
- "I like writers. If you speak to a writer, you often get an answer."
- Woman says about husband that he keeps bringing whole great masses of dogs back from the pound.
- "We haven't got any more gin," he said. "Will you have a bromide?" he added hopefully.
- Long engagement: nothing to do but to marry or quarrel, so I decided to quarrel.
- "*I* didn't do it," he said, using the scented "I."
- "Remember you're physically repulsive to me."
- "Learn young about hard work and good manners—and you'll be through the whole dirty mess and nicely dead again before you know it."
- Now it's all as useless as repeating a dream.
- "I'm going to break that stubborn stupid part of you that thinks that any American woman who has met Brancusi is automatically a genius and entitled ever after to leave the dishes and walk around with her head in the clouds."
- "You look to me like a very ordinary three-piece suit."
- Man to Woman: "You look as if you wanted excitement—is that true?"
- "Go to sleep with a cheapskate—go on—it'd do you good. It would take another little tuck in your soul and you'd fit better, be more comfortable."
- "Francis says he wants to go away and try his personality on a lot of new people."
- "You went out of your way to make a preposterous attack on an old gentlewoman who had given you nothing but courtesy and consideration."

- "I have decided that the office cannot continue to hold both you and me. One of us must go—which shall it be?"
  "Well, Mr. Wrackham, your name is painted on the doors—I suppose it would be simpler if you stayed."
- "My last husband was thrown from his horse. You must learn to ride." He takes one look around uneasily for a horse.
- "We throw in one of these flowers. You know how frails are—if a stone sails in, they put up a yelp—if it's a rose, they think there's the Prince of Wales at last."
- "That one about the four girls named Meg who fall down the rabbit hole."
- "He wants to make a goddess out of me and I want to be Mickey Mouse."
- "Yes mam, if necessary. Look here, you take a girl and she goes into some cafe where she's got no business to go. Well, then, her escort he gets a little too much to drink an' he goes to sleep an' then some fella comes up and says, 'Hello, sweet mamma,' or whatever one of those mashers says up here. What does she do? She can't scream, on account of no real lady will scream nowadays—no—she just reaches down in her pocket and slips her fingers into a pair of Powell's defensive brass-knuckles, debutante's size, executes what I call the Society Hook, and Wham! that big fella's on his way to the cellar."

How Do You Respond?

1. Fitzgerald notes, "The cartoon cat licked the cartoon kitten and a girl behind me said, 'Isn't that sweet?'" Compare this sort of observation with Thoreau's encounter with a woodchuck.

2. Fitzgerald's notebooks consist of unrelated jottings and fragments. Do you think his quotations are made up or taken from life? What makes you think so? How would he use them in his fiction?

3. From the material selected for his notebooks, what kind of writer do you think that Fitzgerald is? Summarize briefly Fitzgerald's view of life. Is it comic? tragic? cynical? optimistic? other?

DOROTHY WORDSWORTH

> Dorothy Wordsworth (1771–1855) was the diffident and unsung heroine of her brother William's life: only with the posthumous publication of her Journal did it become clear how much she had contributed to his life's work. Again and again, she had given him the germ or seed of a poem. Self-denying, dutiful, sensitive, and totally dependable, she devoted all her days to the service of his needs. Her journals are perfectly matter of fact and unaffected: their main theme is that of sheer goodness of soul and clarity of perception. She is refreshingly free of any consciousness of self, and for that reason Virginia Woolf characteristically celebrated her.

From *THE GRASMERE JOURNALS*

March 12, 1802

Friday. A very fine morning. We went to see Mr. Clarkson off. Then we went up towards Easedale but a shower drove us back. The sun shone while it rained, and the stones of the walls and the pebbles on the road glittered like silver. When William was at Keswick I saw Jane Ashburner driving the cow along the high road from the well where she had been watering it. She had a stick in her hand and came tripping along in the Jig step, as if she were dancing—Her presence was bold and graceful, her cheeks flushed with health and her countenance was free and gay. William finished his poem of the singing bird. In the meantime I read the remainder of Lessing. In the Evening after tea William wrote Alice Fell—he went to bed tired with a wakeful mind and a weary Body. A very sharp clear night.

March 13

Saturday Morning. It was as cold as ever it has been all winter very hard frost. I baked pies Bread, and seed-cake for Mr Simpson. William finished Alice Fell, and then he wrote the Poem of the Beggar woman* taken from a Woman whom I had seen in May—

---

*The poem was ultimately named "Beggars."

(now nearly 2 years ago) when John and he were at Gallow Hill. I sate with him at Intervals all the morning, took down his stanzas etc. After dinner we walked to Rydale, for letters—it was terribly cold we had 2 or 3 brisk hail showers. The hail stones looked clean and pretty upon the dry clean Road. Little Peggy Simpson was standing at the door catching the Hail-stones in her hand. She grows very like her Mother. When she is sixteen years old I daresay, that to her Grandmother's eye she will seem as like to what her Mother was as any rose in her garden is like the Rose that grew there years before. No letters at Rydale. We drank tea as soon as we reached home. After tea I read to William that account of the little Boys belonging to the tall woman* and an unlucky thing it was for he could not escape from those very words, and so he could not write the poem. He left it unfinished and went tired to Bed. In our walk from Rydale he had got warmed with the subject and had half cast the Poem.

March 14

Sunday Morning. William had slept badly—he got up at 9 o'clock, but before he rose he had finished the Beggar Boys—and while we were at Breakfast that is (for I had breakfasted) he, with his Basin of Broth before him untouched and a little plate of Bread and butter he wrote the Poem to a Butterfly! He ate not a morsel, nor put on his stockings but sate with his shirt neck unbuttoned, and his waistcoat open while he did it. The thought first came upon him as we were talking about the pleasure we both always feel at the sight of a Butterfly. I told him that I used to chase them a little but that I was afraid of brushing the dust off their wings, and did not catch them— He told me how they used to kill all the white ones when he went to school because they were frenchmen. Mr Simpson came in just as he was finishing the Poem. After he was gone I wrote it down and the other poems and I read them all over to him. We then called at Mr Olliff's. Mr O. walked with us to within sight of Rydale—the sun shone very pleasantly, yet it was extremely cold. We dined and then Wm went to bed. I lay upon the fur gown before the fire but I could not sleep—I lay there a long time—it is now half past 5 I am going to write letters. I began to write to Mrs Rawson—

*the beggar boys.

William rose without having slept we sate comfortably by the fire till he began to try to alter the butterfly, and tired himself—he went to bed tired.

March 15

Monday Morning We sate reading the poems and I read a little German. Mr Luff came in at one o'clock. He had a long talk with William—he went to Mr Olliff's after dinner and returned to us to tea. During his absence a sailor who was travelling from Liverpool to Whitehaven called he was faint and pale when he knocked at the door, a young Man very well dressed. We sate by the kitchen fire talking with him for 2 hours—he told us [? most] interesting stories of his life. His name was Isaac Chapel—he had been at sea since he was 15 years old. He was by trade a sail-maker. His last voyage was to the Coast of Guinea. He had been on board a slave ship the Captain's name Maxwell where one man had been killed a Boy put to lodge with the pigs and was half eaten, one Boy set to watch in the hot sun till he dropped down dead. He had been cast away in North America and had travelled 30 days among the Indians where he had been well treated—He had twice swum from a King's ship in the night and escaped, he said he would rather be in hell than be pressed. He was now going to wait in England to appear against Captain Maxwell. "O he's a Rascal, Sir, he ought to be put in the papers!" The poor man had not been in bed since Friday Night. He left Liverpool at 2 o'clock on Saturday morning. He had called at a farm house to beg victuals and had been refused. The woman said she would give him nothing. "Won't you? Then I can't help it." He was excessively like my Brother John. A letter was brought us at tea time by John Dawson from M. H. I wrote to her, to Sara about Mr Olliff's gig, and to Longman and Rees*—I wrote to Mrs Clarkson by Mr Luff.

March 16

Tuesday. A very fine morning. Mrs Luff called. William went up into the orchard while she was here and wrote a part of The Emigrant Mother. After dinner I read him to sleep—I read Spenser while he leaned upon my shoulder. We walked to look at Rydale. Then

*Wordsworth's publishers.

we walked towards Goan's. The moon was a good height above the mountains. She seemed far and distant in the sky there were two stars beside her, that twinkled in and out, and seemed almost like butterflies* in motion and lightness. They looked to be far nearer to us than the Moon.

March 17
Wednesday. William went up into the orchard and finished the Poem. Mrs Luff and Mrs Olliff called I went with Mrs O. to the top of the White Moss—Mr O. met us and I went to their house he offered me manure for the garden. I went and sate with W. and walked backwards and forwards in the orchard till dinner time—he read me his poem. I broiled Beefsteaks. After dinner we made a pillow of my shoulder, I read to him and my Beloved slept—I afterwards got him the pillows and he was lying with his head on the table when Miss Simpson came in. She stayed tea. I went with her to Rydale. No letters! A sweet Evening as it had been a sweet day, a grey evening, and I walked quietly along the side of Rydale Lake with quiet thoughts—the hills and the lake were still—the Owls had not begun to hoot, and the little Birds had given over singing. I looked before me and I saw a red light upon Silver How as if coming out of the vale below,

> "There was a light of most strange birth
> A Light that came out of the earth
> And spread along the dark hill-side."†

Thus I was going on when I saw the shape of my Beloved in the Road at a little distance—we turned back to see the light but it was fading—almost gone. The owls hooted when we sate on the Wall at the foot of White Moss. The sky broke more and more and we saw the moon now and then. John Green passed us with his cart—we sate on. When we came in sight of our own dear Grasmere, the Vale looked fair and quiet in the moonshine,‡ the Church was there

*Two words erased: "or skylarks".
†Might these be lost lines from *Peter Bell*, which D. W. was copying about this time? (H. D.)
‡D. W. wrote first, "quiet and fair in the moonlight," then erased it.

and all the cottages. There were high slow-travelling clouds in the sky that threw large masses of Shade upon some of the Mountains. We walked backwards and forwards between home and Oliffs till I was tired. William kindled and began to write the poem.* We carried cloaks into the orchard and sate a while there, I left him and he nearly finished the poem. I was tired to death and went to bed before him—he came to me and read the Poem to me in bed.—A sailor begged here today going to Glasgow he spoke cheerfully in a sweet tone.

How Do You Respond?

1. Would Dorothy Wordsworth's Journals interest us if her brother were not famous? Are you interested in them in their own right? Why?

2. How does Dorothy Wordsworth reveal herself in these selections? Discuss.

3. Write a short character sketch of Dorothy Wordsworth, based on these extracts from her journals.

*Probably "The Emigrant Mother."

MAY SARTON

> *Novelist, poet, playwright, autobiographer, journal-keeper, May Sarton (born in Belgium in 1912) has written over two dozen volumes, including* The Bridge of Years, Shadow of a Man, Inner Landscape, *and* Collected Poems, 1930–1973. *She has said, "It is my hope that all my work may come to be seen as a whole, the communication of a vision of life that is unsentimental, humorous, passionate, and in the end, timeless." The following selection is from her* Journal of a Solitude.

From JOURNAL OF A SOLITUDE

September 15th

. . . It is raining. I look out on the maple, where a few leaves have turned yellow, and listen to Punch, the parrot, talking to himself and to the rain ticking gently against the windows. I am here alone for the first time in weeks, to take up my "real" life again at last. That is what is strange—that friends, even passionate love, are not my real life unless there is time alone in which to explore and to discover what is happening or has happened. Without the interruptions, nourishing and maddening, this life would become arid. Yet I taste it fully only when I am alone here and "the house and I resume old conversations."

On my desk, small pink roses. Strange how often the autumn roses look sad, fade quickly, frost-browned at the edges! But these are lovely, bright, singing pink. On the mantel, in the Japanese jar, two sprays of white lilies recurved, maroon pollen on the stamens, and a branch of peony leaves turned a strange pinkish-brown. It is an elegant bouquet; *shibui,* the Japanese would call it. When I am alone the flowers are really seen; I can pay attention to them. They are felt as presences. Without them I would die. Why do I say that? Partly because they change before my eyes. They live and die in a few days; they keep me closely in touch with process, with growth, and also with dying. I am floated on their moments.

The ambience here is order and beauty. That is what frightens me when I am first alone again. I feel inadequate. I have made an open place, a place for meditation. What if I cannot find myself inside it?

I think of these pages as a way of doing that. For a long time now, every meeting with another human being has been a collision. I feel too much, sense too much, am exhausted by the reverberations after even the simplest conversation. But the deep collision is and has been with my unregenerate, tormenting, and tormented self. I have written every poem, every novel, for the same purpose—to find out what I think, to know where I stand. I am unable to become what I see. I feel like an inadequate machine, a machine that breaks down at crucial moments, grinds to a dreadful halt, "won't go," or, even worse, explodes in some innocent person's face.

Plant Dreaming Deep has brought me many friends of the work (and also, harder to respond to, people who think they have found in me an intimate friend). But I have begun to realize that, without my own intention, that book gives a false view. The anguish of my life here—its rages—is hardly mentioned. Now I hope to break through into the rough rocky depths, to the matrix itself. There is violence there and anger never resolved. I live alone, perhaps for no good reason, for the reason that I am an impossible creature, set apart by a temperament I have never learned to use as it could be used, thrown off by a word, a glance, a rainy day, or one drink too many. My need to be alone is balanced against my fear of what will happen when suddenly I enter the huge empty silence if I cannot find support there. I go up to Heaven and down to Hell in an hour, and keep alive only by imposing upon myself inexorable routines. I write too many letters and too few poems. It may be outwardly silent here but in the back of my mind is a clamor of human voices, too many needs, hopes, fears. I hardly ever sit still without being haunted by the "undone" and the "unsent." I often feel exhausted, but it is not my work that tires (work is a rest): it is the effort of pushing away the lives and needs of others before I can come to the work with any freshness and zest.

September 17th

Cracking open the inner world again, writing even a couple of pages, threw me back into depression, not made easier by the weather, two gloomy days of darkness and rain. I was attacked by a storm of tears, those tears that appear to be related to frustration, to buried anger, and come upon me without warning. I woke yesterday so depressed that I did not get up till after eight.

I drove to Brattleboro to read poems at the new Unitarian church there in a state of dread and exhaustion. How to summon the vitality needed? I had made an arrangement of religious poems, going back to early books and forward into the new book not yet published. I suppose it went all right—at least it was not a disaster—but I felt (perhaps I am wrong) that the kind, intelligent people gathered in a big room looking out on pine trees did not really want to think about God, His absence (many of the poems speak of that) or His presence. Both are too frightening. . . .

September 18th

The value of solitude—one of its values—is, of course, that there is nothing to *cushion* against attacks from within, just as there is nothing to help balance at times of particular stress or depression. A few moments of desultory conversation with dear Arnold Miner, when he comes to take the trash, may calm an inner storm. But the storm, painful as it is, might have had some truth in it. So sometimes one has simply to endure a period of depression for what it may hold of illumination if one can live through it, attentive to what it exposes or demands.

The reasons for depression are not so interesting as the way one handles it, simply to stay alive. This morning I woke at four and lay awake for an hour or so in a bad state. It is raining again. I got up finally and went about the daily chores, waiting for the sense of doom to lift—and what did it was watering the house plants. Suddenly joy came back because I was fulfilling a simple need, a living one. Dusting never has this effect (and that may be why I am such a poor housekeeper!), but feeding the cats when they are hungry, giving Punch clean water, makes me suddenly feel calm and happy.

Whatever peace I know rests in the natural world, in feeling myself a part of it, even in a small way. Maybe the gaiety of the Warner family, their wisdom, comes from this, that they work close to nature all the time. As simple as that? But it is not simple. Their life requires patient understanding, imagination, the power to endure constant adversity—the weather, for example! To go with, not against the elements, an inexhaustible vitality summoned back each day to do the same tasks, to feed the animals, clean out barns and pens, keep that complex world alive.

September 19th
The sun is out. It rose through the mist, making the raindrops sparkle on the lawn. Now there is blue sky, warm air, and I have just created a wonder—two large autumn crocuses plus a small spray of pink single chrysanthemums and a piece of that silvery leaf (artemisia? arethusa?) whose name I forget in the Venetian glass in the cosy room. May they be benign presences toward this new day! . . .

How Do You Respond?

1. Do you believe that it is necessary to "get away" in order to think and write? Do you think solitude is a good thing? Do you fear it or welcome it?

2. What, for you, makes an event or occasion important or legitimate? Do you do things that others think is a waste of time? What supports you when you don't have others' approval for an occupation?

3. Sarton refers to a storm inside herself that "might have had some truth in it." What does she mean? Have you experienced storms with truth in them? Tell about one, or about how you become aware of inner feelings.

HENRY DAVID THOREAU

> The voice of Henry David Thoreau (1817–1862) is one of the essentially and distinctively American voices of the nineteenth century. A careful craftsman, he worked to shape a prose that conveys the sheer richness and nervous energy of a person almost intoxicated with the sheer intensity of being alive. His entry of April 12, 1852, reveals him as very much a man of his time, yet every generation discovers a "new" Thoreau: like the natural world that he never tired of celebrating, he is prodigal, enlivening, and inexhaustible. Among other things, we can learn from him—particularly in his Journals and in Walden—the pleasure of losing the self in the act of really paying attention to what is there.

From the JOURNALS

April 1 [1852]

. . . We have had a good solid winter, which has put the previous summer far behind us; intense cold, deep and lasting snows, and clear, tense winter sky. It is a good experience to have gone through with.

April 3

. . . The bluebird carries the sky on his back.

April 12

. . . I am made somewhat sad this afternoon by the coarseness and vulgarity of my companion, because he is one with whom I have made myself intimate. He inclines latterly to speak with coarse jesting of facts which should always be treated with delicacy and reverence. I lose my respect for the man who can make the mystery of sex the subject of a coarse jest, yet, when you speak earnestly and seriously on the subject, is silent. I feel that this is to be truly irreligious. Whatever may befall me, I trust that I may never lose my respect for purity in others. The subject of sex is one on which I do not wish to meet a man at all unless I can meet him on the most inspiring ground—if his view degrades, and does not elevate.

I would preserve purity in act and thought, as I would cherish the memory of my mother.

April 16

. . . As I turned round the corner of Hubbard's Grove, saw a woodchuck, the first of the season, in the middle of the field, six or seven rods from the fence which bounds the wood, and twenty rods distant. I ran along the fence and cut him off, or rather overtook him, though he started at the same time. When I was only a rod and a half off, he stopped, and I did the same; then he ran again, and I ran up within three feet of him, when he stopped again, the fence being between us. I squatted down and surveyed him at my leisure. His eyes were dull black and rather inobvious, with a faint chestnut (?) iris, with but little expression and that more of resignation than of anger. The general aspect was a coarse grayish brown, a sort of grisel (?). A lighter brown next the skin, then black or very dark brown and tipped with whitish rather loosely. The head between a squirrel and a bear, flat on the top and dark brown, and darker still or black on the tip of the nose. The whiskers black, two inches long. The ears very small and roundish, set far back amd nearly buried in the fur. Black feet, with long and slender claws for digging. It appeared to tremble, or perchance shivered with cold. When I moved, it gritted its teeth quite loud, sometimes striking the under jaw against the other chatteringly, sometimes grinding one jaw on the other, yet as if more from instinct than anger. Whichever way I turned, that way it headed. I took a twig a foot long and touched its snout, at which it started forward and bit the stick, lessening the distance between us to two feet, and still it held all the ground it gained. I played with it tenderly awhile with the stick, trying to open its gritting jaws. Ever its long incisors, two above and the two below, were presented. But I thought it would go to sleep if I stayed long enough. It did not sit upright as sometimes, but *standing* on its fore feet with its head down, i.e. half sitting, half standing. We sat looking at one another about half an hour, till we began to feel mesmeric influences. When I was tired, I moved away, wishing to see him run, but I could not start him. He would not stir as long as I was looking at him or could see him. I walked round him; he turned as fast and fronted me still. I sat down by his side within a foot. I talked to him *quasi* forest lingo, baby-talk, at any rate in a conciliatory tone, and thought that I had some influence on him. He gritted his teeth less. I chewed checkerberry leaves and presented them to his nose at last without a grit; though I saw that by so much gritting of the teeth he had worn them rapidly and they were covered with a fine white powder, which, if you measured it thus, would have made his anger terrible. He did not mind any noise I might make. With a little stick I lifted one of his paws to examine it, and held it up at pleasure. I turned him over to see what color he was beneath (darker or more purely brown), though he turned himself back again sooner than I could have wished. His tail was also all brown, though not very dark, rat-tail like, with loose hairs standing out on all sides like a caterpillar brush. He had a rather mild look. I spoke kindly to him. I reached checkerberry leaves to his mouth. I stretched my hands over him, though he turned up his head and still gritted a little. I laid my hand on him, but immediately took it off again, instinct not being wholly overcome. If I had had a few fresh bean leaves, thus in advance of the season, I am sure I should have tamed him completely. It was a frizzy tail. His is a humble, terrestrial color like a partridge's, well concealed where dead wiry grass rises above darker brown or chestnut dead leaves—a modest color. If I had had some food, I should have ended with stroking him at my leisure. Could easily have wrapped him in my handkerchief. He was not fat nor particularly lean. I finally had to leave him without seeing him move from the place. A large, clumsy, burrowing squirrel. *Arctomys*, bear-mouse. I respect him as one of the natives. He lies there, by his color and habits so naturalized amid the dry leaves, the withered grass, and the bushes. A sound nap, too, he has enjoyed in his native fields, the past winter. I think I might learn some wisdom of him. His ancestors have lived here longer than mine. He is more thoroughly acclimated and naturalized than I. Bean leaves the red man raised for him, but he can do without them.

April 24

. . . I know two species of men. The vast majority are men of society. They live on the surface; they are interested in the transient and fleeting; they are like driftwood on the flood. They ask forever and only the news, the froth and scum of the eternal sea. They use policy; they make up for want of matter with manner. They have many letters to write. Wealth and the approbation of men is to them success. The enterprises of society are something final and sufficing for them. The world advises them, and they listen to its advice. They live wholly an evanescent life, creatures of circumstance. It is of prime importance to them who is the president of the day. They have no knowledge of truth, but by an exceedingly dim and transient instinct, which stereotypes the church and some other institutions. They dwell, they are ever, right in my face and eyes like gnats; they are like motes, so near the eyes that, looking beyond, they appear like blurs; they have their being between my eyes and the end of my nose. The *terra firma* of my existence lies far beyond, behind them and their improvements. If they write, the best of them deal in "elegant literature." Society, man, has no prize to offer me that can tempt me; not one. That which interests a town or city or any large number of men is always something trivial, as politics. It is impossible for me to be interested in what interests men generally. Their pursuits and interests seem to me frivolous. When I am most myself and see the clearest, men are least to be seen; . . . and that they are seen at all is the proof of imperfect vision. These affairs of men are so narrow as to afford no vista, no distance; it is a shallow foreground only, no large extended views to be taken. Men put to me frivolous questions: When did I come? where am I going? That was a more pertinent question—what I lectured for?—which one auditor put once to another. What an ordeal it were to make men pass through, to consider how many ever put to you a vital question! Their knowledge of something better gets no further than what is called religion and spiritual knockings.

May 8
. . . No tarts that I ever tasted at any table possessed such a refreshing, cheering, encouraging acid that literally put the heart in you and set you on edge for this world's experiences, bracing the spirit, as the cranberries I have plucked in the meadows in the spring. They cut the winter's phlegm, and now I can swallow another year of this world without other sauce. Even on the Thanksgiving table they are comparatively insipid, have lost as much flavor as beauty, are never so beautiful as in water.

April 23 [1857]
I saw at Daniel Ricketson's a young woman, Miss Kate Brady, twenty years old, her father an Irishman, a worthless fellow, her mother a

smart Yankee. The daughter formerly did sewing, but now keeps school for a livelihood. She was born at the Brady house, I think in Freetown, where she lived till twelve years old and helped her father in the field. There she rode horse to plow and was knocked off the horse by apple tree boughs, kept sheep, caught fish, etc., etc. I never heard a girl or woman express so strong a love for nature. She purposes to return to that lonely ruin, and dwell there alone, since her mother and sister will not accompany her; says that she knows all about farming and keeping sheep and spinning and weaving, though it would puzzle her to shingle the old house. There she thinks she can "live free." I was pleased to hear of her plans, because they were quite cheerful and original, not professedly reformatory, but growing out of her love for "Squire's Brook and the Middleborough ponds." A strong love for outward nature is singularly rare among both men and women. The scenery immediately about her homestead is quite ordinary, yet she appreciates and can use that part of the universe as no other being can. Her own sex, so tamely bred, only jeer at her for entertaining such an idea, but she has a strong head and a love for good reading, which may carry her through. I would by no means discourage, nor yet particularly encourage her, for I would have her so strong as to succeed in spite of all ordinary discouragements.

April 26
... A great part of our troubles are literally domestic or originate in the house and from living indoors. I could write an essay to be entitled "Out of Doors"—undertake a crusade against houses. What a different thing Christianity preached to the house-bred and to a party who lived out of doors! Also a sermon is needed on economy of fuel. What right has my neighbor to burn ten cords of wood, when I burn only one? Thus robbing our half-naked town of this precious covering. Is he so much colder than I? It is expensive to maintain him in our midst. If some earn the salt of their porridge, are we certain that they earn the fuel of their kitchen and parlor? One man makes a little of the driftwood of the river or of the dead and refuse (unmarketable!) wood of the forest suffice, and Nature rejoices in him. Another, Herod-like, requires ten cords of the best of young white oak or hickory, and he is commonly esteemed a virtuous man. He who burns the most wood on his hearth is the

least warmed by the sight of it growing. Leave the trim wood-lots to widows and orphan girls. Let men tread gently through nature. Let us religiously burn stumps and worship in groves, while Christian vandals lay waste the forest temples to build miles of meeting houses and horse-sheds and feed their box stoves.

May 3

. . . Up and down the town, men and boys that are under subjection are polishing their shoes and brushing their go-to-meeting clothes. I, a descendant of Northmen who worshipped Thor, spend my time worshipping neither Thor nor Christ; a descendant of Northmen who sacrificed men and horses, sacrifice neither men nor horses. I care not for Thor nor for the Jews. I sympathize not today with those who go to church in newest clothes and sit quietly in straight-backed pews. I sympathize rather with the boy who has none to look after him, who borrows a boat and paddle and in common clothes sets out to explore these temporary vernal lakes. I meet such a boy paddling along under a sunny bank, with bare feet and his pants rolled up above his knees, ready to leap into the water at a moment's warning. . . .

May 8

. . . Within a week I have had made a pair of corduroy pants, which cost when done $1.60. They are of that peculiar clay color, reflecting the light from portions of their surface. They have this advantage, that, beside being very strong, they will look about as well three months hence as now—or as ill, some would say. Most of my friends are disturbed by my wearing them. I can get four of five pairs for what one ordinary pair would cost in Boston, and each of the former will last two or three times as long under the same circumstances. The tailor said that the stuff was not made in this country; that it was worn by the Irish at home, and now they would not look at it, but others would not wear it, durable and cheap as it is, because it is worn by the Irish. Moreover, I like the color on other accounts. Anything but black clothes.

How Do You Respond?

1. Have you ever paid attention to an animal as closely as Thoreau did the woodchuck? Has such a close examination ever changed your way

of looking at things? As an exercise, choose a partner and take turns, one talking and the other taking notes, while attending to an animal. Look for a squirrel or dog on campus, or, ideally, observe an unfamiliar animal, perhaps in a zoo.

2. What do you suppose that the woodchuck would have written in its journal after its encounter with Thoreau? (Would it have felt that he had "respected" it?)

3. Write a journal entry by one of the "men of society" (April 24) about Thoreau and his values. Do you think that either Thoreau or the people who seek success are entirely right? Where do you think the balance lies?

VIRGINIA WOOLF

> *The* Diaries *of Virginia Woolf (1882–1941) reveal the writer as heroine: frequently preyed on by profound depressions, she found her salvation in work and friendship. Of her* Diaries, *W. H. Auden wrote: "I have never read any book that more truthfully conveyed what a writer's life is like. . . ." Anyone wishing to learn how the vocation of writing can bring absorption, delight, self-transcendence, and a deep sense of personal meaning, need look no further. She was always a remarkable writer and is known best for her novels,* To The Lighthouse, Mrs. Dalloway, The Waves, *and for her feminist essay,* A Room of One's Own. *Her* Diaries *reveal her, as well, as a great human being.*

From *A WRITER'S DIARY*

Friday, January 3rd 1936

I began the year with three entirely submerged days, headache, head bursting, head so full, racing with ideas; and the rain pouring; the floods out; when we stumbled out yesterday the mud came over my great rubber boots; the water squelched in my soles; so this Christmas has been, as far as country is concerned, a failure, and in spite of what London can do to chafe and annoy I'm glad to go back and have, rather guiltily, begged not to stay here another week. Today it is a yellow grey foggy day; so that I can only see the hump, a wet gleam, but no Caburn. I am content though because I think that I have recovered enough balance in the head to begin *The Years*, I mean the final revision on Monday. This suddenly becomes a little urgent, because for the first time for some years, L. says I have not made enough to pay my share of the house, and have to find £70 out of my hoard. This is now reduced to £700 and I must fill it up. Amusing, in its way, to think of economy again. But it would be a strain to think seriously; and worse—a brutal interruption—had I to make money by journalism. The next book I think of calling *Answers to Correspondents* . . . But I must not at once stop and make it up. No, I must find a patient and quiet method of soothing that excitable nerve to sleep until *The Years* is on the table—finished. In February? Oh the relief—as if a vast—what can I say—bony excrescence—bag of muscle—were cut out of my brain. Yet it's better to write that than the other. A queer light on my psychology. I can no longer write for papers. I must write for my own book. I mean I at once adapt what I'm going to say, if I think of a newspaper.

Saturday, January 4th

The weather has improved and we have decided to stay till Wednesday. It will now of course rain. But I will make some good resolutions: to read as few weekly papers, which are apt to prick me into recollection of myself, as possible, until this *Years* is over: to fill my brain with remote books and habits; not to think of *Answers to Correspondents;* and altogether to be as fundamental and as little superficial, to be as physical, as little apprehensive, as possible. And now to do Roger; and then to relax. For, to tell the truth, my head is still all nerves; and one false move means racing despair, exaltation, and all the rest of that familiar misery: that long scale of unhappiness. So I have ordered a sirloin and we shall go for a drive.

Sunday, January 5th

I have had another morning at the old plague. I rather suspect that I have said the thing I meant, and any further work will only muddle. Further work must be merely to tidy and smooth out. This seems likely because I'm so calm. I feel well, that's done. I want to be off on something else. Whether good or bad, I don't know. And my head is quiet today, soothed by reading *The Trumpet Major* last night and a drive to the floods. The clouds were an extraordinary tropical birds wing colour: an impure purple; and the lakes reflected it, and there were droves of plover, black and white; and all very linear in line and pure and subtle in colour. How I slept!

Tuesday, January 7th
I have again copied out the last pages, and I think got the spacing better. Many details and some fundamentals remain. The snow scene for example, and I suspect a good many unfaced passages remain. But I preserve my sense that it's stated; and I need only use my craft, not my creation.

Thursday, January 16th
Seldom have I been more completely miserable than I was about 6:30 last night, reading over the last part of *The Years*. Such feeble twaddle—such twilight gossip it seemed; such a show up of my own decrepitude, and at such huge length. I could only plump it down on the table and rush upstairs with burning cheeks to L. He said: "This always happens." But I felt, No, it has never been so bad as this. I make this note should I be in the same state after another book. Now this morning, dipping in, it seems to me, on the contrary, a full, bustling live book. I looked at the early pages. I think there's something to it. But I must now force myself to begin regular sending to Mabel. 100 pages go tonight I swear.

Tuesday, February 25th
And this will show how hard I work. This is the first moment—this five minutes before lunch—that I've had to write here. I work all the morning: I work from 5 to 7 most days. Then I've had headaches: vanquish them by lying still and binding books and reading *David Copperfield*. I have sworn that the script shall be ready, typed and corrected, on 10th March. L. will then read it. And I've still all the Richmond and El. scene to type out: many corrections in that most accursed raid scene to make: all this to have typed: if I can by the 1st which is Sunday; and then I must begin at the beginning and read straight through. So I'm quite un-

able either to write here or to do Roger. On the whole, I'm enjoying it—that's odd—though in the ups and downs and with no general opinion.

Wednesday, March 4th

Well, I'm almost through copying the raid scene, I should think for the 13th time. Then it will go tomorrow; and I shall have I think one day's full holiday—if I dare—before re-reading. So I'm in sight of the end: that is in sight of the beginning of the other book which keeps knocking unmercifully at the door. Oh to be able once more to write freely every morning, spinning my own words afresh—what a boon—what a physical relief, rest, delight after these last months—since October year more or less—of perpetual compressing and re-writing always at that one book.

Sunday, June 21st

. . . A very strange, most remarkable summer. New emotions: humility, impersonal joy, literary despair. I am learning my craft in the most fierce conditions. Really reading Flaubert's letters I hear my own voice cry out Oh art! Patience: find him consoling, admonishing. I must get this book quietly, strongly, daringly into shape. But it won't be out till next year. Yet I think it has possibilities, could I seize them. I am trying to cut the characters deep in a phrase: to pare off and compact scenes: to envelop the whole in a medium.

Tuesday, June 23rd

A good day—a bad day—so it goes on. Few people can be so tortured by writing as I am. Only Flaubert I think. Yet I see it now, as a whole. I think I can bring it off, if I only have courage and patience: take each scene quietly: compose: I think it may be a good book. And then—oh when it's finished!

Not so clear today, because I went to dentist and then shopped. My brain is like a scale: one grain pulls it down. Yesterday it balanced: today dips.

Friday, October 30th

I do not wish for the moment to write out the story of the months since I made the last mark here. I do not wish, for reasons I cannot now develop, to analyse that extraordinary summer. It will be more helpful and healthy for me to write scenes; to take up my pen and describe actual events: good practice too for my stumbling and doubting pen. Can I still "write"? That is the question, you see. And now I will try to prove if the gift is dead, or dormant.

How Do You Respond?

1. Do you think that Virginia Woolf records things in her diary that she has thought out, or does she write to find out what she thinks?

2. Virginia Woolf distinguishes between craft (revision) and creation (writing a first draft). Compare these two activities, referring to her entries for January 7 and March 4.

3. Virginia Woolf argues with herself in her diary. Choose such a passage and discuss how her fears and her reason contend in it.

ANNE FRANK

> *Anne Frank (1929–1945) left a classic account of adolescence, of how an intelligent girl perceived the life of her emotions, her mind, and her body. As with others of genius who died young, there is little point in speculating about what she might have become had she survived her early years. Her* Diary *is one of the quintessential statements of what growing up feels like from the inside. That she fell prey to the Nazi reign of terror is an inescapable part of the poignancy and tragic irony of her* Diary; *but even had she not been killed at the hands of the Nazis, her diary would still exert its power and truth over us.*

From *THE DIARY OF A YOUNG GIRL*

Sunday, 14 June, 1942

On Friday, June 12th, I woke up at six o'clock and no wonder; it was my birthday. But of course I was not allowed to get up at that hour, so I had to control my curiosity until a quarter to seven. Then I could bear it no longer, and went to the dining room, where I received a warm welcome from Moortje (the cat).

Soon after seven I went to Mummy and Daddy and then to the sitting room to undo my presents. The first to greet me was *you*, possibly the nicest of all. Then on the table there were a bunch of roses, a plant, and some peonies, and more arrived during the day.

I got masses of things from Mummy and Daddy, and was thoroughly spoiled by various friends. Among other things I was given *Camera Obscura*, a party game, lots of sweets, chocolates, a puzzle, a brooch, *Tales and Legends of the Netherlands* by Joseph Cohen, *Daisy's Mountain Holiday* (a terrific book), and some money. Now I can buy *The Myths of Greece and Rome*—grand!

Then Lies called for me and we went to school. During recess I treated everyone to sweet biscuits, and then we had to go back to our lessons.

Now I must stop. Bye-bye, we're going to be great pals!

Monday, 15 June, 1942

I had my birthday party on Sunday afternoon. We showed a film *The Lighthouse Keeper* with Rin-Tin-Tin, which my school friends thoroughly enjoyed. We had a lovely time. There were lots of girls and boys. Mummy always wants to know whom I'm going to marry. Little does she guess that it's Peter Wessel; one day I managed, without blushing or flickering an eyelid, to get that idea right out of her mind. For years Lies Goosens and Sanne Houtman have been my best friends. Since then, I've got to know Jopie de Waal at the Jewish Secondary School. We are together a lot and she is now my best girl friend. Lies is more friendly with another girl, and Sanne goes to a different school, where she has made new friends.

Saturday, 20 June, 1942

I haven't written for a few days, because I wanted first of all to think about my diary. It's an odd idea for someone like me to keep a diary; not only because I have never done so before, but because it seems to me that neither I—nor for that matter anyone else—will be interested in the unbosomings of a thirteen-year-old schoolgirl. Still, what does that matter? I want to write, but more than that, I want to bring out all kinds of things that lie buried deep in my heart.

There is a saying that "paper is more patient than man"; it came back to me on one of my slightly melancholy days, while I sat chin in hand, feeling too bored and limp even to make up my mind whether to go out or stay at home. Yes, there is no doubt that paper is patient and as I don't intend to show this cardboard-covered notebook, bearing the proud name of "diary," to anyone, unless I find a real friend, boy or girl, probably nobody cares. And now I come to the root of the matter, the reason for my starting a diary: it is that I have no such real friend.

Let me put it more clearly, since no one will believe that a girl of thirteen feels herself quite alone in the world, nor is it so. I have darling parents and a sister of sixteen. I know about thirty people whom one might call friends—I have strings of boy friends, anxious to catch a glimpse of me and who, failing that, peep at me through mirrors in class. I have relations, aunts and uncles, who are darlings too, a good home, no—I don't seem to lack anything. But it's the same with all my friends, just fun and joking, nothing more. I can never bring myself to talk of anything outside the common round. We don't seem to be able to get any closer, that is the root of the trouble. Perhaps I lack confidence, but anyway, there it is, a stubborn fact and I don't seem to be able to do anything about it.

Hence, this diary. In order to enhance in my mind's eye the picture of the friend for whom I have waited so long, I don't want to set down a series of bald facts in a diary like most people do, but I want this diary itself to be my friend, and I shall call my friend Kitty. No one will grasp what I'm talking about if I begin my letters to Kitty just out of the blue, so albeit unwillingly, I will start by sketching in brief the story of my life.

My father was thirty-six when he married my mother, who was then twenty-five. My sister Margot was born in 1926 in Frankfort-on-Main, I followed on June 12, 1929, and, as we are Jewish, we emigrated to Holland in 1933, where my father was appointed Managing Director of Travies N.V. This firm is in close relationship with the firm of Kolen & Co. in the same building, of which my father is a partner.

The rest of our family, however, felt the full impact of Hitler's anti-Jewish laws, so life was filled with anxiety. In 1938 after the pogroms, my two uncles (my mother's brothers) escaped to the U.S.A. My old grandmother came to us, she was then seventy-three. After May 1940 good times rapidly fled: first the war, then the capitulation, followed by the arrival of the Germans, which is when the sufferings of us Jews really began. Anti-Jewish decrees followed each other in quick succession. Jews must wear a yellow star, Jews must hand in their bicycles, Jews are banned from trains and are forbidden to drive. Jews are only allowed to do their shopping between three and five o'clock and then only in shops which bear the placard "Jewish shop." Jews must be indoors by eight o'clock and cannot even sit in their own gardens after that hour. Jews are forbidden to visit theaters, cinemas, and other places of entertainment. Jews may not take part in public sports. Swimming baths, tennis courts, hockey fields, and other sports grounds are all prohibited to them. Jews may not visit Christians. Jews must go to Jewish schools, and many more restrictions of a similar kind.

So we could not do this and were forbidden to do that. But life went on in spite of it all. Jopie used to say to me, "You're scared to do anything, because it may be forbidden." Our freedom was strictly limited. Yet things were still bearable.

Granny died in January 1942; no one will ever know how much she is present in my thoughts and how much I love her still.

In 1934 I went to school at the Montessori Kindergarten and continued there. It was at the end of the school year, I was in form 6B, when I had to say good-by to Mrs. K. We both wept, it was very sad. In 1941 I went, with my sister Margot, to the Jewish Secondary School, she into the fourth form and I into the first.

So far everything is all right with the four of us and here I come to the present day.

Saturday, 20 June, 1942

Dear Kitty,

I'll start straight away. It is so peaceful at the moment, Mummy and Daddy are out and Margot has gone to play ping-pong with some friends.

I've been playing ping-pong a lot myself lately. We ping-pongers are very partial to an ice cream, especially in summer, when one gets warm at the game, so we usually finish up with a visit to the nearest ice-cream shop, Delphi or Oasis, where Jews are allowed. We've given up scrounging for extra pocket money. Oasis is usually full and among our large circle of friends we always manage to find some kindhearted gentleman or boy friend, who presents us with more ice cream than we could devour in a week.

I expect you will be rather surprised at the fact that I should talk of boy friends at my age. Alas, one simply can't seem to avoid it at our school. As soon as a boy asks if he may bicycle home with me and we get into conversation, nine out of ten times I can be sure that he will fall head over heels in love immediately and simply won't allow me out of his sight. After a while it cools down of course, especially as I take little notice of ardent looks and pedal blithely on.

If it gets so far that they begin about "asking Father" I swerve slightly on my bicycle, my satchel falls, the young man is bound to get off and hand it to me, by which time I have introduced a new topic of conversation.

These are the most innocent types; you get some who blow kisses or try to get hold of your arm, but then they are definitely knocking at the wrong door. I get off my bicycle and refuse to go further in their company, or I pretend to be insulted and tell them in no uncertain terms to clear off.

There, the foundation of our friendship is laid, till tomorrow!

Yours, Anne

How Do You Respond?

1. Would you be interested in Anne Frank's diary if you knew nothing of her fate? How far do the circumstances that you live in give meaning to your life?

2. If you had kept a diary when you were thirteen, how would it have compared with Anne Frank's? Would you have taken the same delight in ordinary matters? Did you also feel that there was a serious part of you unknown to your friends or family?

3. Is there something about Anne Frank that you think gives her short life meaning for you?

GEORGE ORWELL

> *George Orwell (1903–1950) will be remembered above all as the voice of the social conscience. With the steep decline in the influence of official religion in Britain, he filled the void with a stream of writings—Down and Out in Paris and London, Homage to Catalonia, Animal Farm, 1984—that express an incorruptible moral sensitivity, a strenuous conscience. A socialist from the time he achieved maturity, he was also his own man, a non-joiner, prickly, ironic, undeceived, bright-eyed, and perfectly disinterested—in the best sense of the word. Political cant he despised, whether it came from right or left. Predictably enough, both sides hated and feared him: not only would he not be bought, but he would not keep quiet. Always he would ask the uncomfortable questions and point out that the emperor was stark-naked. He died, characteristically, of self-neglect in middle-age.*

From *WAR-TIME DIARY: 1940*

8 June

In the middle of a fearful battle in which, I suppose, thousands of men are being killed every day, one has the impression that there is no news. The evening papers are the same as the morning ones, the morning ones are the same as those of the night before, and the radio repeats what is in the papers. As to truthfulness of news, however there is probably more suppression than downright lying. Borkenau considers that the effect of the radio has been to make war comparatively truthful, and that the only large-scale lying hitherto has been the German claims of British ships sunk. These have certainly been fantastic. Recently one of the evening papers which has made a note of the German announcements pointed out that in about 10 days the Germans claimed to have sunk 25 capital ships, i.e. 10 more than we ever possessed.

Stephen Spender said to me recently, "Don't you feel that any time during the past ten years you have been able to foretell events better than, say, the Cabinet?" I had to agree to this. Partly it is a question of not being blinded by class interests etc, e.g. anyone not financially interested could see at a glance the strategic danger to

England of letting Germany and Italy dominate Spain, whereas many rightwingers, even professional soldiers, simply could not grasp this most obvious fact. But where I feel that people like us understand the situation better than so-called experts is not in any power to foretell specific events, but in the power to grasp what *kind* of world we are living in. At any rate, I have known since about 1931 (Spender says he has known since 1929) that the future must be catastrophic. I could not say exactly what wars and revolutions would happen, but they never surprised me when they came. Since 1934 I have known war between England and Germany was coming, and since 1936 I have known it with complete certainty. I could feel it in my belly, and the chatter of the pacifists on the one hand, and the Popular Front people who pretended to fear that Britain was preparing for war against Russia on the other, never deceived me. Similarly, such horrors as the Russian purges never surprised me, because I had always felt that—not *exactly* that, but something *like* that—was implicit in Bolshevik rule. I could feel it in their literature. . . . Who would have believed seven years ago that Winston Churchill had any kind of political future before him? A year ago Cripps* was the naughty boy of the Labour Party, who expelled him and refused even to hear his defence. On the other hand, from the Conservative point of view he was a dangerous Red. Now he is ambassador in Moscow, the Beaverbrook press having led the cry for his appointment. Impossible to say yet whether he is the right man. If the Russians are disposed to come round to our side, he probably is, but if they are still hostile, it would have been better to send a man who does not admire the Russian régime.

10 June
Have just heard, though it is not in the papers, that Italy has declared war. . . . The allied troops are withdrawing from Norway,

---

*Sir Stafford Cripps (1889–1952), started his career as a successful lawyer, becoming a Labour MP in 1931. Frequently in trouble with the Labour Party leadership during the '30s, he was considered a brilliant theoretical mind, while his personal austerity and the rigidity of his Socialism gained him respect if not affection. He was Ambassador to Moscow 1940–42. He then joined the War Cabinet in February 1942 as Lord Privy Seal and Leader of the House of Commons. In the post-war Labour Government he was Chancellor of the Exchequer 1947–50.

the reason given being that they can be used elsewhere and Narvik after its capture was rendered useless to the Germans. But in fact Narvik will not be necessary to them till the winter, it wouldn't have been much use anyway when Norway had ceased to be neutral, and I shouldn't have thought the allies had enough troops in Norway to make much difference. The real reason is probably so as not to have to waste warships.

This afternoon I remembered very vividly that incident with the taxi-driver in Paris in 1936, and was going to have written something about it in this diary. But now I feel so saddened that I can't write it. Everything is disintegrating. It makes me writhe to be writing book reviews etc at such a time, and even angers me that such time-wasting should still be permitted. The interview at the War Office on Saturday *may* come to something, if I am clever at faking my way past the doctor. If once in the army, I know by the analogy of the Spanish war, that I shall cease to care about public events. At present I feel as I felt in 1936 when the Fascists were closing in on Madrid, only far worse. But I will write about the taxi-driver some time.

12 June

E and I last night walked through Soho to see whether the damage to Italian shops etc was as reported. It seemed to have been exaggerated in the newspapers, but we did see, I think, 3 shops which had had their windows smashed. The majority had hurriedly labelled themselves "British". Gennari's, the Italian grocer's, was plastered all over with printed placards saying "This establishment is entirely British". The Spaghetti House, a shop specialising in Italian foodstuffs, had renamed itself "British Food Shop". Another shop proclaimed itself Swiss, and even a French restaurant had labelled itself British. The interesting thing is that all these placards must evidently have been printed beforehand and kept in readiness.
. . . Disgusting though these attacks on harmless Italian shopkeepers are, they are an interesting phenomenon, because English people, i.e. people of a kind who would be likely to loot shops, don't as a rule take a spontaneous interest in foreign politics. I don't think there was anything of this kind during the Abyssinian war, and the Spanish war simply did not touch the mass of the people. Nor was

there any popular move against the Germans resident in England until the last month or two. The low-down, cold-blooded meanness of Mussolini's declaration of war at that moment must have made an impression even on people who as a rule barely read the newspapers.

13 June

Yesterday to a group conference of the LDV,* held in the Committee Room at Lord's. . . . Last time I was at Lord's[†] must have been at the Eton-Harrow match in 1921. At that time I should have felt that to go into the Pavilion, not being a member of the MCC, was on a par with pissing on the altar, and years later would have had some vague idea that it was a legal offence for which you could be prosecuted.

I notice that one of the posters recruiting for the Pioneers, of a foot treading on a swastika with the legend "Step on it", is cribbed from a Government poster of the Spanish war, i.e. cribbed as to the idea. Of course it is vulgarised and made comic, but its appearance at any rate shows that the Government are beginning to be willing to learn.

The Communist candidate in the Bow by-election got about 500 votes. This is a new depth-record, though the Blackshirts have often got less (in one case about 150). The more remarkable because Bow was Lansbury's[‡] seat, and might be expected to contain a lot of pacifists. The whole poll was very low, however.

14 June

The Germans are definitely in Paris, one day ahead of schedule. It can be taken as a certainty that Hitler will go to Versailles. Why don't they mine it and blow it up while he is there? Spanish troops have occupied Tangier, obviously with a view to letting the Italians use it as a base. To conquer Spanish Morocco from French Morocco would probably be easy at this date, and to do so, ditto the other

---

*Local Defence Volunteers, which later became the Home Guard.
†Cricket grounds in London, home of the Marylebone Cricket Club.
‡George Lansbury (1859–1940), Labour MP and leader of the Labour Party 1931–35, a fervent advocate of pacifism.

Spanish colonies, and set up Negrin* or someone of his kind as an alternative government, would be a severe blow at Franco. But even the present British Government would never think of doing such a thing. One has almost lost the power of imagining that the Allied governments can ever take the initiative.

Always, as I walk through the Underground stations, sickened by the advertisements, the silly staring faces and strident colours, the general frantic struggle to induce people to waste labour and material by consuming useless luxuries or harmful drugs. How much rubbish this war will sweep away, if only we can hang on throughout the summer. War is simply a reversal of civilised life; its motto is "Evil be thou my good", and so much of the good of modern life is actually evil that it is questionable whether on balance war does harm.

15 June

It has just occurred to me to wonder whether the fall of Paris means the end of the Albatross Library,[†] as I suppose it does. If so, I am £30 to the bad. It seems incredible that people still attach any importance to long-term contracts, stocks and shares, insurance policies, etc in such times as these. The sensible thing to do now would be to borrow money right and left and buy solid goods. A short while back E made enquiries about the hire-purchase terms for sewing machines and found they had agreements stretching over two and a half years.

P. W. related that Unity Mitford,[‡] besides having tried to shoot

---

*Juan Negrin, Prime Minister of the Spanish Government during the last phase of the civil war, after which he set up a Spanish Government in exile.

†One of the earliest publishers in Paris producing books in English for the continental market. Their publications included many of the most interesting books of the time, several of which were banned in Britain.

‡Victor William (Peter) Watson (1908–56), a rich young man who after much travel decided in about 1939 to devote his life to the arts. He was co-founder with his friend Cyril Connolly of the magazine *Horizon* which he financed himself besides providing all the material for the art section. In 1948 he was one of the founders of the Institute of Contemporary Arts. He was always an admirer of Orwell's writing.

The Hon. Unity Valkyrie Mitford (1914–48), fourth daughter of the second Lord Redesdale. From 1934, when she first met Hitler, she was his admirer. In January 1940 she was brought back to England from Germany suffering from bullet wounds in the head. Thereafter she lived in retirement.

herself while in Germany, is going to have a baby. Whereupon a little man with a creased face, whose name I forget, exclaimed, "The Fuehrer wouldn't do such a thing!"

16 June

This morning's papers make it reasonably clear that, at any rate until after the Presidential election, the USA will not do anything, i.e. will not declare war, which in fact is what matters. For, if the USA is not actually in the war, there will never be sufficient control of either business or labour to speed up production of armaments. In the last war this was the case even when the USA was a belligerent.

It is impossible even yet to decide what to do in the case of German conquest of England. The one thing I will not do is to clear out, at any rate not further than Ireland, supposing that to be feasible. If the fleet is intact and it appears that the war is to be continued from America and the Dominions, then one must remain alive if possible, if necessary in the concentration camp. If the USA is going to submit to conquest as well, there is nothing for it but to die fighting, but one must above all die *fighting* and have the satisfaction of killing somebody else first.

Talking yesterday to M, one of the Jewish members of my LDV section, I said that if and when the present crisis passed there would be a revolt in the Conservative Party against Churchill and an attempt to force wages down again, etc. He said that in that case there would be revolution, "or at least he hoped so". M is a manufacturer and I imagine fairly well off.

17 June

The French have surrendered. This could be foreseen from last night's broadcast and in fact should have been foreseeable when they failed to defend Paris, the one place where it might have been possible to stop the German tanks. Strategically all turns on the French fleet, of which there is no news yet. . . .

Considerable excitement today over the French surrender, and people everywhere to be heard discussing it. Usual line, "Thank God we've got a navy". A Scottish private, with medals of the last war, partly drunk, making a patriotic speech in a carriage in the Underground which the other passengers seemed rather to like.

Such a rush on evening papers that I had to make four attempts before getting one.

Nowadays, when I write a review, I sit down at the typewriter and type it straight out. Till recently, indeed till six months ago, I never did this and would have said that I could not do it. Virtually all that I wrote was written at least twice, and my books as a whole three times—individual passages as many as five or ten times. It is not really that I have gained in facility, merely that I have ceased to care, so long as the work will pass inspection and bring in a little money. It is deterioration directly due to the war.

Considerable throng at Canada House, where I went to make enquiries, As G* contemplates sending her child to Canada. Apart from mothers, they are not allowing anyone between 16 and 60 to leave, evidently fearing a panic rush.

*Gwen O'Shaughnessy, widow of Laurence (Eric), Eileen Blair's brother.

How Do You Respond?

1. What is the difference between "having convictions" and "being opinionated"? How would you characterize Orwell?

2. Compare Orwell's entries for June 10 ("I feel so saddened . . .") and June 17 ("I have ceased to care . . ."). What do these say about Orwell's attitude toward life?

3. Discuss the place of anger in Orwell's writing. Does his anger seem justified or self-serving?

KEEPING A JOURNAL

The following are suggestions, invitations for you, as you begin or continue a journal:

1. In your journal, write about the various ways you read and have read:

- Write about those times in your life when you were possessed by reading. Did you ever hide, after the lights were turned out, with book and flashlight, under the bedcovers? What were you reading? What was it that captivated you?
- Write about those times in your life when you "went off" reading,

the phases when reading seemed to have little or nothing to offer.
- Write about what you read. What books/stories/magazines have you recommended to friends? What have been your favorite "reads"? What do you consider a "good read"? Who are your favorite writers? Why? Ask half-a-dozen people at random the same questions.

2. Observe readers reading, noting their posture, their movements, their shufflings, their unconscious gestures, their handling of the book. Characterize these readers. Would you say they are affected by what they read? Any signs of pleasure? Pain? Amazement?

3. Write about what induces you to open a book. The title? The cover? Biographical notes on the author? A photograph of the author?

4. Write about your expectations. What does a title arouse in you? What do you expect after reading a first line? After ten minutes of reading? What keeps you reading? When do you know a book is not for you? What do you do to resolve the tension that sometimes arises when you *have* to read something required of you?

5. Write about your satisfaction and dissatisfactions. Write about a half-dozen works that have given you pleasure, that have meant something to you. Characterize the various kinds of pleasure and satisfaction these works have offered. Write about books you tried to read and didn't finish. Why did you give up?

6. Write about your associations. What personal experiences, events, thoughts, questions, images, memories, are evoked in you when you read? As you read the various works in *Responding to Prose*, keep a running dialogue with the writer, following the suggestions offered in Chapter 1.

7. Imitate one or several of the ways the writers in this chapter use a journal: Observe closely a natural object or animal, following the lead of Thoreau when he notices in great detail the movements of the woodchuck. Speak to your journal as a close confidant, as Anne Frank does. Write jottings of what you see, what you hear. Don't censor; don't worry about seeming odd or crazy. Don't worry about grammar or spelling. Write down what strikes you, what moves you, what disturbs you, what annoys you, what delights you.

8. Accept Virginia Woolf's invitation (Chapter 1, p. 11) to get inside reading by writing. Recall an "event that has left a distinct impression on you—how at the corner of the street, perhaps you passed two people talking. A tree shook; an electric light danced; the tone of the talk was comic, but also tragic; a whole vision, an entire conception, seemed contained in that moment."

Writing for Oneself 65

9. Use your journal to discover what you think, what you experience, what you want to write about, what you think of what you're reading. Make the journal *your own*.

10. Distinguish between the parts of your journal—those parts for which you are the only reader; those you may share with friends; those you can share with the class; those that are part of your conversation with your instructor.

THE WRITER'S FORMS

Chapter 3

❖❖ ─────────────────────────────

"Once Upon a Time"

NARRATING

The teacher Akiba, a noted scholar of the first century, told his students this story:

> There was once a young man who decided to trick a wise old man. He caught a small bird and held it, fluttering, in one hand behind his back. The boy approached the wise man and said, "Old man, I have a question to test you. I want to see how wise you are. I am holding a bird in my hand. Is it alive, or is it dead?"
>
> The boy speculated that if the old man said the bird was dead, he would open his hand to reveal the live bird, but if the old man called the bird alive, he would crush the bird, dead. The old man looked steadily into the eyes of the boy and said, "The answer, my young friend, is in your hands."

What do you make of this story? What is memorable about it? Why do you suppose a teacher would tell it to his students? If Akiba had wanted to instruct, to teach his students a lesson, then why didn't he say, simply, "You can't fool a wise man," or "The wise see what fools cannot," or "Within our own hands, we often hold life or death."

Why do you suppose that we tell stories? We tell stories and listen to them, first, because stories give us pleasure. Through jokes, anecdotes, news accounts, soap operas, short stories, novels, histories, we share in the living of others—those who are like us, and those who are not. We tell stories, also, because we remember stories. While we may hold onto a saying—that the wise are indeed wise—we remember the *stuff* of stories: the boy and the teacher, the bird and its peril. We remember characters, their words, their plights, the tension as the story builds and then releases, beginnings and endings. We remember stories because our minds are drawn to the *concrete*, the specific events of living.

"We tell ourselves stories," says the writer Joan Didion, "in order to live":

> The princess is caged in the consulate. The man with the candy will lead the children into the sea. The naked woman on the ledge outside the window on the sixteenth floor is a victim of accidie,* or the naked woman is an exhibitionist, and it would be "interesting" to know which. We tell ourselves that it makes some difference whether the naked woman is about to commit a mortal sin or is about to register a political protest or is about to be, the Aristophanic view, snatched back to the human condition by the fireman in priest's clothing just visible in the window behind her, the one smiling at the telephoto lens. We look for the sermon in the suicide, for the social and moral lesson in the murder of five. We interpret what we see, select the most workable of the multiple choices. We live entirely, especially if we are writers, by the imposition of a narrative line upon disparate images, by the "ideas" with which we have learned to freeze the shifting phantasmagoria which is our actual experience.
>
> FROM *The White Album*

We tell stories in order to make sense out of the world, to make sense out of what William James calls the "buzzing, booming mass" about us, the swirl and whirl of faces, voices, colors, sounds, lights, shapes. We shape all that "out there," and one of the most powerful ways of shaping is through story, through putting things into a chronological order. We construct beginnings and endings; we interpret. We make sense out of the raw data of our lives, the "concrete" (the tangible, what we see and hear and touch), by forming the

---

*spiritual torpor, apathy.

"abstract" (the organizing idea, our interpretation of the concrete). We offer ourselves lessons, sayings, morals. "The meek shall inherit the earth." "Necessity is the mother of invention." "As you sow, so shall you reap." We take these lessons along with us as we confront the future, so that if the moral fades, we may still hold on to a way of looking at things. Maxine Hong Kingston in "No Name Woman" says that whenever her mother "had to warn us about life," she told *a story to grow up on*. The child hears the story, the concrete, and the lesson as well, the abstract. We need both.

All cultures throughout history have their stories: to explain natural phenomena, to tell histories, to teach the young, to share common experiences, to make sense of the world. Stories are powerful bonds of a community; they often pass from one generation to the next. Stories take different forms: fables, myths, family legends, parables, short stories, histories, essays. In this chapter, you will see how narrative takes different forms, from the Biblical story of Abraham and Isaac to the Greek myth of Echo and Narcissus, from fables by Aesop and James Thurber to the short stories of Ernest Hemingway and Grace Paley, from the autobiographical writings of Benjamin Franklin, Maxine Hong Kingston, and Richard Wright to the essays of Pearl Rowe and George Orwell.

❖ ❖ ───

AS YOU READ

The Concrete and the Abstract

In the fable, the form of a story is plain to see; a fable has two parts, the story and the moral, the concrete and the abstract. As we have seen, the events of the story as they happen in time—the setting, the dialogues, the characters talking to each other, indeed, all the story of our lives, the tangible, that which we see and hear and touch—we call the concrete. The moral at the end—the attempt to interpret, to make sense of it all—is the abstract, what we will see later as the *evaluation*. Read the two fables in this chapter, Aesop's and James Thurber's, to see how the abstraction at the end, the moral, offers an interpretation of story itself.*

---
*I owe this view of the fable as a play between the concrete and abstract to my two colleagues, Rosemary Deen and Marie Ponsot.

The Once

Every story, every telling of an event, every narrative, includes a "once," an event that took place as it did only once. That particular event, with its characters, their dialogue, its tension, will never be repeated in the same way again. The signal of the *once* may appear at the very beginning of the narrative in the "once upon a time" of the fairy tale, or it may appear after the stage is set, after a place is described or a character or a situation is sketched. It may follow a brief summary of what the story is about. The *once* is the concrete, the event that happened, that encompasses a small universe: a time, a place, an event that evolves among people in a situation, often fraught with conflict and tension.

The *once* implies narrative. Narrative is the chronological telling of an event, often characterized by the recurring phrase *and then, and then, and then.* First A happened *and then* B *and then* C. Narrative provides shape for events; it traces the history of a people or a history of a life; it records a news event or shows a process (as you will see in Chapter 4).

Ordinary/Extraordinary

Every story contrasts the ordinary and the extraordinary. The "once," that one concrete happening, is set against the pattern of how things usually are. Out of the ordinary, the dailiness, the expected, we meet the surprising, the strange, the unusual, the extraordinary, even the fabulous. In fact, we tell a story because we perceive that things *are different.* "That night," says the narrator in "Cookies at Midnight," "I stayed up into the middle of the night." That night was different. Never before had things happened that way.

Tension

Every story is an answer to a question, a solution to a problem. Whenever questions are raised, whenever problems arise, tension results. Will I pass or fail that exam? Will our team win or lose that lacrosse game? Will Sue marry John? Will Abraham kill Isaac? Will Benjamin Franklin eat the fish, now that he is tempted? As readers of narrative, our expectations center firmly on the question, on the problem. We want to know how things work out; we want to understand why they turn out as they do.

Evaluation

What is the point? What does it matter? Every storyteller tells a story for a reason. William Labov, a sociolinguist, has studied the ways we tell stories, and he has found that every story has two chief features: the narrative itself, the *once*, the events as they occurred in time, and *evaluation*, the story's reason for being, the answer to the question, *so what?*

Think for a moment of a friend telling you a story—a long story—of something that happened on the job. The story goes on and on. Close to the surface of your inner response is the question: *so what? Why* are you telling me this story? We expect to know why the story is being told. Is the event to be taken as funny, strange, mysterious, a powerful lesson about life, silly, sad? We want to know. Storytellers, either implicitly or explicitly, are answering that question, *so what?* In some narratives, as in the fable, writers draw an explicit lesson or a moral from the event, a statement about meaning. "This was a story to grow up on," says Maxine Hong Kingston. It is convenient "to be a reasonable creature," says Ben Franklin. This is "my first lesson in how to live as a Negro," says Richard Wright. In some selections—in the essay by Pearl Rowe, in the short stories by Ernest Hemingway and Grace Paley—we are offered no explicit moral, no explicit lesson, no explicit interpretation. We are to interpret for ourselves, we infer—"carry in"—the meanings, the messages, the values. When you read a narrative and find yourself shrugging your shoulders and saying to yourself, "So what?" then the text is probably too far removed from your present needs or concerns. You may want to put the text aside for a while or talk to others about their interpretations or write about where you and the text part company.

AS YOU WRITE

Generating Material

All of us have stories to tell; all of us are storytellers. In your journal, write down some of these stories that you find yourself repeating to others. Recall stories that have been told to you by close family members and friends, or stories that you might want to pass on to close friends or to your own children. Record stories of how you were named or how your parents met or how they came to this country. Write stories of your first date, your first job; stories of the surprising, the shocking, the miraculous. We all construct our lives around telling stories. We tell ourselves stories as we reconstruct the events of a day in our minds; we regale our friends as we bring them into our own lives and form bonds. Recall some of your stories. Write them down without deliberation; write quickly a number of stories that make up the fabric of your life. Write a half-dozen or nine or ten.

Reading Your Writing

Once you have recorded a number of stories, read them, noting how each piece begins, how each piece ends, discovering where the tension lies, what the problem is and how it is resolved, what the question is and how it is answered. Notice where the *once* appears, whether it occurs at the beginning or is preceded by a setting, a description of character, a statement pointing to the abstraction. Now think about what the story says. What message or messages are you trying to deliver? Find the *so what?* of the story, what it is that matters, what the matter is. Notice that the "message," the "point," may not have been at the conscious level of your mind as you were telling or writing.

Shaping Your Writing

Given what you have observed about beginnings and endings, in your own stories and those you have read, decide how you want to begin. Do you want the abstraction right up front? Do you want to reinforce it at the end? Do you want a sandwich, like this?

Abstraction
Concrete (the once)
Abstraction

Do you want to lead your reader gradually into the abstraction?

Concrete (the once)
Abstraction

The moves you make as a writer of narrative will be guided by your awareness of the audience and by your own purposes—whether you want to lay things out at the beginning or whether you want to hold off, building and building the suspense, to offer at the end both the ending and your message.

As you go, keep in mind the ways that writers intensify the telling of a story: bringing character to life through description, through dialogue, through allowing different voices to be heard.

THE BIBLE

The story of Abraham and Isaac has haunted the mind of the Western world for more than two thousand years. We can interpret—make sense of—it in many ways: as a manifestation of absolute power; as a story of a test; as one view of how power is to be tempered with mercy; as an account of the powerlessness of unquestioning belief. The English poet, Wilfred Owen, writing in the battlefield of the First World War, saw it as a parable of how old men are always willing to sacrifice young men. How do you read it?

ABRAHAM AND ISAAC

The time came when God put Abraham to the test. "Abraham," he called, and Abraham replied, "Here I am." God said, "Take your son, Isaac, your only son, whom you love, and go to the land of Moriah. There you shall offer him as a sacrifice on one of the hills which I will show you." So Abraham rose early in the morning and saddled his ass, and he took with him two of his men and his son Isaac; and he split the firewood for the sacrifice, and set out for the place of which God had spoken. On the third day Abraham looked up and saw the place in the distance. He said to his men, "Stay here with the ass while I and the boy go over there; and when we have worshipped we will come back to you." So Abraham took the wood for the sacrifice and laid it on his son Isaac's shoulder; he himself carried the fire and the knife, and the two of them went on together. Isaac said to Abraham, "Father," and he answered, "What is it, my son?" Isaac said, "Here are the fire and the wood, but where is the young beast for a sacrifice?" Abraham answered, "God will provide himself with a young beast for a sacrifice, my son." And the two of them went on together and came to the place of which God had spoken. There Abraham built an altar and arranged the wood. He bound his son Isaac and laid him on the altar on top of the wood. Then he stretched out his hand and took the knife to kill his son; but the angel of the LORD called to him from heaven, "Abraham, Abraham." He answered, "Here I am." The angel of the LORD said, "Do not raise your hand against the boy; do not touch him. Now I know you are a God-fearing man. You have not withheld from me your one, your only son." Abraham looked up, and there he saw a ram caught by its horns in a thicket. So he went and took the ram and offered it as a sacrifice instead of his son. Abraham named that place Jehovah-jireh, and to this day the saying is: "In the mountain of the LORD it was provided." Then the angel of the LORD called from heaven a second time to Abraham, "This is the word of the LORD: By my own self I swear: inasmuch as you have done this and have not withheld your son, your only son, I will bless you abundantly and greatly multiply your descendants until they are as numerous as the stars in the sky and the grains of sand on the sea-shore. Your descendants shall possess the cities of their enemies. All nations on earth shall pray to be blessed as your descendants are blessed, and this because you have obeyed me."

How Do You Respond?

1. If this is narrative, who is the narrator? Think of other Bible stories. Are you aware of a narrator in them? How is your acceptance of the story affected by your knowing or not knowing who is talking?

2. The story is about how Abraham obeys God, but as striking is how Isaac obeys his father. Discuss the patriarchal qualities of this narrative.

3. Tell the story with Isaac as the central character. Tell it as a report by a spokesperson for the Society for Prevention of Cruelty to Children.

AESOP

> If the narratives of the Bible have filtered deeply into the minds of Western peoples, the same is true of the Fables of Aesop. For centuries they were a staple part of the early reading of persons born to power and given an education appropriate to their social status. With the discovery of folk-tales in the early nineteenth century, however, readers began to turn away from Aesop's explicit moralizings. Today's reader tends to feel that if there is a meaning anywhere, it must be found in the story.

THE NORTH WIND AND THE SUN

The North Wind and the Sun had an argument over who was the most powerful. They agreed to settle their disagreement by a contest: whoever could take the coat off a traveler would be declared the winner.

The North Wind tried first. He blew and blew and blew with all his might, but the harder he blew, the closer the traveler wrapped his coat around him. At last the North Wind gave up. Then the Sun had a try.

He shone out in all his warmth. The traveler, feeling the warmth of his rays, began to take off one garment after another. At last, almost overcome by the heat, he took off his clothing and bathed in a stream by the roadside.

Moral: Persuasion is better than force.

How Do You Respond?

1. Aesop's moral implies that the North Wind used force and the Sun used persuasion. Do you think that the Sun's action was actually less "forceful"? What implications would this story have as part of the education of a person "born to power"?

2. Tell the story so that the Wind wins. What would the moral be?

3. Make up a modern situation that would have the same point as "The North Wind and the Sun"—perhaps an anecdote like those printed in the *Readers' Digest*.

OVID

> *If the Bible and Aesop's* Fables *were fundamental elements in the education of Western civilization over many centuries, Ovid's* Metamorphoses *had to wait for the Renaissance before they came into their own. They comprise one of the richest and most moving collections of myths ever made: myths of the seasons, of natural processes, of night and day, of birth and death. Through the windows of such myths, we see the natural world taking on a great wealth of meaning, meaning that is not concerned with "scientific" explanation but with how such matters touch us as human beings who need coherent patterns of feeling to deal with the brute facts and hazards of phenomena such as storm, night, and death.*

ECHO AND NARCISSUS

Echo was a beautiful nymph, fond of the woods and hills, where she devoted herself to woodland sports. She was a favourite of Diana, and attended her in the chase. But Echo had one failing; she was fond of talking and, whether in chat or argument, would have the last word. One day Juno was seeking her husband, who, she had reason to fear, was amusing himself among the nymphs. Echo by her talk contrived to detain the goddess till the nymphs made their escape. When Juno discovered it, she passed sentence upon Echo in these words: "You shall forfeit the use of that tongue with which you cheated me, except for that one purpose you are so fond of—reply. You shall still have the last word, but no power to speak first."

This nymph saw Narcissus, a beautiful youth, as he pursued the chase upon the mountains. She loved him and followed his footsteps. O how she longed to address him in the softest accents, and win him to converse! but it was not in her power. She waited with impatience for him to speak first, and had her answer ready. One day the youth, being separated from his companions, shouted aloud, "Who's here?" Echo replied, "Here." Narcissus looked around, but seeing no one, called out, "Come." Echo answered, "Come." As no one came, Narcissus called again, "Why do you shun me?" Echo asked the same question. "Let us join one another," said the youth.

The maid answered with all her heart in the same words, and hastened to the spot, ready to throw her arms about his neck. He started back, exclaiming, "Hands off! I would rather die than you should have me!" "Have me," said she; but it was all in vain. He left her, and she went to hide her blushes in the recesses of the woods. From that time forth she lived in caves and among mountain cliffs. Her form faded with grief, till at last all her flesh shrank away. Her bones were changed into rocks and there was nothing left of her but her voice. With that she is still ready to reply to any one who calls her, and keeps up her old habit of having the last word.

Narcissus's cruelty in this case was not the only instance. He shunned all the rest of the nymphs, as he had done poor Echo. One day a maiden who had in vain endeavoured to attract him uttered a prayer that he might some time or other feel what it was to love and meet no return of affection. The avenging goddess heard and granted the prayer.

There was a clear fountain, with water like silver, to which the shepherds never drove their flocks, nor the mountain goats resorted, nor any of the beasts of the forest; neither was it defaced with fallen leaves or branches; but the grass grew fresh around it, and the rocks sheltered it from the sun. Hither came one day the youth, fatigued with hunting, heated and thirsty. He stooped down to drink, and saw his own image in the water; he thought it was some beautiful water-spirit living in the fountain. He stood gazing with admiration at those bright eyes, those locks curled like the locks of Bacchus or Apollo, the rounded cheeks, the ivory neck, the parted lips, and the glow of health and exercise over all. He fell in love with himself. He brought his lips near to take a kiss; he plunged his arms in to embrace the beloved object. It fled at the touch, but returned again after a moment and renewed the fascination. He could not tear himself away; he lost all thought of food or rest, while he hovered over the brink of the fountain gazing upon his own image. He talked with the supposed spirit: "Why, beautiful being, do you shun me? Surely my face is not one to repel you. The nymphs love me, and you yourself look not indifferent upon me. When I stretch forth my arms you do the same; and you smile upon me and answer my beckonings with the like." His tears fell into the water and disturbed the image. As he saw it depart, he exclaimed, "Stay, I entreat you! Let me at least gaze upon you, if I may not touch you." With this, and much more of the same kind, he cherished the flame that consumed him so that by degrees he lost his colour, his vigour, and the beauty which formerly had so charmed the nymph Echo. She kept near him, however, and when he exclaimed, "Alas! alas!" she answered him with the same words. He pined away and died; and when his shade passed the Stygian river, it leaned over the boat to catch a look of itself in the waters. The nymphs mourned for him, especially the water-nymphs; and when they smote their breasts Echo smote hers also. They prepared a funeral pyre and would have burned the body, but it was nowhere to be found; but in its place a flower, purple within, and surrounded with white leaves, which bears the name and preserves the memory of Narcissus.

How Do You Respond?

1. How do you interpret or make sense of this myth of metamorphoses, of the nymph Echo and the youth Narcissus being changed into elements of nature? Do you believe the events to be true? If not, what do you think of a civilization that did?

2. Compare this myth to modern "explanation" stories, such as Kipling's *Just So Stories*.

3. Choose a natural phenomenon (a nearby geological formation, a familiar plant, muggy summer days) and wrote a short myth to account for it.

JAMES THURBER

> *If you have ever tried to be amusing for more than two minutes, you will already have discovered that it is impossible to be funny by taking thought: it seems that it was either meant to come or it was not. To be funny, to enjoy a comic vision of life—it seems that these are ways of being, for some blessed souls, and we must be thankful for their existence. James Thurber (1894–1961) seems to have been born with a good story on his lips: it is as if he could not help being funny.*
>
> *Since his death, some aspects of his comedy have faded, but much—in his drawings for the* New Yorker, *and in his writings,* The Secret Life of Walter Mitty, My Life and Hard Times—*is still as fresh as when his typewriter was convulsed. See his collection,* The Thurber Carnival.

THE UNICORN IN THE GARDEN

Once upon a sunny morning a man who sat in a breakfast nook looked up from his scrambled eggs to see a white unicorn with a gold horn quietly cropping the roses in the garden. The man went up to the bedroom where his wife was still asleep and woke her. "There's a unicorn in the garden," he said. "Eating roses." She opened one unfriendly eye and looked at him. "The unicorn is a mythical beast," she said, and turned her back on him. The man walked slowly downstairs and out into the garden. The unicorn was still there; he was now browsing among the tulips. "Here, unicorn," said the man, and he pulled up a lily and gave it to him. The unicorn ate it gravely. With a high heart, because there was a unicorn in his garden, the man went upstairs and roused his wife again. "The unicorn," he said, "ate a lily." His wife sat up in bed and looked at him, coldly. "You are a booby," she said, "and I am going to have you put in the booby-hatch." The man, who had never liked the words "booby" and "booby-hatch," and who liked them even less on a shining morning when there was a unicorn in the garden, thought for a moment. "We'll see about that," he said. He walked over to the door. "He has a golden horn in the middle of his forehead," he told her. Then he went back to the garden to watch the unicorn; but the unicorn had gone away. The man sat down among the roses and went to sleep.

As soon as the husband had gone out of the house, the wife got up and dressed as fast as she could. She was very excited and there was a gloat in her eye. She telephoned the police and she telephoned a psychiatrist; she told them to hurry to her house and bring a strait-jacket. When the police and the psychiatrist arrived they sat down in chairs and looked at her, with great interest. "My husband," she said, "saw a unicorn this morning." The police looked at the psychiatrist and the psychiatrist looked at the police. "He told me it ate a lily," she said. The psychiatrist looked at the police and the police looked at the psychiatrist. "He told me it had a golden horn in the middle of its forehead," she said. At a solemn signal from the psychiatrist, the police leaped from their chairs and seized the wife. They had a hard time subduing her, for she put up a terrific struggle, but they finally subdued her. Just as they got her into the strait-jacket, the husband came back into the house.

"Did you tell your wife you saw a unicorn?" asked the police. "Of course not," said the husband. "The unicorn is a mythical beast." "That's all I wanted to know," said the psychiatrist. "Take her away. I'm sorry, sir, but your wife is as crazy as a jay bird." So they took her away, cursing and screaming, and shut her up in an institution. The husband lived happily ever after.

Moral: Don't count your boobies until they are hatched.

How Do You Respond?

1. Since this story deals with an unhappy marriage and a woman being dragged off to an institution, how do you recognize that it is comic? Why do you suppose the husband and wife sought to have each other legally removed rather than just separating?

2. Why aren't the characters given names? Compare this practice with the conventional folk tale.

3. Thurber tells the story from the man's side. Do you see it that way? What does the story say about relations between men and women? What feeling on the subject do you sense in Thurber?

BENJAMIN FRANKLIN

> "Time is money." "The early bird catches the worm." "Snug as a bug in a rug." Benjamin Franklin's sayings have persisted to this day. The fifteenth child of Bostonian parents, Franklin grew up to be a prominent statesman, scientist, publisher, and writer. His Autobiography, *begun in 1771 and published posthumously in 1867, shows him as a modest, sober, thoughtful man. No doubt he was—as we see in the following excerpt—but for another side of Franklin, delve into his collection of irreverent essays*, The Bagatelles. *You are in for a treat.*

From BENJAMIN FRANKLIN's *AUTOBIOGRAPHY*

I believe I have omitted mentioning that, in my first voyage from Boston, being becalmed off Block Island, our people set about catching cod, and hauled up a great many. Hitherto I had stuck to my resolution of not eating animal food, and on this occasion I considered, with my master Tryon, the taking of every fish as a kind of unprovoked murder, since none of them had, or ever could do us any injury that might justify the slaughter. All this seemed very reasonable. But I had formerly been a great lover of fish, and, when this came hot out of the frying-pan, it smelled admirably well. I balanced some time between principle and inclination, till I recollected that, when the fish were opened, I saw smaller fish taken out of their stomachs; then thought I, "if you eat one another, I don't see why we mayn't eat you." So I dined upon cod very heartily, and continued to eat with other people, returning only now and then occasionally to a vegetable diet. So convenient a thing it is to be a *reasonable creature,* since it enables one to find or make a reason for everything one has a mind to do.

How Do You Respond?

1. The external events of this story are few. A man is on a ship. People on the ship catch fish. The man eats some of the fish. Why does the story matter? What arouses your interest in Franklin's tale?
2. How old do you think Franklin was at the time he resolved to

become a vegetarian? Does this affect how you feel about his change of opinion? When you were younger, did you take moral stands that you later talked yourself out of? Do you still?

3. Notice how Franklin's sentences are longer than those of most modern writers, how they amble over more content but still come to a tidy ending. Rewrite the story in shorter sentences. Does your version have the charm of Franklin's original?

PHILIP SLATER

> *Philip Slater (born in 1927) is a distinguished sociologist, whose best known book is* The Pursuit of Loneliness: American Culture at the Breaking Point, *from which the following passage is taken.*

A MODERN FABLE

Once upon a time there was a man who sought escape from the prattle of his neighbors and went to live alone in a hut he had found in the forest. At first he was content, but a bitter winter led him to cut down the trees around his hut for firewood. The next summer he was hot and uncomfortable because his hut had no shade, and he complained bitterly of the harshness of the elements.

He made a little garden and kept some chickens, but rabbits were attracted by the food in the garden and ate much of it. The man went into the forest and trapped a fox, which he tamed and taught to catch rabbits. But the fox ate up the man's chickens as well. The man shot the fox and cursed the perfidy of the creatures of the wild.

The man always threw his refuse on the floor of his hut and soon it swarmed with vermin. He then built an ingenious system of hooks and pulleys so that everything in the hut could be suspended from the ceiling. But the strain was too much for the flimsy hut and it soon collapsed. The man grumbled about the inferior construction of the hut and built himself a new one.

One day he boasted to a relative in his old village about the peaceful beauty and plentiful game surrounding his forest home. The relative was impressed and reported back to his neighbors, who began to use the area for picnic and hunting excursions. The man was upset by this and cursed the intrusiveness of mankind. He began posting signs, setting traps, and shooting at those who came near his dwelling. In revenge groups of boys would come at night from time to time to frighten him and steal things. The man took to sleeping every night in a chair by the window with a loaded shotgun across his knees. One night he turned in his sleep and shot off his foot. The villagers were chastened and saddened by this misfortune and thereafter stayed away from his part of the forest. The man became lonely and cursed the unfriendliness and indifference of his former neighbors. And in all this the man saw no agency except what lay outside himself, for which reason, and because of his ingenuity, the villagers called him the American.

How Do You Respond?

1. Slater repeats the word *but* at critical intervals. What would happen if the buts were replaced by ands?
2. Compare the purposes of the fables by Aesop, Thurber, and Slater. How are their tones related to their purposes? Can you supply a moral for Slater's fable?
3. Do you feel that Slater's last sentence is a deft stroke or a heavy-handed blow? Can you think of another conclusion—perhaps a happy ending in which the man learns his lesson?

MAXINE HONG KINGSTON

> "I have no idea," says Maxine Hong Kingston (born 1940), "how people who don't write endure their lives." Born of Chinese immigrants, Kingston heard the voices of the "new" land all about her in California, where she grew up, contrasting with the persistent voice of her mother, who wanted to retain the customs, traditions, and rituals of her native China. These conflicts of old and new infuse her two books, China Men and The Woman Warrior. *The following selection is from* The Woman Warrior.

NO NAME WOMAN

"You must not tell anyone," my mother said, "what I am about to tell you. In China your father had a sister who killed herself. She jumped into the family well. We say that your father has all brothers because it is as if she had never been born.

"In 1924 just a few days after our village celebrated seventeen hurry-up weddings—to make sure that every young man who went 'out on the road' would responsibly come home—your father and his brothers and your grandfather and his brothers and your aunt's new husband sailed for America, the Gold Mountain. It was your grandfather's last trip. Those lucky enough to get contracts waved good-bye from the decks. They fed and guarded the stowaways and helped them off in Cuba, New York, Bali, Hawaii. 'We'll meet in California next year,' they said. All of them sent money home.

"I remember looking at your aunt one day when she and I were dressing; I had not noticed before that she had such a protruding melon of a stomach. But I did not think, 'She's pregnant,' until she began to look like other pregnant women, her shirt pulling and the white tops of her black pants showing. She could not have been pregnant, you see, because her husband had been gone for years. No one said anything. We did not discuss it. In early summer she was ready to have the child, long after the time when it could have been possible.

"The village had also been counting. On the night the baby was to be born the villagers raided our house. Some were crying. Like a great saw, teeth strung with lights, files of people walked zigzag across our land, tearing the rice. Their lanterns doubled in the disturbed black water, which drained away through the broken bunds. As the villagers closed in, we could see that some of them, probably men and women we knew well, wore white masks. The people with long hair hung it over their faces. Women with short hair made it stand up on end. Some had tied white bands around their foreheads, arms, and legs.

"At first they threw mud and rocks at the house. Then they threw eggs and began slaughtering our stock. We could hear the animals scream their deaths—the roosters, the pigs, a last great roar from the ox. Familiar wild heads flared in our night windows; the villagers encircled us. Some of the faces stopped to peer at us, their eyes rushing like searchlights. The hands flattened against the panes, framed heads, and left red prints.

"The villagers broke in the front and the back doors at the same time, even though we had not locked the doors against them. Their knives dripped with the blood of our animals. They smeared blood on the doors and walls. One woman swung a chicken, whose throat she had slit, splattering blood in red arcs about her. We stood together in the middle of our house, in the family hall with the pictures and tables of the ancestors around us, and looked straight ahead.

"At that time the house had only two wings. When the men came back, we would build two more to enclose our courtyard and a third one to begin a second courtyard. The villagers pushed through both wings, even your grandparents' rooms, to find your aunt's, which was also mine until the men returned. From this room a new wing for one of the younger families would grow. They ripped up her clothes and shoes and broke her combs, grinding them underfoot. They tore her work from the loom. They scattered the cooking fire and rolled the new weaving in it. We could hear them in the kitchen breaking our bowls and banging the pots. They overturned the great waisthigh earthenware jugs; duck eggs, pickled fruits, vegetables burst out and mixed in acrid torrents. The old woman from the next field swept a broom through the air and loosed the spirits of the broom over our heads. 'Pig.' 'Ghost.' 'Pig,' they sobbed and scolded while they ruined our house.

"When they left, they took sugar and oranges to bless themselves.

They cut pieces from the dead animals. Some of them took bowls that were not broken and clothes that were not torn. Afterward we swept up the rice and sewed it back up into sacks. But the smells from the spilled preserves lasted. Your aunt gave birth in the pigsty that night. The next morning when I went for the water, I found her and the baby plugging up the family well.

"Don't let your father know that I told you. He denies her. Now that you have started to menstruate, what happened to her could happen to you. Don't humiliate us. You wouldn't like to be forgotten as if you had never been born. The villagers are watchful."

Whenever she had to warn us about life, my mother told stories that ran like this one, a story to grow up on.

How Do You Respond?

1. Two *once*s interact here: the story of the aunt's death and the story of the narrator's being told a story. What written signals indicate the telling of these two stories? How would you characterize the tension in this piece?

2. This story of community judgement and punishment is told objectively, as though the neighbor's action followed the aunt's offense as naturally as the flood follows the bursting dam. Does this strengthen or weaken the effect? How would the story be different if the narrator took sides—condemning the aunt or bewailing the family's loss?

3. Did your parents (or other authorities) tell you any "cautionary tales" to encourage you to follow family or community standards? Did such horror stories impress you? Compare them with Kingston's narrative.

PEARL ROWE

> We think of journalism as ephemeral—here today and gone tomorrow—but once in a while we discover stories in the pages of a newspaper that we feel are worth holding on to, because they repay many readings. Such a one is Pearl Rowe's story. It is a privilege to snatch it from the oblivion that overtakes most newspaper stories.

COOKIES AT MIDNIGHT

My mother and I stayed up almost all night once when I was 9. She sat at the kitchen table laboring over a letter that she was writing in Yiddish. (She was unable to write English; even Yiddish was hard for her.)

Like a restless puppy, I circled the kitchen table, sensing that something was wrong. My mother always sent me to bed early on school nights. But not that night.

"Ma, don't you think I should be in bed by now?" I asked, uncomfortable with the lawless freedom.

"I want you should stay up for a while yet. It wouldn't hurt one night."

My four brothers, sister, and father, all older than I, were properly asleep. I took my rag doll by the arm and swung her around over my head, trying to get some attention. "Dolly's dizzy, Ma."

"Put her head between her legs."

"Could I have some cookies?"

She answered without looking up. "Take some out of the box, but close it tight, I think I saw a rat in the pantry."

It was unheard of. Cookies at midnight. I threw in some heavy artillery. "They sent Ida home from school today with nits. Teacher said you should wash my hair with kerosene because I sat next to her."

"That's nice."

"Maaa!" I started to cry.

My mother looked up.

"Ma, are you smoking?"

"Just for a change. Only for a change."

That was some crazy night. My mother was so different from how I had ever seen her before. I decided it would be a good time to sneak in the important question. At least she wasn't busy plucking dead chickens or washing laundry on the scrub board. In her preoccupation she seemed somehow more accessible to me.

"Ma, do some people live forever?"

I had reached her. She looked up, "Yes, baby. Special people."

"Am I special?"

"Absolutely. Positively. You're one of the special people who will live forever."

Boy, was that a relief. I had needed to know that for a long time. I was sure glad to finally get it cleared up. My eyelids grew heavy. The prospect of living forever had made me even sleepier. I stretched out on a step and put my doll beneath my head for a pillow. The next thing I knew, my mother was shaking me awake.

"I finished my letter. Now I want you to do something real nice for me. I want you should write something on the envelope in English."

I was sleepy and cranky. "Maaa, I want to go to bed. And I don't like writing. I only like printing big."

"Then print big."

"Can't I go to bed instead? My head's loose on my neck."

"Just do this one thing and you can go right upstairs—Okay, baby?" My mother led me over to the table and sat me down on the wooden kitchen chair and pushed the chair way under the table as far as it would go. She put the envelope down on the worn oilcloth, right under my chin.

"I want a red crayon."

She rummaged around in a drawer and found one.

"But I don't know what to print. You'll have to tell me."

"I'll tell you exactly." She dictated silly words. Words I was too sleepy to understand or spell right. I sounded them out like in school, moving my mouth as I put them down. My head nodded lower and lower over the paper. When I finished, my mother slid the envelope from under my limp hand.

"Did you finish, baby? Did you put all the words down? All the words like I told you?"

"Yeah. Now can I go to bed?"

She helped me up the stairs to where my sister, Anna, was sleeping. I collapsed into bed beside her. I felt my mother cover and kiss me. Finally. I was fast asleep before she left the room.

That's all I remember from the night my mother seemed to be under a gypsy spell. The next morning it was no better. I sat in the kitchen before school, tracing stick men on the steamy windows, noticing that my mother and father were all dressed up before breakfast, and it wasn't even a holiday.

My father said to my mother, "We have to go now, Freida. You said you wanted to stop at Mr. Moscowitz's grocery."

Before they went out the back door, my mother turned and looked around the room at all six of us kids, her eyes like the lens of a camera, taking pictures fast, before clouds blocked the sun. My father was carrying a small suitcase. My mother told me not to forget to wash my socks for school the next day, and then they were gone.

We all stared at the closed door. Nobody had kissed anybody. Nobody had even said goodby. Everything was tangled and different from ever before, and everybody was just letting it be that way. My big brother Harry would explain it to me, I thought. He knew everything. He could even mix chemicals in his laboratory in the attic and make real crystal out of milk bottles. I asked him where Ma and Pa had gone.

"To the hospital. Ma's having an operation tomorrow."

"Like my tonsils?"

"Something like that."

That night I dreamed that I washed my red socks and something in the red dye in the water scared me and I awoke hugging my doll tight, with my thumb in my mouth and my forefinger in my ear. It was Saturday. I didn't need to go to school or wash my socks after all. My father left for the hospital early, and only Morry and I were in the kitchen. Harry was in the attic making gold. I was sitting on the floor playing jacks. Morry was doing his favorite thing—eating. I don't remember about the other kids.

The doorbell rang. It was always exciting when that happened, because our friends usually just walked in. A doorbell meant something special, like somebody selling encyclopedias or potato peelers. Morry answered the door. It was a telegram for my father. Morry opened it. I stood on my toes behind him and read. "Your wife

Freida died . . ." The rest got all blurred up. Morry ran upstairs to the attic.

"It's my fault," I thought to myself. I hadn't asked my mother if she was one of the special people who would never die, like me.

That night Mr. Moscowitz came over. He looked at my father: "Your missus told me to give you this if . . ." Mr. Moscowitz covered his face with his hand and I could hear him choking and sobbing. He handed my father a thick letter. My father opened it and laid the envelope on the dining-room table. I read the big letters printed crookedly in red crayon across the front of the envelope. I sounded the awful words out as I read them:

"MY LAST WILL AND TESTIMINT. DO NOT OPIN UNTILL I AM DETH."

How Do You Respond?

1. The narrator reconstructs an event of her youth. How do we know that the narrator is not *now* nine years old? Tension often arises out of innocence remembered from the point of view of experience. How does the narrator bring herself and us, as readers, out of innocence and into experience?

2. At what point did you realize that the purpose of the story was not simple humor or nostalgia? Do you mind that the story is much grimmer than it seemed at the beginning?

3. How does the child's confusion further the telling of the story? Why do you think that the words, "Do not opin untill I am deth," made no impression on the girl at the time she wrote them?

ERNEST HEMINGWAY

> *Ernest Hemingway (1899–1961), like his contemporary, Scott Fitzgerald, tried to live out his own myths, and turned his life into an adventure story. The expression, "Men will be boys," could have been invented to characterize the immature, "jock," side of Hemingway's personality, always in search of a "macho" kind of achievement. His preoccupation with war seems perfectly appropriate. But as a writer he made spare, athletic prose, pared down to lean muscle and straight bones. At his best—the stories of* In Our Time, *and his novels*, The Sun Also Rises, A Farewell to Arms, *and* The Old Man and the Sea—*he was an exceptional storyteller, and he characteristically ended the last sentence of the story of his life with a shotgun.*

HILLS LIKE WHITE ELEPHANTS

The hills across the valley of the Ebro were long and white. On this side there was no shade and no trees and the station was between two lines of rails in the sun. Close against the side of the station there was the warm shadow of the building and a curtain, made of strings of bamboo beads, hung across the open door into the bar, to keep out flies. The American and the girl with him sat at a table in the shade, outside the building. It was very hot and the express from Barcelona would come in forty minutes. It stopped at this junction for two minutes and went on to Madrid.

"What should we drink?" the girl asked. She had taken off her hat and put it on the table.

"It's pretty hot," the man said.

"Let's drink beer."

"Dos cervezas," the man said into the curtain.

"Big ones?" a woman asked from the doorway.

"Yes. Two big ones."

The woman brought two glasses of beer and two felt pads. She put the felt pads and the beer glasses on the table and looked at the man and the girl. The girl was looking off at the line of hills. They were white in the sun and the country was brown and dry.

"They look like white elephants," she said.

"I've never seen one," the man drank his beer.

"No, you wouldn't have."

"I might have." the man said. "Just because you say I wouldn't have doesn't prove anything."

The girl looked at the bead curtain. "They've painted something on it," she said. "What does it say?"

"Anis del Toro. It's a drink."

"Could we try it?"

The man called "Listen" through the curtain. The woman came out from the bar.

"Four reales."

"We want two Anis del Toro."

"With water?"

"Do you want it with water?"

"I don't know," the girl said. "Is it good with water?"

"It's all right."

"You want them with water?" asked the woman.

"Yes, with water."

"It tastes like licorice," the girl said and put the glass down.

"That's the way with everything."

"Yes," said the girl. "Everything tastes of licorice. Especially all the things you've waited so long for, like absinthe."

"Oh, cut it out."

"You started it," the girl said. "I was being amused. I was having a fine time."

"Well, let's try and have a fine time."

"All right. I was trying. I said the mountains looked like white elephants. Wasn't that bright?"

"That was bright."

"I wanted to try this new drink. That's all we do, isn't it—look at things and try new drinks?"

"I guess so."

The girl looked across at the hills.

"They're lovely hills," she said. "They don't really look like white elephants. I just meant the coloring of their skin through the trees."

"Should we have another drink?"

"All right."

The warm wind blew the bead curtain against the table.

"The beer's nice and cool," the man said.

"It's lovely," the girl said.

"It's really an awfully simple operation, Jig," the man said. "It's not really an operation at all."

The girl looked at the ground the table legs rested on.

"I know you wouldn't mind it, Jig. It's really not anything. It's just to let the air in."

The girl did not say anything.

"I'll go with you and I'll stay with you all the time. They just let the air in and then it's all perfectly natural."

"Then what will we do afterward?"

"We'll be fine afterward. Just like we were before."

"What makes you think so?"

"That's the only thing that bothers us. It's the only thing that's made us unhappy."

The girl looked at the bead curtain, put her hand out and took hold of two of the strings of beads.

"And you think then we'll be all right and be happy."

"I know we will. You don't have to be afraid. I've known lots of people that have done it."

"So have I," said the girl. "And afterward they were all so happy."

"Well," the man said, "if you don't want to you don't have to. I wouldn't have you do it if you didn't want to. But I know it's perfectly simple."

"And you really want to?"

"I think it's the best thing to do. But I don't want you to do it if you don't really want to."

"And if I do it you'll be happy and things will be like they were and you'll love me?"

"I love you now. You know I love you."

"I know. But if I do it, then it will be nice again if I say things are like white elephants, and you'll like it?"

"I'll love it. I love it now but I just can't think about it. You know how I get when I worry."

"If I do it you won't ever worry?"

"I won't worry about that because it's perfectly simple."

"Then I'll do it. Because I don't care about me."

"What do you mean?"

"I don't care about me."

"Well, I care about you."

"Oh, yes. But I don't care about me. And I'll do it and then everything will be fine."

"I don't want you to do it if you feel that way."

The girl stood up and walked to the end of the station. Across, on the other side, were fields of grain and trees along the banks of the Ebro. Far away, beyond the river, were mountains. The shadow of a cloud moved across the field of grain and she saw the river through the trees.

"And we could have all this," she said. "And we could have everything and every day we make it more impossible."

"What did you say?"

"I said we could have everything."

"We can have everything."

"No, we can't."

"We could have the whole world."

"No, we can't."

"We can go everywhere."

"No, we can't. It isn't ours any more."

"It's ours."

"No, it isn't. And once they take it away, you never get it back."

"But they haven't taken it away."

"We'll wait and see."

"Come on back in the shade," he said. "You mustn't feel that way."

"I don't feel any way," the girl said. "I just know things."

"I don't want you to do anything that you don't want to do—"

"Not that isn't good for me," she said. "I know. Could we have another beer?"

"All right. But you've got to realize—"

"I realize," the girl said. "Can't we maybe stop talking?"

They sat down at the table and the girl looked across at the hills on the dry side of the valley and the man looked at her and at the table.

"You've got to realize," he said, "that I don't want you to do it if you don't want to. I'm perfectly willing to go through with it if it means anything to you."

"Doesn't it mean anything to you? We could get along."

"Of course it does. But I don't want anybody but you. I don't want any one else. And I know it's perfectly simple."

"It's all right for you to say that, but I do know it."

"Would you do something for me now?"

"I'd do anything for you."

"Would you please please please please please please please stop talking?"

He did not say anything but looked at the bags against the wall of the station. There were labels on them from all the hotels where they had spent nights.

"But I don't want you to," he said, "I don't care anything about it."

"I'll scream," the girl said.

The woman came out through the curtains with two glasses of beer and put them down on the damp felt pads. "The train comes in five minutes," she said.

"What did she say?" asked the girl.

"That the train is coming in five minutes."

The girl smiled brightly at the woman, to thank her.

"I'd better take the bags over to the other side of the station," the man said. She smiled at him.

"All right. Then come back and we'll finish the beer."

He picked up the two heavy bags and carried them around the station to the other tracks. He looked up the tracks but could not see the train. Coming back, he walked through the barroom, where people waiting for the train were drinking. He drank an Anis at the bar and looked at the people. They were all waiting reasonably for the train. He went out through the bead curtain. She was sitting at the table and smiled at him.

"Do you feel better?" he asked.

"I feel fine," she said. "There's nothing wrong with me. I feel fine."

How Do You Respond?

1. After the narrator sets the scene, the characters speak for themselves, so that we seem to be overhearing a conversation where less, rather than more, is offered. As readers, we must infer a great deal; we must fill in gaps. What must you bring to the text in order to fill in the gaps? What *is* going on? How do you know?

2. What tension do you feel between the man and the woman in the

story? Within each character individually? Why does Hemingway call the woman "the girl"?

3. What is the relationship between the characters? Who do you feel most controls the situation? Why do you think so?

RICHARD WRIGHT

> Black Boy *by Richard Wright (1908–1960), from which "My Library Card" is taken, is accounted one of the masterpieces of American prose. The book is alive with an urgent sense of desperate need and a powerful energy of aspiration. The novel of the individual's climb through childhood and adolescence toward life's larger possibilities—the "bildungsroman"—had become a major form during the nineteenth century. In many ways, Wright's book is close to autobiography, but it also clearly reflects the archetypal form of quest and escape. Wright's quest was, of course, the great search for autonomy, self-respect, and human identity. He had to transcend not only economic poverty but also conditions that denied the human value of the oppressed individual.*

THE ETHICS OF LIVING JIM CROW

My first lesson in how to live as a Negro came when I was quite small. We were living in Arkansas. Our house stood behind the railroad tracks. Its skimpy yard was paved with black cinders. Nothing green ever grew in that yard. The only touch of green we could see was far away, beyond the tracks, over where the white folks lived. But cinders were good enough for me and I never missed the green growing things. And anyhow cinders were fine weapons. You could always have a nice hot war with huge black cinders. All you had to do was crouch behind the brick pillars of a house with your hands full of gritty ammunition. And the first woolly black head you saw pop out from behind another row of pillars was your target. You tried your very best to knock it off. It was great fun.

I never fully realized the appalling disadvantages of a cinder environment till one day the gang to which I belonged found itself engaged in a war with the white boys who lived beyond the tracks. As usual we laid down our cinder barrage, thinking that this would wipe the white boys out. But they replied with a steady bombardment of broken bottles. We doubled our cinder barrage, but they hid behind trees, hedges, and the sloping embankments of their lawns. Having no such fortifications, we retreated to the brick pillars of our homes. During the retreat a broken milk bottle caught me behind the ear, opening a deep gash which bled profusely. The sight of blood pouring over my face completely demoralized our ranks. My fellow-combatants left me standing paralyzed in the center of the yard and scurried for their homes. A kind neighbor saw me and rushed me to a doctor, who took three stitches in my neck.

I sat brooding on my front steps, nursing my wound and waiting for my mother to come from work. I felt that a grave injustice had been done me. It was all right to throw cinders. The greatest harm a cinder could do was leave a bruise. But broken bottles were dangerous; they left you cut, bleeding, and helpless.

When night fell, my mother came from the white folks' kitchen. I raced down the street to meet her. I could just feel in my bones that she would understand, I knew she would tell me exactly what to do next time. I grabbed her hand and babbled out the whole story. She examined my wound, then slapped me.

"How come yuh didn't hide?" she asked me. "How come yuh awways fightin'?"

I was outraged and bawled. Between sobs I told her that I didn't have any trees or hedges to hide behind. There wasn't a thing I could have used as a trench. And you couldn't throw very far when you were hiding behind the brick pillars of a house. She grabbed a barrel stave, dragged me home, stripped me naked, and beat me till I had a fever of one hundred and two. She would smack my rump with the stave, and, while the skin was still smarting, impart to me gems of Jim Crow wisdom. I was never to throw cinders any more. I was never to fight any more wars. I was never, never, under any conditions, to fight *white* folks again. And they were absolutely right in clouting me with the broken milk bottle. Didn't I know she was working hard every day in the hot kitchens of the white folks to make money to take care of me? When was I ever going to learn to be a good boy? She couldn't be bothered with my fights. She finished by telling me that I ought to be thankful to God as long as I lived that they didn't kill me.

All that night I was delirious and could not sleep. Each time I closed my eyes I saw monstrous white faces suspended from the ceiling, leering at me.

From that time on, the charm of my cinder yard was gone. The green trees, the trimmed hedges, the cropped lawns grew very meaningful, became a symbol. Even today when I think of white folks, the hard, sharp outlines of white houses surrounded by trees, lawns, and hedges are present somewhere in the background of my mind. Through the years they grew into an overreaching symbol of fear.

How Do You Respond?

1. Wright associates green trees, trim lawns, and white frame houses—Norman Rockwell America—with fear. What personal associations do you have that run counter to common stereotypes?

2. Were you surprised at the reaction of Wright's mother to his injury? Why did she react as she did? Do you think she showed love and concern?

3. Trace the flow of emotion through the story. What agency changed Wright's carefree childhood days to a continuing time of fear? Have you ever had to adjust to dangers so overwhelming that you could not hope to master them?

GRACE PALEY

> Grace Paley (born 1922) is a virtuoso. If she were a musician, we would hear her playing all those pieces that most musicians do not play because they are impossibly difficult: her writing is full of cadenzas, trills, unexpected and breathtaking changes of key. Always, on every page, she lives dangerously, takes crazy risks, and pulls it off. She is capable of shocking her readers and of making them laugh out loud: her only failing is to have written too little—two collections of stories, The Little Disturbances of Man and Enormous Changes at the Last Minute, from which "Wants" is taken.

WANTS

I saw my ex-husband in the street. I was sitting on the steps of the new library.

Hello, my life, I said. We had once been married for twenty-seven years, so I felt justified.

He said, What? What life? No life of mine.

I said, O.K. I don't argue when there's real disagreement. I got up and went into the library to see how much I owed them.

The librarian said $32 even and you've owed it for eighteen years. I didn't deny anything. Because I don't understand how time passes. I have had those books. I have often thought of them. The library is only two blocks away.

My ex-husband followed me to the Books Returned desk. He interrupted the librarian, who had more to tell. In many ways, he said, as I look back, I attribute the dissolution of our marriage to the fact that you never invited the Bertrams to dinner.

That's possible, I said. But really, if you remember: first, my father was sick that Friday, then the children were born, then I had those Tuesday-night meetings, then the war began. Then we didn't seem to know them any more. But you're right. I should have had them to dinner. I gave the librarian a check for $32. Immediately she trusted me, put my past behind her, wiped the record clean, which is just what most other municipal and/or state bureaucracies will *not* do.

I checked out the two Edith Wharton books I had just returned because I'd read them so long ago and they are more apropos now than ever. They were *The House of Mirth* and *The Children*, which is about how life in the United States in New York changed in twenty-seven years fifty years ago.

A nice thing I do remember is breakfast, my ex-husband said. I was surprised. All we ever had was coffee. Then I remembered there was a hole in the back of the kitchen closet which opened into the apartment next door. There, they always ate sugar-cured smoked bacon. It gave us a very grand feeling about breakfast, but we never got stuffed and sluggish.

That was when we were poor, I said.

When were we ever rich? he asked.

Oh, as time went on, as our responsibilities increased, we didn't go in need. You took adequate financial care, I reminded him. The children went to camp four weeks a year and in decent ponchos with sleeping bags and boots, just like everyone else. They looked very nice. Our place was warm in winter, and we had nice red pillows and things.

I wanted a sailboat, he said. But you didn't want anything.

Don't be bitter, I said. It's never too late.

No, he said with a great deal of bitterness. I may get a sailboat. As a matter of fact, I have money down on an eighteen-foot two-rigger. I'm doing well this year and can look forward to better. But as for you, it's too late. You'll always want nothing.

He had had a habit throughout the twenty-seven years of making a narrow remark which, like a plumber's snake, could work its way through the ear down the throat, halfway to my heart. He would then disappear, leaving me choking with equipment. What I mean is, I sat down on the library steps and he went away.

I looked through *The House of Mirth*, but lost interest. I felt extremely accused. Now, it's true, I'm short of requests and absolute requirements. But I do want *something*.

I want, for instance, to be a different person. I want to be the woman who brings these two books back in two weeks. I want to be the effective citizen who changes the school system and addresses the Board of Estimate on the troubles of this dear urban center.

I *had* promised my children to end the war before they grew up.

I wanted to have been married forever to one person, my ex-husband or my present one. Either had enough character for a whole life, which as it turns out is really not such a long time. You couldn't exhaust either man's qualities or get under the rock of his reasons in one short life.

Just this morning I looked out the window to watch the street for a while and saw that the little sycamores the city had dreamily planted a couple of years before the kids were born had come that day to the prime of their lives.

Well! I decided to bring those two books back to the library. Which proves that when a person or an event comes along to jolt or appraise me I *can* take some appropriate action, although I am better known for my hospitable remarks.

How Do You Respond?

1. Describe Paley's tone. What do you think of it? What do you think of the way she deals with grave, serious matters?

2. What does the narrator *want*? How do her wants conflict with her ex-husband's expectations? Why does the narrator's ex-husband think that her wanting nothing was a fault? Was it?

3. Paley treats years like weeks and trivial obligations such as borrowed library books as major crises. How is her story like and how is it different from the work of a humorist, say, the writer of a funny newspaper column?

GEORGE ORWELL

> Eric Blair's adoption of the pen-name, George Orwell, signalled a major shift in his life. After a privileged education—he was educated at prep-school and at England's most exclusive boarding school, Eton—he went to work for the British colonial police in Burma, keeping the native Burmese "in their place." What he witnessed there—British colonial arrogance—drove him toward a democratic anti-imperialist socialism: so his life story encapsulates one of the major strands of twentieth century history, the demise of colonialism. He had the strength and the courage to pay for his conversion, and for many years had difficulty in making ends meet. Orwell retained throughout his life a natural sympathy for the nobodies of the world: in the last analysis, his concern was rooted in a reverence for life, but his way of putting it was always modest and low-keyed. Orwell had the intelligence to see the abuse of power for what it was and the courage to say so: he could not be silenced.

A HANGING

It was in Burma, a sodden morning of the rains. A sickly light, like yellow tinfoil, was slanting over the high walls into the jail yard. We were waiting outside the condemned cells, a row of sheds fronted with double bars, like small animal cages. Each cell measured about ten feet by ten and was quite bare within except for a plank bed and a pot for drinking water. In some of them brown silent men were squatting at the inner bars, with their blankets draped round them. These were the condemned men, due to be hanged within the next week or two.

One prisoner had been brought out of his cell. He was a Hindu, a puny wisp of a man, with a shaven head and vague liquid eyes. He had a thick, sprouting moustache, absurdly too big for his body, rather like the moustache of a comic man on the films. Six tall Indian warders were guarding him and getting him ready for the gallows. Two of them stood by with rifles and fixed bayonets, while the others handcuffed him, passed a chain through his handcuffs and fixed it to their belts, and lashed his arms tight to his sides.

They crowded very close about him, with their hands always on him in a careful, caressing grip, as though all the while feeling him to make sure he was there. It was like men handling a fish which is still alive and may jump back into the water. But he stood quite unresisting, yielding his arms limply to the ropes, as though he hardly noticed what was happening.

Eight o'clock struck and a bugle call, desolately thin in the wet air, floated from the distant barracks. The superintendent of the jail, who was standing apart from the rest of us, moodily prodding the gravel with his stick, raised his head at the sound. He was an army doctor, with a gray toothbrush moustache and a gruff voice. "For God's sake hurry up, Francis," he said irritably. "The man ought to have been dead by this time. Aren't you ready yet?"

Francis, the head jailer, a fat Dravidian in a white drill suit and gold spectacles, waved his black hand. "Yes sir, yes sir," he bubbled. "All iss satisfactorily prepared. The hangman iss waiting. We shall proceed."

"Well, quick march, then. The prisoners can't get their breakfast till this job's over."

We set out for the gallows. Two warders marched on either side of the prisoner, with their rifles at the slope; two others marched close against him, gripping him by arm and shoulder, as though at once pushing and supporting him. The rest of us, magistrates and the like, followed behind. Suddenly, when we had gone ten yards, the procession stopped short without any order or warning. A dreadful thing had happened—a dog, come goodness knows whence, had appeared in the yard. It came bounding among us with a loud volley of barks, and leapt round us wagging its whole body, wild with glee at finding so many human beings together. It was a large woolly dog, half Airedale, half pariah. For a moment it pranced round us, and then, before anyone could stop it, it had made a dash for the prisoner and, jumping up, tried to lick his face. Everyone stood aghast, too taken aback even to grab at the dog.

"Who let that bloody brute in here?" said the superintendent angrily. "Catch it, someone!"

A warder, detached from the escort, charged clumsily after the dog, but it danced and gamboled just out of his reach, taking everything as part of the game. A young Eurasian jailer picked up a handful of gravel and tried to stone the dog away, but it dodged the stones and came after us again. Its yaps echoed from the jail walls. The prisoner, in the grasp of the two wardens, looked on incuriously, as though this was another formality of the hanging. It was several minutes before someone managed to catch the dog. Then we put my handkerchief through its collar and moved off once more, with the dog still straining and whimpering.

It was about forty yards to the gallows. I watched the bare brown back of the prisoner marching in front of me. He walked clumsily with his bound arms, but quite steadily, with that bobbing gait of the Indian who never straightens his knees. At each step his muscles slid neatly into place, the lock of hair on his scalp danced up and down, his feet printed themselves on the wet gravel. And once, in spite of the men who gripped him by each shoulder, he stepped slightly aside to avoid a puddle on the path.

It is curious, but till that moment I had never realized what it means to destroy a healthy, conscious man. When I saw the prisoner step aside to avoid the puddle I saw the mystery, the unspeakable wrongness of cutting a life short when it is in full tide. This man was not dying, he was alive just as we are alive. All the organs of his body were working—bowels digesting food, skin renewing itself, nails growing, tissues forming—all toiling away in solemn foolery. His nails would still be growing when he stood on the drop, when he was falling through the air with a tenth of a second to live. His eyes saw the yellow gravel and the gray walls, and his brain still remembered, foresaw, reasoned—reasoned even about puddles. He and we were a party of men walking together, seeing, hearing, feeling, understanding the same world; and in two minutes, with a sudden snap, one of us would be gone—one mind less, one world less.

The gallows stood in a small yard, separate from the main grounds of the prison, and overgrown with tall prickly weeds. It was a brick erection like three sides of a shed, with planking on top, and above that two beams and a crossbar with the rope dangling. The hangman, a gray-haired convict in the white uniform of the prison, was waiting beside his machine. He greeted us with a servile crouch as we entered. At a word from Francis the two warders, gripping the prisoner more closely than ever, half led half pushed him to the gallows and helped him clumsily up the ladder. Then the hangman climbed up and fixed the rope round the prisoner's neck.

We stood waiting, five yards away. The warders had formed in a rough circle round the gallows. And then, when the noose was fixed, the prisoner began crying out to his god. It was a high, reiterated cry of "Ram! Ram! Ram! Ram!" not urgent and fearful like a prayer or cry for help, but steady, rhythmical, almost like the tolling of a bell. The dog answered the sound with a whine. The hangman, still standing on the gallows, produced a small cotton bag like a flour bag and drew it down over the prisoner's face. But the sound, muffled by the cloth, still persisted, over and over again: "Ram! Ram! Ram! Ram! Ram!"

The hangman climbed down and stood ready, holding the lever. Minutes seemed to pass. The steady, muffled crying from the prisoner went on and on, "Ram! Ram! Ram!" never faltering for an instant. The superintendent, his head on his chest, was slowly poking the ground with his stick; perhaps he was counting the cries, allowing the prisoner a fixed number—fifty, perhaps, or a hundred. Everyone had changed color. The Indians had gone gray like bad coffee, and one or two of the bayonets were wavering. We looked at the lashed, hooded man on the drop, and listened to his cries— each cry another second of life; the same thought was in all our minds: oh, kill him quickly, get it over, stop that abominable noise!

Suddenly the superintendent made up his mind. Throwing up his head he made a swift motion with his stick. "Chalo!" he shouted almost fiercely.

There was a clanking noise, and then dead silence. The prisoner had vanished, and the rope was twisting on itself. I let go of the dog, and it galloped immediately to the back of the gallows; but when it got there it stopped short, barked, and then retreated into a corner of the yard, where it stood among the weeds, looking timorously out at us. We went round the gallows to inspect the prisoner's body. He was dangling with his toes pointed straight downward, very slowly revolving, as dead as a stone.

The superintendent reached out with his stick and poked the bare brown body; it oscillated slightly. "*He's* all right," said the superintendent. He backed out from under the gallows, and blew out a deep breath. The moody look had gone out of his face quite suddenly. He glanced at his wrist watch. "Eight minutes past eight. Well, that's all for this morning, thank God."

The warders unfixed bayonets and marched away. The dog, sobered and conscious of having misbehaved itself, slipped after them. We walked out of the gallows yard, past the condemned cells with their waiting prisoners, into the big central yard of the prison. The convicts, under the command of warders armed with lathis, were already receiving their breakfast. They squatted in long rows, each man holding a tin pannikin, while two warders with buckets marched around ladling out rice; it seemed quite a homely, jolly scene, after the hanging. An enormous relief had come upon us now that the job was done. One felt an impulse to sing, to break into a run, to snigger. All at once everyone began chattering gaily.

The Eurasian boy walking beside me nodded towards the way we had come, with a knowing smile: "Do you know, sir, our friend (he meant the dead man) when he heard his appeal had been dismissed, he pissed on the floor of his cell. From fright. Kindly take one of my cigarettes, sir. Do you not admire my new silver case, sir? From the boxwallah, two rupees eight annas. Classy European style."

Several people laughed—at what, nobody seemed certain.

Francis was walking by the superintendent, talking garrulously: "Well, sir, all has passed off with the utmost satisfactoriness. It was all finished—flick! like that. It iss not always so—oah, no! I have known cases where the doctor wass obliged to go beneath the gallows and pull the prissoner' legs to ensure decease. Most disagreeable!"

"Wriggling about, eh? That's bad," said the superintendent.

"Ach, sir, it iss worse when they become refractory! One man, I recall, clung to the bars of hiss cage when we went to take him out. You will scarcely credit, sir, that it took six warders to dislodge him, three pulling at each leg. We reasoned with him, 'My dear fellow,' we said, 'think of all the pain and trouble you are causing to us!' But, no, he would not listen! Ach, he wass very troublesome!"

I found that I was laughing quite loudly. Everyone was laughing. Even the superintendent grinned in a tolerant way. "You'd better all come out and have a drink," he said quite genially. "I've got a bottle of whisky in the car. We could do with it."

We went through the big double gates of the prison into the road. "Pulling at his legs!" exclaimed a Burmese magistrate suddenly, and burst into a loud chuckling. We all began laughing again. At that moment Francis's anecdote seemed extraordinarily funny. We all had a drink together, native and European alike, quite amicably. The dead man was a hundred yards away.

How Do You Respond?

1. When the state does something that individuals are forbidden to do, why is the action usually formalized in a ceremony? How does the dog subvert the formal impersonality wanted by those in charge? How would the story be different without the dog?

2. Both Slater's fable and Wright's biography turn on *buts*—expectations that are denied by what follows. Orwell puts a *but* in the center of his narrative—"It is curious, but till that moment . . ." How does this affect the story? Does this explicit moralizing strengthen or weaken the narrative?

3. Orwell does not mention the crime committed by the condemned man. Does the omission matter? Think of different things that he may have done. How would each change your feeling toward him?

FOCUS ON YOUR READING

1. Observe the way each selection begins. The story of Abraham and Isaac begins abruptly. Suddenly, we hear that the time "came when God put Abraham to the test." Richard Wright begins with an evaluative statement when he says he learned "a first lesson in how to live as a Negro." Observe the ways other writers in this chapter begin their works.

2. In each narrative, no matter how it begins, a *once* appears, that one day or one time when the event written of happened. Observe in each selection where the *once* appears.

3. Study the time path in each selection; that is, observe the way writers tell their stories chronologically. Does time progress from the beginning of an event to the end? Do you notice any shifts in verb tense or any places where the writer offers comments not dependent on the time in the story? At the end of "Echo and Narcissus," which has been told in past time, verbs are framed in the present: we are told that a flower *bears* the name and *preserves* the memory of Narcissus. Why do you suppose the verbs are cast in the present tense?

4. Writers of narratives use a variety of techniques to build tension, which is a conflict between two forces. The opposing forces or

conflict may reside within a single character, as they do in Ben Franklin when he wants to maintain his vegetarianism but is tempted by the sight of the fish. Or the tension may rise between two characters, as it does in the Hemingway and Paley stories. Observe in several selections the ways that writers build and then release tension.

5. Details, those particular descriptions that allow us to see the particular world created by a writer, bring a piece of writing to life. Observe the way Maxine Hong Kingston, for example, describes the villagers' attack on her aunt's house, how they "overturned the great waist high earthenware jugs; duck eggs; pickled fruits. . . ." Observe how George Orwell describes the nervous "chattering" of the witnesses in "A Hanging." Observe ways other writers realize—make real—scenes, people, situations.

FOCUS ON YOUR WRITING

6. Tell a story, as Maxine Hong Kingston has done, to "grow up on," one that you have been told as a child, or one that you would tell your own children. Draw two or three inferences—or evaluative statements—from the story. In other words, answer the question, *so what?* Choose those statements that best fit your idea of how to answer that question.

7. Tell a story where the conflict between opposing forces is clear. You want to do something, but you are torn. You want to listen to the "authorities"—your parents, perhaps—but you are tempted not to. You want to take a stand for something you believe in, yet you hold back.

8. Tell a story where the lesson you have learned is clear. You may begin: *This was my first lesson in how to. . . .*

9. Study a narrative you have written. How does it begin? Where does the *once* appear? Now try another beginning. Which do you prefer? Do you tell all that needs to be told? Do you tell "too much"? Do you think you might reduce or expand any section? Can you add descriptive details to provide sharper images?

10. Pearl Rowe in "Cookies at Midnight" offers no explicit statement about why this story matters. The evaluative statements are implied. Write a brief essay in which you offer evaluative statements to fit Pearl Rowe's narrative. Answer the question *so what?* Why does this story matter?

Chapter 4

❖ ❖

"How Do You Get to Route 95?"

PROCEDURES

There you are, walking down the road, when a driver in a green Trans Am stops to ask, "How do you get to the Sheltaire Motel on Route 95?"

"Well," you say, thinking hard, "follow this road a little ways. Turn right by some white houses on the corner—that's where the Smiths live—and keep going. When you come to a four-lane road, that's Route 95. The Sheltaire is around there somewhere."

A little ways? Keep going? Around there somewhere? If the driver is lucky, these directions may lead to someone else who can give better instructions: "You're close—it's about half a mile from here. Go down this road about a half-mile, turn right at the white church, and go another quarter-mile. You'll come to Route 95 and the Sheltaire is about 500 yards to your right, just past the lake."

Procedures are very much a part of our daily lives, whether we are giving directions to a driver, describing an accident to the police, giving our secret recipe for pea soup to a friend, or trying to set a new digital watch. When we must tell how to do something or how something happened, we follow certain rules. We have an audience in mind, we stay close to the sequence of events as they occur, and we provide signal words like *first, second, third* to break down the process into manageable steps. (The instructions with digital watches may not follow all these rules.) We offer description when it's needed, provide examples, and define the terms that need to be defined. In this way, we give clear, direct, precise information or instructions.

HOW TO DO SOMETHING

Take a look at Craig Claibourne's recipe for cheese soufflé, which is a light and puffy cheese and egg dish.

CHEESE SOUFFLÉ 4 to 6 servings

¼ cup butter
¼ cup flour
1½ cups milk
Salt
Worcestershire sauce
Cayenne pepper
½ pound Cheddar cheese, finely grated
4 eggs, separated

1. Preheat oven to moderate (375°F).
2. In a saucepan melt the butter over low heat and add flour; stir with a wire whisk until blended. Meanwhile, bring the milk to a boil and add all at once to the butter-flour mixture, stirring vigorously with the whisk. Season to taste with salt, Worcestershire, and cayenne pepper.
3. Turn off the heat and let the mixture cool two to three minutes. Add the cheese and stir until melted. Beat in the egg yolks one at a time and cool.
4. Beat the egg whites until they stand in peaks, but do not overbeat. Cut and fold the egg whites into the mixture. Turn into a two-quart casserole (greased or ungreased, as desired) and bake thirty to forty-five minutes.

If that is not clear enough, Claibourne illuminates the procedure with graphic illustrations.

Soufflés are tricky to make—a step out of order, an overbeaten egg, or overcooking will cause the soufflé to fall. A recipe provides a good model for writing about a procedure. The recipe writer first sets out the ingredients and then breaks down the procedure into

112 THE WRITER'S FORMS

1. To make a soufflé, first prepare a basic white sauce.

2. Let white sauce cool. Beat in egg yolks one at a time. Add seasonings.

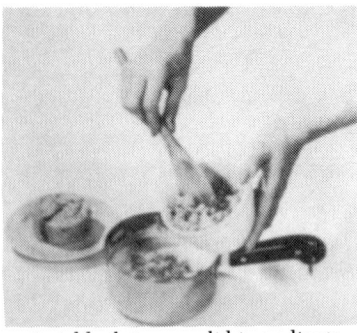

3. Add whatever solid ingredients are to be used—such as salmon—and blend well into the white sauce and egg yolk mixture.

4. Using a rotary beater or an electric mixer, beat egg whites until they stand in peaks; do not overbeat.

5. Gently fold the beaten egg whites into the sauce, using a rubber spatula or wooden spoon. Do not overblend.

6. Pour into a soufflé dish and bake until firm in a moderate oven.

the essential and sequential steps. In making soufflés, you first turn on the oven so that it will be ready when you have beaten and mixed the ingredients. When you are fixing a broken window, you first gather the necessary equipment so that you don't have to dash up and down a ladder, collecting tools and materials from the basement and garage as you work. In the same way, as you write, you set out the ingredients, you gather your tools, when you offer your readers an overview, telling them what they will need in order to complete the procedure.

After giving the overview, you break down what needs to be done into a sequence of actions—first, second, third. You describe whenever possible to help your readers visualize the procedure. Since your readers are not *actually* present, your task is to represent the procedure in such a way that they are *virtually* present: you imagine them looking over your shoulder. Notice how Claibourne describes parts of the procedure: the heat should be *low*; the stirring should be *vigorous*; and the egg whites should be beaten *until they stand in peaks*. Through graphic illustrations, Claibourne shows how those peaks should look.

In the following selections, Jean John writes about the "how to" of making a terrarium. Notice how carefully she sets out the ingredients and then takes us through the procedure. Scissors Sam tells precisely and humorously how to sharpen a knife. In Dick Gregory's personal account, the "how to" of giving up food is blended with his reasons for putting himself on a fast. Here the writer uses the "how-to's" of a procedure for a larger, more serious purpose.

HOW WAS IT DONE?

Procedure is also involved when we look back to see how something was done or how something happened. In the following brief account, a survivor recounts what he witnessed when a dam broke in his home town of Buffalo Creek, West Virginia:

> I walked to the back porch and saw my neighbors running and screaming. I heard one say "the dam." I then came running through the house and told my wife to head for the hills. When I got to the living room I saw the water rolling by the window. I knew then there was no way out of the house, and all hope

vanished. My wife started crying and praying. I saw a housetop going by with a friend of mine on top. Then I heard a big crash and saw the big wave of water coming with houses and trash in it. There was nothing we could do but watch and pray for the best and wonder how long our house would stand. I saw four or five of our neighbor's homes go by. I tried to think of a way out, but there just wasn't any. The water was thirty or forty minutes passing, but it seemed like it would never pass. Then finally it was gone and left a dead body lying on the hood of my car.*

The speaker, here, relies on chronology, telling the events as they happened in time. His verbs are active and in the past tense: *I walked . . . saw . . . heard . . . came . . . told.*

Eyewitnesses try to get it straight, to tell it the way it happened, whether they are sports announcers or witnesses to a crime. They try to anticipate what their audiences need to know. They don't throw in the Smiths' house when talking to a stranger. They tell what a soufflé is before offering a recipe. They detail an account of the dam breaking, creating a vivid word picture for the listener who wasn't there.

Procedure or process analysis is similar to narrative; it follows an *and then, and then* development. "What did you do today?" the husband asks his wife as she comes home from work. And she tells him: *first I did this and then I did that and then I did this,* relating the story of her day. In the following selections, notice how Kate Chopin blends procedure and narrative to tell what happened in an hour as she creates a startling story. The procedure takes in not only what happened in the hour but also what happened to the character.

Alvin and Heidi Toffler analyze the American family by looking back at a series of changes in the concept and construction of family. Here cause and effect work closely with procedure as we see how a particular procedure affects institutions and social structure. George Orwell in "Some Thoughts on the Common Toad" describes the emergence of spring in London of the 1940s, implicitly offering reassurance in the teeth of terrifying events. His essay recalls the words of the poet, Gerard Manley Hopkins:

> As sure as what is most sure, sure as that spring primroses
> Shall new-dapple next year, sure as tomorrow morning,

*From Kai T. Erikson, *Everything in Its Path* (New York: Simon and Schuster, 1976), p. 161.

> Amongst come-back-again things, things with a revival, things with a recovery . . .
>
> St. Winefred's Well

Despite the ravages of winter, despite the despair wrought by war, spring—"as sure as what is most sure"—each year surfaces anew. And finally, the chapter closes with poet Muriel Rukeyser recounting the creative procedure of writing a poem.

❖ ❖ ───────────────────────────────

AS YOU READ

Evaluation

A procedure is naturally set within a frame of *implicit* evaluations: A writer tells how to save money through buying government bonds because she thinks it *wise* to save money, or because she thinks it urgent to support the government. A cookbook writer offers a recipe because he approves of it. The implicit evaluation is: This is a terrific recipe; try it! He does not need to add, "This is the best beef stew you've ever tasted," or, "The lemon meringue pie is heavenly."

When set into an essay, the procedure is often framed by an *explicit* evaluation; that is, the writer tells about a procedure for an explicit purpose. Jean John writes about building a terrarium because, to her, terrariums are worthy of attention. But Dick Gregory talks of fasting not simply to tell how to do it but to show the purpose of his fasting: to protest the war in Viet Nam.

In the same way as in narratives, then, the *evaluation* answers the question *So what?* As you read the selections in this chapter, note passages that point up what the writers think of the subject, the point of view, the tone. Those very elements that we considered when looking at narrative cut across all writing.

Procedures rely on selecting—choosing relevant details—and sequencing—ordering through time: first *a*, then *b*, then *c*. The Tofflers, in their sweep through ten thousand years, *select* what they see as three waves of family development. Those three waves are not naturally "out there" in the world, like mammoth bones; the Tofflers select from masses of information and construct a sequence from what they see. In the same way, George Orwell could have written about other signs that show the emergence of spring. He selects the "common toad," and then convinces us that his choice is apt by telling how the toad surfaces "from a hole in the ground, where it has lain buried since the previous autumn." Sequencing is not automatic. Writers select among many details and then set them into an order governed by time, by what comes first, second, third.

Change

Change is fundamental to procedures. In carrying out a procedure, we expect something to change, to become different. The dull knife becomes sharp; the raw eggs and milk and other ingredients turn into a soufflé; the raw material in a writer's mind becomes a poem. Pay attention, as you read, to changes that occur and to ways that writers signal the changes to come.

AS YOU WRITE

Generating Material

Our daily life is made up of procedures we automatically follow: We no longer think about how to make a cup of instant coffee or tie a shoe or drive a car. We simply do so. Think about activities that you perform daily: making a scrambled egg, walking the dog, taking a particular route to work. Jot down some of these daily acts in your journal, and write about them, quickly, selecting details that are relevant and placing them in a sequence.

Now think about the complex procedures of your life—deciding on a new job, confronting death, dealing with loss, stopping smoking, learning to swim, writing a poem. Current magazines and books are filled with self-help procedures: how to handle guilt, how to tell children about divorce, how to be a success on the job, how to lose ten pounds in seven days. Write up a batch of procedures from your own life and from the world about you. Keep track of procedures you might like to pursue in your own writing.

Reading Your Writing

As you scan your informal writings, think about a potential audience. Can you expect your readers to be naturally interested in your subject? Will you need to captivate them, to make your evaluations explicit: learn how to make *this* chicken soup or *this* herbal tea because.... If you write about how to stop smoking, your audience will probably know the problems smokers face; your job may be to convince them that your method will work. You'll need to consider how much knowledge you can assume in your readers; you won't need to tell them what a chicken is, but you will have to identify and describe dill, turnips, parsley. Writing about the coming of spring, you can assume, as Orwell does, that an audience will know about toads. But if you're writing about photography, you'll need to anticipate what your audience needs to know about focusing, about lenses, about distance.

Shaping Your Writing

As you write, set the procedure within a context: the motel is about a mile from here; we are going to make a soufflé. With a framework in mind, the sequencing will be clear as the whole is broken down into parts. Be sure that the words signalling one step and then another are obvious, and that, throughout, you provide details, descriptions, instructions, definitions to help your reader along. *You* may know precisely how to get to Route 95, but unless you give an overview and make the steps along the way clear, your readers may be lost. If Route 95 is not one mile away but thirty, that is crucial information. Think of yourself riding and riding and riding, wondering when that white church will appear. Give your reader a sense of the whole as well as of the parts.

JEAN JOHN

> Fall is the best time to make terrariums, according to Jean John of New York City. "When you live in the city," she says, "you need to remind yourself that there's a world outside—trees, rocks, flowers. A terrarium brings the outside in."

THE "HOW TO" OF TERRARIUMS

TERRARIUM PLANTS

Small	Medium	Tall
Baby's tears (Heixine)	Strawberry begonia	Boxwood
Running myrtle (Periwinkle)	Pachysandra	Euonymus
	Wandering Jew	Aluminum plant
	Ajuga	Coleus
Small leaf ivy	Pipple Peperomia	Wax begonia
Irish shamrock	Pilea	Patience
	Purple passion	Oxalis
	Philodendron	

The first terrariums were called Wardian Cases in honor of their discoverer, Dr. Nathaniel Ward, an English surgeon and botanist whose work more than 100 years ago led to the development of greenhouses. He experimented with plants in containers and found that if plants had light, air and humidity they could thrive without care or fresh water.

As a result of this discovery, plants unable to survive long voyages could be shipped to distant ports. The tea industry was established in India because tea plants could be shipped this way from Shanghai.

Almost any clear glass container (light amber or green-tinted glass) that you can plug, cork, or cover has the makings of an attractive garden setting. Fish bowls, brandy snifters, liquor and wine bottles, and mason jars may be used. Not all glass gardens need to sit. They can hang from a wire wrapped around the neck.

Harmony and simplicity are important principles. Don't overcrowd the scene, as the purpose of a garden is to grow. A single terrarium has to have a relatively homogeneous selection of plants with compatible soil, light, and temperature predilections.

You can devise an interesting landscape design simply by sloping the soil upward against the glass, giving the effect of a hillside in the background. Start with the taller material planted in the rear then work forward, filling the central focal area and finally the foreground with a low creeping or sprawling plant. The foreground serves as an invitation, its function being to lead the eye onward to further exploration.

Adding interest are accessories such as featherrock, driftwood, sea shells, Japanese stones, gravel, pebbles, miniature figurines or garden ornaments—lanterns, bridges, Buddhas, pagodas, and attractive rocks.

You will need sphagnum moss, gravel for drainage, charcoal chips to sweeten the soil, sterile soil, and tools, which include long sticks, scissors for pruning, a mister or atomizer, and an artist's or bottle brush.

Plant selection is wide (see box) and there is no need to use or exhibit plants that are on the New York State Conservation List.

To make the terrarium: First, line it with moss that has been soaked in water then drained; secrete bits of charcoal in the moss. Now spread gravel over the bottom for drainage. Add soil in proportion either to the size of the container or the height of the vegetation. Make a depression in the soil using a long stick or pencil as you plant your selection.

Plant taller background material first, medium-sized plants second, and low growth in the foreground last. Cover roots carefully with soil. Water the garden thoroughly, then cover it.

Put the newly planted garden in a cool place without sun for several days to give the plants time to adjust to their new surroundings. Lastly, move the glass garden to a light but not sunny site, relax, and watch it grow.

A well-balanced terrarium soil retains moisture but is porous enough to assure good drainage.

For an all-purpose soil, take two parts topsoil to one part sand and add one part milled sphagnum and leaf mold. Vermiculite ensures sturdy root growth. Packaged terrarium soil is available at garden supply stores.

The first watering, using an atomizer or mister, should be thorough enough to get the rainmaking cycle functioning.

From the soil, plants absorb water, which is then evaporated.

This evaporated water, when confined in a terrarium, can't dissolve into the atmosphere; therefore it is condensed by the glass. Beadlike patches of moisture form which, like rain clouds, become heavy and then break, trickling down the sides of the glass like rain, to be absorbed by the soil. Water may not be needed again for three months.

How Do You Respond?

1. When does Jean John get to the "how to" of making a terrarium? Why do you think she waits until halfway into the article?
2. If you were reducing this article to 100 words to accompany a terrarium kit, would you include anything from the first half of the article? What?
3. Do you feel the need for pictures to go with this article? Why?

SAM LONG

> Sam Long in a brief autobiographical note to his manual on sharpening scissors and tools says that he was born on June 24, 1912, "amongst the foothills of Laurel Ridge in western Pennsylvania." For years, he was a drifter, moving from one job to another, until in 1957 he capitalized on the skills his father taught him and became "Scissors Sam," the knife sharpener, traveling across the United States, meeting and talking with people along the way. "Now, that I am about to retire," he said in 1972, "it is my pleasure and duty to write this book."

KNIVES

Volumes of books could be written about knives, but let's keep it simple. When I was a boy and lived on our small farm, my mother whetted her knife on the top of one of the milk crocks. Anyone who can't learn to sharpen a knife after reading my instructions is pretty dumb.

← CUTTING EDGE

Let's start off with the ordinary, old-fashioned knife. Naturally the best test of dullness is when it quits cutting. Surprisingly, how many housewives hand me their knives and ask, "Can you tell me if they need sharpening?" Yes I can—always.

If you hold the cutting edge straight toward the eye, and the knife is dull, you will notice a blunt edge. Let's say it is somewhat comparable to the back of the knife, although not nearly so. When a knife is perfectly sharp, one can look straight at the cutting side and see no blunt edge.

Many people hand me a knife and ask, "Can you put an edge on this knife?" In reality, I take the edge *off* the knife.

The most convenient method of sharpening a knife is to lay it across the corner of a table with the back down. Hold the blade at a 60 degree angle. With the other hand stroke the stone downward away from the cutting edge. Either a file or stone may be used, depending on the hardness of the knife. Another method is to rest the knife on a block of wood across your lap. Hone both sides of the cutting edge equally.

In early days there was only one conventional knife. Today we still have the conventional knife which is still the best. Then we have added hollowground knives which are good. Now the nitwits come out with all styles of serrated knives which I wouldn't give a hoot for, except for two purposes. Serrated knives, mostly of the round tooth type, have long been used for cutting bread, and they answer the purpose very well. Steak knives are much more efficient with about two inches of the front of the blade serrated. For other purposes than these two, I wouldn't give a nickle for all the serrated knives made.

Knives vary from very hard metal to very soft. If knives are too hard to the point where the metal is crystallized, they won't take a good cutting edge and tend to chip easily. On the other hand I have sharpened some cheap knives that are so soft a sardine can fashioned into a blade would make a better cutting edge. The medium temper steel always makes the best knife. Steel is very similar to the

DULL   SHOULDER   MEDIUM   SHARP

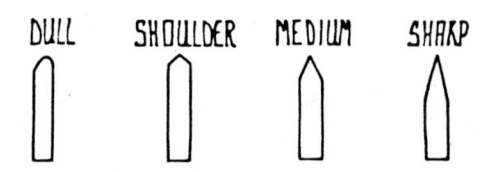

dress or shirt you wear. It's not the hardness nor how soft, but the fine texture of the material.

There are so many brands on the market, it would be useless to mention a few, were it my intention to mention brand names. An ordinary priced knife with a common wood handle usually is the best kitchen knife. When you get into real expensive knives with fancy handles, you usually pay for the handle, not the knife blade.

Softer knives usually take a better sharpening edge with an ordinary file. One point I have observed for many years is that a file works better on softer metal and a stone on hard metal. The most efficient knife sharpener ever was the old fashioned "huge" sandstone with water dripping on it. If an electric grinder is used, keep moving the blade and stop frequently to avoid burning the knife. Mechanical devices, such as electric can openers, sharpen only a very small fraction of the blade and soon leave what is known as a shoulder.

Hollow ground knives can be sharpened more often by the novice without leaving a shoulder. Never lay a knife on frozen or hard food and attempt hitting it with a hammer. Cleavers are made for that purpose.

Oil stones are efficient, but very slow if the knife is very dull, especially when the shoulder needs to be taken off.

Once I called on a house and some young "green" gentleman informed me I was a few days too late. He explained that he bought a butcher steel the Saturday night before—as if that was to answer all his sharpening needs. A butcher steel is a very temporary sharpening device. Every fifteen minutes the butcher picks up his steel, but periodically sharpens all his knives on a grinder.

Some housewives tell me, "Don't make it too sharp." I prefer my knives with a razor edge. Again, buy a common knife for general kitchen work. Knives are made to cut with, not to look at.

If your knives are always in excellent cutting condition, you will be able to cut the roast very thin, and reduce your hubby's waistline.

How Do You Respond?

1. Do you think Long's tone is refreshing or distracting? How do you feel when he says that *you* will be "pretty dumb" if you can't follow his instruction? What do you think of his instructions?

2. Suggest improvements in his ordering of details and his sequencing. Write a short list of sharpening instructions that could be put in a package with a new knife.

3. Think back over the opinions and information offered by Long. Do you remember them in detail? Do you remember them better than you would an impersonal list of instructions?

DICK GREGORY

> *Dick Gregory (born 1932) wears two hats: those of comedian and of political activist, but they are, to switch the metaphor, two sides of the same coin. He is a member of a great generation of stand-up comedians—possibly the most brilliant that America has ever produced—that included Mort Sahl and Lenny Bruce. They used the resources and the sheer power of comedy to say very serious things, to throw a blinding light on forms of folly and hypocrisy, greed and wickedness, in such a way that you could never again say: but nobody told me! Gregory's autobiographies,* Nigger *and* Up From Nigger, *from which the following selection is taken, show the stand-up comedian and political activist wearing a third hat—that of an able, poignant writer.*

FAREWELL TO FOOD

During the long marches in Milwaukee, I had time to do a lot of thinking. My thoughts kept returning to how I could personally help to bring an end to the Vietnam war. I decided not to get a haircut until the war was over, and I urged others to join my Samsonesque protest. I figured if enough people stopped getting haircuts, it would create a large lobby of barbers who would instantaneously join the anti-war effort. I also urged people not to shave until after the war, reasoning that even old ladies who owned stock in Gillette Blue Blades would join the peace movement.

I also began thinking about going on a long fast. I had been hearing and reading about fasting, and I thought an extended fast would be the best possible witness I could make, considering the publicity it would inevitably attract. I kept thinking of Mahatma Gandhi and his nonviolent movement in India. It seemed to me that fasting was the ultimate weapon in the nonviolent arsenal.

So I held a press conference and announced that I would fast for thirty-two days, beginning on Thanksgiving and ending on Christmas Day. In my press conference opening statement, I said, "I am determined to set an example as an individual American, lawfully protesting against my government's policy in Vietnam. From Thanksgiving until Christmas, I will fast in sympathy with the millions of Americans who are also opposed to the war in Vietnam. I will not eat, drink juice, or take prepared vitamins or other food supplements.

"I suggest that true Christians and humanitarians celebrate Christmas this year in simplicity and sacrifice, and, in sympathy with the suffering on both sides of the war, avoid traditional decorations, Christmas trees, lights, ornaments, toys, and the exchange of gifts and presents, until peace on earth and goodwill to men become a reality."

I realized that there would be doubters and scoffers who would insist that I was sneaking food during the fast. So I asked Jimmy Smith, editor and publisher of the *Chicago Gazette*, and Irv Kupcinet, *Chicago Sun-Times* columnist and television personality, to hold a $1,000 bond against any challenge to my fasting fidelity. I said that I would willingly submit to a medical examination to see if any food had entered my digestive system, as long as a doctor of my own choice was allowed to be present during the exam. I was betting a thousand dollars that an honest medical exam would prove that I was living only on distilled water. I also asked any potential challengers to post a $100 contribution to SNCC against my $1,000.

Whether by accident or by Providence, I happened to be going through some papers and I came across a name and address: Dr. Alvenia Fulton, The Fultonia Health Food Center, 521 East Sixty-third Street. I said to Lillian, "Look, Lil, here's the name and address of that lady who sent those salads to the campaign headquarters. We really should go by and thank her."

We did, and that visit changed my life. I had no idea that Dr. Fulton knew anything about fasting. But it turned out that she is one of the world's leading authorities on the subject and had personally fasted many, many times before. She had read about my impending fast in the newspaper, and she asked if I had ever fasted before. I told her I hadn't. She began immediately to teach me the techniques of scientific fasting. She told me to begin cleaning out my body by drinking only freshly squeezed juices for seven days before Thanksgiving. She explained the condition of toxemia, the retention of poisonous toxins in the body as a result of bad eating habits and improper elimination. She told me how the poisons would be flushed out of my body during the period of fasting. She told me to cleanse my colon with enemas and to continue the enemas after my fast began. I couldn't help thinking about the irony of my original reaction to her salads. I had suspected her of possibly trying to poison me, and here she was telling me how to get the poisons out of my system!

Dr. Fulton was so excited about my fast that she promised to fast along with me. Under the tutelage of Dr. Fulton, my "hunger strike" became a "scientific fast." What began as a protest against the war was later to become a way of life, a whole new understanding of the functioning of the human body and the laws of Mother Nature.

On Thanksgiving Day, I began my fast. But I maintained my hectic schedule of college lectures, benefits, nightclub dates, and radio and television shows: the Wesley South show in Chicago, a benefit for Imamu Baraka (LeRoi Jones) in Newark, the Merv Griffin show in New York, a lecture at Brown University, a benefit in McKeesport, Pennsylvania, a benefit at New York's Town Hall with Sidney Poitier, the Senior Class Dinner at Yale University, college lectures in the South, the Midwest and on the West Coast—Iowa, Texas, California, West Virginia, Colorado, Wisconsin. In a forty-day period I visited fifty-seven cities and gave sixty-three lectures.

Every night I would call Dr. Fulton. Her knowledge of fasting was so complete, she knew in advance—each day of the fast—what feelings and sensations I would be experiencing. For example, she told me that I would experience a sudden burst of energy at the end of the third week. It was difficult for me to believe, especially at those times when I felt weak during the *first* three weeks. But she was absolutely right. At the end of three weeks, the body begins *consuming itself*, thoroughly ridding itself of stored-up poisons which have been accumulating for a lifetime. And there is an accompanying resurgence of energy.

She also warned me to beware of lifting anything heavy as the fast progressed, and also to avoid sudden movements, like getting up suddenly or changing positions suddenly. Again, since the body was going through such a thorough cleansing process, especially the cleansing of the bloodstream, any sudden movement would be a shock to the system in the process of renewing itself. Her words of advice were especially valuable to me, since I was a man on the move with loads and loads of luggage. During that fast I came to have a special appreciation for my skycap brothers!

Even with Dr. Fulton's wise counsel, I still went through some mental changes. Everywhere I went, I could tell people really thought I was going to die. Before long I began to share their concern. I would come back to the hotel room after a lecture, flop down on the bed, and pass out in slumber. Then I'd wake up in the middle of the night. The room would be dark and everything would be quiet and I'd wonder if I was dead or alive. Then I would get to thinking, maybe that's what death feels like. Since I'd never died before, I thought death might be "one eternal pinch!"

I also found that my hunger disappeared after the third or fourth day of the fast. But the temptations to *get hungry* were all around me. You don't realize how many food commercials there are on TV, how many restaurants, lunch counters, and hot dog stands, until you go on a fast. Then they all seem to jump out at you.

I would go to sleep, and the "hot dog parade" would start marching through my dreams, even though I'd long since given up hot dogs. I came to realize the great extent to which hunger is a mental attitude rather than an actual physical need. And I realized why there are so many overweight folks in America. The temptations to eat are all around, appealing to people's minds, whether their bodies need the food or not.

For two successive weekends before Christmas, I played the Village Gate, sharing the stage with an old friend, jazzman Charles Lloyd. I did three shows a night, Friday and Saturday nights. The room was packed. I don't know if folks came to hear my funnies as a standup comedian, or if they came thinking it was funny that I could still stand up!

Of course I had to talk about the fast during my act:

"Everybody keeps asking me about my fast. A reporter asked me the other day if I had any unusual things happen to me as a result of the fast. I said, 'Yes. Yesterday I had a button drop off.' He said, 'What's so unusual about a button dropping off?' I told him, 'It was my belly button.'"

"People ask if I have to take any special precautions. Well, after the third week of the fast, I started wearing a protective covering around my knees—my jockey shorts! I've lost so much weight, I look like Wilt 'The Stilt' Chamberlain, after taxes. My stomach is so shrunk, if I swallowed a marshmallow, I'd look pregnant."

"But I don't mind telling you, I'm hungry. I don't dare allow myself to be near anybody with food, even if it's meat. And I don't ordinarily eat meat. I'm so hungry, do you know what NAACP means to me these days? Never Associate with Anyone Carrying Porkchops!"

On the Friday before Christmas, I got into New York City early and held a press conference at the Village Gate. I announced that I was extending my fast until New Year's Day. "When I began this personal, nonviolent demonstration as an American citizen and a Christian," I told the press, "I chose to make it during the Thanksgiving and Christmas holidays because of their significance to me as days of peace and thankfulness and blessing. I have received an enormous number of communications from all over the world. I now realize that this time of year is also precious to many other people of different faiths and nationalities, and in respect to those throughout the world who celebrate Hannukah as Jews, Ramadan as Moslems, and Tet as Buddhists, I have resolved to extend my fast until the New Year."

Some of the reporters asked me again what I hoped to accomplish by my fasting. I answered, "This is the only country in the world where more people die each year from overeating than undereating. So I've deduced that America's conscience must lie in her stomach. I just hope my fast will locate that American conscience and cause people to think about the war in Vietnam. Everywhere I go people are worrying about the possibility of my dying. Perhaps they will also begin worrying about the *reality* of people dying every hour of every day in Vietnam."

Once again, *The New York Times* probed deeper than the press conference in covering the story. *Times* reporter J. Anthony Lukas checked with doctors at the Columbia Presbyterian Medical Center for expert medical opinion. The doctors said that my forty-nine pound weight loss was "about right" for someone who was doing what I was doing. When asked if they thought I was really fasting, the doctors were noncommittal, but observed that it was "not at all impossible for a man as deeply committed as Mr. Gregory."

A medical opinion of a different sort came from my friend and physician, Dr. Charles Lee Williams, in Chicago. He was really worried about my health, and his concern was recorded in an article in the *Chicago Courier* written by Wesley South. Dr. Williams had examined me and found acetone in my blood, indicating that the remaining fats in my body were rapidly breaking down. He said the ingredient acts like alcohol in the blood and makes a person behave like he is drunk. Dr. Williams seemed to feel that my extension of the fast was the act of a drunken fool. He was quoted as saying:

"I warned him to stop this fast a long time ago. He is fast approaching the point of no return. He has made his point, and I can see no reason why he should continue it.

"Whenever a person survives a fast for thirty days, we write them up in the medical journals. Now Dick is planning to go even further. The prisoners in the Nazi concentration camps were better off than Dick. Those unfortunates were on a starvation diet. They were at least eating some food. They were partially starved. Dick is completely starved.

"If you don't put gasoline in an automobile, it will stop. If you don't put fuel in the human body, it will die. Dick is playing a game more dangerous than Russian roulette. Instead of using a revolver with five empty chambers and one bullet, by extending his fast, Dick is using a revolver with five bullets and one empty chamber."

At the time I was examined by Dr. Williams, a Cook County circuit court judge was also visiting the office. He suggested that it might be necessary for the courts to declare me incompetent in order to save my life. In other words, the judge seemed to feel, as the title of a record album by my friend and colleague-in-comedy Richard Pryor would declare, "That nigger's crazy!"

While I appreciated the love and concern about my health, I knew I wasn't crazy, nor was I playing Russian roulette. I had already learned from Dr. Fulton how Mother Nature would tell me when I was in real danger. During the period in which the body is cleansing itself of all impurities, a chalky coating, sometimes yellow and sometimes white, will appear on the surface of the tongue. As long as the coating is on the tongue, there is no danger of dying from starvation. When the coating disappears, the fast must be broken because starvation has set in. And at that point, true hunger returns.

My tongue was still coated. So even though my doctor thought I was foolish and the judge thought I was crazy, the true momma of us all, Mother Nature, was saying, "You're all right, son. I'll tell you when to quit."

I was losing weight from head to toe. And one night onstage at the Village Gate, I found out I was losing weight in my fingers too. Well into my performance, I got up from the stool I usually use in my act and was pacing back and forth aross the stage, microphone in hand. At one point I made a dramatic gesture, swinging my arm away from my body. My wedding band went sailing across the room! My fingers had gotten so skinny that the ring no longer fit. Fortunately my wedding band was recovered by a customer, and I returned it to my finger after I had fattened up a bit.

I broke my fast on New Year's Day. Of course, I couldn't eat solid food. After a long fast, a person must gradually return to eating by remaining on a diet of juice one day for every ten days of fasting. During the fast, the villi in the stomach have gone to sleep, and they must be awakened gradually.

But that first sip of juice is a real trip! You can feel those stomach villi waking up. You can almost hear the stomach sending a message to the brain, "Hey, he's eating again. Get ready. Here it comes!" You close your eyes and it seems like every star in the heavens comes down to introduce itself to you personally! It is Mother Nature's trip, a real mind-blowing experience, which does not need to be induced by unnatural and artificial substances.

I had a party to go to that night. It was inauguration day in Gary,

Indiana, for the city's new mayor, Richard Hatcher. Lil and I attended the swearing-in ceremony and the inaugural ball. I knew I had gotten down to ninety-eight pounds during the fast, but I didn't fully realize how much weight I had lost until I was being fitted for a tuxedo. All my life I've been fighting against being called "boy," and here I was back in the boy's department!

It was like a double celebration for me. It seemed so appropriate to be at Dick Hatcher's inaugural on the same day that I had broken my fast. Both Dick Hatcher and I had been through a period of struggle and testing, and we had both emerged victorious. We had seen our respective ordeals through to the end.

Dick Hatcher had overcome all kinds of obstacles to become the mayor of Gary. The Indiana State Legislature had even passed new laws to try to stop him. But he brought together that growing northern Black political power that was beginning to say in Cleveland, in Newark, and now in Gary, "No longer will the office of mayor be viewed as a job for whites only!" Just as my fast had thoroughly cleansed my body, Black power was beginning to cleanse the American political system. Dick Hatcher's victory and my fast were symbolically related.

The next day I held a press conference at the Knickerbocker Hotel in Chicago to release a letter I had just sent to the White House. A copy was sent to John M. Bailey, chairman of the Democratic National Committee.

I told the president and the chairman that the selection of Chicago as the site of the 1968 Democratic National Convention was a "cruel insult" to all those progressive Democrats, both Black and white, who would see the choice as an endorsement of the repressive local Democratic administration headed by Mayor Daley. I said further that if five steps were not taken immediately, the convention would be held in Chicago only over my dead body. The five conditions were: (1) enacting a fair housing bill for Chicago, with a guarantee that anyone could walk anywhere in Chicago without fear of racial attack; (2) appointing a Black to the top echelon of the police department; (3) guaranteeing the safety of the Reverend Jesse Jackson, founder of Operation Breadbasket, who had received many threats on his life; (4) lifting the injunction against Martin Luther King, Jr., and others on marching in the Chicago suburbs; and (5) making the Chicago police and fire fighters the highest paid in the nation.

I sent similar letters to Mayor Daley, to each of the fifty aldermen in the Chicago City Council, and to the police and fire commissioners. I personally delivered Mayor Daley's letter to his office, along with a copy of the book *Before the Mayflower* by *Ebony* magazine Senior Editor Lerone Bennett, Jr.

The next day some headlines read: DICK GREGORY VOWS CONVENTION HELD OVER HIS DEAD BODY. I thought of the line I'd used at the Selma march about Sheriff Jim Clark. I'm sure some Democrats felt that wouldn't be a bad route either!

How Do You Respond?

1. Gregory mixes the story of his fast with information about fasting. How does he blend narrative and an account of a procedure? What do you think of the result?

2. If this narrative were written as a medical document, what parts would be omitted? What changes would be made in structure and tone? Write a physician's report on this fast in the passive voice about an anonymous subject. Eliminate the personal and narrative elements altogether by reducing Gregory's story to a chart or graph. What are the differences in these forms of the information?

3. Even in an impersonal report about an anonymous subject, the personal element is still there. The writer is present even when invisible; the subject exists even when unnamed. What are the advantages of "scientific" reports? The disadvantages? Is the formal, impersonal and objective approach misleading in any way?

KATE CHOPIN

> The writings of Kate O'Flaherty (Chopin), (1851–1904) have had their fair share of trouble with the censors, those who would prevent us from reading books that make them feel uncomfortable: her great novel, The Awakening, which appeared in 1899, was banned by the library in her hometown, St. Louis, and after a reprint in 1906, it was out of print for over fifty years. She raised six children and after her husband died, when she was about 30, she managed the family plantation in addition to the work of writing. The question of women's emancipation was a big one in the 1890s, and it is out of her defense of woman's right to a decent degree of self-determination that her most compelling writing came.

THE STORY OF AN HOUR

Knowing that Mrs. Mallard was afflicted with a heart trouble, great care was taken to break to her as gently as possible the news of her husband's death.

It was her sister Josephine who told her, in broken sentences, veiled hints that revealed in half concealing. Her husband's friend Richards was there, too, near her. It was he who had been in the newspaper office when intelligence of the railroad disaster was received, with Brently Mallard's name leading the list of "killed." He had only taken the time to assure himself of its truth by a second telegram, and had hastened to forestall any less careful, less tender friend in bearing the sad message.

She did not hear the story as many women have heard the same, with a paralyzed inability to accept its significance. She wept at once, with sudden, wild abandonment, in her sister's arms. When the storm of grief had spent itself she went to her room alone. She would have no one follow her.

There stood, facing the open window, a comfortable, roomy armchair. Into this she sank, pressed down by a physical exhaustion that haunted her body and seemed to reach into her soul.

She could see in the open square before her house the tops of trees that were all aquiver with the new spring life. The delicious breath of rain was in the air. In the street below a peddler was crying his wares. The notes of a distant song which some one was singing reached her faintly, and countless sparrows were twittering in the eaves.

There were patches of blue sky showing here and there through the clouds that had met and piled above the other in the west facing her window.

She sat with her head thrown back upon the cushion of the chair quite motionless, except when a sob came up into her throat and shook her, as a child who has cried itself to sleep continues to sob in its dreams.

She was young, with a fair, calm face, whose lines bespoke repression and even a certain strength. But now there was a dull stare in her eyes, whose gaze was fixed away off yonder on one of those patches of blue sky. It was not a glance of reflection, but rather indicated a suspension of intelligent thought.

There was something coming to her and she was waiting for it, fearfully. What was it? She did not know; it was too subtle and elusive to name. But she felt it, creeping out of the sky, reaching toward her through the sounds, the scents, the color that filled the air.

Now her bosom rose and fell tumultuously. She was beginning to recognize this thing that was approaching to possess her, and she was striving to beat it back with her will—as powerless as her two white slender hands would have been.

When she abandoned herself a little whispered word escaped her slightly parted lips. She said it over and over under her breath: "Free, free, free!" The vacant stare and the look of terror that had followed it went from her eyes. They stayed keen and bright. Her pulses beat fast, and the coursing blood warmed and relaxed every inch of her body.

She did not stop to ask if it were not a monstrous joy that held her. A clear and exalted perception enabled her to dismiss the suggestion as trivial.

She knew that she would weep again when she saw the kind, tender hands folded in death; the face that had never looked save with love upon her, fixed and gray and dead. But she saw beyond that bitter moment a long procession of years to come that would belong to her absolutely. And she opened and spread her arms out to them in welcome.

There would be no one to live for during those coming years; she would live for herself. There would be no powerful will bending her in that blind persistence with which men and women believe they have a right to impose a private will upon a fellow-creature. A kind intention or a cruel intention made the act seem no less a crime as she looked upon it in that brief moment of illumination.

And yet she had loved him—sometimes. Often she had not. What did it matter! What could love, the unsolved mystery, count for in face of this possession of self-assertion which she suddenly recognized as the strongest impulse of her being!

"Free! Body and soul free!" she kept whispering.

Josephine was kneeling before the closed door with her lips to the keyhole, imploring for admission. "Louise, open the door! I beg; open the door—you will make yourself ill. What are you doing, Louise? For heaven's sake open the door."

"Go away. I am not making myself ill." No; she was drinking in a very elixir of life through that open window.

Her fancy was running riot along those days ahead of her. Spring days, and summer days, and all sorts of days that would be her own. She breathed a quick prayer that life might be long. It was only yesterday she had thought with a shudder that life might be long.

She arose at length and opened the door to her sister's importunities. There was a feverish triumph in her eyes, and she carried herself unwittingly like a goddess of Victory. She clasped her sister's waist, and together they descended the stairs. Richards stood waiting for them at the bottom.

Some one was opening the front door with a latchkey. It was Brently Mallard who entered, a little travel-stained, composedly carrying his grip-sack and umbrella. He had been far from the scene of accident, and did not even know there had been one. He stood amazed at Josephine's piercing cry; at Richards's quick motion to screen him from the view of his wife.

But Richards was too late.

When the doctors came they said she had died of heart disease—of joy that kills.

How Do You Respond?

1. Chopin gives us a sequential narrative of how a woman died, an account of cause and effect, and a short story. Translate the facts of the story into an autopsy report. What is lost in the translation?
2. Were you surprised when the woman felt freed by the news of her husband's death? What would your mother or grandmother have thought about the woman's reaction?
3. How do you feel about the view that widowhood can mean freedom? How can one partner's expectations be experienced by the other partner as limitations?

ALVIN AND HEIDI TOFFLER

> *"Western society for the past three hundred years has been caught up in a fire storm of change," says Alvin Toffler (born 1928). With his wife Heidi, co-author of the following article, he pursues a passionate interest in change—how people respond to the change that invades their lives from the arena of super-technology to the living room of the nuclear family.* Future Shock, The Futurists, *and* Learning for Tomorrow *are among his many works.*

THE CHANGING AMERICAN FAMILY

The American family is not dying. It is diversifying. This is the "secret" to understanding what is happening to ourselves, our children, and our society. Millions of people today are frightened about the future of the family. Dire predictions pour from the pulpit, the press, even from the White House. Emotional oratory about the need to "restore" the family is echoing through the nation.

Unfortunately, our attempts to strengthen family life are doomed unless we first understand what is happening. And all the evidence suggests we don't.

Despite misconceptions, the American family system is not falling apart because of immoral television programs or permissive child-rearing or because of some sinister conspiracy. If that were the problem, the solutions would be simpler.

To begin with, it is worth noticing that whatever is happening to family life is *not* just happening in the United States. Many of today's trends in divorce, remarriage, new family styles, and attitudes toward children are present in Britain, France, Sweden, Germany, Canada, even in the Soviet Union and Eastern Europe. Something is happening to families in all these countries at once.

What is happening is that the existing family system is fracturing—and taking on a new, more diversified form—because of powerful pressures arising from revolutionary changes in energy, technology, work, economics, and communications. If permissiveness and immorality play a role, they are far less important than these other, larger pressures.

The whole world is changing rapidly, and it seems reasonable that you cannot have a revolution in all these fields without expecting a revolution in family life as well.

Human history has gone through successive phases—each characterized by a certain kind of family. In greatly simplified terms we can sketch these:

The First Wave family: Ten thousand years ago, the invention of agriculture launched the First Wave of change in history. As people shifted from hunting, fishing, and foraging, the typical peasant-style family spread: a large household, with grandparents and children, uncles and aunts and sometimes nonblood relatives, as well as neighbors, boarders or others, all living together and—most important—working together as a production team in the fields.

This kind of "extended" family was found all over the world, from Japan to Eastern Europe to France to the American colonies. It is still the dominant type of family in the nonindustrial, agricultural countries today.

The Second Wave family: Three hundred years ago, the Industrial Revolution exploded in England and triggered the Second Wave of change.

The old style family which worked so well as a production team in the fields did not fit well in the new evolving world of factories and offices. The elderly couldn't keep up with the clattering machines. Children were too undisciplined to be really efficient factory hands. And the industrial economy needed workers who could move from city to city as jobs opened up or closed. That was hard to do with a big family.

Gradually, under these pressures, families became smaller, more streamlined, with the husband going out to work in a factory or office, the wife staying home, and the kids marching off to school. Old folks were farmed out to their own apartments or nursing homes. Young people moved into their own apartments as soon as they could afford it. The family adapted to the new conditions and the so-called "nuclear" family became the most popular model.

This is the type of family that most of today's evangelists, politicians, and others have in mind when they say we must "protect" the family or "restore" it. They act as though the nuclear family were the only acceptable form of family life.

Yet today, as society is struck by a new shock-wave of technological, economic, ecological, and energy changes, the family system is adapting once more, just as it did three hundred years ago.

Because the economic and other conditions that made the nuclear family popular are changing, the nuclear family itself is less and less popular. America is no longer a nation of poorly educated blue-collar workers. Most of us work in service occupations or spend our time processing information. And today only some 7 percent of Americans still live in classical nuclear families. The nuclear family is simply no longer the norm—and it is not likely to become the norm again, no matter how much pulpit-pounding or breast-beating we do about it. In its place, a new family system is emerging.

The Third Wave family: This new system is harder to describe because it is not based on a single dominant family form but on a dazzling diversity of household structures.

For example, look at what is happening to single life. Between 1970 and 1978 alone, the number of people aged 14 to 34 who live alone nearly tripled in the United States. Today fully one-fifth of all households are live-alones. Some are alone out of necessity, others prefer it. Then there are the child-free couples. As James Ramey of the Center for Policy Research has pointed out, we are seeing a massive shift from "child-centered" to "adult-centered" homes. The number of couples who deliberately decide not to have children—whether for economic, psychological, or ecological reasons—has increased dramatically.

Next come the single-parent households. Divorce rates may be leveling out in this country, depending upon how they are measured, but broken nuclear households are so widespread that today as many as one out of seven children are raised by a single parent. In big cities that may run as high as one in four.

In many countries at once, the single-parent household is becoming a key family form. Sweden gives one-parent households first crack at nursery and day-care facilities. Germany is building special blocks of apartments for them.

Then there is what we have called the "aggregate family." That's where two divorced people—each with kids—marry, and the kids from both sides come to know each other and form a kind of tribe. Often the kids get on better than the parents. It has been estimated that, before long, 25 percent of American kids may be part of such "aggregate families."

Trial marriages . . . single-sex households . . . communes . . . all can be found as people struggle to find alternatives to the nuclear model. Some of these will turn out to be workable alternatives; others will fall by the wayside.

We can also expect to see an increasing number of "electronic cottage" families—families in which one or both spouses work at home instead of commuting to the job. As the cost of gasoline skyrockets and the cost of computers and communication plummets, companies will increasingly supply their employees with simple work-at-home electronic equipment.

In such homes, we may well find husband and wife sharing the same work. Even children and old folks might pitch in, as they once did in the agricultural household. In our day, such "electronic cottage" families are as much an outgrowth of changes in energy, technology, and communications, as the nuclear family was a response to the factory system at the time of the Industrial Revolution.

In the new environment, nuclear households will no doubt continue to survive. For many people, they work. But this Second Wave family form will hardly dominate the future, as it did the recent past.

What we are seeing today, therefore, is not the death of the family, but the rapid emergence of a Third Wave family system based on many different types of family.

This historic shift to new, more varied and flexible family arrangements is rooted in and related to parallel changes now fast developing in other fields. In fact, we find the same push toward diversity at every level.

The energy system is diversifying, shifting from a near-total reliance on fossil fuels to new, alternative sources of energy. In the world of work, we see a similar trend: Older Second Wave industries engaged in mass production—turning out millions of identical items. Newer Third Wave industries, based on computers, numerical controls, and robots, custom-tailor their goods and turn them out in small runs. At the consumer level, we see an increasing variety of products.

The same shift toward diversity is even stronger in communications where the power of the great mass media is increasingly challenged by new "mini-media"—cable television, satellite-based networks, special-interest magazines. This shift toward diversity amounts to the demassificaton of the media.

In short, the whole structure of society is moving toward increased diversity. It is hardly surprising that the family system is in tune with this shift. The recent startling changes in American family structure are part of this larger move from a mass society to one that offers a far greater variety of life choice.

Any attempt to go backward to a simpler system dominated by the nuclear family—or by any one model—will fail, just as our attempts to save the economy by "reindustrializing" have failed. For in both cases we are looking backward rather than forward.

To help families adapt to the new Third Wave society, with its diversified energy, production, communications, and politics, we should encourage innovations that permit employees to adjust their work hours to personal needs. We should favor "flex-time," part-time work arrangements, job-sharing. We should eliminate housing, tax, and credit regulations that discriminate against non-nuclear families. We need more imaginative day-care facilities.

An idea put forward by one businesswoman: a bank of word-processors and a nursery located in a suburban shopping center, so that busy housewives or husbands can put in an hour or two of paid work whenever it is convenient for them, and actually have their kids right there with them.

In short, anything that makes it easier to combine working and self-help, job-work with housework, easier to enter and leave the labor force, could smooth the transition for millions of people who are now caught, as it were, between the old, Second Wave, family arrangements and the fast-emerging Third Wave family system.

Rather than wallowing in nostalgia and praising the "good old days"—which were never as good as they may seem in retrospect—we ought to be finding ways to make the new system more decent, responsible, morally satisfying, and humane. The first step is an understanding of the Third Wave.

How Do You Respond?

1. In this article, what is the Tofflers' purpose in writing? Do they present a villain? What is their method of developing their ideas?

2. The Tofflers argue both vertically—up and down history—and horizontally—across national boundaries. That is, they trace the development of the family through time and look at what is happening to it in many different places today. Do the people disturbed by modern developments take a similarly wide view? Is there a current issue that you would *not* like to see subjected to such a critical examination? Why?

3. The Tofflers' essay is taken from a newspaper magazine distributed on Sundays in mostly small cities in the U.S.A. It is, however, based on Alvin Toffler's book, *The Third Wave*. What do you think was done to adapt the information for a popular audience? Comment on the vocabulary, tone, and sentence and paragraph length.

GEORGE ORWELL

> *In this selection, one of four by Orwell offered in* Responding to Prose, *Orwell, like Thoreau, appears as a close observer of the natural environment. Characteristically, however, Orwell moves quickly to deal with politics and the human condition.*

SOME THOUGHTS ON THE COMMON TOAD

Before the swallow, before the daffodil, and not much later than the snowdrop, the common toad salutes the coming of spring after his own fashion, which is to emerge from a hole in the ground, where he has lain buried since the previous autumn, and crawl as rapidly as possible towards the nearest suitable patch of water. Something—some kind of shudder in the earth, or perhaps merely a rise of a few degrees in the temperature—has told him that it is time to wake up: though a few toads appear to sleep the clock round and miss out a year from time to time—at any rate, I have more than once dug them up, alive and apparently well, in the middle of the summer.

At this period, after his long fast, the toad has a very spiritual look, like a strict Anglo-Catholic toward the end of Lent. His movements are languid but purposeful, his body is shrunken, and by contrast his eyes look abnormally large. This allows one to notice, what one might not at another time, that a toad has about the most beautiful eye of any living creature. It is like gold, or more exactly it is like the golden-colored semi-precious stone which one sometimes sees in signet rings, and which I think is called a chrysoberyl.

For a few days after getting into the water the toad concentrates on building up his strength by eating small insects. Presently he has swollen to his normal size again, and then he goes through a phase of intense sexiness. All he knows, at least if he is a male toad, is that he wants to get his arms round something, and if you offer him a stick, or even your finger, he will cling to it with surprising strength and take a long time to discover that it is not a female toad. Frequently one comes upon shapeless masses of ten or twenty toads rolling over and over in the water, one clinging to another without distinction of sex. By degrees, however, they sort themselves out into couples, with the male duly sitting on the female's back. You can distinguish males from females, because the male is smaller, darker and sits on top, with his arms tightly clasped round the female's neck. After a day or two the spawn is laid in long strings which wind themselves in and out of the reeds and soon become invisible. A few more weeks, and the water is alive with masses of tiny tadpoles which rapidly grow larger, sprout hind legs, then forelegs, then shed their tails: and finally, about the middle of the summer, the new generation of toads, smaller than one's thumbnail but perfect in every particular, crawl out of the water to begin the game anew.

I mention the spawning of the toads because it is one of the phenomena of spring which most deeply appeal to me, and because the toad, unlike the skylark and the primrose, has never had much of a boost from the poets. But I am aware that many people do not like reptiles or amphibians, and I am not suggesting that in order to enjoy the spring you have to take an interest in toads. There are also the crocus, the missel thrush, the cuckoo, the blackthorn, etc. The point is that the pleasures of spring are available to everybody, and cost nothing. Even in the most sordid street the coming of spring will register itself by some sign or other, if it is only a brighter blue between the chimney pots or the vivid green of an elder sprouting on a blitzed site. Indeed it is remarkable how Nature goes on existing unofficially, as it were, in the very heart of London. I have seen a kestrel flying over the Deptford gasworks, and I have heard a first-rate performance by a blackbird in the Euston Road. There must be some hundreds of thousands, if not millions, of birds living inside the four-mile radius, and it is rather a pleasing thought that none of them pays a half-penny of rent.

As for spring, not even the narrow and gloomy streets round the Bank of England are quite able to exclude it. It comes seeping in everywhere, like one of those new poison gases which pass through all filters. The spring is commonly referred to as "a miracle," and during the past five or six years this worn-out figure of speech has taken on a new lease of life. After the sort of winters we have had to endure recently, the spring does seem miraculous, because it has become gradually harder and harder to believe that it is actually going to happen. Every February since 1940 I have found myself thinking that this time winter is going to be permanent. But Persephone, like the toads, always rises from the dead at about the same moment. Suddenly, toward the end of March, the miracle happens and the decaying slum in which I live is transfigured. Down in the square the sooty privets have turned bright green, the leaves are thickening on the chestnut trees, the daffodils are out, the wallflowers are budding, the policeman's tunic looks positively a pleasant shade of blue, the fish-monger greets his customers with a smile, and even the sparrows are quite a different color, having felt the balminess of the air and nerved themselves to take a bath, their first since last September.

Is it wicked to take a pleasure in spring, and other seasonal changes? To put it more precisely, is it politically reprehensible, while we are all groaning under the shackles of the capitalist system, to point out that life is frequently more worth living because of a blackbird's song, a yellow elm tree in October, or some other natural phenomenon which does not cost money and does not have what the editors of the left-wing newspapers call a class angle? There is no doubt that many people think so. I know by experience that a favorable reference to "Nature" in one of my articles is liable to bring me abusive letters, and though the keyword in these letters is usually "sentimental," two ideas seem to be mixed up in them. One is that any pleasure in the actual process of life encourages a sort of political quietism. People, so the thought runs, ought to be discontented, and it is our job to multiply our wants and not simply to increase our enjoyment of the things we have already. The other idea is that this is the age of machines and that to dislike the machine, or even to want to limit its domination, is backward-looking, reactionary, and slightly ridiculous. This is often backed up by the statement that a love of Nature is a foible of urbanized people who have no notion what Nature is really like. Those who really have to deal with the soil, so it is argued, do not love the soil, and do not take the faintest interest in birds or flowers, except from a strictly utilitarian point of view. To love the country one must live in the town, merely taking an occasional week-end ramble at the warmer times of year.

This last idea is demonstrably false. Medieval literature, for instance, including the popular ballads, is full of an almost Georgian enthusiasm for Nature, and the art of agricultural peoples such as the Chinese and Japanese centers always round trees, birds, flowers, rivers, mountains. The other idea seems to me to be wrong in a subtler way. Certainly we ought to be discontented, we ought not simply to find out ways of making the best of a bad job, and yet if we kill all pleasure in the actual process of life, what sort of future are we preparing for ourselves? If a man cannot enjoy the return of spring, why should he be happy in a labor-saving Utopia? What will he do with the leisure that the machine will give him? I have always suspected that if our economic and political problems are ever really solved, life will become simpler instead of more complex, and that the sort of pleasure one gets from finding the first primrose will loom larger than the sort of pleasure one gets from eating an ice to the tune of a Wurlitzer. I think that by retaining one's childhood love of such things as trees, fishes, butterflies, and—to return to my first instance—toads, one makes a peaceful and decent future a little more probable, and that by preaching the doctrine that nothing is to be admired except steel and concrete, one merely makes it a little surer that human beings will have no outlet for their surplus energy except in hatred and leader-worship.

At any rate, spring is here, even in London, N.1, and they can't stop you enjoying it. This is a satisfying reflection. How many a time have I stood watching the toads mating, or a pair of hares having a boxing match in the young corn, and thought of all the important persons who would stop me enjoying this if they could. But luckily they can't. So long as you are not actually ill, hungry, frightened, or immured in a prison or a holiday camp, spring is still spring. The atom bombs are piling up in the factories, the police are prowling through the cities, the lies are streaming from the loudspeakers, but the earth is still going round the sun, and neither the dictators nor the bureaucrats, deeply as they disapprove of the process, are able to prevent it.

How Do You Respond?

1. Orwell begins by observing the spring emergence of the common toad; he ends with an assertion of the joys of freedom and the cosmic image of the earth going around the sun. How does he make the leap from toad to earth and sun? How does his beginning, middle, and end work together to make a whole?

2. Do you feel that Orwell is present in his essay in a way that the Tofflers are not? Does Orwell seem to enjoy the act of writing more? Do you feel that the Tofflers are passionate about the point they wish to make? What makes you think so?

3. What unusual signs of the change to summer or winter can you think of—something truly significant but uncelebrated, like Orwell's toad?

MURIEL RUKEYSER

> Muriel Rukeyser (1913–1980) was a prolific poet who also wrote biography, books for children, and two remarkable books that cannot be categorized—The Life of Poetry and The Orgy. At one of her poetry readings in New York, the time arrived for questions. A man in the audience started by confessing nervously that his question might be foolish and pointed out that he was an engineer; at this point some of the audience snickered foolishly. He then asked, "To get the most out of one's reading, what should one bring to a poem?" Muriel Rukeyser respected the seriousness of the speaker and replied: "It's not a foolish question. It's a question everyone has to ask, all of us. And I think what must be brought to a poem is what must be brought to anything you care about, to anything in life that really matters: all of yourself."

THE PROCESS OF WRITING A POEM

The process of writing a poem represents work done on the self of the poet, in order to make form. That this form has to do with the relationships of sounds, rhythms, imaginative beliefs does not isolate the process from any other creation. A total imaginative response is involved, and the first gestures of offering—even if the offering is never completed, and indeed even if the poem falls short. If it does, it has fallen in the conception, for the conception and the execution are identified here—whatever is conceived *is* made, is written.

Essentials are here, as in mathematical or musical creation—we need no longer distinguish, for we are speaking of the process itself, except for our illustrations. Only the essential is true; Joseph Conrad, in a letter of advice, drives this home by recommending deletions, explaining that these words are "not essential and therefore not true to the fact."

The process has very much unconscious work in it. The conscious process varies: my own experience is that the work on a poem "surfaces" several times, with new submergence after each rising. The "idea" for the poem, which may come as an image thrown against memory, as a sound of words that sets off a travelling of sound and meaning, as a curve of emotion (a form) plotted by certain crises of events or image or sound, or as a title which evokes a sense of inner relations; this is the first "surfacing" of a poem. Then a period of stillness may follow. The second surfacing may find the poem filled in, its voices distinct, its identity apparent, and another deep dive to its own depth of sleep and waiting. A last surfacing may find you ready to write. You may have jotted down a course of images, or a first line, or a whole verse, by now. This last conscious period finds you with all the work on yourself done—at least this is typical of the way I write a fairly sustained poem—and ready for the last step of all, the writing of the poem. Then the experience is followed, you reach its conclusion with the last word of your poem. One role is accomplished. At this point, you change into the witness. You remember what you may, and much or little critical work—re-writing—may be done.

I know most clearly the process of writing a recent, fairly extended poem, "Orpheus." The beginnings go far back, to childhood and a wish for identity, as rebirth, as co-ordination, as form. My interests here are double: a desire for form, and perhaps a stronger desire to understand the wish for form. The figure of Orpheus stands for loss and triumph over loss, among other things: the godhead of music and poetry, yes, in a mythology I was always familiar with a distance at which it could be better dealt with than the mythology, say, of the Old Testament. In a poem written when I was nineteen, after a long hospitalization for typhoid fever contracted in an Alabama station-house during the second Scottsboro trial—a poem called "In Hades, Orpheus", I focussed on Eurydice, the ill woman who yearns backward from the burning green of the world to the paleness and rest—and death—of the hospital. Then the interest in Orpheus himself took precedence: I was at the brilliant performance of Gluck's *Orpheus* which Tchelitchew designed for the Metropolitan Opera, and was moved by that play of loss and the dragging loves and the music and thorny volcanic Hell; so moved and disturbed that, years later, I wished to go on from there, not to revisit those scenes of Hell.

On Forty-Second Street, late one night, I saw the nightwalkers go past the fifth-run movie houses, the Marine Bar, the Flea Circus, not as whole people, but as a leg, part of a shoulder, an eye askew. Pieces of people. This went into notes for a poem that never was written. They say "MARINE BAR, portraits of an eye and the mouth, blue leg and half a face." This was eight years before the poem was written. Then there was a period of writing other poems and prose, of being away from New York and returning, and then a time of great scattering, a year later, when I wrote what became the beginning of "The Antagonists":

> Pieces of animals, pieces of all my friends
> prepare assassinations while I sleep . . .

This was a poem that began with the tearing of the "I" and moved on to a reconciliation in love and intensity. Near the phrases, in my notebook, I wrote "bringing the dead back to life."

Four years later, reading Thomson and Geddes' *Life*, I became interested again in morphology and specifically in the fact that no part of the body lives or dies to itself. I read what I could about the memory and lack of memory of fragments, of amputees, and of dislocated nerve centers. And at the same time I was writing, as part of another poem,

> Orpheus in hell remembered rivers
> and a music rose
> full of all human voices;
> all words you wish are in that living sound
> and even torn to pieces
> one piece sang
> Come all ye torn and wounded here
> together
> and one sang to its brother
> remembering.

There, in Carmel, the course of the poem suddenly became clear. It did not concern Eurydice—not directly—it was of a later time. The murder of Orpheus began it; that early unsolved murder. Why did the women kill him? Reinach has written a paper about the murder. Was it because he loved Eurydice and would not approach them? Was it because he was homosexual, and they were losing their lovers to him? Was it because he had seen their orgies without taking part? All these theories had been advanced. But my poem started a moment later. I had it now! "Pieces of Orpheus," I wrote: that would be the title. The scene is the mountaintop, just after the murder. The hacked pieces lie in their blood, the women are running down the slope, there is only the mountain, the moon, the river, the cloud. He was able to make all things sing. Now they begin: "the voice of the Cloud to the killers of Orpheus," I wrote. I knew what would follow. The pieces of the body would begin to talk, each according to its own nature, but they would be lost, they would be nothing, being no longer together. Like those in love, apart, I thought. No, not like anything. Like pieces of the body, knowing there had been pain, but not able to remember what pain— knowing they had loved, but not remembering whom. They know there must be some surpassing effort, some risk. The hand moves, finds the lyre, and throws it upward with a fierce gesture. The lyre flies upward in night, whistling through the black air to become the constellation; as it goes up, hard, the four strings sing *Eurydice*. And *then* the pieces begin to remember; they begin to come together; he turns into god. He is music and poetry; he is Orpheus.

I was not able to write the poem. I went back to Chicago and to New York that winter, and, among a hundred crucial pressures, looked up some of the Orphic hymns in the New York Public Library. I wrote "The mountaintop, in silence, after the murder" and "lions and towers of the sky" and "The pieces of the body begin to remember" and "He has died the death of the god." Now there begin to be notes. This is the middle of winter, six years after the night on Forty-Second Street.

Again in California, in a year of intense physical crisis, threat, renewal, loss, and beginning. Now the notes begin to be very full. He did not look at Eurydice. He looked past her, at Hell. Now the wounds are the chorus: Touch me! Love me! Speak to me! This goes back to the yearning and self-pity of early love-poems, and a way must be found to end the self-pity.

Months later, the phrases begin to appear in fuller relationship. "The body as a circus, these freaks of Orpheus." Body Sonnets is one rejected notion. "Air-tree, nerve-tree, blood-maze"; Pindar said of him "Father of Songs."

"Sing in me, days and voices," I write; and a form takes shape. I will solve a problem that has been moving toward solution. My longer poems, like the "Elegies" and "The Soul and Body of John Brown," contained songs. This poem will move toward its song: its own song and Orpheus' song. A poem that leads to a song! The pieces that come together, become a self, and sing.

Now I was ready to write. There were pages of notes and false starts, but there was no poem. There were whole lines, bits of drawing, telephone messages in the margin. Now something was ready; the poem began, and the first section was written.

It was slower to come to the second and third sections; as they were finished, the song too was ready; but now I turned into reader. The resurrection itself needed sharpening. These symbols must not be finished; the witness himself wants to finish. But this friend is right, the women must be part of his song, the god must include his murderers if murder is part of his life. And this correspondent is right, pain is not *forgotten*. All of this re-writing is conscious throughout, as distinct from the writing of the poem, in which suggestions, relations, images, phrases, sailed in from everywhere. For days of reminder and revery, everything became Orpheus. Until it was time to go back to the title. The working title was "Pieces of Orpheus." But that was for myself. No longer the pieces, but the rebirth, stands clear. The name alone should head the poem. So: two words are crossed out: it is ready.

How Do You Respond?

1. The making of a poem—a work of art—is a complex procedure, with many stages; some are relatively active; others relatively passive. What do you think of Rukeyser's account of this often mysterious, delicate balance of acting and waiting?

2. Does Rukeyser's account of the writing of a poem make you think of similar acts, where you are both active and passive? Discuss.

3. From Rukeyser's account, do you think that writing a poem is essentially different from writing prose? Of the other selections in this chapter, which do you feel were *willed*, which imagined? Why?

FOCUS ON YOUR READING

1. Observe the way each selection begins. How does each writer introduce the subject? Jean John in "The 'How To' of Terrariums" begins with a brief history of terrariums, and then she describes the kinds of container one might use. Scissors Sam Long begins with a challenge, "Anyone who can't learn to sharpen a knife after reading my instructions is pretty dumb." Muriel Rukeyser begins with an abstraction: "The process of writing a poem represents a work done on the self of the poet, in order to make form." See how the other writers in this chapter open their essays.

2. Note how the steps of a process are presented in Craig Claibourne's recipe, Jean John's instructions, and Sam Long's procedures. Note how Dick Gregory takes us with him through the days of his fast. What words do these writers use to signal their breaking down of a continuous process into manageable steps?

3. Look at the specific directions given by Claibourne, John, and Long. Note the directions that are vague and those that are precise. Do you know, for example, *how much* salt, sauce, or pepper to put in your cheese soufflé? Is this a *serious* weakness in the recipe? How can you gauge "to taste" unless you have used this recipe before? Can you visualize Sam Long's process of sharpening a knife? What's the "back" of a knife? What does he mean by holding the "blade at a 60 degree angle"? Can you follow these instructions? Is he "pretty dumb?"

4. When we tell how something happened, as in Kate Chopin's "Story of an Hour" or in Dick Gregory's "Farewell to Food," we rely on narrative, on telling of a *once*. What distinguishes these two selections from the essays by the Tofflers and Orwell?

5. When we speak of *tone* in writing, as in speech, we mean the way the words sound in our ear. Tone is the author's voice. It may be soothing and quiet, loud and brassy, harsh and irritating. Read a bit of Sam Long's instructions on sharpening a knife. How would you classify Long's tone—how does he sound to you? Is he chatty? Relaxing? Aggressive? Genial? Familiar? Does he sound like a "professional" writer? Now read a bit from Orwell. How does he sound to you?

FOCUS ON YOUR WRITING

1. Turn one of the pieces from your journal into an essay that charts the change from one form to another. You may write of a birth or a death; you may write of discovering something within yourself or something within a friend that you never knew before.

2. Write instructions for performing an everyday task—following a particular route to work, operating a CB radio, making a peanut butter and jelly sandwich, tying a shoe. Imagine your readers looking over your shoulder and talk to them as you engage in each step of the procedure. Now write the same instructions for a child who is unfamiliar with the task you are performing.

3. Give a blow-by-blow account of an event you witnessed—an accident, a fire, a meeting between long-lost friends, a musical performance. What is your attitude toward the event? How do you capture that attitude in your tone, your point of view, your evaluative statements?

4. Gregory's perceptions about food change as he endures his fast. Write of a situation, an event in your life where, as a result of actions you took, your perceptions changed.

5. Write about your family history over the past three or four generations. Does it correspond to the patterns described by the Tofflers? If not, what are the main differences?

6. Describe an intricate, complex process that involves your inventing or creating or discovering: your writing a poem, discovering an idea, coming to know something you didn't know before.

7. Write about your own writing. In how many different ways do you write? Do ideas flow quickly? Do you need to take long walks so that ideas can ferment? Where do you do your best thinking?

KEEPING YOUR JOURNAL

Gregory gave up food to demonstrate his political ideas. Have you ever felt so strongly about an issue that you might take similar action?

How do you write? Jot down as quickly as you can in your journal the ways in which you write. Do ideas flow quickly? Do you need to take long walks so that ideas can ferment? Where do you do your best thinking?

A process involves change from one form to another. The dull knife becomes sharp; the raw eggs and milk and other ingredients are turned into a soufflé; the raw material of a writer's mind becomes a poem. In your journal, write of processes—the ordinary and the extraordinary—that come to mind. As you write, write quickly.

Chapter 5

❖ ❖

"Why Is the Sky Blue?"

CAUSE AND EFFECT

"Why do the Cheerios melt?" the five-year-old asks her mother as she watches the small doughnuts soften in her cereal bowl. And "Why is the sky blue?" "Why are the leaves green?" "Why are oranges round?" "Why can a parrot talk but a dog or fish can't?" "Why does it thunder?" "Why can't I watch television now?" Searching for causes, searching for reasons are fundamental acts of mind. We want to know *why*. We need to find causes that satisfy us.

Mythologies are stories about gods and goddesses who were imagined to be the forces behind all natural phenomena. Myths explain how and why things came into existence—people, animals, trees, flowers, the sun, moon, stars, storms, eruptions, earthquakes. The Greeks saw Zeus as the great god of the sky. He reigned over all atmospheric events as lord of winds and clouds, of rains both gentle and torrential. He lived in the upper parts of the air and on mountain tops, and, when he was angry, he bolted his thunder. Myths impose human patterns on natural events. Humanity's first attempts to understand and explain the natural world were expressed as myths.

Now our talk of thunder reflects modern scientific observations. We say thunder is sound caused by a lightning discharge. The heat of the discharge expands the air around it and forms a compression wave that we call thunder. Scientists talk of transmitting flows of current, of the durations of these channels of current, of the time lag between the distant lightning flash and the arrival of the sound of thunder.

No longer do we look to a Zeus in the sky when it thunders, yet we retain our need to know reasons—to ask *why*—and to wonder about the effects of our actions. We wonder about natural phenomena, about earthquakes and floods; and we wonder about human failings, about plane crashes and fires; we wonder about war and economic crisis; we wonder about human nature, about character and personality; we wonder about life and death. Parents look at their teenager who runs away from home and wonder why: have they erred? Were they too hard on her or too soft? Is she just like her Uncle Joe—a "bad lot" from the beginning? We speculate about heredity and environment. The child psychiatrist, Selma Fraiberg, offers this fable of modern parents who tried to mold their child:

A FABLE

There once was a boy named Frankie who was going to be the very model of a modern, scientifically reared child. His mother and his father consulted the writings of experts, subscribed to lecture series, and educated themselves in all the rites and practices of child rearing sacred to these times. They knew how children develop fears and neurotic symptoms in early childhood and with the best intentions in the world they set out to rear a child who would be free—oh, as free as any child can be in this world of ours—of anxiety and neurotic tendencies.

So Frankie was breast-fed and weaned and toilet-trained at the proper ages and in the proper manner. A baby sister was provided for him at a period in his development best calculated to avoid trauma. It goes without saying that he was prepared for the new baby by approved techniques. His sex education was candid and thorough.

The probable sources of fear were located and systematically decontaminated in the program devised by Frankie's parents. Nursery rhymes and fairy tales were edited and revised; mice and their tails were never parted and ogres dined on Cheerios instead of human flesh. Witches and evil-doers practiced harmless forms of sorcery and were easily reformed by a light sentence or a mild rebuke. No one died in the fairy-tale world and no one died in Frankie's world. When Frankie's parakeet was stricken by a fatal disease, the corpse was removed and a successor installed before Frankie awakened from his afternoon nap. With all these precautions Frankie's parents found it difficult to explain why Frankie should have any fears. But he did.

At the age of two when many children are afraid of disappearing down the bath-tub drain, Frankie (quite independently and without the influence of wayward companions) developed a fear of going down the bath-tub drain.

In spite of all the careful preparations for the new baby, he was not enthusiastic about her arrival and occupied himself with the most unfilial plots for her disposal. Among the more humane proposals he offered was that the baby should be taken back to the dime store. (And you know how thorough his sex education had been!)

And that wasn't all. At an age when other children waken from bad dreams, Frankie also wakened from bad dreams. Incomprehensibly (for you know how ogres were reformed in Frankie's nursery) Frankie was pursued in his bad dreams by a giant who would eat him up!

And that wasn't all. In spite of the merciful treatment accorded to witches in Frankie's education, Frankie disposed of evil-doers in his own way when he made up stories. He got rid of witches in his stories by having their heads chopped off.

FROM *The Magic Years*

Fraiberg goes on to talk of the complexity of character, of how we cannot know the effects of our actions. No matter what parents do, children naturally develop anxieties and fears. Parents cannot shape and mold a child as they cut a cookie.

Searching for causes and speculating about effects are complex activities. We think we nail down reasons, that we control outcomes, and yet mysteries remain. People in Lisbon in 1755 believed they lived in a secure, benign world. The earthquake that devastated their city and most of its population shook their beliefs. *Why,* they wanted to know. Why would the most civilized and cultured of cities be destroyed? We in the 1980s look at those who seem to have had everything, particularly stars like Judy Garland, Marilyn Monroe, Elvis Presley, and we wonder what went wrong with their lives.

What is it within success and fame that destroys? Similarly, scientists chart the migration of birds but cannot yet say why the Golden Plover migrates from the arctic regions of Canada to the southernmost tip of South America and back again, a round trip of 15,000 miles.

When we look for causes, we begin with the *concrete*, with the event we observe, and then we work back in time, trying to understand how that something came to be. We look at processes. We look for patterns.

$$\text{Causes} \longleftarrow \text{EVENT}$$

When we look to effects, we move forward in time, trying to anticipate how an action will affect future events.

$$\text{EVENT} \longrightarrow \text{Effects}$$

There is often a simultaneous moving back and forth: we move back to uncover causes and we move forward to speculate on effects. You may wonder how you have come to the end of the month with only $20 in your pocket and you search back to remember how you spent your money. Or you may think ahead to the effects of your spending: "If I buy this coat for $150, how will I live for the rest of the month?" You may look at a present relationship and wonder how it became a problem, or you may wonder how it will develop in the future: "If I marry Sue, what will my life be like?"

When we search for causes, we ask *why?* We look for patterns in the past; we interpret and reshape our histories. Why did Joe turn out bad? Why did the United States become involved in the Viet Nam war? Why are we suffering from high inflation? When we speculate on effects, we ask *then what?* If I take this job, then what? If the United States produces neutron bombs, then what? If the President changes his economic policies, then what? We use an *if—then* form to deal with effects.

In this chapter's selections, we see the interplay of cause and effect. An unfortunate bricklayer in "Falling Bricks" becomes entangled in a Chaplinesque state of affairs, where each move causes another disastrous effect. Selma Fraiberg in "Why Does the Baby Smile?" looks at a baby's first smile and considers "the early phases of human attachment." Tillie Olsen in her short story, "I Stand Here Ironing," takes us into the mind of a mother, who wonders how her daughter has come to be as she is. Richard Wright weaves cause and effect in "My Library Card"; he describes the processes that led him to read and tells how his learning to read opened to him new worlds of thought and action.

Wright begins with personal ponderings and moves on to larger social and political questions; he considers Abraham Lincoln's prayer in the "Gettysburg Address," that the destruction of the Civil War will benefit the entire nation. Ellen Willis and John Holt each look at schooling, with Willis talking of the effects of being a high-school misfit in "Memoirs of a Non-Prom Queen," and Holt talking of the effects of poor teaching in "How Teachers Make Children Hate Reading." Tom Wolfe offers a historical reading as he looks back to the 1940s, the age of the boom of booms, to find the roots of the sexual revolution of the 1970s in "The Sexed-Up, Doped-Up, Hedonistic Heaven of the Boom-Boom '70s."

❖❖ ───────────────────────────────

AS YOU READ

Seeing Questions

Selma Fraiberg asks right out, "Why does the baby smile?" John Holt asks, "Why should it be that children intensely dislike to read?" Once you see such a question, reading the text becomes a search for answers. Often the questions reflect the writer's knowledge that the answers cannot fully satisfy. The mother in Tillie Olsen's, "I Stand Here Ironing," in her search for answers, asks, "Why should I put that first? I do not even know if it matters, or if it explains anything."

Often the question is implicit. Tom Wolfe's title, "The Sexed-Up, Doped-Up, Hedonistic Heaven of the Boom-Boom 70s" invites us to ask, "Well, how did the 70s get that way?" Wolfe's essay responds to that implicit question, as he searches through history for answers. As you read, watch for implicit and explicit questions that shape a piece of writing.

Observing and Inferring

Selma Fraiberg answers her question, "Why does the baby smile?" by referring to careful observations she and other researchers have made. She notices that "even in the early weeks" of life, the mouth relaxes "in a little smile" during or after nursing, and she then *infers* that this is a smile of contentment and satisfaction. Throughout, she makes observations of the baby's responses to the mother, to familiar faces, eventually to the stranger who is at first welcomed and then rejected as the baby becomes more and more aware of the world about. Fraiberg records the *concrete* evidence and infers that these early smiles are "a matter of some significance in understanding the early phases of human attachment in the infant." Throughout, Fraiberg weaves together her close concrete observations and what she makes out of them. Throughout, she observes and infers. As you read, notice these patterns of setting out observations and then drawing inferences.

The Narratives Within Cause and Effect

"One day about 40 minutes before lunch, I asked my students to take pencil and paper and start writing about anything they wanted to . . . ," says John Holt in "How Teachers Make Children Hate Reading." Throughout the essay, Holt relies on a number of *once*'s. These examples, beginning with *once* or *one day*, are brief, condensed narratives that support Holt's assertions about reading. Our friend, the bricklayer, also uses narrative as he recounts what happened, the *and then, and then, and then,* of his unhappy experience with falling bricks. His narrative is a back and forth motion between cause and effect. A happened, and B resulted, and because of B, C resulted. In the narrative, the causes are obvious, for we see how one physical action resulted in another. The whole is framed in the telling of a *once*.

AS YOU WRITE

Generating Material

Ask *why* questions. In your journal, jot down as many *why* questions as come to you without deliberation, without worrying about whether or not you know answers:

Why am I going to college?

Why has the world become embroiled in a potentially deadly nuclear build-up?

Why am I an accounting major when I love literature?

Why do I love that man?

Why do my parents still seem to control me, even though I'm in Michigan and they're in Ohio, and I see them twice a year?

And then, just as quickly, write down *then what* questions:

If I take my savings and go off to Europe for the summer, then what?

If the President reduces funding for college loans, then what?

If I drop out of college, then what?

If I stop smoking, then what?

Let the questions come, and then take one question that nags at you, and write quick spontaneous responses that "answer" the question.

Reading Your Writing

Your varied responses will probably be complex and jumbled. Answering the question, "Why am I going to college?" is not a simple matter. You must take into account your own expectations of yourself, what you want to do "in life," what your parents think, what jobs are out there. You must think about your real interests and what college offers you. As you read through your list of rough responses, try to cluster them. Do they fall into categories? Can you supply concrete, tangible events from your life? You remember, "When I was a kid, I always liked to build things; I was always building bridges, using the furniture in the living room. I made scores of bridges across little streams." Pull out the narratives, the specific events that demonstrate those early interests: "I remember that when I walked to school, I would stop to study the slant of a roof or count the number of windows in a house. Once, I was so absorbed, that. . . ."

Shaping Your Writing

The search for causes takes you back in time to what you remember from the past, to what you observed and may still observe. You put pieces together by inferring. You try to make sense out of what you have experienced and what you have seen. "I am now in college," you say, and then you go back in time, keeping in mind that you're trying to make sense for yourself and for your audience—of how *you think* things have come to be. Your reader doesn't know what you mean when you say, "I'm in college because I loved to build bridges over streams when I was a kid." What was that early interest like? What pleasures did you get from building things? What did you learn? How has that interest shaped your reading, now, in art history, in architecture? Keep in mind that you are attempting to answer the question *why*, knowing full well that the answers, in many cases, will be partial ones, for one never knows, *completely*, how things have come to be. Allow yourself room for wondering, speculating, and surmising.

And as you look to effects, keep in mind the *then what* questions as you speculate on how things might turn out if you, say, drop out of college, again knowing full well that you're anticipating effects, you're guessing about the future. You might know: (a) your parents will disapprove; (b) you'll be leaving a relatively safe, secure environment; (c) you'll need to get a job—but, then what? You'll know when you get there.

JEAN L'ANSELME

> Jean L'Anselme's story of the bricklayer achieved overnight fame when it was told to an audience of students in Oxford by the great English humorist, Gerard Hoffnung. The occasion was fortunately recorded; Hoffnung died shortly after in early middle age. If you are ever fortunate enough to get your hands on the recording, you will hear him—in the words of the old cliché—bringing down the house; you will hear the audience cracking up, convulsed; and I swear you will hear the sound of falling bricks, disintegrating roofs, and collapsing bricklayers.

FALLING BRICKS

Dear Sir,

By the time I arrived at the house where you sent me to make repairs, the storm had torn a good fifty bricks from the roof. So I set up on the roof of the building a beam and a pulley and I hoisted up a couple of baskets of bricks. When I had finished repairing the building there were a lot of bricks left over since I had brought up more than I needed and also because there were some bad, reject bricks that I still had left to bring down. I hoisted the basket back up again and hitched up the line at the bottom. Then I climbed back up again and filled up the basket with the extra bricks. Then I went down to the bottom and untied the line. Unfortunately, the basket of bricks was much heavier than I was and before I knew what was happening, the basket started to plunge down, lifting me suddenly off the ground. I decided to keep my grip and hang on, realizing that to let go would end in disaster—but halfway up I ran into the basket coming down and received a severe blow on the shoulder. I then continued to the top, banging my head against the beam and getting my fingers jammed in the pulley. When the basket hit the ground it burst its bottom, allowing all the bricks to spill out. Since I was now heavier than the basket I started back down again at high speed. Halfway down, I met the basket coming up, and received several severe injuries on my shins. When I hit the ground, I landed on the bricks, getting several more painful cuts and bruises from the sharp edges.

At this moment I must have lost my presence of mind, because I let go of the line. The basket came down again, giving me another heavy blow on the head, and putting me in the hospital. I respectfully request sick leave.

How Do You Respond?

1. Diagram the escalations of this calamity, showing how the first act caused a second and the second caused the third. Is the diagram clearer than the prose? Explain. Is it as funny as the prose? Discuss.
2. What evidence is there in the text that this is a work of fiction?
3. Diagram one of your own calamities as cause and effect. Write an account of it.

SELMA FRAIBERG

> *Selma Fraiberg (born 1918) brings to her classic text,* The Magic Years, *her knowledge as a child psychoanalyst and her experiences as a parent. To Fraiberg, the child is a magician who "believes his actions and his thoughts can bring about events." Fraiberg summons parents, teachers, psychologists—adults, in general—"to drop down on all fours" and accompany children on their explorations. "It is probably many years," she says, "since you last studied the underside of a dining room chair." As Thoreau is the loving observer of the natural environment, so is Fraiberg an affectionate observer of children. Her* Magic Years, *from which the following selection is taken, is for all who want to keep in touch with the child still in them.*

WHY DOES THE BABY SMILE?

The response smile which occurs around two months is a significant milestone in the baby's development. Scientists have been much slower to grasp the significance of this event than a baby's parents. This is the occasion for great excitement. The news is transmitted to grandparents and all interested relatives. No trumpets are blown, no formal holidays proclaimed, but everyone concerned seems to understand that this smile is very special.

Now no parent cares in the least *why* the baby smiles, or why the psychologists think he smiles, and you might wish to skip the next few paragraphs except that I hope you don't. Why the baby smiles is a matter of some significance in understanding the early phases of human attachment in the infant.

First of all, let's remember that this response smile has had antecedents. Even in the early weeks we will notice that satisfaction in the course of nursing or at the end of the nursing period will cause the mouth to relax in a little smile of contentment. This early smile of satisfaction is an instinctive reaction and is not yet a response to a human face.

Now let's watch this baby as he nurses. If he is not too sleepy his eyes fix solemnly on the face of his mother. We have learned experimentally that he does not take in the whole face before him, only the upper part of the face, the eyes and forehead. Through repetition of the experience of nursing and its regular accompaniment, the human face, an association between nursing and the human face will be established. But more than this, the pleasure, the satisfactions of nursing become associated with the human face. Repetition of this pleasurable experience gradually traces an image of the face on the surface of the memory apparatus and the foundations of memory are established. When the mental image is firmly established the visual image of the human face is "recognized" (very crudely), that is, the sight of the human face evokes the mental image and it is "remembered." Now comes the turning point. This is not just a memory based on pictures, but a memory derived from image plus pleasure, the association established through nursing. The baby's response to the sight of the human face is now seen as a response of pleasure. He smiles at the sight of the human face. The little smile which had originated as an instinctive reaction to satisfaction in nursing is now produced occasionally, then more and more, at the sight of the face, as if the face evokes the memory of satisfaction and pleasure. The baby has made his first human connections.

We should not be disappointed to learn that the baby does not yet discriminate his mother's face from other human faces. "How can they prove *that*?" we'd like to know. "That smile certainly *looks* very special." We know this from two sets of observations. For many weeks after the response smile has been established, almost any human face that presents itself to the baby can elicit the smile. (Ironically, a mask representing the eyes and forehead of the human face can be presented to the baby of this age and this, too, will bring forth a pleasure response.) We may not find this so convincing a proof. How do we know this isn't just a sociable little guy who likes his mother *and* the rest of the human race? And maybe his response to the mask only proves that he has a sense of humor. Perhaps the second set of observations will be more convincing. Psychologists place the positive identification and differentiation of the mother's face around eight months because of certain responses of the infant which are familiar to all of us. He no longer smiles at any face that swims into view. On the contrary, let your jolliest uncle approach with beaming face and twenty keys on a chain to dangle before his eyes and he may be greeted by a quizzical look, an uncomprehending stare or—worse for family relations—a howl! Now let mother or father come over to offer reassurances to the baby and apologies to the uncle, and upon seeing these two faces, the baby relaxes, wriggles, and smiles. He may study these three sets of faces for a few minutes and, finally satisfied that the familiar faces are re-established, he turns to the unfamiliar face and permits his uncle to jingle keys and make comical faces for which he may later be rewarded with a smile. Or let Grandma who is a frequent, but not constant visitor, offer to take over a bottle feeding. He is hungry, shows eagerness for the bottle, but when he takes in the face that is not mother's he looks dismayed, his face puckers, and he howls in protest. "He never did *that* before!" says his grandmother. And it is true that several weeks ago when Grandma had taken over a feeding he had polished off his bottle with as much zest as when his mother fed him.

This reaction to the strange face, the not-mother face, is the first positive evidence that he differentiates his mother's face from others. (We should not fail to mention that if father has had close contact with the baby and if there are sisters and brothers, these faces will be differentiated, too. We use "mother" as a convenient reference point and with the understanding that for the period of infancy she will be the primary love object.) The reaction to being fed by Grandma shows us, too, that pleasure in eating is no longer simply a matter of biological need and satisfaction, but is bound to the person of his mother. He has finally linked this face, this person, with the satisfaction of his needs and regards her as the source of satisfaction. The pleasure and satisfaction given him through feeding and caring for him are now transferred to her image, and the sight of her face, her presence, will bring forth such crowing and joyful noises, and the disappearance of her face such disappointment, that we can say that he loves his mother as a person.

That has a curious sound! "Loves his mother as a person." Obviously, since she is a person how else could he love her? And if we say that we mean "loves her as a person outside himself," that sounds just as foolish to our adult ears. Of course, she is a person outside himself. We know that! But the baby did not. He learned this slowly, awkwardly, in the course of the first months of life. For during the early months the infant doesn't differentiate between his body and other bodies, or between mental images and perceptions, between inner and outer. Everything is undifferentiated oneness, the oneness being centered in the baby himself.

At the time that the baby discovers that his mother is a person outside himself a tremendous amount of learning has taken place. In order to achieve something that seems commonplace to us he had to engage in hundreds of experiments over a period of months. He had to assemble hundreds of pieces in a vast and intricate jigsaw puzzle in order to establish a crude picture of the person-mother and a crude image of his own body. We can reconstruct these experiments largely through observation.

How Do You Respond?

1. Into how many stages or phases does Fraiberg break the baby's development, before it reaches the point of loving its mother "as a person"? Discuss how dividing a continuous process into stages may result in distortions.

2. How would you characterize the tone of this piece? What is the relationship between the tone and the author's purpose? How does the tone affect our reading of the text?

3. Discuss Fraiberg's handling of the tension between common assumptions about her subject and what science has discovered.

TILLIE OLSEN

> *Tillie Olsen (born 1913) came out of Nebraska, the birthplace of other remarkable writers—John Neihardt, Willa Cather, and Wright Morris. Her great theme is the denial or thwarting of the individual life's promise. Yet, oddly, the effect of reading her is not one of gloom or depression but of a deep and quiet exhilaration. She celebrates not personality but character, shaped in stoicism and resilience by unkind circumstance. Her book,* Silences, *explores the lives of women writers, the long and deep silences in their lives, the gaps when writing was denied or frustrated by the sheer pressure of circumstance. Her famous collection of stories is* I Stand Here Ironing.

I STAND HERE IRONING

I stand here ironing, and what you asked me moves tormented back and forth with the iron.

"I wish you would manage the time to come in and talk with me about your daughter. I'm sure you can help me understand her. She's a youngster who needs help and whom I'm deeply interested in helping."

"Who needs help. . . ." Even if I came, what good would it do? You think because I am her mother I have a key, or that in some way you could use me as a key? She has lived for nineteen years. There is all that life that has happened outside of me, beyond me.

And when is there time to remember, to sift, to weigh, to estimate, to total? I will start and there will be an interruption and I will have to gather it all together again. Or I will become engulfed with all I did or did not do, with what should have been and what cannot be helped.

She was a beautiful baby. The first and only one of our five that was beautiful at birth. You do not guess how new and uneasy her tenancy in her now-loveliness. You did not know her all those years she was thought homely, or see her poring over her baby pictures, making me tell her over and over how beautiful she had been—and would be, I would tell her—and was now, to the seeing eye. But the seeing eyes were few or nonexistent. Including mine.

I nursed her. They feel that's important nowadays. I nursed all the children, but with her, with all the fierce rigidity of first motherhood, I did like the books said. Though her cries battered me to trembling and my breasts ached with swollenness, I waited till the clock decreed.

Why do I put that first? I do not even know if it matters, or if it explains anything.

She was a beautiful baby. She blew shining bubbles of sound. She loved motion, loved light, loved color and music and textures. She would lie on the floor in her blue overalls patting the surface so hard in ecstasy her hands and feet would blur. She was a miracle to me, but when she was eight months old I had to leave her daytimes with the woman downstairs to whom she was no miracle at all, for I worked or looked for work and for Emily's father, who "could no longer endure" (he wrote in his goodbye note) "sharing want" with us.

I was nineteen. It was the pre-relief, pre-WPA* world of the depression. I would start running as soon as I got off the streetcar, running up the stairs, the place smelling sour, and, awake or asleep to startle awake, when she saw me she would break into a clogged weeping that could not be comforted, a weeping I can yet hear.

After a while I found a job hashing at night so I could be with her days, and it was better. But it came to where I had to bring her to his family and leave her.

It took a long time to raise the money for her fare back. Then she got chicken pox and I had to wait longer. When she finally came, I hardly knew her, walking quick and nervous like her father, looking like her father, thin, and dressed in a shoddy red that yellowed her skin and glared at the pock marks. All the baby loveliness gone.

She was two. Old enough for nursery school, they said, and I did not know then what I know now—the fatigue of the long day, and the lacerations of group life in the kinds of nurseries that are only parking places for children.

Except that it would have made no difference if I had known. It was the only place there was. It was the only way we could be together, the only way I could hold a job.

And even without knowing, I knew. I knew that the teacher was

*Works Progress Administration, a government jobs program of the 1930s.

evil because all these years it has curdled into my memory, the little boy hunched in the corner, her rasp, "Why aren't you outside, because Alvin hits you? That's no reason, go out, scaredy." I knew Emily hated it even if she did not clutch and implore, "Don't go, Mommy," like the other children, mornings.

She always had a reason why we should stay home. Momma, you look sick. Momma, I feel sick. Momma, the teachers aren't there today, they're sick. Momma, we can't go, there was a fire there last night. Momma it's a holiday today, no school, they told me.

But never a direct protest, never rebellion. I think of our others in their three-, four-year-oldness—the explosions, the tempers, the denunciations, the demands—and I feel suddenly ill. I put the iron down. What in me demanded that goodness in her? And what was the cost, the cost to her of such goodness?

The old man living in the back once said in his gentle way, "You should smile at Emily more when you look at her." What *was* in my face when I looked at her? I loved her. There were all the acts of love.

It was only with the others I remembered what he said, and it was the face of joy, and not of care or tightness or worry I turned to them—too late for Emily. She does not smile easily, let alone almost always, as her brothers and sisters do. Her face is closed and sombre, but when she wants, how fluid. You must have seen it in her pantomimes, you spoke of her rare gift for comedy on the stage that rouses a laughter out of the audience so dear they applaud and applaud and do not want to let her go.

Where does it come from, that comedy? There was none of it in her when she came back to me that second time, after I had had to send her away again. She had a new daddy now to learn to love, and I think perhaps it was a better time. Except when we left her alone nights, telling ourselves she was old enough.

"Can't you go some other time, Mommy, like tomorrow?" she would ask. "Will it be just a little while you'll be gone? Do you promise?"

The time we came back, the front door open, the clock on the floor in the hall. She rigid awake. "It wasn't just a little while. I didn't cry. Three times I called you, just three times, and then I went downstairs to open the door so you could come faster. The clock talked loud, I threw it away, it scared me what it talked."

She said the clock talked loud that night I went to the hospital to have Susan. She was delirious with the fever that comes before red measles, but she was fully conscious all the week I was gone and the week after we were home when she could not come near the new baby or me.

She did not get well. She stayed skeleton thin, not wanting to eat, and night after night she had nightmares. She would call for me, and I would rouse from exhaustion to sleepily call back, "You'll all right, darling, go to sleep, it's just a dream," and if she still called, in a sterner voice, "now go to sleep, Emily, there's nothing to hurt you." Twice, only twice, when I had to get up for Susan anyhow, I went in to sit with her.

Now when it is too late (as if she would let me hold and comfort her like I do the others) I get up and go to her at her moan or restless stirring. "Are you awake, Emily? Can I get you something?" And the answer is always the same: "No, I'm all right, go back to sleep, Mother."

They persuaded me at the clinic to send her away to a convalescent home in the country where "she can have the kind of food and care you can't manage for her, and you'll be free to concentrate on the new baby." They still send children to that place. I see pictures on the society page of sleek young women planning affairs to raise money for it, or dancing at the affairs, or decorating Easter eggs or filling Christmas stockings for the children.

They never have a picture of the children, so I do not know if they still wear those gigantic red bows and the ravaged looks on the every other Sunday when parents can come to visit "unless otherwise notified"—as we were notified the first six weeks.

Oh it is a handsome place, green lawns and tall trees and fluted flower beds. High up on the balconies of each cottage the children stand, the girls in their red bows and white dresses, the boys in white suits and giant red ties. The parents stand below shrieking up to be heard and the children shriek down to be heard, and between them the invisible wall "Not To Be Contaminated by Parental Germs or Physical Affection."

There was a tiny girl who always stood hand in hand with Emily.

Her parents never came. One visit she was gone. "They moved her to Rose Cottage," Emily shouted in explanation. "They don't like you to love anybody here."

She wrote once a week, the labored writing of a seven-year-old. "I am fine. How is the baby. If I write my leter nicly I will have a star. Love." There never was a star. We wrote every other day, letters she could never hold or keep but only hear read—once. "We simply do not have room for children to keep any personal possessions," they patiently explained when we pieced one Sunday's shrieking together to plead how much it would mean to Emily to be allowed to keep her letters and cards.

Each visit she looked frailer. "She isn't eating," they told us. (They had runny eggs for breakfast or mush with lumps, Emily said later, I'd hold it in my mouth and not swallow. Nothing ever tasted good, just when they had chicken.)

It took us eight months to get her released home, and only the fact that she gained back so little of her seven lost pounds convinced the social worker.

I used to try to hold and love her after she came back, but her body would stay stiff, and after a while she'd push away. She ate little. Food sickened her, and I think much of life too. Oh, she had physical lightness and brightness, twinkling by on skates, bouncing like a ball up and down up and down over the jump rope, skimming over the hill; but these were momentary.

She fretted about her appearance, thin and dark and foreign-looking at a time when every little girl was supposed to look or thought she should look a chubby blond replica of Shirley Temple. The doorbell sometimes rang for her, but no one seemed to come and play in the house or be a best friend. Maybe because we moved so much.

There was a boy she loved painfully through two school semesters. Months later she told me how she had taken pennies from my purse to buy him candy. "Licorice was his favorite and I brought him some every day, but he still liked Jenifer better'n me. Why, Mommy?" the kind of question for which there is no answer.

School was a worry to her. She was not glib or quick, in a world where glibness and quickness were easily confused with ability to learn. To her overworked and exasperated teachers she was an overconscientious "slow learner" who kept trying to catch up and was absent entirely too often.

I let her be absent, though sometimes the illness was imaginary. How different from my now-strictness about attendance with the others. I wasn't working. We had a new baby, I was home anyhow. Sometimes, after Susan grew old enough, I would keep her home from school, too, to have them all together.

Mostly Emily had asthma, and her breathing, harsh and labored, would fill the house with a curiously tranquil sound. I would bring the two old dresser mirrors and her boxes of collections to her bed. She would select beads and single earrings, bottle tops and shells, dried flowers and pebbles, old postcards and scraps, all sorts of oddments; then she and Susan would play Kingdom, setting up landscapes and furniture, peopling them with action.

Those were the only times of peaceful companionship between her and Susan. I have edged away from it, that poisonous feeling between them, that terrible balancing of hurts and needs I had to do between the two, and did so badly, those earlier years.

Oh there are conflicts between the others too, each one human, needing, demanding, hurting, taking—but only between Emily and Susan, no, Emily toward Susan, that corroding resentment. It seems so obvious on the surface, yet it is not obvious. Susan, the second child, Susan, golden and curly-haired and chubby, quick and articulate and assured, everything in appearance and manner Emily was not; Susan, not able to resist Emily's precious things, losing or sometimes clumsily breaking them; Susan telling jokes and riddles to company for applause while Emily sat silent (to say to me later: That was *my* riddle, Mother, I told it to Susan); Susan, who for all the five years' difference in age was just a year behind Emily in developing physically.

I am glad for that slow physical development that widened the difference between her and her contemporaries, though she suffered over it. She was too vulnerable for that terrible world of youthful competition, of preening and parading, of constant measuring of yourself against every other, of envy, "If I had that copper hair," or "If I had that skin. . . ." She tormented herself enough about not looking like the others, there was enough of the unsureness, the having to be conscious of words before you speak, the constant caring—what are they thinking of me?—without having it all magnified unendurably by the merciless physical drives.

Ronnie is calling. He is wet and I change him. It is rare there is such a cry now. That time of motherhood is almost behind me when the ear is not one's own but must always be racked and listening for the child cry, the child call. We sit for a while and I hold him, looking out over the city spread in charcoal with its soft aisles of light. "Shoogily," he breathes and curls closer. I carry him back to bed, asleep. *Shoogily.* A funny word, a family word, inherited from Emily, invented by her to say: *comfort.*   In this and other ways she leaves her seal, I say aloud. And startle at my saying it. What do I mean? What did I start to gather together, to try and make coherent? I was at the terrible, growing years. War years. I do not remember them well. I was working, there were four smaller ones now, there was not time for her. She had to help be a mother, and housekeeper, and shopper. She had to set her seal. Mornings of crisis and near-hysteria trying to get lunches packed, hair combed, coats and shoes found, everyone to school or Child Care on time, the baby ready for transportation. And always the paper scribbled on by a smaller one, the book looked at by Susan then mislaid, the homework not done. Running out to that huge school where she was one, she was lost, she was a drop; suffering over the unpreparedness, stammering and unsure in her classes.

There was so little time left at night after the kids were bedded down. She would struggle over books, always eating (it was in those years she developed her enormous appetite that is legendary in our family) and I would be ironing, or preparing food for the next day, or writing V-mail to Bill, or tending the baby. Sometimes, to make me laugh, or out of her despair, she would imitate happenings or types at school.

I think I said once, "Why don't you do something like this in the school amateur show?" One morning she phoned me at work, hardly understandable through the weeping: "Mother, I did it. I won, I won; they gave me first prize; they clapped and clapped and wouldn't let me go."

Now suddenly she was Somebody, and as imprisoned in her difference as she had been in her anonymity.

She began to be asked to perform at other high schools, even in colleges, then at city and state-wide affairs. The first one we went

"Why Is the Sky Blue?" 173

to, I only recognized her that first moment when, thin, shy, she almost drowned herself into the curtains. Then: Was this Emily? The control, the command, the convulsing and deadly clowning, the spell, then the roaring, stamping audience, unwilling to let this rare and precious laughter out of their lives.

Afterwards: You ought to do something about her with a gift like that—but without money or knowing how, what does one do? We have left it all to her, and the gift has as often eddied inside, clogged and clotted, as been used and growing.

She is coming. She runs up the stairs two at a time with her light graceful step, and I know she is happy tonight. Whatever it was that occasioned your call did not happen today.

"Aren't you ever going to finish the ironing, Mother? Whistler painted his mother in a rocker. I'd have to paint mine standing over an ironing board." This is one of her communicative nights and she tells me everything and nothing as she fixes herself a plate of food out of the icebox.

She is so lovely. Why did you want me to come in at all? Why were you concerned? She will find her way.

She starts up the stairs to bed. "Don't get me up with the rest in the morning." "But I thought you were having midterms." "Oh those," she comes back in, kisses me, and says quite lightly, "in a couple of years when we'll all be atom-dead they won't matter a bit."

She has said it before. She *believes* it. But because I have been dredging the past, and all that compounds a human being is so heavy and meaningful in me, I cannot endure it tonight.

I will never total it all. I will never come in to say: she was a child seldom smiled at. Her father left me before she was a year old. I had to work her first six years when there was work, or I sent her home and to his relatives. There were years she had care she hated. She was dark and thin and foreign-looking in a world where the prestige went to blondness and curly hair and dimples; she was slow where glibness was prized. She was a child of anxious, not proud, love. We were poor and could not afford for her the soil of easy growth. I was a young mother, I was a distracted mother. There were the other children pushing up, demanding. Her younger sister seemed all that she was not. There were years she did not want me to touch her. She kept too much in herself, her life was such she had to keep too much in herself. My wisdom came too late. She has much to her and probably little will come of it. She is a child of her age, of depression, of war, of fear.

Let her be. So all that is in her will not bloom—but in how many does it? There is still enough left to live by. Only help her to know—help make it so there is cause for her to know–that she is more than this dress on the ironing board, helpless before the iron.

How Do You Respond?

1. How much of the story takes place in the mother's mind as she recalls the past and how much in the present as she is ironing? Cite some signals in the text that indicate the back-and-forth motion in time.

2. Compare the cause-and-effect in this piece with the exploration in Fraiberg's essay. What is the difference in tone, in purpose?

3. Did you have a relationship—with a brother, sister, friend, teacher—that did not work out as you would have liked? In your journal, explore the cause and effect of this relationship. Can you explain why it turned out as it did?

ABRAHAM LINCOLN

> *A collection of America's great speeches would include several by Abraham Lincoln: "The Emancipation Proclamation," the "Second Inaugural Address," and, undoubtedly, "The Gettysburg Address," delivered on that dark battlefield of the Civil War. Stories about Lincoln—his honesty, his poring over books by candlelight, his rise from near poverty to the Presidency—are American legends.*

THE GETTYSBURG ADDRESS

Four score and seven years ago our fathers brought forth on this continent, a new nation, conceived in Liberty, and dedicated to the proposition that all men are created equal.

Now we are engaged in a great civil war, testing whether that nation, or any nation so conceived and so dedicated, can long endure. We are met on a great battle-field of that war. We have come to dedicate a portion of that field, as a final resting place for those who here gave their lives that that nation might live. It is altogether fitting and proper that we should do this.

But, in a larger sense, we can not dedicate—we can not consecrate—we can not hallow—this ground. The brave men, living and dead, who struggled here, have consecrated it, far above our poor power to add or detract. The world will little note, nor long remember what we say here, but it can never forget what they did here. It is for us the living, rather, to be dedicated here to the unfinished work which they who fought here have thus far so nobly advanced. It is rather for us to be here dedicated to the great task remaining before us—that from these honored dead we take increased devotion to that cause for which they gave the last full measure of devotion—that we here highly resolve that these dead shall not have died in vain—that this nation, under God, shall have a new birth of freedom—and that government of the people, by the people, for the people, shall not perish from the earth.

How Do You Respond?

1. Why does Lincoln begin with a reference to an event that happened eighty-seven years before? How does this event affect what he says about the Civil War? About the future?

2. Does Lincoln invite his listeners to mourn the soldiers killed at Gettysburg? Discuss whether we can mourn the loss of people we haven't known.

3. How does Lincoln's rhetoric indicate that he is dealing formally with a serious matter? Write a version of the address as if Lincoln were expressing the same thoughts to a few friends who had dropped by while he was thinking about his speech.

RICHARD WRIGHT

> *One of the young Richard Wright's discoveries was that the writer is necessarily and irresistibly a reader; that it is through the continuous absorption of other's writings that one internalizes unconsciously the resources and possibilities of the written word. And that to sweat over the grammarian's text-books is precisely* not *the way in which to learn to write: the one thing necessary is immersion in the real thing—writing. The following selection is taken from* Black Boy.

MY LIBRARY CARD

One morning I arrived early at work and went into the bank lobby where the Negro porter was mopping. I stood at a counter and picked up the Memphis *Commercial Appeal* and began my free reading of the press. I came finally to the editorial page and saw an article dealing with one H. L. Mencken. I knew by hearsay that he was the editor of the *American Mercury*, but aside from that I knew nothing about him. The article was a furious denunciation of Mencken, concluding with one, hot, short sentence: Mencken is a fool.

I wondered what on earth this Mencken had done to call down upon him the scorn of the South. The only people I had ever heard denounced in the South were Negroes, and this man was not a Negro. Then what ideas did Mencken hold that made a newspaper like the *Commercial Appeal* castigate him publicly? Undoubtedly he must be advocating ideas that the South did not like. Were there, then, people other than Negroes who criticized the South? I knew that during the Civil War the South had hated northern whites, but I had not encountered such hate during my life. Knowing no more of Mencken than I did at that moment, I felt a vague sympathy for him. Had not the South, which had assigned me the role of a non-man, cast at him its hardest words?

Now, how could I find out about this Mencken? There was a huge library near the riverfront, but I knew that Negroes were not allowed to patronize its shelves any more than they were the parks and playgrounds of the city. I had gone into the library several times to get books for the white men on the job. Which of them would now help me to get books? And how could I read them without causing concern to the white men with whom I worked? I had so far been successful in hiding my thoughts and feelings from them, but I knew that I would create hostility if I went about this business of reading in a clumsy way.

I weighed the personalities of the men on the job. There was Don, a Jew; but I distrusted him. His position was not much better than mine and I knew that he was uneasy and insecure; he had always treated me in an offhand, bantering way that barely concealed his contempt. I was afraid to ask him to help me to get books; his frantic desire to demonstrate a racial solidarity with the whites against Negroes might make him betray me.

Then how about the boss? No, he was a Baptist and I had the suspicion that he would not be quite able to comprehend why a black boy would want to read Mencken. There were other white men on the job whose attitudes showed clearly that they were Kluxers or sympathizers, and they were out of the question.

There remained only one man whose attitude did not fit into an anti-Negro category, for I had heard the white men refer to him as a "Pope lover." He was an Irish Catholic and was hated by the white Southerners. I knew that he read books, because I had got him volumes from the library several times. Since he, too, was an object of hatred, I felt that he might refuse me but would hardly betray me. I hesitated, weighing and balancing the imponderable realities.

One morning I paused before the Catholic fellow's desk.

"I want to ask you a favor," I whispered to him.

"What is it?"

"I want to read. I can't get books from the library. I wonder if you'd let me use your card?"

He looked at me suspiciously.

"My card is full most of the time," he said.

"I see," I said and waited, posing my question silently.

"You're not trying to get me into trouble, are you, boy?" he asked, staring at me.

"Oh, no, sir."

"What book do you want?"

"A book by H. L. Mencken."

"Which one?"

"I don't know. Has he written more than one?"

"He has written several."

"I didn't know that."

"What makes you want to read Mencken?"

"Oh, I just saw his name in the newspaper," I said.

"It's good of you to want to read," he said. "But you ought to read the right things."

I said nothing. Would he want to supervise my reading?

"Let me think," he said. "I'll figure out something."

I turned from him and he called me back. He stared at me quizzically.

"Richard, don't mention this to the other white men," he said.

"I understand," I said. "I won't say a word."

A few days later he called me to him.

"I've got a card in my wife's name," he said. "Here's mine."

"Thank you, sir."

"Do you think you can manage it?"

"I'll manage fine," I said.

"If they suspect you, you'll get in trouble," he said.

"I'll write the same kind of notes to the library that you wrote when you sent me for books," I told him. "I'll sign your name."

He laughed.

"Go ahead. Let me see what you get," he said.

That afternoon I addressed myself to forging a note. Now, what were the names of books written by H. L. Mencken? I did not know any of them. I finally wrote what I thought would be a foolproof note: *Dear Madam: Will you please let this nigger boy*—I used the word "nigger" to make the librarian feel that I could not possibly be the author of the note—*have some books by H. L. Mencken?* I forged the white man's name.

I entered the library as I had always done when on errands for whites, but I felt that I would somehow slip up and betray myself. I doffed my hat, stood a respectful distance from the desk, looked as unbookish as possible, and waited for the white patrons to be taken care of. When the desk was clear of people, I still waited. The white librarian looked at me.

"What do you want, boy?"

As though I did not possess the power of speech, I stepped forward and simply handed her the forged note, not parting my lips.

"What books by Mencken does he want?" she asked.

"I don't know, ma'am," I said, avoiding her eyes.

"Who gave you this card?"

"Mr. Falk," I said.

"Where is he?"

"He's at work, at the M---- Optical Company," I said. "I've been in here for him before."

"I remember," the woman said. "But he never wrote notes like this."

Oh, God, she's suspicious. Perhaps she would not let me have the books? If she had turned her back at that moment, I would have ducked out the door and never gone back. Then I thought of a bold idea.

"You can call him up, ma'am," I said, my heart pounding.

"You're not using these books, are you?" she asked pointedly.

"Oh, no, ma'am. I can't read."

"I don't know what he wants by Mencken," she said under her breath.

I knew now that I had won; she was thinking of other things and the race questions had gone out of her mind. She went to the shelves. Once or twice she looked over her shoulder at me, as though she was still doubtful. Finally she came forward with two books in her hand.

"I'm sending him two books," she said. "But tell Mr. Falk to come in next time, or send me the names of the books he wants. I don't know what he wants to read."

I said nothing. She stamped the card and handed me the books. Not daring to glance at them, I went out of the library, fearing that the woman would call me back for further questioning. A block away from the library I opened one of the books and read a title: *A Book of Prefaces*. I was nearing my nineteenth birthday and I did not know how to pronounce the word "preface." I thumbed the pages and saw strange words and strange names. I shook my head, disappointed. I looked at the other book; it was called *Prejudices*. I knew what that word meant; I had heard it all my life. And right off I was on guard against Mencken's books. Why would a man want to call a book *Prejudices*? The word was so stained with all my memories of racial hate that I could not conceive of anybody using it for a title. Perhaps I had made a mistake about Mencken? A man who had prejudices must be wrong.

When I showed the books to Mr. Falk, he looked at me and frowned.

"That librarian might telephone you," I warned him.

"That's all right," he said. "But when you're through reading those books, I want you to tell me what you get out of them."

That night in my rented room, while letting the hot water run over my can of pork and beans in the sink, I opened *A Book of Prefaces* and began to read. I was jarred and shocked by the style, the clear, clean, sweeping sentences. Why did he write like that? And how did one write like that? I pictured the man as a raging demon, slashing with his pen, consumed with hate, denouncing everything American, extolling everything European or German, laughing at the weaknesses of people, mocking God, authority. What was this? I stood up, trying to realize what reality lay behind the meaning of the words . . . Yes, this man was fighting, fighting with words. He was using words as a weapon, using them as one would use a club. Could words be weapons? Well, yes, for here they were. Then, maybe, perhaps, I could use them as a weapon? No. It frightened me. I read on and what amazed me was not what he said, but how on earth anybody had the courage to say it.

Occasionally I glanced up to reassure myself that I was alone in the room. Who were these men about whom Mencken was talking so passionately? Who was Anatole France? Joseph Conrad? Sinclair Lewis, Sherwood Anderson, Dostoevski, George Moore, Gustave Flaubert, Maupassant, Tolstoy, Frank Harris, Mark Twain, Thomas Hardy, Arnold Bennett, Stephen Crane, Zola, Norris, Gorky, Bergson, Ibsen, Balzac, Bernard Shaw, Dumas, Poe, Thomas Mann, O. Henry, Dreiser, H. G. Wells, Gogol, T. S. Eliot, Gide, Baudelaire, Edgar Lee Masters, Stendhal, Turgenev, Huneker, Nietzsche, and scores of others? Were these men real? Did they exist or had they existed? And how did one pronounce their names?

I ran across many words whose meanings I did not know, and I either looked them up in a dictionary or, before I had a chance to do that, encountered the word in a context that made its meaning clear. But what strange world was this? I concluded the book with the conviction that I had somehow overlooked something terribly important in life. I had once tried to write, had once reveled in feeling, had let my crude imagination roam, but the impulse to dream had been slowly beaten out of me by experience. Now it surged up again and I hungered for books, new ways of looking and seeing. It was not a matter of believing or disbelieving what I read, but of feeling something new, of being affected by something that made the look of the world different.

As dawn broke I ate my pork and beans, feeling dopey, sleepy. I went to work, but the mood of the book would not die; it lingered, coloring everything I saw, heard, did. I now felt that I knew what the white men were feeling. Merely because I had read a book that had spoken of how they lived and thought. I identified myself with that book. I felt vaguely guilty. Would I, filled with bookish notions, act in a manner that would make the whites dislike me?

I forged more notes and my trips to the library became frequent. Reading grew into a passion. My first serious novel was Sinclair Lewis's *Main Street*. It made me see my boss, Mr. Gerald, and identify him as an American type. I would smile when I saw him lugging his golf bags into the office. I had always felt a vast distance separating me from the boss, and now I felt closer to him though still distant. I felt now that I knew him, that I could feel the very limits of his narrow life. And this had happened because I had read a novel about a mythical man called George Babbitt.

The plots and stories in the novels did not interest me so much as the point of view revealed. I gave myself over to each novel without reserve, without trying to criticize it; it was enough for me to see and feel something different. And for me, everything was something different. Reading was like a drug, a dope. The novels created moods in which I lived for days. But I could not conquer my sense of guilt, my feeling that the white men around me knew that I was changing, that I had begun to regard them differently.

Whenever I brought a book to the job, I wrapped it in newspaper—a habit that was to persist for years in other cities and under other circumstances. But some of the white men pried into my packages when I was absent and they questioned me.

"Boy, what are you reading those books for?"

"Oh, I don't know, sir."

"That's deep stuff you're reading, boy."

"I'm just killing time, sir."

"You'll addle your brains if you don't watch out."

I read Dreiser's *Jennie Gerhardt* and *Sister Carrie* and they revived in me a vivid sense of my mother's suffering; I was overwhelmed. I grew silent, wondering about the life around me. It would have been impossible for me to have told anyone what I derived from these novels, for it was nothing less than a sense of life itself. All my life had shaped me for the realism, the naturalism of the modern novel, and I could not read enough of them.

Steeped in new moods and ideas, I bought a ream of paper and tried to write; but nothing would come, or what did come was flat beyond telling. I discovered that more than desire and feeling were necessary to write and I dropped the idea. Yet I still wondered how it was possible to know people sufficiently to write about them? Could I ever learn about life and people? To me, with my vast ignorance, my Jim Crow station in life, it seemed a task impossible of achievement. I now knew what being a Negro meant. I could endure the hunger. I had learned to live with hate. But to feel that there were feelings denied me, that the very breath of life itself was beyond my reach, that more than anything else hurt, wounded me. I had a new hunger.

In buoying me up, reading also cast me down, made me see what was possible, what I had missed. My tension returned, new, terrible, bitter, surging, almost too great to be contained. I no longer *felt* that the world about me was hostile, killing; I *knew* it. A million times I asked myself what I could do to save myself, and there were no answers. I seemed forever condemned, ringed by walls.

I did not discuss my reading with Mr. Falk, who had lent me his library card; it would have meant talking about myself and that would have been too painful. I smiled each day, fighting desperately to maintain my old behavior, to keep my disposition seemingly sunny. But some of the white men discerned that I had begun to brood.

"Wake up there, boy!" Mr. Olin said one day.

"Sir!" I answered for the lack of a better word.

"You act like you've stolen something," he said.

I laughed in the way I knew he expected me to laugh, but I resolved to be more conscious of myself, to watch my every act, to guard and hide the new knowledge that was dawning within me.

If I went north, would it be possible for me to build a new life then? But how could a man build a life upon vague, unformed yearnings? I wanted to write and I did not even know the English language. I bought English grammars and found them dull. I felt that I was getting a better sense of the language from novels than from grammars. I read hard, discarding a writer as soon as I felt that I had grasped his point of view. At night the printed page stood before my eyes in sleep.

Mrs. Moss, my landlady, asked me one Sunday morning: "Son, what is this you keep on reading?"

"Oh, nothing. Just novels."

"What you get out of 'em?"

"I'm just killing time," I said.

"I hope you know your own mind," she said in a tone which implied that she doubted if I had a mind.

I knew of no Negroes who read the books I liked and I wondered if any Negroes ever thought of them. I knew that there were Negro doctors, lawyers, newspapermen, but I never saw any of them. When I read a Negro newspaper I never caught the faintest echo of my preoccupation in its pages. I felt trapped and occasionally, for a few days, I would stop reading. But a vague hunger would come over me for books, books that opened up new avenues of feeling and seeing, and again I would forge another note to the white librarian. Again I would read and wonder as only the naïve and unlettered can read and wonder, feeling that I carried a secret, criminal burden about with me each day.

That winter my mother and brother came and we set up housekeeping, buying furniture on the installment plan, being cheated and yet knowing no way to avoid it. I began to eat warm food and to my surprise found that regular meals enabled me to read faster. I may have lived through many illnesses and survived them, never suspecting that I was ill. My brother obtained a job and we began to save toward the trip north, plotting our time, setting tentative dates for departure. I told none of the white men on the job that I was planning to go north; I knew that the moment they felt I was thinking of the North they would change toward me. It would have made them feel that I did not like the life I was living, and because my life was completely conditioned by what they said or did, it would have been tantamount to challenging them.

I could calculate my chances for life in the South as a Negro fairly clearly now.

I could fight the southern whites by organizing with other Negroes, as my grandfather had done. But I knew that I could never

184 THE WRITER'S FORMS

win that way; there were many whites and there were but few blacks. They were strong and we were weak. Outright black rebellion could never win. If I fought openly I would die and I did not want to die. News of lynchings were frequent.

I could submit and live the life of a genial slave, but that was impossible. All of my life had shaped me to live by my own feelings, and thoughts. I could make up to Bess and marry her and inherit the house. But that, too, would be the life of a slave; if I did that, I would crush to death something within me, and I would hate myself as much as I knew the whites already hated those who had submitted. Neither could I ever willingly present myself to be kicked, as Shorty had done. I would rather have died than do that.

I could drain off my restlessness by fighting with Shorty and Harrison. I had seen many Negroes solve the problem of being black by transferring their hatred of themselves to others with a black skin and fighting them. I would have to be cold to do that, and I was not cold and I could never be.

I could, of course, forget what I had read, thrust the whites out of my mind, forget them; and find release from anxiety and longing in sex and alcohol. But the memory of how my father had conducted himself made that course repugnant. If I did not want others to violate my life, how could I voluntarily violate it myself?

I had no hope whatever of being a professional man. Not only had I been so conditioned that I did not desire it, but the fulfillment of such an ambition was beyond my capabilities. Well-to-do Negroes lived in a world that was almost as alien to me as the world inhabited by whites.

What, then, was there? I held my life in my mind, in my consciousness each day, feeling at times that I would stumble and drop it, spill it forever. My reading had created a vast sense of distance between me and the world in which I lived and tried to make a living, and that sense of distance was increasing each day. My days and nights were one long, quiet, continuously contained dream of terror, tension, and anxiety. I wondered how long I could bear it.

How Do You Respond?

1. Perhaps, in planning to write this selection, Richard Wright listed the positive and negative effects of his reading. Imagine that you are

Wright and make such a list of good and bad effects. How are the two sides of the list related? What pattern do you see?

2. Why was the community opposed to reading on the part of people like Wright? List the bad effects that they might have expected to result from Wright's reading.

3. This passage by Wright is part of an autobiography. What do you think was his purpose in writing his story? List several goals that you think he may have had in writing.

ELLEN WILLIS

> Music critic, film critic, commentator on the women's movement, Ellen Willis (born 1941) writes forcefully about contemporary culture—particularly about women and their changing roles. Beginning to See the Light, *a collection of essays, and her many contributions to the* New Yorker, Rolling Stone, *and the* Village Voice *mark her as one of America's leading journalists.*

MEMOIRS OF A NON-PROM QUEEN

There's a book out called *Is There Life after High School?* It's a fairly silly book, maybe because the subject matter is the kind that only hurts when you think. Its thesis—that most people never get over the social triumphs or humiliations of high school—is not novel. Still, I read it with the respectful attention a serious hypochondriac accords the lowliest "dear doctor" column. I don't know about most people, but for me, forgiving my parents for real and imagined derelictions has been easy compared to forgiving myself for being a teenage reject.

Victims of high school trauma—which seems to have afflicted a disproportionate number of writers, including Ralph Keyes, the author of this book—tend to embrace the ugly duckling myth of adolescent social relations: the "innies" (Keyes's term) are good-looking, athletic mediocrities who will never amount to much, while the "outies" are intelligent, sensitive, creative individuals who will do great things in an effort to make up for their early defeats. Keyes is partial to this myth. He has fun with celebrity anecdotes: Kurt Vonnegut receiving a body-building course as a "gag prize" at a dance; Frank Zappa yelling "fuck you" at a cheerleader; Mike Nichols, as a nightclub comedian, insulting a fan—an erstwhile overbearing classmate turned used-car salesman. In contrast, the ex-prom queens and kings he interviews slink through life, hiding their pasts lest someone call them "dumb jock" or "cheerleader type," perpetually wondering what to do for an encore.

If only it were that simple. There may really be high schools where life approximates an Archie comic, but even in the Fifties, my large (5,000 students), semisuburban (Queens, New York), heterogeneous high school was not one of them. The students' social life was fragmented along ethnic and class lines; there was no universally recognized, schoolwide social hierarchy. Being an athlete or a cheerleader or a student officer didn't mean much. Belonging to an illegal sorority or fraternity meant more, at least in some circles, but many socially active students chose not to join. The most popular kids were not necessarily the best looking or the best dressed or the most snobbish or the least studious. In retrospect, it seems to me that they were popular for much more honorable reasons. They were attuned to other people, aware of subtle social nuances. They projected an inviting sexual warmth. Far from being slavish followers of fashion, they were self-confident enough to set fashions. They suggested, initiated, led. Above all—this was their main appeal for me—they knew how to have a good time.

True, it was not particularly sophisticated enjoyment—dancing, pizza eating, hand holding in the lunchroom, the usual. I had friends—precocious intellectuals and bohemians—who were consciously alienated from what they saw as all that teenage crap. Part of me identified with them, yet I badly wanted what they rejected. Their seriousness engaged my mind, but my romantic and sexual fantasies, and my emotions generally, were obsessively fixed on the parties and dances I wasn't invited to, the boys I never dated. I suppose what says it best is that my "serious" friends hated rock & roll; I loved it.

If I can't rationalize my social ineptitude as intellectual rebellion, neither can I blame it on political consciousness. Feminism has inspired a variation of the ugly duckling myth in which high school wallflower becomes feminist heroine, suffering because she has too much integrity to suck up to boys by playing a phony feminine role. There is a tempting grain of truth in this idea. Certainly the self-absorption, anxiety, and physical and social awkwardness that made me a difficult teenager were not unrelated to my ambivalent awareness of women's oppression. I couldn't charm boys because I feared and resented them and their power over my life; I couldn't be sexy because I saw sex as a mine field of conflicting, confusing rules that gave them every advantage. I had no sense of what might make me attractive, a lack I'm sure involved unconscious resistance to the game girls were supposed to play (particularly all the rigmarole surrounding clothes, hair, and cosmetics); I was a clumsy dancer because I could never follow the boy's lead.

Yet ultimately this rationale misses the point. As I've learned from comparing notes with lots of women, the popular girls were in fact more in touch with the reality of the female condition than I was. They knew exactly what feminist organizers call denying the awful truth. I was a bit schizy. Desperate to win the game but unwilling to learn it or even face my feelings about it, I couldn't really play, except in fantasy; paradoxically, I was consumed by it much more thoroughly than the girls who played and played well. Knowing what they wanted and how to get it, they preserved their sense of self, however compromised, while I lost mine. Which is why they were not simply better game players but genuinely more likable than I.

The ugly duckling myth is sentimental. It may soothe the memory of social rejection, but it falsifies the experience, evades its cruelty and uselessness. High school permanently damaged my self-esteem. I learned what it meant to be impotent; what it meant to be invisible. None of this improved my character, spurred my ambition, or gave me a deeper understanding of life. I know people who were popular in high school who later became serious intellectuals, radicals, artists, even journalists. I regret not being one of those people. To see my failure as morally or politically superior to their success would be to indulge in a version of the Laingian fallacy—that because a destructive society drives people crazy, there is something dishonorable about managing to stay sane.

How Do You Respond?

1. Where are the causes here and where are the effects? Are they easy to sort out? Cite places in the text where Willis may be trying to show how difficult it is to analyze cause and effect.
2. How does Willis use her own experience in constructing her essay? What is the relationship between her personal experience and her purpose in writing?
3. List the generalizations that Willis disputes. Discuss how far your experience shows them to be true or false.

JOHN HOLT

> *Every society, if it is to stay healthy in mind and spirit, needs critics, skeptics, people who, like Socrates, insist on asking awkward and unsettling questions: John Holt (born 1923) is such a one. For the last twenty years, he has been looking hard at "education" or, rather, at the ways in which many of our institutions that are theoretically committed to education, are in effect defeating and denying it. He is a freespirit who challenges unthinking infatuation with compulsion and competitiveness. Have a look at his book,* How Children Fail.

HOW TEACHERS MAKE CHILDREN HATE READING

When I was teaching English at the Colorado Rocky Mountain School, I used to ask my students the kinds of questions that English teachers usually ask about reading assignments—questions designed to bring out the points that *I* had decided *they* should know. They, on their part, would try to get me to give them hints and clues as to what I wanted. It was a game of wits. I never gave my students an opportunity to say what they really thought about a book.

I gave vocabulary drills and quizzes too. I told my students that every time they came upon a word in their book they did not understand, they were to look it up in the dictionary. I even devised special kinds of vocabulary tests, allowing them to use their books to see how the words were used. But looking back, I realize that these tests, along with many of my methods, were foolish.

My sister was the first person who made me question my conventional ideas about teaching English. She had a son in the seventh grade in a fairly good public school. His teacher had asked the class to read Cooper's *The Deerslayer*. The choice was bad enough in itself; whether looking at man or nature, Cooper was superficial, inaccurate, and sentimental, and his writing is ponderous and ornate. But to make matters worse, this teacher had decided to give the book the microscope and x-ray treatment. He made the students look up and memorize not only the definitions but the derivations of every big word that came along—and there were plenty. Every chapter was followed by close questioning and testing to make sure the students "understood" everything.

Being then, as I said, conventional, I began to defend the teacher, who was a good friend of mine, against my sister's criticisms. The argument soon grew hot. What was wrong with making sure that children understood everything they read? My sister answered that until this class her boy had always loved reading, and had read a lot on his own; now he had stopped. (He was not really to start again for many years.)

Still I persisted. If children didn't look up the words they didn't know, how would they ever learn them? My sister said, "Don't be silly! When you were little you had a huge vocabulary, and were always reading very grown-up books. When did you ever look up a word in a dictionary?"

She had me. I don't know that we had a dictionary at home; if we did, I didn't use it. I don't use one today. In my life I doubt that I have looked up as many as fifty words, perhaps not even half that.

Since then I have talked about this with a number of teachers. More than once I have said, "according to tests, educated and literate people like you have a vocabulary of about twenty-five thousand words. How many of these did you learn by looking them up in a dictionary?" They usually are startled. Few claim to have looked up even as many as a thousand. How did they learn the rest?

They learned them just as they learned to talk—by meeting words over and over again, in different contexts, until they saw how they fitted.

Unfortunately, we English teachers are easily hung up on this matter of understanding. Why should children understand everything they read? Why should anyone? Does anyone? I don't, and I never did. I was always reading books that teachers would have said were "too hard" for me, books full of words I didn't know. That's how I got to be a good reader. When about ten, I read all the D'Artagnan stories and loved them. It didn't trouble me in the least that I didn't know why France was at war with England or who was quarreling with whom in the French court or why the Musketeers should always be at odds with Cardinal Richelieu's men. I didn't even know who the Cardinal was, except that he was a dangerous and powerful man that my friends had to watch out for. This was all I needed to know.

Having said this, I will now say that I think a big, unabridged dictionary is a fine thing to have in any home or classroom. No book is more fun to browse around in—*if* you're not made to. Children, depending on their age, will find many pleasant and interesting things to do with a big dictionary. They can look up funny-sounding words, which they like, or words that nobody else in the class has ever heard of, which they like, or long words, which they like, or forbidden words, which they like best of all. At a certain age, and particularly with a little encouragement from parents or teachers, they may become very interested in where words came from and when they came into the language and how their meanings have changed over the years. But exploring for the fun of it is very different from looking up words out of your reading because you're going to get into trouble with your teacher if you don't.

While teaching fifth grade two years or so after the argument with my sister, I began to think again about reading. The children in my class were supposed to fill out a card—just the title and author and a one-sentence summary—for every book they read. I was not running a competition to see which child could read the most books, a competition that almost always leads to cheating. I just wanted to know what the children were reading. After a while it became clear that many of these very bright kids, from highly literate and even literary backgrounds, read very few books and deeply disliked reading. Why should this be?

At this time I was coming to realize, as I described in my book

How Children Fail, that for most children school was a place of danger, and their main business in school was staying out of danger as much as possible. I now began to see also that books were among the most dangerous things in school.

From the very beginning of school we make books and reading a constant source of possible failure and public humiliation. When children are little we make them read aloud, before the teacher and other children, so that we can be sure they "know" all the words they are reading. This means that when they don't know a word, they are going to make a mistake, right in front of everyone. Instantly they are made to realize that they have done something wrong. Perhaps some of the other children will begin to wave their hands and say, "Ooooh! O-o-o-oh!" Perhaps they will just giggle, or nudge each other, or make a face. Perhaps the teacher will say, "Are you sure?" or ask someone else what he thinks. Or perhaps, if the teacher is kindly, she will just smile a sweet, sad smile—often one of the most painful punishments a child can suffer in school. In any case, the child who has made the mistake knows he has made it, and feels foolish, stupid, and ashamed, just as any of us would in his shoes.

Before long many children associate books and reading with mistakes, real or feared, and penalties and humiliation. This may not seem sensible, but it is natural. Mark Twain once said that a cat that sat on a hot stove lid would never sit on one again—but it would never sit on a cold one either. As true of children as of cats. If they, so to speak, sit on a hot book a few times, if books cause them humiliation and pain, they are likely to decide that the safest thing to do is to leave all books alone.

After having taught fifth-grade classes for four years I felt quite sure of this theory. In my next class were many children who had had great trouble with schoolwork, particularly reading. I decided to try at all costs to rid them of their fear and dislike of books, and to get them to read oftener and more adventurously.

One day soon after school had started, I said to them, "Now I'm going to say something about reading that you have probably never heard a teacher say before. I would like you to read a lot of books this year, but I want you to read them only for pleasure. I am not going to ask you questions to find out whether you understand the books or not. If you understand enough of a book to enjoy it and want to go on reading it, that's enough for me. Also I'm not going to ask you what words mean.

"Finally," I said, "I don't want you to feel that just because you start a book, you have to finish it. Give an author thirty or forty pages or so to get his story going. Then if you don't like the characters and don't care what happens to them, close the book, put it away, and get another. I don't care whether the books are easy or hard, short or long, as long as you enjoy them. Furthermore I'm putting all this in a letter to your parents, so they won't feel they have to quiz and heckle you about books at home."

The children sat stunned and silent. Was this a teacher talking? One girl, who had just come to us from a school where she had had a very hard time, and who proved to be one of the most interesting, lively, and intelligent children I have ever known, looked at me steadily for a long time after I had finished. Then, still looking at me, she said slowly and solemnly, "Mr. Holt, do you really mean that?" I said just as solemnly, "I mean every word of it."

Apparently she decided to believe me. The first book she read was Dr. Seuss's *How the Grinch Stole Christmas,* not a hard book even for most third graders. For a while she read a number of books on this level. Perhaps she was clearing up some confusion about reading that her teachers, in their hurry to get her up to "grade level," had never given her enough time to clear up. After she had been in the class six weeks or so and we had become good friends, I very tentatively suggested that, since she was a skillful rider and loved horses, she might like to read *National Velvet*. I made my sell as soft as possible, saying only that it was about a girl who loved and rode horses, and that if she didn't like it, she could put it back. She tried it, and though she must have found it quite a bit harder than what she had been reading, finished it and liked it very much.

During the spring she really astonished me, however. One day, in one of our many free periods, she was reading at her desk. From a glimpse of the illustrations I thought I knew what the book was. I said to myself, "It can't be," and went to take a closer look. Sure enough, she was reading *Moby Dick* in the edition with woodcuts by Rockwell Kent. When I came close to her desk she looked up. I said, "Are you really reading that?" She said she was. I said, "Do you like it?" She said, "Oh, yes, it's neat!" I said, "Don't you find parts of it rather heavy going?" She answered "Oh, sure, but I just skip over those parts and go on to the the next good part."

This is exactly what reading should be and in school so seldom is—an exciting, joyous adventure. Find something, dive into it, take the good parts, skip the bad parts, get what you can out of it, go on to something else. How different is our mean-spirited, picky insistence that every child get every last little scrap of "understanding" that can be dug out of a book.

For teachers who really enjoy doing it, and will do it with gusto, reading aloud is a very good idea. I have found that not just fifth graders but even ninth and eleventh graders enjoy it. Jack London's "To Build a Fire" is a good read-aloud story. So are ghost stories; and "August Heat," by W. F. Harvey, and "The Monkey's Paw," by W. W. Jacobs, are among the best. Shirley Jackson's "The Lottery" is sure-fire, and will raise all kinds of questions for discussion and argument. Because of a television program they had seen and that excited them, I once started reading to my fifth graders William Golding's *Lord of the Flies*, thinking to read only a few chapters, but they made me read it to the end.

In my early fifth-grade classes the children usually were of high IQ, came from literate backgrounds, and were generally felt to be succeeding in school. Yet it was astonishingly hard for most of those children to express themselves in speech or in writing. I have known a number of five-year olds who were considerably more articulate than most of the fifth graders I have known in school. Asked to speak, my fifth graders were covered with embarrassment; many refused altogether. Asked to write, they would sit for minutes on end, staring at the paper. It was hard for most of them to get down a half page of writing, even on what seemed to be interesting topics or topics they chose themselves.

In desperation I hit on a device that I named the Composition Derby. I divided the class into teams, and told them that when I said, "Go," they were to start writing something. It could be about anything they wanted, but it had to be about something—they couldn't just write "dog dog dog dog" on the paper. It could be true stories, descriptions of people or places or events, wishes, made-up stories, dreams—anything they liked. Spelling didn't count, so they didn't have to worry about it. When I said, "Stop," they were to stop and count up the words they had written. The team that wrote the most words would win the derby.

It was a success in many ways and for many reasons. The first surprise was that the two children who consistently wrote the most words were two of the least successful students in the class. They were bright, but they had always had a very hard time in school. Both were very bad spellers, and worrying about this had slowed down their writing without improving their spelling. When they were free of this worry and could let themselves go, they found hidden and unsuspected talents.

One of the two, a very driven and anxious little boy, used to write long adventures, or misadventures, in which I was the central character—"The Day Mr. Holt Went to Jail," "The Day Mr. Holt Fell Into the Hole," "The Day Mr. Holt Got Run Over," and so on. These were very funny, and the class enjoyed hearing me read them aloud. One day I asked the class to write a derby on a topic I would give them. They groaned; they liked picking their own. "Wait till you hear it," I said. "It's 'The Day the School Burned Down.'"

With a shout of approval and joy they went to work, and wrote furiously for 20 minutes or more, laughing and chuckling as they wrote. The papers were all much alike; in them the children danced around the burning building, throwing in books and driving me and the other teachers back in when we tried to escape.

In our first derby the class wrote an average of about 10 words a minute; after a few months their average was over 20. Some of the slower writers tripled their output. Even the slowest, one of whom was the best student in the class, were writing 15 words a minute. More important, almost all the children enjoyed the derbies and wrote interesting things.

Some time later I learned that Professor S. I. Hayakawa, teaching freshman English, had invented a better technique. Every day in class he asked his students to write without stopping for about half an hour. They could write on whatever topic or topics they chose, but the important thing was not to stop. If they ran dry, they were to copy their last sentence over and over again until new ideas came. Usually they came before the sentence had been copied once. I use this idea in my own classes, and call this kind of paper a Non-Stop. Sometimes I ask students to write a Non-Stop on an assigned topic, more often on anything they choose. Once in a while I ask them to count up how many words they have written, though I rarely ask them to tell me; it is for their own information. Sometimes these papers are to be handed in; often they are what I call private papers, for the students' eyes alone.

The private paper has proved very useful. In the first place, in any English class—certainly any large English class—if the amount the students write is limited by what the teacher can find time to correct, or even to read, the students will not write nearly enough. The only remedy is to have them write a great deal that the teacher does not read. In the second place, students writing for themselves will write about many things that they would never write on a paper to be handed in, once they have learned (sometimes it takes a while) that the teacher means what he says about the papers' being private. This is important, not just because it enables them to get things off their chest, but also because they are most likely to write well, and to pay attention to how they write, when they are writing about something important to them.

Some English teachers, when they first hear about private papers, object that students do not benefit from writing papers unless the papers are corrected. I disagree for several reasons. First, most students, particularly poor students, do not read the corrections on their papers; it is boring, even painful. Second, even when they do read these corrections, they do not get much help from them, do not build the teacher's suggestions into their writing. This is true even when they really believe the teacher knows what he is talking about.

Third, and most important, we learn to write by writing, not by reading other people's ideas about writing. What most students need above all else is practice in writing, and particularly in writing about things that matter to them, so that they will begin to feel the satisfaction that comes from getting important thoughts down in words and will care about stating these thoughts forcefully and clearly.

Teachers of English—or, as some schools say (ugh!), Language Arts—spend a lot of time and effort on spelling. Most of it is wasted; it does little good, and often more harm than good. We should ask ourselves, "How do good spellers spell? What do they do when they are not sure which spelling of a word is right?" I have asked this of a number of good spellers. Their answer never varies. They do not rush for a dictionary or rack their brains trying to remember some rules. They write down the word both ways, or several ways, look at them and pick the one that looks best. Usually they are right.

Good spellers know what words look like and even, in their writing muscles, feel like. They have a good set of word images in their minds, and are willing to trust these images. The things we do to "teach" spelling to children do little to develop these skills or talents, and much to destroy them or prevent them from developing.

The first and worst thing we do is to make children anxious about spelling. We treat a misspelled word like a crime and penalize the misspeller severely; many teachers talk of making children develop a "spelling conscience," and fail otherwise excellent papers because of a few spelling mistakes. This is self-defeating. When we are anxious, we don't perceive clearly or remember what we once perceived. Everyone knows how hard it is to recall even simple things when under emotional pressure; the harder we rack our brains, the less easy it is to find what we are looking for. If we are anxious enough, we will not trust the messages that memory sends us. Many children spell badly because although their first hunches about how to spell a word may be correct, they are afraid to trust them. I have often seen on children's papers a word correctly spelled, then crossed out and misspelled.

There are some tricks that might help children get sharper word images. Some teachers may be using them. One is the trick of air writing; that is, of "writing" a word in the air with a finger and "seeing" the image so formed. I did this quite a bit with fifth graders, using either the air or the top of a desk, on which their fingers left no mark. Many of them were tremendously excited by this. I can still hear them saying, "There's nothing there, but I can see it." It seemed like black magic. I remember that when I was little I loved to write in the air. It was effortless, voluptuous, satisfying, and it was fun to see the word appear in the air. I used to write "Money Money Money," not so much because I didn't have any as because I liked the way it felt, particularly that y at the end, with its swooping tail.

Another thing to help sharpen children's image-making machinery is taking very quick looks at words—or other things. The conventional machine for doing this is the tachistoscope. But these are expensive, so expensive that most children can have few chances to use them, if any at all. With some three-by-five and four-by-eight file cards you can get the same effect. On the little cards you put the words or the pictures that the child is going to look at. You hold the larger card over the card to be read, uncover it for a split second with a quick wrist motion, then cover it up again. Thus you have a tachistoscope that costs one cent and that any child can work by himself.

Once when substituting in a first-grade class, I thought that the children, who were just beginning to read and write, might enjoy some of the kind of free, non-stop writing that my fifth graders had. One day about 40 minutes before lunch, I asked them all to take pencil and paper and start writing about anything they wanted to. They seemed to like the idea, but right away one child said anxiously, "Suppose we can't spell a word."

"Don't worry about it." I said. "Just spell it the best way you can."

A heavy silence settled on the room. All I could see were still pencils and anxious faces. This was clearly not the right approach. So I said, "All right, I'll tell you what we'll do. Any time you want to know how to spell a word, tell me and I'll write it on the board."

They breathed a sigh of relief and went to work. Soon requests for words were coming fast; as soon as I wrote one, someone asked me another. By lunchtime, when most of the children were still busily writing, the board was full. What was interesting was that most of the words they had asked for were much longer and more complicated than anything in their reading books or workbooks. Freed from worry about spelling, they were willing to use the most difficult and interesting words that they knew.

The words were still on the board when we began school next day. Before I began to erase them, I said to the children, "Listen everyone, I have to erase these words, but before I do, just out of curiosity, I'd like to see if you remember some of them."

The result was surprising. I had expected that the child who had asked for and used a word might remember it, but I did not think many others would. But many of the children still knew many of the words. How had they learned them? I suppose each time I wrote a word on the board a number of children had looked up, relaxed yet curious, just to see what the word looked like, and these images and the sound of my voice saying the word had stuck in their minds until the next day. This, it seems to me, is how children may best learn to write and spell.

What can a parent do if a school, or a teacher, is spoiling the language for a child by teaching it in some tired way? First, try to get them to change, or at least let them know that you are eager for change. Talk to other parents; push some of these ideas in the PTA; talk to the English department at the school; talk to the child's own teacher. Many teachers and schools want to know what the parents want.

If the school or teacher cannot be persuaded, then what? Perhaps all you can do is try not to let your child become too bored or discouraged or worried by what is happening in school. Help him meet the school's demands, foolish though they may seem, and try to provide more interesting alternatives at home—plenty of books and conversation, and a serious and respectful audience when a child wants to talk. Nothing that ever happened to me in English classes at school was as helpful to me as the long conversations I used to have every summer with my uncle, who made me feel that the difference in our ages was not important and that he was really interested in what I had to say.

At the end of her freshman year in college a girl I know wrote home to her mother, "Hooray! Hooray! Just think—I never have to take English any more!" But this girl had always been an excellent English student, had always loved books, writing, ideas. It seems unnecessary and foolish and wrong that English teachers should so often take what should be the most flexible, exciting, and creative of all school courses and make it into something that most children can hardly wait to see the last of. Let's hope that we can and soon will begin to do much better.

How Do You Respond?

1. John Holt says that he used to see things one way and now he sees them differently. How would you say he sees his former behavior?

2. Are you convinced by Holt's arguments in favor of his new way of reading? Support it or dispute it from your own experience.

3. Select the main points of Holt's argument. Note how they apply to your own encounters with reading and writing.

TOM WOLFE

> *Tom Wolfe (born 1931) has been credited with the invention of "the new journalism." But he demurs, saying that it was all the result of an accident. One day he was late in delivering an assignment to a magazine: "Just type up your notes and we'll get them rewritten," he was told. So he ran to his typewriter and bashed away. In the next two hours, he saw a new kind of prose emerging on his paper: it was serendipitous, vivid, chancy, unpredictable, chatty, sometimes vulgar, even shocking, a kind of frenetic verbal bombardment, a linguistic carnival. What he brought to the typewriter was, of course, a witty, well-stocked, sharp, humorous mind. Try his* Electric Kool-Aid Acid Test *and* The Pump-House Gang.

THE SEXED-UP, DOPED-UP, HEDONISTIC HEAVEN OF THE BOOM-BOOM '70s

For me the 1970s began the moment I saw Harris, on a little surprise visit to the campus, push open the door of his daughter Laura's dormitory room. Two pairs of eyes popped up in one of the beds, blazing like raccoons' at night by the garbage cans . . . illuminating the shanks, flanks, glistening haunches and cloven declivities of a boy and girl joined mons-to-mons. Harris backed off, one little step after another. He looked as if he were staring down the throat of a snake. He pulled the door shut, ever so gingerly.

The girl in the bed was not his daughter, but that didn't calm him in the slightest. For an hour we lurched around the campus, looking for little Laura. Finally we went back to her room, on the chance she might have returned. This time Harris knocked on the door, and a girl's voice said, "Come in." Quite a cheery voice it was, too.

"Laura?"

But it wasn't Laura. Inside, in the bed, was the same couple—except that they were no longer in medias res. They were sitting up with the covers pulled up to about collarbone level, looking perfectly relaxed. *At home,* as it were.

"Hi," says the girl. "Can we help you?"

Their aplomb is more than Harris can deal with. He takes on the look of a man who, unaccountably, feels that *he* has committed the gaffe. He begins to croak. He sounds ashamed.

"I'm Laura's . . . I'm looking for my . . . I want . . ."

"Laura's at the library," says the boy. He's just as relaxed and cheery as the girl.

Harris backs out and closes the door once more . . . very diffidently. . . . At the library we find his missing daughter. She has long, brown Pre-Raphaelite hair, parted in the middle, a big floppy crew-neck sweater, jeans and clogs. She's 18 years old and looks about 12 and is not the least bit embarrassed by what her father tells her.

"Daddy, really. Don't pay any attention to that." she says. "I mean, my *God*, everybody used to have to use the *kitchen!* There was a mattress on the floor in there, and you used to have to jump over the mattress to get to the refrigerator-sort-of-thing. So we made a schedule, and everybody's room is a Free Room a couple of days a month, and if your room's a Free Room, you just go to the library-sort-of-thing. I mean, the kitchen was . . . *so* . . . *gross!*"

All Harris does is nod slowly, as if some complex but irresistible logic is locking into place. In the time it takes us to drive back to New York, Harris works it out in his mind. . . . The kitchen was *so gross*-sort-of-thing. . . . That's all. . . . By nightfall he has dropped the entire incident like a rock into a lake of amnesia.

By the next morning he has accepted the new order as *the given,* and in that moment he becomes a true creature of the 1970s.

How quickly we swallowed it all over the past 10 years! I keep hearing the 1970s described as a lull, a rest period, following the uproars of the 1960s. I couldn't disagree more. With the single exception of the student New Left movement—which to me evaporated mysteriously in 1970—the uproars did not subside in the least. On the contrary, their level remained so constant, they became part of the background noise, like a new link of I-95 opening up.

The idea of a coed dorm, with downy little Ivy Leaguers copulating in Free Rooms like fox terriers, was a lurid novelty even as late as 1968. Yet in the early 1970s the coed dorm became *the standard.* Fathers, daughters, faculty—no one so much as blinked any longer. It was in the 1970s, not the 1960s, that the ancient wall around sexual promiscuity fell. And it fell like the wall of Jericho; it didn't require a shove. By the mid-1970s, any time I reached a city of 100,000 to 200,000 souls, the movie fare available on a typical evening seemed to be: two theaters showing *Jaws,* one showing *Benji* and 11 showing pornography of the old lodge smoker sort, now dressed up in color and 35 mm stock. Two of the 11 would be drive-in theaters, the better to beam the various stiffened giblets and moist folds and nodules out into the night air to become part of the American Scene. Even in the rural South the *typical* landscape of the 1970s included—shank to flank with the Baptist and United Brethren churches and the hot-wax car wash and the Arby's—the roadside whorehouse, a windowless shack painted black or maroon with a shopping mall-style back-lit plastic marquee saying: MASSAGE PARLOR—TOTALLY NUDE GIRLS—SAUNA ENCOUNTER SESSIONS.

The wall around promiscuity was always intended to protect the institution of the family. In the 1970s one had a marvelous, even bizarre opportunity to see what happens to that institution when it is left unprotected. The 1970s will be remembered as the decade of the great Divorce Epidemic; or, to put it another way, the era of the New Cookie. The New Cookie is the girl in her 20s for whom the American male now *customarily* chucked his wife of two to four decades when the electrolysis gullies appeared above her upper lip. In 1976 Representative Wayne Hays of Ohio, one of the most powerful figures in the House of Representatives, was ruined when it was discovered that he had put his New Cookie, a girl named Elizabeth Ray, on his office payroll. It was this bureaucratic lapse that was his undoing, however, not the existence of the New Cookie. Six months before, when he had divorced his wife of 38 years, it hadn't caused a ripple.

Ways of life that as late as 1969 had seemed intolerable scarcely drew a second glance in 1979. In 1969 I was invited to address a group of Texas corporation heads on the subject of "the drug culture." The meeting was held on the back lawn of the home of one of the group in a pavilion with a hardwood floor below and striped tenting above, the sort of rigging that is set up for deb season dances in the fall. Why these 80 or 90 businessmen had set up this edifice to hear a talk about the dopers I couldn't make out . . . until one of them spoke up in the middle of my talk and said: "Listen, half the people here already know it, and so I'm gonna tell you, too: my son was arrested two nights ago for possession of marijuana, and that's the third goddamned time in ten goddamned months for that little peckerwood! Now . . . what are we gonna *do* about it?"

This was greeted with shouts of "Yeah!" . . . "Mine, too!" . . . "My daughter—four times, goddamn it!" . . . "You tell 'em, Bubba!" . . . "Form a mullyfoggin' committee!"

Somehow I knew at that moment it was only a matter of time before marijuana was legalized in the United States, and it had nothing to do with medical facts, juridical reasoning, or the Epicurean philosophies of the weed's proponents. It had to do solely with the fact that people of wealth and influence were getting tired of having to extract their children from the legal machinery. That was getting worse than dope itself. By 1979 it had come to pass. My book *The Electric Kool-Aid Acid Test* had been about a man, the novelist Ken Kesey, who had been arrested twice in California for possession of a few ounces of marijuana. Facing a probable five-year jail sentence, he had fled to the jungles of Mexico to live among the dapple-wing Anopheles, the verruga-crazed Phlebotomus, and Pacific Coast female ticks. That was in 1966. Today, on sunny days in Manhattan, one can see young office workers sitting on the Contempo Slate terraces out front of the glass buildings along Park Avenue and the Avenue of the Americas wearing Ralph Lauren Saville Pseud suits and Calvin Klein clings, taking coffee breaks and toking their heads off, passing happy sopping joints from fingertip to fingertip and goofing in the open air. In New York, as in California and most other states, possession of a small amount of marijuana has been reduced to a misdemeanor and, in effect, taken off the books, since the police, with the tacit consent of the citizenry, usually ignore it.

As the moral ground shifted, like the very templates of the earth, matters of simple decorum were not spared, either. To me the most fascinating side of Watergate was the ease and obvious relish with which men and women on both sides of the Senate hearing room table and the bar of justice, the sheriffs as well as the bandits, the winners as well as the losers, capitalized on the event in the form of book deals and television commercials. The Watergate book was one of the decade's new glamour industries, like the desk calculator business or the digital watch game. Nixon, Haldeman, Ehrlichman, Magruder, McCord, Hunt, and the Deans (John and Mo) published their side of it. And the winners? His Honor Judge Sirica, His Probity Leon Jaworski, His Jurisprudence Samuel Dash . . . As they piously cranked out their best-sellers, it became obvious that to fix blame, obtain convictions, and ruin great reputations in a case like Watergate was worth . . . *millions of dollars.* None of them, I assume, entered or carried out the good fight with any such thought in mind. Nevertheless, the lesson was there when it was all over, and the rush to line up the book contracts began. How very *seventies* it was that the books came out, all the same, and hardly anyone, in or out of government, so much as arched an eyebrow!

The great Senate hero of Watergate, Senator Sam Ervin of North Carolina, retired and made commercials for American Express. *Ave atque vale,* Defender of the Constituton! Selling off chunks of one's righteous stuff via television commercials became not merely acceptable but *conventional* behavior for famous people in the 1970s. In 1969 the first man to set foot on the moon, Neil Armstrong, delivered, via television, a cosmic symploce measuring the stride of mankind itself in the new age of exploration. In 1979 Armstrong was on television in a Sales Rep sack suit delivering Cordobas, Newports, and LeBarons for the Chrysler Corporation. *Non sibi sed patriae,* Apollo!

The hedonism of the 1970s derives, in my opinion, from a development so stupendous, so long in the making, and so obvious that, like the Big Dipper or the curvature of the Earth, it is barely noticed any longer. Namely, the boom of the booms. Wartime spending in the United States in the early 1940s brought the Depression to an end and touched off a boom that has continued for nearly 40 years. The wave of prosperity had its dips, but they were mere wrinkles in a soaring curve. The boom pumped money into *every* class level of the population on a scale such as history has never known. Truck dispatchers, duplicator machine repairmen, bobbin cleaners, policemen, firemen, and garbage men were making so much money— $15,000 to $20,000 (and more) per year—and taking so many vacations on tropical littorals and outfitting their $12,000 RVs with so many micro-wave ovens and micro-sauna booths, it was impossible to use the word "proletarian" any longer with a straight face.

By the late 1970s these *new masses* began appearing also in France, West Germany, Switzerland, England, Norway, Sweden, Japan and, to a lesser extent, Italy—which is to say, throughout the *capitalist* world. By 1977 per capita incomes in these countries were catching up with those of the United States and outstripping the rate of inflation in most cases. In England the average family's "disposable" or "discretionary" income—the surplus wealth that new ways of living are made of—had risen 26.5 percent in 10 years, and the increase was greatest among working-class people. It had become common for skilled workers to make as much as $20,000 a year, bringing them up even, in income, with middle-level executives and top corporate salesmen. In early 1979 the average hourly wage for workers in manufacturing plants was $6.49 in the United States, the same in West Germany, $7.29 in Norway and $8.46 in Switzerland. Despite inflation, the European workers' second homes, sports cars, vacations in Venice, and calfskin trench coats were real.

The old utopian socialists of the 19th century—the Saint-Simons, the Owens, the Fouriers—*lived* for the day when industrial workers would command the likes of $6.49 or more per hour. They foresaw a day when industrialization (Saint-Simon coined the word) would give the common man the things he needed in order to realize his potential as an intelligent being: surplus (discretionary) income, political freedom, free time (leisure), and freedom from grinding drudgery. They never dreamed that their blissful Utopia would be achieved not under socialism but as the result of a hard-charging, go-getter business boom. To heighten the irony, it was in the 1970s that socialism was dealt a blow from which it is never likely to recover. Starting with the publication of Solzhenitsyn's *Gulag Archipelago* in 1973, the repressive nature of socialism as a monolithic system of government became too obvious to ignore any longer. By the 1970s there was no possible ideological detour around concentration camps, and under the pure socialism the concentration camps were found again and again—in the Soviet Union, in Cambodia, in Cuba, in the new United Vietnam. By 1979 Marxism was finished as a spiritual force, although the ideologues lingered on. In objective terms, then, the time was ripe for a development that would have confounded all the twilight theories of the past 100 years: namely the Rise of the West.

In subjective terms, however, the story was different. There was no moral force, no iron in the soul, not even a reigning philosophy, to give spiritual strength to the good times being had by all.

Solzhenitsyn, for his part, was not enchanted with American life, once he settled into his rural redoubt in Vermont. In his famous Harvard commencement speech of June 1978, he characterized the American way as soft, materialistic, morally impoverished. "The human soul," he said, "longs for things higher, warmer, and purer than those offered by today's mass living habits, introduced by the revolting invasion of publicity, by TV stupor, and by intolerable music. . . . Two hundred or even fifty years ago, it would have seemed quite impossible, in America, that an individual could be granted boundless freedom simply for the satisfaction of his instincts or whims." What Solzhenitsyn was looking at, utterly stupefied, was the first era of: *every man an aristocrat.*

In 1976 I wrote an essay entitled "The Me Decade and the Third Great Awakening." I soon found the phrase "the Me Decade" being used in many publications as a way of characterizing this as an age of narcissism, greed, or simple rut-boar wallowing. In the essay I was referring to something that I still find considerably more subtle:

America's extraordinary boom began in the early 1940s, but it was not until the 1960s that the *new masses* began to regard it as a permanent condition. Only then did they spin out the credit line and start splurging and experimenting with ways of life heretofore confined to the upper orders. In the 1970s they moved from the plateau of the merely materialistic to a truly aristocratic luxury: the habit of putting oneself on stage, analyzing one's conduct, one's *relationships,* one's hang-ups, one's personality, precisely the way noblemen did it during the age of chivalry. This secret vice was one of the dividends of the feminist movement of the 1970s. An ordinary status—woman, housewife—was elevated to the level of drama. One's existence as a *woman* . . . as *Me* . . . became something all the world analyzed, agonized over, drew cosmic conclusions from, or, in any event, took seriously. Books were written about *being a woman,* meetings were held, consciousnesses were raised (as the phrase went), television specials were produced, and magazines were founded upon that single notion. Every woman became a heroine of the great epic of the sexes. Out of such intense concentration upon the self, however, came a feeling that was decidedly religious, binding one beaming righteous soul to the other in the name of the cause.

And there you had the paradox of the 1970s: it was both the most narcissistic of decades and the least. In fact, such has been the paradox of hedonism itself for some 2,300 years. In the third century B.C. Epicurus, now remembered as the greatest of the hedonistic philosophers, lived a life that today would earn him the designation of "cult leader." At his home in Athens he established what would now be called a commune. The commingling of men and women within the Garden of Epicurus, as it was called, was viewed by many as depraved. Epicurus and his disciples developed the proposition that all truth is derived from the senses and the highest truth is derived from pleasure. Or as Hemingway would put it in our time: "Morality is what you feel good after." Yet the pursuit of pleasure, like most monomanias, carries the seeds of spirituality. Epicureanism became one of the most powerful pre-Christian religions, and in no time the Epicurean emphasis on pleasure became spiritual and, in fact, quite juiceless. Likewise, in the 1970s spirituality gushed forth in the most unexpected places, even among *swingers,* as the decade's most dedicated sexual-obsessives became known.

At a sex farm in the Santa Monica mountains of Los Angeles, people of all class levels gathered for weekends in the nude. They copulated in the living room, by the chess table, out by the pool, on the tennis courts, in the driveway, with the same open, free, liberated spirit as dogs in the park or baboons in a tree. In conversation, however, the atmosphere was quite different. The air became humid with solemnity. If you closed your eyes, you thought you were at a 19th century Wesleyan church encampment at Oak Bluffs. It's the soul that gets a workout here, brethren. . . . At the apex of my soul is a spark of the Divine . . . and I perceive it in the pure moment of ecstasy . . . which your textbooks call "the orgasm," but which I know to be Heaven. . . .

And in this strange progress from sexology to theology was added another rogue surge to what I think of as the Third Great Awakening, namely the third great religious wave in American history and the most extraordinary development of the 1970s. Such was the hunger for some form of spiritual strength that any obsession was sufficient to found a faith upon: jogging, flying, UFOs, ESP, health foods, or drug rehabilitation. No terrain was too barren or too alien to support a messiah. It was the Third Awakening that made possible the election as President of that curious figure Jimmy Carter, an evangelical Baptist who had recently been "born again" and "saved," who had "accepted Jesus Christ as my personal Savior." Jimmy Carter seemed to come straight from the tent meeting where Sister Martha played the Yamaha piano and the sisters and the brethren stood up and gave witness and shouted. "Share it, brother!" "Share it, sister!" And praised God. In the four years that followed, Jimmy Carter never seemed to understand the power that flowed through his piney wood veins. He dissipated the power and the glory and threw away all his trump cards. The people yearned for hallelujah, testifying, and the blood of the lamb, and he gave them position statements from the Teleprompter.

America now tingles with the things of the flesh while roaring drunk on things of the spirit. We are in that curious interlude of the 20th century that Nietzsche foretold a century ago: the time of the *reevaluation,* the devising of new values to replace the osteoporotic skeletons of the old. God is dead, and 40 new gods live, prancing like mummers. Behold, it is not the ending but the beginning! Ecce America—in her Elizabethan period, her Bourbon Louis romp, her season of rude animal health and rising sap! Sisters and brethren, it is written that these are evil days, but I say unto you: the holiest of spirits are even now bubbling up into every brain. . . .

How Do You Respond?

1. Wolfe has fashioned a distinctive way of writing, offering fast, punchy anecdotes, interspersing dialogue, using unconventional words and punctuation, setting out contradictions and paradoxes. Discuss your reaction to this style of writing, which draws attention to itself.

2. Wolfe proposes to explain the decade of the 70s. What do you think of his confidence that he can make sense of what others see as confusion and chaos? What in his writing style lets him get away with setting himself up as a know-it-all? *Does* he get away with it, in your opinion?

3. Sophistication is generally thought of as being cool and detached. Wolfe presents himself as knowing but enthusiastic. Would you say that he is sophisticated? If not sophisticated, what is he?

FOCUS ON YOUR READING

1. Note the title and opening line of each selection. Characterize the expectations it arouses in you. When you meet Tom Wolfe's spunky title, for example, "The Sexed-Up, Doped-Up, Hedonistic Heaven of the Boom-Boom 70s"—what do you imagine will follow? When you meet Tillie Olsen's "I Stand Here Ironing," what associations do you bring to the word *ironing*? Even if you do not read through all the selections in the chapter, glance at the openings to observe how, in fact, writers begin, and how you, as a reader, respond.

2. Notice how many of these selections build on narrative. Make a chronology, for example, of Emily's years in "I Stand Here Ironing." Fill in the main events of her life. The chronology may help you fix the outline of the story in your mind.

3. Tom Wolfe says, "The hedonism of the 1970s derives, in my opinion, from a development so stupendous, so long in the making, and so obvious that, like the Big Dipper or the curvature of the earth, it is barely noticed any longer, namely, the boom of the booms." And John Holt asks in his essay, "Why should it be that children intensely dislike to read?" Where in the other selections do you observe the writer pointing to a *search for causes*?

4. Richard Wright talks about the effects of his learning to read; Ellen Willis talks of the effects of her being an "outie," a "reject" in her high school. Observe how these writers take events out of their past and project to a future time, where they study the effects of their past experiences.

5. John Holt says that his original methods of teaching reading were "foolish" because they never gave students "an opportunity to say what they really thought about a book." He then *contrasts* his new ways of teaching to these older, foolish ones. In "I Stand Here Ironing," the mother *contrasts* the raising of her daughter Emily to the raising of her other children. Observe in these pieces and in others in the chapter how contrasting is a fundamental way of perceiving experiences.

6. Tom Wolfe says, "Two pairs of eyes popped up in one of the beds, blazing like raccoons at night by the garbage cans. . . ." He describes a young woman: "She has long, brown pre-Raphaelite hair, parted in the middle, a big floppy crew-neck sweater, jeans and clogs. She's 18 years old and looks about 12 and is not the least

embarrassed by what we tell her." Wolfe is a master of *descriptive* detail. Note how he and other writers in the chapter bring their writing alive and sharpen our perceptions through their close attention to detail.

FOCUS ON YOUR WRITING

1. English is "something that most children can hardly wait to see the last of," says Holt. Write about your experiences in English classes. Were they anything like the negative situations Holt describes? Or were you fortunate in having enlightened teachers like Holt?

2. Write of an intricate series of events following the pattern of "Falling Bricks," where each action led to an immediate and irreversible reaction.

3. Following the pattern of Tillie Olsen's "I Stand Here Ironing," write a reflective piece, imagining yourself in a situation where someone asks you to reflect on the causes and effects of events in your own life: moving to a new place, losing someone you loved, being raised by your parents.

4. Does Ellen Willis's essay on high-school trauma strike familiar notes for you? If so, write of your own experiences of being an "outie" or a "reject." Were you popular and successful? How did that feel?

5. Write about your own reading, keeping Wright's words in mind: "My reading had created a vast sense of distance between me and the world in which I lived. . . ."

CHAPTER 6

❖ ❖

"What's It Like?"

DESCRIBING

"What's it like?" a husband asks his wife when she tells him she has seen an available apartment, one she very much wants to rent.

"Well, it's on the third floor of an old Victorian house," she says. "There's no elevator, of course, only a private staircase, which leads right up to the apartment. It's the only one on the floor, so it's quiet. There are three big rooms and a bath and a very quaint kitchen. What struck me right away as I walked into the living room was the airiness, the feeling of space. Two whole walls are windowed. You feel as if you're sitting in a tree house, and you can look down over the lake. You go down a small hall off the living room, and there's one bedroom with two small windows, but they face east, so we'd get the morning sun. . . ."

Why describe? Let's explore the question for a moment by taking a close look at this situation. One person, in this case the wife, is "in the know." She has seen something, an apartment, that she wants someone else, her husband, to "see." He hasn't yet been there, and so she attempts to *represent* the apartment to him through words. She could take a photograph; she could draw a diagram; she chooses, as most of us would in this situation, to describe. Describing is what we naturally do when we want to tell someone else what we have seen. Like telling a story, like telling how to do something or what causes something, describing is a form of life. We both tell stories and describe things because we want to bring someone into a world we have experienced. We need to share. We want, in certain situations like this one, to convince another person that what we see is worth considering—and perhaps worth "buying."

The husband, here, is in the dark. He doesn't know what the apartment is like, and he wants to know. The wife tells him what it's like according to her observations and colored by her preferences. She first gives him a sense of the whole. She tells him where the apartment is—on the third floor of an old Victorian building—and how large it is—three rooms and a bath. Then she describes the place, weaving together the concrete—her observations of the particular—and the abstract—her generalizations. The place strikes her as quiet. Why? Because it's the only apartment on that floor. The place strikes her as airy and spacious. Why? Because of the windows and the setting outside. The kitchen strikes her as quaint. Why? Presumably, she will tell her husband what it is about the kitchen that adds up to quaintness. As she talks, she places herself physically in relation to what she is describing: she enters into the living room; she moves down a small hall. Her words try to bring him into the actual setting.

What's it like? How does it strike you? Where are you when you're describing a place or a person? What is your angle of vision? What is your attitude toward your subject? How do you generalize about the concrete, about what you actually see? These considerations are fundamental to the act of describing, when we attempt to represent what we have seen through the filter of our own self. Because each of us experiences the world in an individual way, our renditions, our attempts to make real for others what we see or hear or taste or feel, are individual. "There is no such thing as pure *objective* observation," says Thoreau. "Your observation, to be interesting, i.e. to be significant, must be *subjective*. The sum of what the writer of whatever class has to report is simply some human experience, whether he be poet or philosopher or man of science. . . ."

The husband, entering the same apartment, may very well see it quite differently. The private staircase? How in the world are they going to lug their six-foot couch up all those stairs? The windows?

He may like less exposed rooms. He may wonder whether so much glass will admit the winter cold. The "quaint" kitchen? The refrigerator is a 1950s model and makes strange noises. The sink is shallow, the stove rusty, the linoleum stained. To the husband, the kitchen is hardly quaint—it is obsolete.

The Snapshot

Stand in front of a building or at the entrance to a room. Choose a place where you can see the whole, and pretend that you are snapping a photo. Hold things in your vision and describe them so that you can bring someone else into your realm. Where do you begin? At the doorway to the room? Do your eyes travel from left to right, around the room? Do you focus on the center of the room, on the most dominant piece of furniture, or on the windows? The writer of the following piece focuses on one item in her mother's kitchen:

> The white metal cabinet was the center of the kitchen. There was a built-in cupboard that stored the dishes and china, the pots and pans; a red formica-top table and four chairs sat in the dead center; and white wooden cabinets squared the large, sunny space; but the metal cabinet was the real center. Everything there was placed just so. The boxes were kept with the boxes, the cans kept with the cans, vegetables with vegetables, fruit with fruit by kind and label: pears with pears, fruit cocktail with fruit cocktail, peaches with peaches, Delmonte with Delmonte, Libby with Libby, sliced with sliced, halves with halves. Labels faced front.

Now, follow the same procedure of snapping a word-photo by observing a person. Hold him or her still. How do you begin? Feet first? Head first? How do you move—from the bottom up, or from the top down? Or do you snap a striking feature, as Richard Selzer does in this passage:

> Save for the white fringe open at the front, Elihu Koontz is bald. The hair has grown too long and is wilted. He wears it as one would wear a day-old laurel wreath. He is naked to the waist, so that I can see his breasts. They are the breasts of Buddha, inverted triangles from which the nipples swing, dark as garnets.

We hold things still when we take this kind of photograph with words. We observe and we record what strikes us. We compare, we contrast, we use metaphor to render our subject alive, as Selzer does when he sees Koontz as having "the breasts of Buddha," with nipples "dark as garnets." When we describe in these ways, the action is zero—we are freezing things in time and holding them still. The sequence is no longer one of "and then, and then" but of more striking and less striking elements in a scene that is present all at once.

The Moving Picture

Description can also take moving pictures as we pass through a scene or tell a story. Description is a part of any kind of writing. The writer describes while journeying through an event or through an experience. The writer moves through space while describing, and we move as well. In the following selection from Charles Dickens's *Great Expectations*, the speaker Pip takes us with him into a house he has not entered before. As he moves through the scene, we see what he sees, and we register, with him, the surprise and fear he experiences in being in such an extraordinary place:

> We went into the house by a side door—the great front entrance had two chains across it outside—and the first thing I noticed was, that the passages were all dark, and that she had left a candle burning there. She took it up, and we went through more passages and up a staircase, and still it was all dark, and only the candle lighted us.
>
> At last we came to the door of a room, and she said, "Go in." I answered, more in shyness than politeness, "After you, miss."
>
> To this she returned: "Don't be ridiculous, boy; I am not going in." And scornfully walked away, and—what was worse— took the candle with her.
>
> This was very uncomfortable, and I was half afraid. However, the only thing to be done being to knock at the door, I knocked, and was told from within to enter. I entered, therefore, and found myself in a pretty large room, well lighted with wax candles. No glimpse of daylight was to be seen in it. It was a dressing-room, as I supposed from the furniture, though much of it was of forms and uses then quite unknown to me. But prominent in it was a draped table with a gilded looking-glass,

and that I made out at first sight to be a fine lady's dressing table.

Whether I should have made out this object so soon, if there had no fine lady sitting at it, I cannot say. In an arm-chair, with an elbow resting on the table and her head leaning on that hand, sat the strangest lady I have ever seen, or shall ever see.

She was dressed in rich materials—satins, and lace, and silks— all of white. Her shoes were white. And she had a long white veil dependent from her hair, and she had bridal flowers in her hair, but her hair was white. Some bright jewels sparkled on her neck and on her hands, and some other jewels lay sparkling on the table. Dresses, less splendid than the dress she wore, and half-packed trunks, were scattered about. She had not quite finished dressing, for she had but one shoe on—the other was on the table near her hand—her veil was but half arranged, her watch and chain were not put on, and some lace for her bosom lay with those trinkets, and with her handkerchief, and gloves, and some flowers, and a Prayer-book, all confusedly heaped about the looking-glass.

It was not in the first moments that I saw all these things, though I saw more of them in the first moments than might be supposed. But, I saw that everything within my view which ought to be white, had been white long ago, and had lost its lustre, and was faded and yellow. I saw that the bride within the bridal dress had withered like the dress, and like the flowers, and had no brightness left but the brightness of her sunken eyes. I saw that the dress had been put upon the rounded figure of a young woman, and that the figure upon which it now hung loose had shrunk to skin and bone. Once, I had been taken to one of our old marsh churches to see a skeleton in the ashes of a rich dress, that had been dug out of a vault under the church pavement. Now, waxwork and skeleton seemed to have dark eyes that moved and looked at me. I should have cried out, if I could.

Point of View

When we describe, we usually have a particular attitude about our subject. A room strikes us as appealing or not. A person strikes us, too, as someone we appreciate or not. The words we choose, the details we select, reveal our attitude. The woman who described the apartment to her husband obviously wanted him to appreciate her representation. She wanted to convince him that it was a suitable place to rent—she *saw* for him what she wanted him to see. In the following two passages, we see the same material, essentially the same actions, represented in two different ways.

When the train came in, he got in quickly. Immediately, he realized that he was in a SMOKING compartment. He looked around, happily. A cheerful red-faced old man was pulling on a cigar with great relish. Two women talked animatedly, their eyes full of laughter, cigarettes bobbing up and down in their lips. Everywhere, a warm cozy haze, a sense of well-being; the windows, bathed in warm breath and smoke, kept out the cold world outside. He sighed contentedly, and lit a cigarette.

❖ ❖

When the train came in, he got in quickly. Immediately, he realized that he was in a SMOKING compartment. He looked around. An old man with signs of high blood pressure, sucked, like a grotesque baby, on a cigar. Two women talked at each other, soggy cigarettes dangling from their nicotine-stained mouths, their eyes screwed up against the smoke. Everywhere, a disgusting smelly stale haze, a sense of claustrophobia; the windows, polluted by all the smoke and stale breath, were opaque; the fresh world of nature was invisible. He groaned and rushed into the next compartment.

When we describe, we *select* the particulars that strike us. We are aware of the whole—of the general features: house, apartment, man, woman—but our focus is usually on the particulars. We offer first the ordinary, the known, and then the extraordinary, the unique. We provide a context for our subject by naming the general characteristic: He is a man who. . . . And then the particulars: He is a man who walks four golden retrievers on an extended leash. When we define—as we shall see in the next chapter—we cite those general characteristics; when we describe, we go for the particular, the specific, the unique, the individual. This play between defining and describing, between focusing on the general or the specific, is a natural way of both putting things into their general classes and making room for the particular.

The writers of the selections in this chapter all use description to convey their attitudes toward their subjects. They choose details that tell us what their subjects are like and how they feel about them. In "Two Homeless Persons Adrift in Grand Central," David Bird gives us a sense of two people, a man and a woman, who live a squalid existence in a railroad station in New York City. He describes their clothes; he lets us listen in on their talk. Bird, the reporter, puts us there, on the spot.

Barbara Meyer looks back and recalls a young man she knew years before when they both were teenagers. Her spilling of memories, the opening of her memory safe, allows us to see Stitch Drewniany as the writer saw him. Meyer's memories of Stitch and their time together as high-school sweethearts breathe life into an obituary column.

Memory plays a large part in Richard Selzer's "The Masked Marvel's Last Toehold." Selzer begins by describing a present situation: he is to amputate a man's leg. The physical features of the patient evoke memories; he knew him before. Through Selzer's retelling of that *story*, through his describing the *process* of a wrestling match he observed, we come to see "The Masked Marvel" as he was then. Now, years later, at his sickbed, Selzer—and we—see him again.

Memory, too, guides Alfred Kazin once more through the kitchen of his Brownsville tenement where, as a child and as a young man, that room was "the center of the household." There is where he did his homework, his first writing; there is where his mother did her work. Kazin offers specific detail and, at the time, infuses those details with his own fond, and at times, painful, recollections. Scott Momaday also takes us to a place, Rainy Mountain in Kiowa County, Oklahoma, where his people, the Kiowa Indians, live and where his grandmother has recently died. Momaday blends description of the place, of his grandmother, of his people, to write a history that includes them all. Joan Didion, too, works with place and with people as she follows the events of a sensational murder in Southern California. Place influences events, says Didion, presenting a golden land where "The future always looks good . . . because no one remembers the past."

Place is central to William Faulkner's short story, "A Rose for

Emily," an old house in a Southern town where an eccentric figure has lived a mysterious existence. Once we meet Emily, we are not likely to forget her, for Faulkner's powers of description render her vividly: "She looked bloated, like a body long submerged in motionless water, and of that pallid hue. Her eyes, lost in the fatty ridges of her face, looked like two small pieces of coal pressed into a lump of dough. . . ."

❖ ❖

AS YOU READ

The Concrete

How do writers make vivid a person, a place, a situation? How do writers realize—make real—what they experience, what they see, hear, touch, smell—and what they imagine? As you read, notice how the writers use words to set before us colors, shapes, sizes; how they try to convey sounds, smells, people talking. "The particular object is a very remarkable phenomenon," said the philosopher Ludwig Wittgenstein. A scene, a person, a situation comes alive by means of the particular detail: the light slanting in on a particular leaf, the single "Caw" of a single crow in an empty lot, the way your grandmother held her teacup at the kitchen table in the late afternoon.

By focusing on the particular, writers *show* as well as *tell*. They show the azaleas, the lilacs, the tulips, blooming in profusion, rather than simply telling, "It was a nice spring day." As you read, notice when a scene, a person, a situation comes to life for you, and then read closely to see how the writer accomplished this feat of sleight-of-pen.

Evaluation/Point of View

When we tell a story (see Chapter 3), we blend the events of the story as they happened in time with our sense of what the events meant. So it is when we describe. We do not simply list what is out there:

218 THE WRITER'S FORMS

- San Bernardino Valley
- California
- Santa Ana wind
- desert
- mountains
- October
- hills
- no rain

We evaluate as we tell. Sometimes we do it implicitly, through selecting words that convey our sense of the wind, whether it is benign or harsh, hot or cold. Sometimes we offer explicit statements, saying straight out: It was a bad, destructive wind. Joan Didion in "Some Dreamers of the Golden Dream," does both.

> This is a story about love and death in the golden land, and begins with the country. The San Bernardino Valley lies only an hour east of Los Angeles by the San Bernardino Freeway but is in certain ways an alien place: not the coastal California of subtropical twilights and the soft westerlies off the Pacific but a harsher California, haunted by the Mojave just beyond the mountains, devastated by the hot dry Santa Ana wind that comes down through the passes at 100 miles an hour and whines through the eucalyptus windbreaks and works on nerves. October is the bad month for the wind, the month when breathing is difficult and the hills blaze up spontaneously. There has been no rain since April. Every voice seems a scream. It is the season of suicide and divorce and prickly dread, wherever the wind blows.

This scene sets the stage for what is to come: the country, the landscape, the weather reflect the alienation of the people she describes. As you read, notice how writers *evaluate* the concrete, how they use words to create a mood, an impression, an image that gives us a sense of their point of view, their way of looking at things.

AS YOU WRITE

Generating Material

Write in your journal, as quickly as you can, words, images, impressions that strike you when you are actually in a place, observing what is around you, taking in smells, sounds, bits of dialogue, colors, shapes. And then, writing from memory, recall a person or a place as Barbara Meyer does in "A Death Gives Life to Fond Memories." Record as much of the concrete as you can, focusing on the particular, noting or remembering what the person wore (your mother's worn black oxfords, the laces tied into small, neat bows). Imagine yourself in each situation as a fly on the wall, taking in all you can, not trying to put things in order.

Reading Your Writing

As you read over your quick jottings, try to discern patterns. See if your notes suggest ways you might render a scene or a person vividly so that a reader, who has not been there with you, can grasp the experience along with you. Think about the dominant impressions the scene or person or situation left with you, the ways you evaluate, make sense, out of what you see. Decide on your point of view, what you think and feel about the subject. Select the details, colors, shapes, sounds, smells, dialogue, that are the most memorable, sharp, poignant, *for you.* These are probably the ones that will make the subject vivid for your reader.

Shaping Your Writing

Keep your reader in mind as you shape a scene or describe a person. Keep in mind that the reader needs to know where you are. Your reader will be jolted if you are describing the inside of a house and then suddenly, without warning, you are outside in the garden describing the lilac trees. Let your reader know—either implicitly or explicitly—your attitudes toward the concrete, how the day strikes you, how a person gives you a sense of wonderment, how a situation is fraught with tension. Let your evaluation, your point of view, your angle of vision surface. Remember that the reader is not there on the spot; the reader cannot read your mind as you observe or recall. *Show* what you can, and *tell* what you think.

DAVID BIRD

> *Everyone has a story to tell, and it is David Bird's particular gift that he can draw stories from seemingly unpromising sources. He also knows how to disappear—to render himself invisible—so as to let people speak for themselves. He is obviously a good listener, and good listeners are rewarded with good stories.*

TWO HOMELESS PERSONS ADRIFT IN GRAND CENTRAL

Her name is Madeline. His name is Lee. They don't know each other, but they are both in their mid-50s and Grand Central Terminal is the closest thing they have to a home.

Madeline and Lee are two of an estimated 36,000 homeless people in New York City. The number has grown so much recently, according to a study released this month by the Community Service Society, a nonprofit, nonsectarian social agency, that public facilities can no longer care for them. Their stories follow.

MADELINE

Madeline is a slender woman who seems larger because of the three sweaters and a layer of plastic sheeting she wears under her coat to ward off the cold. The other night, as the stream of suburbanites hurrying for their trains was slowing to a trickle, she stopped near the entrance to Track 23 and set down the shopping bag that contained all of her possessions, odd bits of paper and clothing.

She walked over to the stainless-steel drinking fountain near the gleaming face of the Manufacturers Hanover Trust cash machine and took a quick drink of water, then rinsed her hands and set out on what she says has become one of her main tasks in life.

"I play football all over this station," she explained to a visitor as she vigorously kicked old cigarette butts and other pieces of litter away from an ever larger arc around her shopping bag. It is, she said, her way of attracting attention to get the cleaners to do a better job of sweeping the station.

"See that Time up there," she said, pointing up to a billboard on the balcony advertising the magazine. "I had a good time playing football up there last week, kicked the trash right down the stairs. They got the message, all right."

Madeline says she cares about Grand Central and spends her time there because of "the quality people" who pass through it. Asked about Pennsylvania Station, she made a face and scoffed: "There's just no comparison."

She was born on a farm in Orangeburg, S. C., Madeline said, "but I received my education on Long Island."

"My parents came up here because they wanted me to have an education," she added, "and it was too far down South to walk from the farm to school. They heard it was a shorter walk up North—and, besides, you didn't have to pay for books. In the South then, you had to pay for your books."

Madeline said her parents died early, so she was raised mostly by her grandmother. She graduated from high school and then worked for several years as a chambermaid in Manhattan hotels. Her last employment, "many years ago," was in a Revlon cosmetics factory, where she met the man who briefly became her husband.

"I made the mistake of moving in with my mother-in-law," she said. "My husband, Leonard, was spoiled. I said to him. 'We're both making good salaries, let's get a place of our own.' He said, 'Well, we don't have to pay rent here.' "

"Finally, I gave him three days to make up his mind. When I asked him what he'd decided, he started to answer, 'Well . . .' I said, 'Stop right there, that's all I need to hear.' I gave Leonard back to his mother, and I moved back to my grandmother's house."

Then Madeline's grandmother died. "I went around crying for days and days, not knowing what to do," she said. Then she came across Grand Central Terminal.

"I saw the opportunity to be secure in Grand Central, to be secure for the rest of my life," she said. "I was able to do something to keep the place clean, to help decent people."

Madeline said she got enough to eat. "There are five people in this station who see that I get food." she said, referring to food stands. "I go to the counter and I get whatever I want."

She sleeps only for short periods, on benches or in movie theaters. She avoids staying at the women's shelter operated by the city at 358 Lafayette Street, she said, because other women made sexual advances.

Madeline does not spend all of her time in Grand Central. "When the weather's nice I walk down to 14th Street," she said. "It's nice down there. I need the air in my lungs. I don't hurry. I stop along the way to talk to people."

Although she talks freely and exchanges greetings with passersby, Madeline says she has no real friends because she might be betrayed by any close relationships.

"I stay alone," she said, "and stay alive."

LEE

Sensing that a police officer was coming, Lee hobbled away from his usual spot on the ledge at the entrance to the subway shuttle at Grand Central.

He used to be a car cleaner in the station on the midnight-to-8 A.M. shift, but that was long ago. Lee is 55 years old now, and he has a hard time remembering when he last worked.

"I lost my job—I'll be honest with you—because I drank too much," he said. "They found me sleeping instead of sweeping. Let's face it—I'm no good. I'm a bum."

If he had his choice, Lee said, he would sit at the shuttle entrance all the time. "Sometimes I'll be there at 6 in the morning, and at 6 the next morning I'll still be there. I know the people that go by. I just sit there smoking a cigarette and taking a drink now and then out of my bottle."

"I don't ask for anything," he said. "People come up and give me money and sandwiches, and they buy me coffee. I get more coffee than I can use."

Lee cannot spend all day and all night at his spot, he said, because the police prod him to get out when the station is closed from 1:30 A.M. to 5:30 A.M. "They chase you out," he said, "and you just come back when they're gone." Like Madeline, he tries to elude them and stay in the station after it is closed. If Lee and Madeline have to leave, they ride the subways until the station is open again.

Lee was born in upstate Oswego, but has lost all contact with any family he had. "I had a sister," he said, "but I haven't seen her in years and don't even know where she is." Lee said he was married once and had two sons, but he has no idea where they are, either.

He joined the Army when he was 17. "I was in the medics," he said. "I drove an ambulance in Germany. I traveled around in the army. I was in Alaska, in Anchorage, too."

Lee said he was entitled to veterans' benefits because he had injured his leg, "but I had to keep a lot of appointments and fill out a lot of forms, and I got to drinking and I just said to hell with it."

Whenever he has the money, Lee said, he cleans up in the terminal's men's room. For 75 cents, he can rent a stall where he can shower and shave. Running a hand over his stubble of beard, he murmured: "Maybe I ought to go down there now. But I don't have a cent in my pocket."

"Being a bum is not the nicest thing in the world," Lee said. "It's not a good life, but when you've got nothing else to do, what are you going to do? It's better than going to jail."

He remembers what life was like when he was working: "At 74th Street and First Avenue, I had a nice room—no, I had two rooms, a kitchenette. I dressed up every day and walked proudly on the street. Then everything went down, down, down."

He fingered his dirty maroon jacket; his only other clothing was a pair of blue pants and a streaked topcoat he kept next to him, with a nearly empty bottle of cheap wine protruding from a pocket.

"I'm pretty far down," Lee said of his life now, running a shaky hand through his thin black hair. "I don't know if I've hit bottom, but I'm close to it."

Like Madeline, he said he had no close associations with other people even though there are many others who inhabit the terminal. "I'm a loner," he said. "No friends."

He has tried joining groups of other men in his situation at places like Alcoholics Anonymous or at religious missions, but he said they did not suit him.

He thought for a while about getting a job again, but the idea soon faded.

"I can't get a job," he said. "Who's going to hire someone who's been on a drunk for years when they can get someone new and fresh? But you know, if things worked and they hired me, they might be getting a good worker who was determined to do better the second time around."

He mulled that idea for a few seconds before adding: "But then they might not."

How Do You Respond?

1. To a great extent, David Bird lets his subjects, Madeline and Lee, speak for themselves. What effect does their talk have on us as readers?

2. How would a social worker describe these people? A policeman? A snob?

3. Does Bird evaluate his subjects; does he judge them? Can you point to any aspect of Bird's writing that reveals his own attitude?

BARBARA MEYER

> *To be able to write with tenderness but to avoid sentimentality; to write openly but without self-display; to celebrate, without effusiveness: these are some of Barbara Meyer's gifts.*

A DEATH GIVES LIFE TO FOND MEMORIES

Stitch Drewniany died Sunday, March 23. Too bad, you say, but who was Stitch Drewniany?

Well, in the whole scheme of living, he was not someone very important. He hadn't even reached the first half-century of his life.

To his family and friends, Stitch might well have been the most important person in their lives, but to the average person perusing the obituary page of a local newspaper, he was just another victim of an untimely death.

Basically, that is what it almost meant to me. Almost, but not quite.

Stitch, you see, was a high-school sweetheart of mine. The romance lasted for only a year, and it was not The Big Love Affair nor was he my first boyfriend.

But it is part of my "memory safe," and when my eye caught the name, the tumblers fell into place, the safe door opened wide and all the memories of Stitch and those high-school days spilled over me.

Stitch was a friend before he was a boyfriend, and I can remember the night when that changed as clearly as I can remember this morning's breakfast.

It was a perfect summer evening, and we were walking home from the park together after hearing the Friday night band concert. It was the kind of night dreams are made of.

Honeysuckle hung heavy in the air, crickets were sending out their love calls and lighting bugs were in abundance, almost lighting the path before us. Just a hint of a breeze stirred the leaves, but not awakening them, and in the black sky the summer constellations looked like an artist's glitter tossed upon it.

No one else was on the path we were taking. Timidly, Stitch reached for my hand. It felt warm and good—and right. We walked a bit farther, then slowed down and stopped. We turned toward each other simultaneously and he bent over and kissed me for the first time.

Why I remember that kiss so well is something I could never understand. It wasn't passionate, rough, or experienced. It was sweet, thoughtful, and innocent. We were both a little embarrassed. He didn't kiss me again that night, but it was an unspoken pledge. From that night on, we were "an item."

In those years, not too many boys had cars. Stitch didn't. And there weren't many places to go. Park concerts, "Y" dances once a month, or the movies. That was about it. Boys didn't have much money to spend on dates.

Our relationship consisted pretty much of walking home after school (holding hands, of course), stopping for a cherry Coke, and spending Friday or Saturday night together, but never both. And there were always a few kisses in the doorway before saying goodnight.

If you had sexual stirrings, chances were that you didn't know it. If you knew it, you didn't act upon it, especially if you were "good."

Stitch was big, like a huge honey bear, but gentle and soft. He was on the football team, but third string, and so he never got into many games.

We never exchanged gifts. Once, in one of his shop classes, Stitch spelled out my name and his with long pieces of copper wire, and I kept them for many years. When I married, my mother must have thrown them out, along with other paraphernalia stored in the attic.

Our romance was low key and ended the same way when my family moved away. I never saw Stitch again, or ever knew what had happened to him until the sad report of his death. Funny, but for the last 20 years he lived only about an hour's drive away from me. I never knew it. He had worked as the manager of a silversmith company after having, according to the obituary, "previously owned a Carvel Ice Cream Shop."

He was a member of a bowling league, he had been a Marine in the Korean War, and he left a wife, three brothers, and a sister. But no children.

A life summed up coldly in a few paragraphs. I can only wonder what caused his early death. An old war injury? A heart attack? Or was it, as Dr. Eric Berne theorizes, part of his script? His father had died young, too.

I wanted to add something a little more personal. People come in and go out of our lives. Some we remember, others we forget completely.

I often wonder who has me in their memory safe. When my obituary turns up, I hope someone will have a few fond memories. It's comforting to think that somewhere along the line you touched someone enough for them to remember the touch.

I hope that, if you had a Stitch in your life, you'll treasure the memory. It was nice, in a sad way, to bring that memory out after all these years and look at it again.

I don't know what kind of person he eventually turned out to be, but 17-year-old Stitch Drewniany was worth remembering today.

How Do You Respond?

1. How would Barbara Meyer have written about Stitch Drewniany if he had died during the time they were dating? Compare the difficulty

of writing about an emotionally charged subject that is still close in time with the greater ease of handling an experience that has become part of the memory bank.

2. Imagine that you meet a grade-school friend who moved away when you both were ten. Tell your friend something of your recent past, conveying where you have been and who you are now.

3. How would you characterize Meyer's tone? Does the title of her piece, "Death Gives Life to Fond Memories," seem a paradox to you? If the newspaper story had reminded her of a friend still alive ("Former City Man Awarded for Bravery"), how would her reaction have been different?

RICHARD SELZER

> *"I spy on my patients," says Richard Selzer (born 1928). Selzer is a surgeon, and he writes out of his experience with patients in hospitals—in recovery rooms and non-recovery rooms. We cannot doubt that Selzer takes us "inside" when we meet his vivid, wrenching descriptions in his short stories,* Rituals of Surgery, *and essays,* Mortal Lessons *and* Confessions of a Knife.

THE MASKED MARVEL'S LAST TOEHOLD

Morning rounds.

On the fifth floor of the hospital, in the west wing, I know that a man is sitting up in his bed, waiting for me. Elihu Koontz is seventy-five, and he is diabetic. It is two weeks since I amputated his left leg just below the knee. I walk down the corridor, but I do not go straight into his room. Instead, I pause in the doorway. He is not yet aware of my presence, but gazes down at the place in the bed where his leg used to be, and where now there is the collapsed leg of his pajamas. He is totally absorbed, like an athlete appraising the details of his body. What is he thinking, I wonder. Is he dreaming the outline of his toes. Does he see there his foot's incandescent ghost? Could he be angry? Feel that I have taken from him something for which he yearns now with all his heart? Has he forgotten so soon the pain? It was a pain so great as to set him apart from all other men, in a red-hot place where he had no kith or kin. What of those black gorilla toes and the soupy mess that was his heel? I watch him from the doorway. It is a kind of spying, I know.

Save for a white fringe open at the front, Elihu Koontz is bald. The hair has grown too long and is wilted. He wears it as one would wear a day-old laurel wreath. He is naked to the waist, so that I can see his breasts. They are the breasts of Buddha, inverted triangles from which the nipples swing, dark as garnets.

I have seen enough. I step into the room, and he sees that I am there.

"How did the night go, Elihu?"

He looks at me for a long moment. "Shut the door," he says.

I do, and move to the side of the bed. He takes my left hand in both of his, gazes at it, turns it over, then back, fondling, at last holding it up to his cheek. I do not withdraw from this loving. After a while he relinquishes my hand, and looks up at me.

"How is the pain?" I ask.

He does not answer, but continues to look at me in silence. I know at once that he has made a decision.

"Ever hear of The Masked Marvel?" He says this in a low voice, almost a whisper.

"What?"

"The Masked Marvel" he says. "You never heard of him?"

"No."

He clucks his tongue. He is exasperated.

All at once there is a recollection. It is dim, distant, but coming near.

"Do you mean the wrestler?"

Eagerly, he nods, and the breasts bob. How gnomish he looks, oval as the huge helpless egg of some outlandish lizard. He has very long arms, which, now and then, he unfurls to reach for things—a carafe of water, a get-well card. He gazes up at me, urging. He *wants* me to remember.

"Well . . . yes," I say. I am straining backward in time. "I saw him wrestle in Toronto long ago."

"Ha!" He smiles. "You saw *me*." And his index finger, held rigid and upright, bounces in the air.

The man has said something shocking, unacceptable. It must be challenged.

"You?" I am trying to smile.

Again that jab of the finger. "You saw *me*."

"No," I say. But even then, something about Elihu Koontz, those prolonged arms, the shape of his head, the sudden agility with which he leans from his bed to get a large brown envelope from his nightstand, something is forcing me toward a memory. He rummages through his papers, old newspaper clippings, and I remember . . .

It is almost forty years ago. I am ten years old. I have been sent to Toronto to spend the summer with relatives. Uncle Max has bought two tickets to the wrestling match. He is taking me that night.

"He isn't allowed," says Aunt Sarah to me. Uncle Max has angina.

"He gets too excited," she says.

"I wish you wouldn't go, Max," she says.

"You mind your own business," he says.

And we go. Out into the warm Canadian evening. I am not only abroad, I am abroad in the *evening*! I have never been taken out in the evening. I am terribly excited. The trolleys, the lights, the horns. It is a bazaar. At the Maple Leaf Gardens, we sit high and near the center. The vast arena is dark except for the brilliance of the ring at the bottom.

It begins.

The wrestlers circle. They grapple. They are all haunch and paunch. I am shocked by their ugliness, but I do not show it. Uncle Max is exhilarated. He leans forward, his eyes unblinking, on his face a look of enormous happiness. One after the other, a pair of wrestlers enter the ring. The two men join, twist, jerk, tug, bend, yank, and throw. They then leave and are replaced by another pair. At last it is the main event. "The Angel vs. The Masked Marvel."

On the cover of the program notes, there is a picture of The Angel hanging from the limb of a tree, a noose of thick rope around his neck. The Angel hangs just so for an hour every day, it is explained, to strengthen his neck. The Masked Marvel's trademark is a black stocking cap with holes for the eyes and mouth. He is never seen without it, states the program. No one knows who The Masked Marvel really is!

"Good," says my Uncle Max. "Now you'll see something." He is fidgeting, waiting for them to appear. They come down separate aisles, climb into the ring from opposite sides. I have never seen anything like them. It is The Angel's neck that first captures the eye. The shaved nape rises in twin columns to puff into the white hood of a sloped and bosselated skull that is too small. As though, strangled by the sinews of that neck, the skull had long since withered and shrunk. The thing about The Angel is the absence of any mystery in his body. It is simply *there*. A monosyllabic announcement. A grunt. One looks and knows everything at once, the fat thighs, the gigantic buttocks, the great spine from which hang knotted ropes and pale aprons of beef. And that prehistoric head. He is all a single hideous piece, The Angel is. No detachables.

The Masked Marvel seems dwarfish. His fingers dangle kneeward. His short legs are slightly bowed as if under the weight of the cask they are forced to heft about. He has breasts that swing when he moves! I have never seen such breasts on a man before.

There is sudden ungraceful movement, and they close upon one another. The Angel stoops and hugs The Marvel about the waist, locking his hands behind The Marvel's back. Now he straightens and lifts The Marvel as though he were uprooting a tree. Thus he holds him, then stoops again, thrusts one hand through The Marvel's crotch, and with the other grabs him by the neck. He rears and . . . The Marvel is aloft! For a long moment, The Angel stands as though deciding where to make the toss. Then throws. Was that board or bone that splintered there? Again and again, The Angel hurls himself upon the body of The Masked Marvel.

Now the Angel rises over the fallen Marvel, picks up one foot in both of his hands, and twists the toes downward. It is far beyond the tensile strength of mere ligament, mere cartilage. The Masked Marvel does not hide his agony, but pounds and slaps the floor with his hand, now and then reaching up toward The Angel in an attitude of supplication. I have never seen such suffering. And all the while his black mask rolls from side to side, the mouth pulled to a tight slit through which issues an endless hiss that I can hear from where I sit. All at once, I hear a shouting close by.

"Break it off! Tear off a leg and throw it up here!"

It is Uncle Max. Even in the darkness I can see that he is gray. A band of sweat stands upon his upper lip. He is on his feet now, panting, one fist pressed at his chest, the other raised warlike toward the ring. For the first time I begin to think that something terrible might happen here. Aunt Sarah was right.

"Sit down, Uncle Max," I say. "Take a pill, please."

He reaches for the pillbox, gropes, and swallows without taking his gaze from the wrestlers. I wait for him to sit down.

"That's not fair," I say, "twisting his toes like that."

"It's the toehold," he explains.

"But it's not *fair*," I say again. The whole of the evil is laid open for me to perceive. I am trembling.

And now The Angel does something unspeakable. Holding the foot of The Marvel at full twist with one hand, he bends and grasps the mask where it clings to the back of The Marvel's head. And he pulls. He is going to strip it off! Lay bare an ultimate carnal mystery! Suddenly it is beyond mere physical violence. Now I am on my feet, shouting into the Maple Leaf Gardens.

"Watch out," I scream. "Stop him. Please, somebody, stop him."

Next to me, Uncle Max is chuckling.

Yet The Masked Marvel hears me, I know it. And rallies from his bed of pain. Thrusting with his free heel, he strikes The Angel at the back of the knee. The Angel falls. The Masked Marvel is on top of him, pinning his shoulders to the mat. One! Two! Three! And it is over. Uncle Max is strangely still. I am grasping for breath. All this I remember as I stand at the bedside of Elihu Koontz.

Once again, I am in the operating room. It is two years since I amputated the left leg of Elihu Koontz. Now it is his right leg which is gangrenous. I have already scrubbed. I stand to one side wearing my gown and gloves. And . . . *I am masked.* Upon the table lies Elihu Koonz, pinned in a fierce white light. Spinal anesthesia has been administered. One of his arms is taped to a board placed at a right angle to his body. Into this arm, a needle has been placed. Fluid drips here from a bottle overhead. With his other hand, Elihu Koontz beats feebly at the side of the operating table. His head rolls from side to side. His mouth is pulled into weeping. It seems to me that I have never seen such misery.

An orderly stands at the foot of the table, holding Elihu Koontz's leg aloft by the toes so that the intern can scrub the limb with antiseptic solutions. The intern paints the foot, ankle, leg, and thigh, both front and back, three times. From a corner of the room where I wait, I look down as from an amphitheater. Then I think of Uncle

Max yelling, "Tear off a leg. Throw it up here." And I think that forty years later I am making the catch.

"It's not fair," I say aloud. But no one hears me. I step forward to break The Masked Marvel's last toehold.

How Do You Respond?

1. Notice how Selzer moves from the present to the future in the first four lines, to the present, and then, later, to the past, as the surgeon retrieves his memory of the wrestler. How many shifts are there? How do they affect us as readers?

2. How does Selzer realize (make real) Koontz? How does he render him vivid?

3. Selzer writes about a painful situation and uses many grotesque images, but you may feel that his tone is at variance with his material. Characterize his tone, and discuss the effect of the writing in relation to the subject matter.

ALFRED KAZIN

> *Alfred Kazin (born 1915) is distinguished by a remarkable zest for life; his autobiographical volumes—the latest is* New York Jew—*give a vivid account of growing up in America and of the life of the professional writer. In some ways his life has been a long love-affair with the typewriter and with New York. When he writes about New York City, it is difficult to separate his delight in words and his affection for the place he writes of. They feed off, and feed, each other. "The Kitchen," taken from* Walker in the City, *is a tribute to a part of his childhood in Brooklyn.*

THE KITCHEN

In Brownsville tenements the kitchen is always the largest room and the center of the household. As a child I felt that we lived in a kitchen to which four other rooms were annexed. My mother, a "home" dressmaker, had her workshop in the kitchen. She told me once that she had begun dressmaking in Poland at thirteen; as far back as I can remember, she was always making dresses for the local women. She had an innate sense of design, a quick eye for all the subtleties in the latest fashions, even when she despised them, and great boldness. For three or four dollars she would study the fashion magazines with a customer, go with the customer to the remnants store on Belmont Avenue to pick out the material, argue the owner down—all remnants stores, for some reason, were supposed to be shady, as if the owners dealt in stolen goods—and then for days would patiently fit and baste and sew and fit again. Our apartment was always full of women in their housedresses sitting around the kitchen table waiting for a fitting. My little bedroom next to the kitchen was the fitting room. The sewing machine, an old nut-brown Singer with golden scrolls painted along the black arm and engraved along the two tiers of little drawers massed with needles and thread on each side of the treadle, stood next to the window and the great coalblack stove which up to my last year in college was our main source of heat. By December the two outer bedrooms were closed off, and used to chill bottles of milk and cream, cold borscht and jellied calves' feet.

The kitchen held our lives together. My mother worked in it all day long, we ate in it almost all meals except the Passover *seder*, I did my homework and first writing at the kitchen table, and in winter I often had a bed made up for me on three kitchen chairs near the stove. On the wall just over the table hung a long horizontal mirror that sloped to a ship's prow at each end and was lined in cherry wood. It took the whole wall, and drew every object in the kitchen to itself. The walls were a fiercely stippled whitewash, so often rewhitened by my father in slack seasons that the paint looked as if it had been squeezed and cracked into the walls. A large electric bulb hung down the center of the kitchen at the end of a chain that had been hooked into the ceiling; the old gas ring and key still jutted out of the wall like antlers. In the corner next to the toilet was the sink at which we washed, and the square tub in which my mother did our clothes. Above it, tacked to the shelf on which were pleasantly ranged square, blue-bordered white sugar and spice jars, hung calendars from the Public National Bank on Pitkin Avenue and the Minsker Progressive Branch of the Workman's Circle; receipts for the payment of insurance premiums, and household bills on a spindle; two little boxes engraved with Hebrew letters.

One of these was for the poor, the other to buy back the Land of Israel. Each spring a bearded little man would suddenly appear in our kitchen, salute us with a hurried Hebrew blessing, empty the boxes (sometimes with a sidelong look of disdain if they were not full), hurriedly bless us again for remembering our less fortunate Jewish brothers and sisters, and so take his departure until the next spring, after vainly trying to persuade my mother to take still another box. We did occasionally remember to drop coins in the boxes, but this was usually only on the dreaded morning of "midterms" and final examinations, because my mother thought it would bring me luck. She was extremely superstitious, but embarrassed about it, and always laughed at herself whenever, on the morning of an examination, she counseled me to leave the house on my right foot. "I know it's silly," her smile seemed to say, "but what harm can it do? It may calm God down."

The kitchen gave a special character to our lives; my mother's character. All my memories of that kitchen are dominated by the nearness of my mother sitting all day long at her sewing machine, by the clacking of the treadle against the linoleum floor, by the patient twist of her right shoulder as she automatically pushed at the wheel with one hand or lifted the foot to free the needle where it had got stuck in a thick piece of material. The kitchen was her life. Year by year, as I began to take in her fantastic capacity for labor and her anxious zeal, I realized it was ourselves she kept stitched together. I can never remember a time when she was not working. She worked because the law of her life was work, work and anxiety; she worked because she would have found life meaningless without work. She read almost no English; she could read the Yiddish paper, but never felt she had time to. We were always talking of a time when I would teach her how to read, but somehow there was never time. When I awoke in the morning she was already at her machine, or in the great morning crowd of housewives at the grocery getting fresh rolls for breakfast. When I returned from school she was at her machine, or conferring over *McCall's* with some neighborhood woman who had come in pointing hopefully to an illustration—"Mrs. Kazin! Mrs. Kazin! Make me a dress like it shows here in the picture!" When my father came home from work she had somehow mysteriously interrupted herself to make supper for us, and the dishes cleared and washed, was back at her machine. When I went to bed at night, often she was still there, pounding away at the treadle, hunched over the wheel, her hands steering a piece of gauze under the needle with a finesse that always contrasted sharply with her swollen hands and broken nails. Her left hand had been pierced through when as a girl she had worked in the infamous Triangle Shirtwaist Factory on the East Side. A needle had gone straight through the palm, severing a large vein. They had sewn it up for her so clumsily that a tuft of flesh always lay folded over the palm.

The kitchen was the great machine that set our lives running; it whirred down a little only on Saturdays and holy days. From my mother's kitchen I gained my first picture of life as a white, overheated, starkly lit workshop redolent with Jewish cooking, crowded with women in housedresses, strewn with fashion magazines, patterns, dress material, spools of thread—and at whose center, so lashed to her machine that bolts of energy seemed to dance out of her hands and feet as she worked, my mother stamped the treadle hard against the floor, hard, hard, and silently, grimly at war, beat out the first rhythm of the world for me.

Every sound from the street roared and trembled at our windows—a mother feeding her child on the doorstep, the screech of the trolley cars on Rockaway Avenue, the eternal smash of a handball against the wall of our house, the clatter of *der Italyéner's* cart packed with watermelons, the sing-song of the old-clothes men walking Chester Street, the cries *"Arbes! Arbes! Kinder! Kinder! Heyse gute árbes!"* All day long people streamed into our apartment as a matter of course—"customers," upstairs neighbors, downstairs neighbors, women who would stop in for a half-hour's talk, salesmen, relatives, insurance agents. Usually they came in without ringing the bell—everyone knew my mother was always at home. I would hear the front door opening, the wind whistling through our front hall, and then some familiar face would appear in our kitchen with the same bland, matter-of-fact inquiring look: no need to stand on ceremony: my mother and her kitchen were available to everyone all day long.

At night the kitchen contracted around the blaze of light on the cloth, the patterns, the ironing board where the iron had burned a black border around the tear in the muslin cover; the finished dresses looked so frilly as they jostled on their wire hangers after all the work my mother had put into them. And then I would get that strangely ominous smell of tension from the dress fabrics and the burn in the cover of the ironing board—as if each piece of cloth and paper crushed with light under the naked bulb might suddenly go up in flames. Whenever I pass some small tailoring shop still lit up at night and see the owner hunched over his steam press; whenever in some poorer neighborhood of the city I see through a window some small crowded kitchen naked under the harsh light glittering in the ceiling, I still smell that fiery breath, that warning of imminent fire. I was always holding my breath. What I must have felt most about ourselves, I see now, was that we ourselves were like kindling—that all the hard-pressed pieces of ourselves and all the hard-used objects in that kitchen were like so many slivers of wood that might go up in flames if we came too near the white-blazing filaments in that naked bulb. Our tension itself was fire, we ourselves were forever burning—to live, to get down the foreboding in our souls, to make good.

Twice a year, on the anniversaries of her parents' deaths, my mother placed on top of the ice-box an ordinary kitchen glass packed with wax, the *yortsayt*, and lit the candle in it. Sitting at the kitchen table over my homework, I would look across the threshold to that mourning-glass, and sense that for my mother the distance from our kitchen to *der heym*, from life to death, was only a flame's length away. Poor as we were, it was not poverty that drove my mother so hard; it was loneliness—some endless bitter brooding over all those left behind, dead or dying or soon to die; a loneliness locked up in her kitchen that dwelt every day on the hazardousness of life and the nearness of death, but still kept struggling in the lock, trying to get us through by endless labor.

With us, life started up again only on the last shore. There seemed to be no middle ground between despair and the fury of our ambition. Whenever my mother spoke of her hopes for us, it was with such unbelievingness that the likes of us would ever come to anything, such abashed hope and readiness for pain, that I finally came to see in the flame burning on top of the ice-box death itself burning away the bones of poor Jews, burning out in us everything but courage, the blind resolution to live. In the light of that mourning-candle, there were ranged around me how many dead and dying—

how many eras of pain, of exile, of dispersion, of cringing before the powers of this world!

It was always at dusk that my mother's loneliness came home most to me. Painfully alert to every shift in the light at her window, she would suddenly confess her fatigue by removing her pince-nez, and then wearily pushing aside the great mound of fabrics on her machine, would stare at the street as if to warm herself in the last of the sun. "How sad it is!" I once heard her say. "It grips me! It grips me!" Twilight was the bottommost part of the day, the chillest and loneliest time for her. Always so near to her moods, I knew she was fighting some deep inner dread, struggling against the returning tide of darkness along the streets that invariably assailed her heart with the same foreboding—Where? Where now? Where is the day taking us now?

Yet one good look at the street would revive her. I see her now, perched against the windowsill, with her face against the glass, her eyes almost asleep in enjoyment, just as she starts up with the guilty cry—"What foolishness is this in me!"—and goes to the stove to prepare supper for us: a moment, only a moment, watching the evening crowd of women gathering at the grocery for fresh bread and milk. But between my mother's pent-up face at the window and the winter sun dying in the fabrics—"Alfred, see how beautiful!"—she has drawn for me one single line of sentience.

How Do You Respond?

1. Characterize Kazin's attitudes toward the kitchen. How does he show us how he *feels* about the place? Are his evaluations implicit or explicit?

2. List the pivotal metaphors used by Kazin to make his points. What is the effect of this kind of writing? How would David Bird have written about Kazin's mother?

3. "The kitchen held our lives together." Do you have a memory that, like the kitchen for Kazin, orders your sense of things? Kazin says that his fears are still aroused by a certain "strangely ominous smell" of burning; is there some cue that brings back to life for you the intense emotions of childhood?

N. SCOTT MOMADAY

> Scott Momaday (born 1934) is a Kiowa Indian who has created two eloquent and powerful memorials of his people: The Way to Rainy Mountain *and* House Made of Dawn. *He not only captures the special qualities of his ancestral culture, but is a great story-teller, able to make his reader's hair stand on end when he has a mind to.*

From THE WAY TO RAINY MOUNTAIN

A single knoll rises out of the plain in Oklahoma, north and west of the Wichita Range. For my people, the Kiowas, it is an old landmark, and they gave it the name Rainy Mountain. The hardest weather in the world is there. Winter brings blizzards, hot tornadic winds arise in the spring, and in summer the prairie is an anvil's edge. The grass turns brittle and brown, and it cracks beneath your feet. There are green belts along the rivers and creeks, linear groves of hickory and pecan, willow and witch hazel. At a distance in July or August the steaming foliage seems almost to writhe in fire. Great green and yellow grasshoppers are everywhere in the tall grass, popping up like corn to sting the flesh, and tortoises crawl about on the red earth, going nowhere in the plenty of time. Loneliness is an aspect of the land. All things in the plain are isolate; there is no confusion of objects in the eye, but *one* hill or *one* tree or *one* man. To look upon that landscape in the early morning, with the sun at your back, is to lose the sense of proportion. Your imagination comes to life, and this, you think, is where Creation was begun.

I returned to Rainy Mountain in July. My grandmother had died in the spring, and I wanted to be at her grave. She had lived to be very old and at last infirm. Her only living daughter was with her when she died, and I was told that in death her face was that of a child.

I like to think of her as a child. When she was born, the Kiowas were living the last great moment of their history. For more than a hundred years they had controlled the open range from the Smoky Hill River to the Red, from the headwaters of the Canadian to the fork of the Arkansas and Cimarron. In alliance with the Comanches, they had ruled the whole of the southern Plains. War was their sacred business, and they were among the finest horsemen the world has ever known. But warfare for the Kiowas was preeminently a matter of disposition rather than of survival, and they never understood the grim, unrelenting advance of the U.S. Cavalry. When at last, divided and ill-provisioned, they were driven onto the Staked Plains in the cold rains of autumn, they fell into panic. In Palo Duro Canyon they abandoned their crucial stores to pillage and had nothing then but their lives. In order to save themselves, they surrendered to the soldiers at Fort Sill and were imprisoned in the old stone corral that now stands as a military museum. My grandmother was spared the humiliation of those high gray walls by eight or ten years, but she must have known from birth the affliction of defeat, the dark brooding of old warriors.

Her name was Aho, and she belonged to the last culture to evolve in North America. Her forebears came down from the high country in western Montana nearly three centuries ago. They were a mountain people, a mysterious tribe of hunters whose language has never been positively classified in any major group. In the late seventeenth century they began a long migration to the south and east. It was a journey toward the dawn, and it led to a golden age. Along the way the Kiowas were befriended by the Crows, who gave them the culture and religion of the Plains. They acquired horses, and their ancient nomadic spirit was suddenly free of the ground. They acquired Tai-me, the sacred Sun Dance doll, from that moment the object and symbol of their worship, and so shared in the divinity of the sun. Not least, they acquired the sense of destiny, therefore courage and pride. When they entered upon the southern Plains they had been transformed. No longer were they slaves to the simple necessity of survival; they were a lordly and dangerous society of fighters and thieves, hunters and priests of the sun. According to their origin myth, they entered the world through a hollow log. From one point of view, their migration was the fruit of an old prophecy, for indeed they emerged from a sunless world.

Although my grandmother lived out her long life in the shadow of Rainy Mountain, the immense landscape of the continental interior lay like memory in her blood. She could tell of the Crows, whom she had never seen, and of the Black Hills, where she had never been. I wanted to see in reality what she had seen more perfectly in the mind's eye, and traveled fifteen hundred miles to begin my pilgrimage.

Yellowstone, it seemed to me, was the top of the world, a region of deep lakes and dark timber, canyons and waterfalls. But, beautiful as it is, one might have the sense of confinement there. The skyline in all directions is close at hand, the high wall of the woods and deep cleavages of shade. There is a perfect freedom in the mountains, but it belongs to the eagle and the elk, the badger and the bear. The Kiowas reckoned their stature by the distance they see, and they were bent and blind in the wilderness.

Descending eastward, the highland meadows are a stairway to the plain. In July the inland slope of the Rockies is luxuriant with flax and buckwheat, stonecrop and larkspur. The earth unfolds and the limit of the land recedes. Clusters of trees, and animals grazing far in the distance, cause the vision to reach away and wonder to build upon the mind. The sun follows a longer course in the day, and the sky is immense beyond all comparison. The great billowing clouds that sail upon it are shadows that move upon the grain like water, dividing light. Farther down, in the land of the Crows and Blackfeet, the plain is yellow. Sweet clover takes hold of the hills and bends upon itself to cover and seal the soil. There the Kiowas paused on their way; they had come to the place where they must change their lives. The sun is at home on the plains. Precisely there does it have the certain character of a god. When the Kiowas came to the land of the Crows, they could see the dark lees of the hills at dawn across the Bighorn River, the profusion of light on the grain shelves, the oldest deity ranging after the solstices. Not yet would they veer southward to the caldron of the land that lay below; they must wean their blood from the northern winter and hold the mountains a while longer in their view. They bore Tai-me in procession to the east.

A dark mist lay over the Black Hills, and the land was like iron. At the top of a ridge I caught sight of Devil's Tower upthrust against the gray sky as if in the birth of time the core of the earth had broken through its crust and the motion of the world was begun. There are things in nature that engender an awful quiet in the heart of man; Devil's Tower is one of them. Two centuries ago, because they could not do otherwise, the Kiowas made a legend at the base of the rock. My grandmother said:

Eight children were there at play, seven sisters and their brother. Suddenly the boy was struck dumb; he trembled and began to run upon his hands and feet. His fingers became claws, and his body was covered with fur. Directly there was a bear where the boy had been. The sisters were terrified; they ran, and the bear after them. They came to the stump of a great tree, and the tree spoke to them. It bade them climb upon it, and as they did so it began to rise into the air. The bear came to kill them, but they were just beyond its reach. It reared against the tree and scored the bark all around with its claws. The seven sisters were borne into the sky, and they became the stars of the Big Dipper.

From that moment, and so long as the legend lives, the Kiowas have kinsmen in the night sky. Whatever they were in the mountains, they could be no more. However tenuous their well-being, however much they had suffered and would suffer again, they had found a way out of the wilderness.

My grandmother had a reverence for the sun, a holy regard that now is all but gone out of mankind. There was a wariness in her, and an ancient awe. She was a Christian in her later years, but she had come a long way about, and she never forgot her birthright. As a child she had been to the Sun Dances; she had taken part in those annual rites, and by them she had learned the restoration of her people in the presence of Tai-me. She was about seven when the last Kiowa Sun Dance was held in 1887 on the Washita River above Rainy Mountain Creek. The buffalo were gone. In order to consummate the ancient sacrifice—to impale the head of a buffalo bull upon the medicine tree—a delegation of old men journeyed into Texas, there to beg and barter for an animal from the Goodnight herd. She was ten when the Kiowas came together for the last time as a living Sun Dance culture. They could find no buffalo; they had to hang an old hide from the sacred tree. Before the dance could begin, a company of soldiers rode out from Fort Sill under orders to disperse the tribe. Forbidden without cause the essential act of their faith, having seen the wild herds slaughtered and left to rot upon the ground, the Kiowas backed away forever from the medicine tree. That was July 20, 1890, at the great bend of the Washita. My grandmother was there. Without bitterness, and for as long as she lived, she bore a vision of deicide.

Now that I can have her only in memory, I see my grandmother in the several postures that were peculiar to her: standing at the wood stove on a winter morning and turning meat in a great iron skillet; sitting at the south window, bent above her beadwork, and afterwards, when her vision failed, looking down for a long time into the fold of her hands; going out upon a cane, very slowly as she did when the weight of age came upon her; praying. I remember her most often at prayer. She made long, rambling prayers out of suffering and hope, having seen many things. I was never sure that I had the right to hear, so exclusive were they of all mere custom and company. The last time I saw her she prayed standing by the side of her bed at night, naked to the waist, the light of a kerosene lamp moving upon her dark skin. Her long, black hair, always drawn and braided in the day, lay upon her shoulders and against her breasts like a shawl. I do not speak Kiowa, and I never understood her prayers, but there was something inherently sad in the sound, some merest hesitation upon the syllables of sorrow. She began in a high and descending pitch, exhausting her breath to silence; then again and again—and always the same intensity of effort, of something that is, and is not, like urgency in the human voice. Transported so in the dancing light among the shadows of her room, she seemed beyond the reach of time. But that was illusion; I think I knew then that I should not see her again.

How Do You Respond?

1. Scott Momaday holds his word-camera still to describe the setting, Rainy Mountain. What other devices does he use to give us a sense of place and a sense of his people?

2. Compare how Kazin and Momaday blend narrative and description, and how they focus on one person who links them to a great variety of meanings.

3. Were you surprised when Momaday revealed that he does not speak Kiowa? How does this affect your perception of his story? What does this detail mean in relation to his search for his people's experience?

JOAN DIDION

> From the very first line of "Some Dreamers of the Golden Dream," Joan Didion infuses the scene—California, the golden land—with cheap metals, so that we immediately sense that the land is tarnished. Didion lives in California; she knows the land, the winds, the people—the "big" people like John Wayne, Howard Hughes, Joan Baez—and the "little" people like the Lucille Millers of her essay.

SOME DREAMERS OF THE GOLDEN DREAM

This is a story about love and death in the golden land, and begins with the country. The San Bernardino Valley lies only an hour east of Los Angeles by the San Bernardino Freeway but is in certain ways an alien place: not the coastal California of the subtropical twilights and the soft westerlies off the Pacific but a harsher California, haunted by the Mojave just beyond the mountains, devasted by the hot dry Santa Ana wind that comes down through the passes at 100 miles an hour and whines through the eucalyptus windbreaks and works on the nerves. October is the bad month for the wind, the month when breathing is difficult and the hills blaze up spontaneously. There has been no rain since April. Every voice seems a scream. It is the season of suicide and divorce and prickly dread, wherever the wind blows.

The Mormons settled this ominous country, and then they abandoned it, but by the time they left the first orange tree had been planted and for the next hundred years the San Bernardino Valley would draw a kind of people who imagined they might live among the talismanic fruit and prosper in the dry air, people who brought with them Midwestern ways of building and cooking and praying and who tried to graft those ways upon the land. The graft took in curious ways. This is the California where it is possible to live and die without ever eating an artichoke, without ever meeting a Catholic or a Jew. This is the California where it is easy to Dial-A-Devotion, but hard to buy a book. This is the country in which a belief in the literal interpretation of Genesis has slipped imperceptibly into a belief in the literal interpretation of *Double Indemnity*, the country of the teased hair and the Capris and the girls for whom all life's promise comes down to a waltz-length white wedding dress and the birth of a Kimberly or a Sherry or a Debbi and a Tijuana divorce and a return to hairdressers' school. "We were just crazy kids," they say without regret, and look to the future. The future always looks good in the golden land, because no one remembers the past. Here is where the hot wind blows and the old ways do not seem relevant, where the divorce rate is double the national average and where one person in every thirty-eight lives in a trailer. Here is the last stop for all those who come from somewhere else, for all those who drifted away from the cold and the past and the old ways. Here is where they are trying to find a new life style, trying to find it in the only places they know to look: the movies and the newspapers. The case of Lucille Marie Maxwell Miller is a tabloid monument to that new life style.

Imagine Banyan Street first, because Banyan is where it happened. The way to Banyan is to drive west from San Bernardino out Foothill Boulevard, Route 66: past the Santa Fe switching yards, the Forty Winks Motel. Past the motel that is nineteen stucco tepees: "Sleep in a wigwam—get more for your wampum." Past Fontana Drag City and the Fontana Church of the Nazarene and the Pit Stop A Go-Go; past Kaiser Steel, through Cucamonga, out to the Kapu Kai Restaurant-Bar and Coffee Shop, at the corner of Route 66 and Carnelian Avenue. Up Carnelian Avenue from the Kapu Kai, which means "Forbidden Seas," the subdivision flags whip in the harsh wind. "Half-acre ranches! Snack bars! Travertine entries! $95 down." It is the trail of an intention gone haywire, the flotsam of the New California. But after a while the signs thin out on Carnelian Avenue, and the houses are no longer the bright pastels of the Springtime Home owners but the faded bungalows of the people who grow a few grapes and keep a few chickens out here, and then the hill gets steeper and the road climbs and even the bungalows are few, and here—desolate, roughly surfaced, lined with eucalyptus and lemon groves—is Banyan Street.

Like so much of this country, Banyan suggests something curious and unnatural. The lemon groves are sunken, down a three- or four-foot retaining wall, so that one looks directly into their dense foliage, too lush, unsettlingly glossy, the greenery of nightmare; the fallen eucalyptus bark is too dusty, a place for snakes to breed. The stones look not like natural stones but like the rubble of some unmentioned upheaval. There are smudge pots, and a closed cistern. To one side of Banyan there is the flat valley, and to the other the San Bernardino Mountains, a dark mass looming too high, too fast, nine, ten, eleven thousand feet, right there above the lemon groves. At midnight on Banyan Street there is no light at all, and no sound except the wind in the eucalyptus and a muffled barking of dogs. There may be a kennel somewhere, or the dogs may be coyotes.

Banyan Street was the route Lucille Miller took home from the twenty-four-hour Mayfair Market on the night of October 7, 1964, a night when the moon was dark and the wind was blowing and she was out of milk, and Banyan Street was where, at about 12:20 A.M., her 1964 Volkswagen came to a sudden stop, caught fire, and began to burn. For an hour and fifteen minutes Lucille Miller ran up and down Banyan calling for help, but no cars passed and no help came. At three o'clock that morning, when the fire had been put out and the California Highway Patrol officers were completing their report, Lucille Miller was still sobbing and incoherent, for her husband had been asleep in the Volkswagen. "What will I tell the children, when there's nothing left, nothing left in the casket," she cried to the friend called to comfort her. "How can I tell them there's nothing left?"

In fact there was something left, and a week later it lay in the Draper Mortuary Chapel in a closed bronze coffin blanketed with pink carnations. Some 200 mourners heard Elder Robert E. Denton of the Seventh-Day Adventist Church of Ontario speak of "the temper of fury that has broken out among us." For Gordon Miller, he said, there would be "no more death, no more heartaches, no more misunderstandings." Elder Ansel Bristol mentioned the "peculiar" grief of the hour. Elder Fred Jensen asked "what shall it profit a man, if he shall gain the whole world, and lose his own soul?" A light rain fell, a blessing in a dry season, and a female vocalist sang "Safe in the Arms of Jesus." A tape recording of the service was made for the widow, who was being held without bail in the San Bernardino County Jail on a charge of first-degree murder.

Of course she came from somewhere else, came off the prairie in search of something she had seen in a movie or heard on the radio, for this is a Southern California story. She was born on January 17, 1930, in Winnipeg, Manitoba, the only child of Gordon and Lily Maxwell, both schoolteachers and both dedicated to the Seventh-Day Adventist Church, whose members observe the Sabbath on Saturday, believe in an apocalyptic Second Coming, have a strong missionary tendency, and, if they are strict, do not smoke, drink, eat meat, use makeup, or wear jewelry, including wedding rings. By the time Lucille Maxwell enrolled at Walla Walla College in College Place, Washington, the Adventist school where her parents then taught, she was an eighteen-year-old possessed of unremarkable good looks and remarkable high spirits. "Lucille wanted to see the world," her father would say in retrospect, "and I guess she found out."

The high spirits did not seem to lend themselves to an extended course of study at Walla Walla College, and in the spring of 1949 Lucille Maxwell met and married Gordon ("Cork") Miller, a twenty-four-year-old graduate of Walla Walla and of the Unversity of Oregon dental school, then stationed at Fort Lewis as a medical officer. "Maybe you could say it was love at first sight," Mr. Maxwell recalls. "Before they were ever formally introduced, he sent Lucille a dozen and a half roses with a card that said even if she didn't come out on a date with him, he hoped she'd find the roses pretty anyway." The Maxwells remember their daughter as a "radiant" bride.

Unhappy marriages so resemble one another that we do not need to know too much about the course of this one. There may or may not have been trouble on Guam, where Cork and Lucille Miller lived while he finished his Army duty. There may or may not have been problems in the small Oregon town where he first set up private practice. There appears to have been some disappointment about their move to California: Cork Miller had told friends that he wanted to become a doctor, that he was unhappy as a dentist and planned to enter the Seventh-Day Adventist College of Medical Evangelists at Loma Linda, a few miles south of San Bernardino. Instead he bought a dental practice in the west end of San Bernardino County, and the family settled there, in a modest house on the kind of street where there are always tricycles and revolving credit and dreams about bigger houses, better streets. That was 1957. By the summer of 1964 they had achieved the bigger house on the better street and the familiar accoutrements of a family on its way up: the $30,000 a year, the three children for the Christmas Card, the picture window, the family room, the newspaper photographs showing "Mrs. Gordon Miller, Ontario Heart Fund Chairman. . . ." They were paying the familiar price for it. And they had reached the familiar season of divorce.

It might have been anyone's bad summer, anyone's siege of heat and nerves and migraine and money worries, but this one began particularly early and particularly badly. On April 24 an old friend, Elaine Hayton, died suddenly; Lucille Miller had seen her only the night before. During the month of May, Cork Miller was hospitalized briefly with a bleeding ulcer, and his usual reserve deepened into depression. He told his accountant that he was "sick of looking at open mouths," and threatened suicide. By July 8, the conventional tensions of love and money had reached the conventional impasse in the new house on the acre lot of 8488 Bella Vista, and Lucille Miller filed for divorce. Within a month, however, the Millers seemed reconciled. They saw a marriage counselor. They talked about a fourth child. It seemed that the marriage had reached the traditional truce, the point at which so many resign themselves to cutting both their losses and their hopes.

But the Millers' season of trouble was not to end that easily. October 7 began as a commonplace enough day, one of those days that sets the teeth on edge with its tedium, its small frustrations. The temperature reached 102 degrees in San Bernardino that afternoon, and the Miller children were home from school because of Teachers' Institute. There was ironing to be dropped off. There was a trip to pick up a prescription for Nembutal, a trip to a self-service dry cleaner. In the early evening, an unpleasant accident with the Volkswagen: Cork Miller hit and killed a German shepherd, and afterward said that his head felt "like it had a Mack truck on it." It was something he often said. As of that evening Cork Miller was $63,479 in debt, including the $29,637 mortgage on the new house, a debt load which seemed oppressive to him. He was a man who wore his responsibilities uneasily, and complained of migraine headaches almost constantly.

He ate alone that night, from a TV tray in the living room. Later the Millers watched John Forsythe and Senta Berger in *See How They Run*, and when the movie ended, about eleven, Cork Miller suggested that they go out for milk. He wanted some hot chocolate. He took a blanket and pillow from the couch and climbed into the passenger seat of the Volkswagen. Lucille Miller remembers reaching over to lock his door as she backed down the driveway. By the time she left the Mayfair Market, and long before they reached Banyan Street, Cork Miller appeared to be asleep.

There is some confusion in Lucille Miller's mind about what happened between 12:30 A.M., when the fire broke out, and 1:50 A.M., when it was reported. She says that she was driving east on Banyan Street at about 35 M.P.H. when she felt the Volkswagen pull sharply to the right. The next thing she knew the car was on the embankment, quite near the edge of the retaining wall, and flames were shooting up behind her. She does not remember jumping out. She does remember prying up a stone with which she broke the window next to her husband, and then scrambling down the retaining wall to try to find a stick. "I don't know how I was going to push him out," she says. "I just thought if I had a stick, I'd push him out." She could not, and after a while she ran to the intersection of Banyan and Carnelian Avenue. There are no houses at that corner, and almost no traffic. After one car had passed without stopping, Lucille Miller ran back down Banyan toward the burning Volkswagen. She did not stop, but she slowed down, and in the flames she could see her husband. He was, she said, "just black."

At the first house up Sapphire Avenue, half a mile from the Volkswagen, Lucille Miller finally found help. There Mrs. Robert Swenson called the sheriff, and then, at Lucille Miller's request, she called Harold Lance, the Millers' lawyer and their close friend. When Harold Lance arrived he took Lucille Miller home to his wife, Joan. Twice Harold Lance and Lucille Miller returned to Banyan Street and talked to the Highway Patrol officers. A third time Harold Lance returned alone, and when he came back he said to Lucille Miller, "O.K. . . . you don't talk any more."

When Lucille Miller was arrested the next afternoon, Sandy Slagle was with her. Sandy Slagle was the intense, relentlessly loyal medical student who used to baby-sit for the Millers, and had been living as a member of the family since she graduated from high school in 1959. The Millers took her away from a difficult home situation, and she thinks of Lucille Miller not only as "more or less a mother or a sister" but as "the most wonderful character" she has ever known. On the night of the accident, Sandy Slagle was in her dormitory at Loma Linda Unversity, but Lucille Miller called her early in the morning and asked her to come home. The doctor was there when Sandy Slagle arrived, giving Lucille Miller an injection of Nembutal. "She was crying as she was going under," Sandy Slagle recalls. "Over and over she'd say, 'Sandy, all the hours I spent trying to save him and now what are they trying to *do* to me?'"

At 1:30 that afternoon, Sergeant William Paterson and Detectives Charles Callahan and Joseph Karr of the Central Homicide Division arrived at 8488 Bella Vista. "One of them appeared at the bedroom door," Sandy Slagle remembers, "and said to Lucille, 'You've got ten minutes to get dressed or we'll take you as you are.' She was in her nightgown, you know, so I tried to get her dressed."

Sandy Slagle tells the story now as if by rote, and her eyes do not waver. "So I had her panties and bra on her and they opened the door again, so I got some Capris on her, you know, and a scarf." Her voice drops. "And then they just took her."

The arrest took place just twelve hours after the first report that there had been an accident on Banyan Street, a rapidity which would later prompt Lucille Miller's attorney to say that the entire case was an instance of trying to justify a reckless arrest. Actually what first caused the detectives who arrived on Banyan Street toward dawn that morning to give the accident more than routine attention were certain apparent physical inconsistencies. While Lucille Miller had said that she was driving about 35 M.P.H. when the car swerved to a stop, an examination of the cooling Volkswagen showed that it was in low gear, and that the parking rather than the driving lights were on. The front wheels, moreover, did not seem to be in exactly the position that Lucille Miller's description of the accident would suggest, and the right rear wheel was dug in deep, as if it had been spun in place. It seemed curious to the detectives, too, that a sudden stop from 35 M.P.H.—the same jolt which was presumed to have knocked over a gasoline can in the back seat and somehow started the fire—should have left two milk cartons upright on the back floorboard, and the remains of a Polaroid camera box lying apparently undisturbed on the back seat.

No one, however, could be expected to give a precise account of what did and did not happen in a moment of terror, and none of these inconsistencies seemed in themselves incontrovertible evidence of criminal intent. But they did interest the Sheriff's Office, as did Gordon Miller's apparent unconsciousness at the time of the accident, and the length of time it had taken Lucille Miller to get help. Something, moreover, struck the investigators as wrong about Harold Lance's attitude when he came back to Banyan Street the third time and found the investigation by no means over. "The way Lance was acting," the prosecuting attorney said later, "they thought maybe they'd hit a nerve."

And so it was that on the morning of October 8, even before the doctor had come to give Lucille Miller an injection to calm her, the San Bernardino County Sheriff's Office was trying to construct another version of what might have happened between 12:30 and 1:50 A.M. The hypothesis they would eventually present was based on the somewhat torturous premise that Lucille Miller had undertaken a plan which failed: a plan to stop the car on the lonely road, spread gasoline over her presumably drugged husband, and, with a stick on the accelerator, gently "walk" the Volkswagen over the embankment, where it would tumble four feet down the retaining wall into the lemon grove and almost certainly explode. If this happened, Lucille Miller might then have somehow negotiated the two miles up Carnelian to Bella Vista in time to be home when the accident was discovered. This plan went awry, according to the Sheriff's Office hypothesis, when the car would not go over the rise of the embankment. Lucille Miller might have panicked then—after she had killed the engine the third or fourth time, say, out there on the dark road with the gasoline already spread and the dogs baying and the wind blowing and the unspeakable apprehension that a pair of headlights would suddenly light up Banyan Street and expose her there—and set the fire herself.

Although this version accounts for some of the physical evidence—the car in low because it had been started from a dead stop, the parking lights on because she could not do what needed doing without some light, a rear wheel spun in repeated attempts to get the car over the embankment, the milk cartons upright because there had been no sudden stop—it did not seem on its own any more or less credible than Lucille Miller's own story. Moreover, some of the physical evidence did seem to support her story: a nail in a front tire, a nine-pound rock found in the car presumably the one with which she had broken the window in an attempt to save her husband. Within a few days an autopsy had established that Gordon Miller was alive when he burned, which did not particularly help the State's case, and that he had enough Nembutal and Sandoptal in his blood to put the average person to sleep, which did: on the other hand Gordon Miller habitually took both Nembutal and Fiorinal (a common headache prescription which contains Sandoptal), and had been ill besides.

It was a spotty case, and to make it work at all the State was going to have to find a motive. There was talk of unhappiness, talk of another man. That kind of motive, during the next few weeks, was what they set out to establish. They set out to find it in accountants' ledgers and double-indemnity clauses and motel registers, set out to determine what might move a woman who believed in all the promises of the middle class—a woman who had been chairman of the Heart Fund and who always knew a reasonable little dressmaker and who had come out of the bleak wild of prairie fundamentalism to find what she imagined to be the good life— what should drive such a woman to sit on a street called Bella Vista and look out her new picture window into the empty California sun and calculate how to burn her husband alive in a Volkswagen. They found the wedge they wanted closer at hand than they might have at first expected, for, as testimony would reveal later at the trial, it seemed that in December of 1963 Lucille Miller had begun an affair with the husband of one of her friends, a man whose daughter called her "Auntie Lucille," a man who might have seemed to have the gift for people and money and the good life that Cork Miller so noticeably lacked. The man was Arthwell Hayton, a well-known San Bernardino attorney and at one time a member of the district attorney's staff.

In some ways it was the conventional clandestine affair in a place like San Bernardino, a place where little is bright or graceful, where it is routine to misplace the future and easy to start looking for it in bed. Over the seven weeks that it would take to try Lucille Miller for murder, Assistant District Attorney Don A. Turner and defense attorney Edward P. Foley would between them unfold a curiously predictable story. There were the falsified motel registrations. There were the lunch dates, the afternoon drives in Arthwell Hayton's red Cadillac convertible. There were the interminable discussions of the wronged partners. There were the confidantes ("I knew everything," Sandy Slagle would insist fiercely later. "I knew every time, places, everything") and there were the words remembered from bad magazine stories ("Don't kiss me, it will trigger things," Lucille Miller remembered telling Arthwell Hayton in the parking lot of Harold's Club in Fontana after lunch one day) and there were the notes, the sweet exchanges: "Hi Sweetie Pie! You are my cup of tea!! Happy Birthday—you don't look a day over 29!! Your baby, Arthwell."

And, toward the end, there was the acrimony. It was April 24, 1964, when Arthwell Hayton's wife, Elaine, died suddenly, and nothing good happened after that. Arthwell Hayton had taken his cruiser, *Captain's Lady*, over to Catalina that weekend; he called home at nine o'clock Friday night, but did not talk to his wife because Lucille Miller answered the telephone and said that Elaine was showering. The next morning the Haytons' daughter found her mother in bed, dead. The newspapers reported the death as accidental, perhaps the result of an allergy to hair spray. When Arthwell Hayton flew home from Catalina that weekend, Lucille Miller met him at the airport, but the finish had already been written.

It was in the breakup that the affair ceased to be in the conventional mode and began to resemble instead the novels of James M. Cain, the movies of the late 1930s, all the dreams in which violence and threats and blackmail are made to seem commonplaces of middle-class life. What was most startling about the case that the State of California was preparing against Lucille Miller was something that had nothing to do with law at all, something that never appeared in the eight-column afternoon headlines but was always there between them: the revelation that the dream was teaching the dreamers how to live. Here is Lucille Miller talking to her lover sometime in the early summer of 1964, after he had indicated that, on the advice of his minister, he did not intend to see her any more: "First, I'm going to go to that dear pastor of yours and tell him a few things. . . . When I do tell him that, you won't be in the Redlands Church any more. . . . Look, Sonny Boy, if you think your reputation is going to be ruined, your life won't be worth two cents." Here is Arthwell Hayton, to Lucille Miller: "I'll go to Sheriff Frank Bland and tell him some things that I know about you until you'll wish you'd never heard of Arthwell Hayton." For an affair between a Seventh-Day Adventist dentist's wife and a Seventh-Day Adventist personal-injury lawyer, it seems a curious kind of dialogue.

"Boy, I could get that little boy coming and going," Lucille Miller later confided to Erwin Sprengle, a Riverside contractor who was a business partner of Arthwell Hayton's and a friend to both the lovers. (Friend or no, on this occasion he happened to have an induction coil attached to his telephone in order to tape Lucille Miller's call.) "And he hasn't got one thing on me that he can prove. I mean, I've got concrete—he has nothing concrete." In the same taped conversation with Erwin Sprengle, Lucille Miller mentioned a tape that she herself had surreptitiously made, months before, in Arthwell Hayton's car.

"I said to him, I said 'Arthwell, I just feel like I'm being used.' . . . He started sucking his thumb and he said 'I love you. . . . This isn't something that happened yesterday. I'd marry you tomorrow if I could. I don't love Elaine.' He'd love to hear that played back, wouldn't he?"

"Yeah," drawled Sprengle's voice on the tape. "That would be just a little incriminating, wouldn't it?"

"Just a *little* incriminating," Lucille Miller agreed. "It really *is*."

Later on the tape, Sprengle asked where Cork Miller was.

"He took the children down to the church."

"You didn't go?"

"No."

"You're naughty."

It was all, moreover, in the name of "love"; everyone involved placed a magical faith in the efficacy of the very word. There was the significance that Lucille Miller saw in Arthwell's saying that he "loved" her, that he did not "love" Elaine. There was Arthwell insisting, later, at the trial, that he had never said it, that he may have "whispered sweet nothings in her ear" (as her defense hinted that he had whispered in many ears), but he did not remember bestowing upon her the special seal, saying the word, declaring "love." There was the summer evening when Lucille Miller and Sandy Slagle followed Arthwell Hayton down to his new boat in its mooring at Newport Beach and untied the lines with Arthwell aboard, Arthwell and a girl with whom he later testified he was drinking hot chocolate and watching television. "I did that on purpose," Lucille Miller told Erwin Sprengle later, "to save myself from letting my heart do something crazy."

January 11, 1965, was a bright warm day in Southern California, the kind of day when Catalina floats on the Pacific horizon and the air smells of orange blossoms and it is a long way from the bleak and difficult East, a long way from the cold, a long way from the past. A woman in Hollywood staged an all-night sit-in on the hood of her car to prevent repossession by a finance company. A seventy-year-old pensioner drove his station wagon at five miles an hour past three Gardena poker parlors and emptied three pistols and a twelve-gauge shotgun through their windows, wounding twenty-nine people. "Many young women became prostitutes just to have enough money to play cards," he explained in a note. Mrs. Nick Adams said that she was "not surprised" to hear her husband announce his divorce plans on the Les Crane Show, and, farther north, a sixteen-year-old jumped off the Golden Gate Bridge and lived.

And, in the San Bernardino County Courthouse, the Miller trial opened. The crowds were so bad that the glass courtroom doors were shattered in the crush, and from then on identification disks were issued to the first forty-three spectators in line. The line began forming at 6 A.M., and college girls camped at the courthouse all night, with stores of graham crackers and No-Cal.

All they were doing was picking a jury, those first few days, but the sensational nature of the case had already suggested itself. Early in December there had been an abortive first trial, a trial at which no evidence was ever presented because on the day the jury was seated the San Bernardino *Sun-Telegram* ran an "inside" story quoting Assistant District Attorney Dan Turner, the prosecutor, as saying, "We are looking into the circumstances of Mrs. Hayton's death. In view of the current trial concerning the death of Dr. Miller, I do not feel I should comment on Mrs. Hayton's death." It seemed that there had been barbiturates in Elaine Hayton's blood, and there had seemed some irregularity about the way she was dressed on that morning when she was found under the covers, dead. Any doubts about the death at the time, however, had never gotten as far as the Sheriff's Office. "I guess somebody didn't want to rock the boat," Turner said later. "These were prominent people."

Although all of that had not been in the *Sun-Telegram's* story, an immediate mistrial had been declared. Almost as immediately, there had been another development: Arthwell Hayton had asked newspapermen to an 11 A.M. Sunday morning press conference in his office. There had been television cameras, and flash bulbs popping. "As you gentlemen may know," Hayton had said, striking a note of stiff bonhomie, "there are very often women who become amorous toward their doctor or lawyer. This does not mean on the physician's or lawyer's part that there is any romance toward the patient or client."

"Would you deny that you were having an affair with Mrs. Miller?" a reporter had asked.

"I would deny that there was any romance on my part whatsoever."

It was a distinction he would maintain through all the wearing weeks to come.

So they had come to see Arthwell, these crowds who now milled beneath the dusty palms outside the courthouse, and they had also come to see Lucille, who appeared as a slight, intermittently pretty woman, already pale from lack of sun, a woman who would turn thirty-five before the trial was over and whose tendency toward haggardness was beginning to show, a meticulous woman who insisted, against her lawyer's advice, on coming to court with her hair piled high and lacquered. "I would've been happy if she'd come in with it hanging loose, but Lucille wouldn't do that," her lawyer said. He was Edward P. Foley, a small, emotional Irish Catholic who several times wept in the courtroom. "She has a great honesty, this woman," he added, "but this honesty about her appearance always worked against her."

By the time the trial opened, Lucille Miller's appearance included maternity clothes, for an official examination on December 18 had revealed that she was then three and a half months pregnant, a fact which made picking a jury even more difficult than usual, for Turner was asking the death penalty. "It's unfortunate but there it is," he would say of the pregnancy to each juror in turn, and finally twelve were seated, seven of them women, the youngest forty-one, an assembly of the very peers—housewives, a machinist, a truck driver, a grocery-store manager, a filing clerk—above whom Lucille Miller had wanted so badly to rise.

That was the sin, more than the adultery, which tended to reinforce the one for which she was being tried. It was implicit in both the defense and the prosecution that Lucille Miller was an erring woman, a woman who perhaps wanted too much. But to the prosecution she was not merely a woman who would want a new house and want to go to parties and run up high telephone bills ($1,152 in ten months), but a woman who would go so far as to murder her husband for his $80,000 in insurance, making it appear an accident in order to collect another $40,000 in double indemnity and straight accident policies. To Turner she was a woman who did not want simply her freedom and a reasonable alimony (she could have had that, the defense contended, by going through with her divorce suit), but wanted everything, a woman motivated by "love and greed." She was a "manipulator." She was a "user of people."

To Edward Foley, on the other hand, she was an impulsive woman who "couldn't control her foolish little heart." Where Turner skirted the pregnancy, Foley dwelt upon it, even calling the dead man's mother down from Washington to testify that her son had told her they were going to have another baby because Lucille felt that it would "do much to weld our home again in the pleasant relations that we used to have." Where the prosecution saw a "calculator," the defense saw a "blabbermouth," and in fact Lucille Miller did emerge as an ingenuous conversationalist. Just as, before her husband's death, she had confided in her friends about her love affair, so she chatted about it after his death, with the arresting sergeant. "Of course Cork lived with it for years, you know," her voice was heard to tell Sergeant Paterson on a tape made the morning after her arrest. "After Elaine died, he pushed the panic button one night and just asked me right out, and that, I think, was when he really— the first time he really faced it." When the sergeant asked why she had agreed to talk to him, against the specific instructions of her lawyers, Lucille Miller said airily, "Oh, I've always been basically quite an honest person. . . . I mean I can put a hat in the cupboard and say it cost ten dollars less, but basically I've always kind of just lived my life the way I wanted to, and if you don't like it you can take off."

The prosecution hinted at men other than Arthwell, and even, over Foley's objections, managed to name one. The defense called Miller suicidal. The prosecution produced experts who said that the Volkswagen fire could not been accidental. Foley produced witnesses who said that it could have been. Lucille's father, now a junior-high school teacher in Oregon, quoted Isaiah to reporters: *"Every tongue that shall rise against thee in judgment thou shalt condemn."* "Lucille did wrong, her affair," her mother said judiciously. "With her it was love. But with some I guess it's just passion." There was Debbie, the Millers' fourteen-year-old, testifying in a steady voice about how she and her mother had gone to a supermarket to buy the gasoline can the week before the accident. There was Sandy Slagle, in the courtroom every day, declaring that on at least one occasion Lucille Miller had prevented her husband not only from committing suicide but from committing suicide in such a way that it would appear an accident and ensure the double-indemnity payment. There was Wenche Berg, the pretty twenty-seven-year-old Norwegian governess to Arthwell Hayton's children, testifying that Arthwell had instructed her not to allow Lucille Miller to see or talk to the children.

Two months dragged by, and the headlines never stopped. Southern California's crime reporters were headquartered in San Bernardino for the duration: Howard Hertel from the *Times,* Jim Bennett and Eddy Jo Bernal from the *Herald-Examiner.* Two months in which the Miller trial was pushed off the *Examiner's* front page only by the Academy Award nominations and Stan Laurel's death. And finally, on March 2, after Turner had reiterated that it was a case of "love and greed," and Foley had protested that his client was being tried for adultery, the case went to the jury.

They brought in the verdict, guilty of murder in the first degree, at 4:50 P.M. on March 5. "She didn't do it," Debbie Miller cried, jumping up from the spectators' section. "She didn't *do* it." Sandy Slagle collapsed in her seat and began to scream. "Sandy, for God's sake please *don't,"* Lucille Miller said in a voice that carried across the courtroom, and Sandy Slagle was momentarily subdued. But as the jurors left the courtroom she screamed again: "You're murderers. . . . Every last one of you is a *murderer."* Sheriff's deputies moved in then, each wearing a string tie that read "1965 SHERIFF'S Rodeo," and Lucille Miller's father, the sad-faced junior-high-school teacher who believed in the word of Christ and the dangers of wanting to see the world, blew her a kiss off his fingertips.

The California Institution for Women at Frontera, where Lucille Miller is now, lies down where Euclid Avenue turns into country road, not too many miles from where she once lived and shopped and organized the Heart Fund Ball. Cattle graze across the road, and Rainbirds sprinkle the alfalfa. Frontera has a softball field and tennis courts, and looks as if it might be a California junior college, except that the trees are not yet high enough to conceal the concertina wire around the top of the Cyclone fence. On visitors' day there are big cars in the parking area, big Buicks and Pontiacs that belong to grandparents and sisters and fathers (not many of them belong to husbands), and some of them have bumper stickers that say "Support Your Local Police."

A lot of California murderesses live here, a lot of girls who somehow misunderstood the promise. Don Turner put Sandra Garner here (and her husband in the gas chamber at San Quentin) after the 1959 desert killings known to crime reporters as "the soda-pop murders." Carole Tregoff is here, and has been ever since she was convicted of conspiring to murder Dr. Finch's wife in West Covina, which is not too far from San Bernardino. Carole Tregoff is in fact a nurse's aide in the prison hospital, and might have attended Lucille Miller had her baby been born at Frontera; Lucille Miller chose instead to have it outside, and paid for the guard who stood outside the delivery room in St. Bernardine's Hospital. Debbie Miller came to take the baby home from the hospital, in a white dress with pink ribbons, and Debbie was allowed to choose a name. She named the baby Kimi Kai. The children live with Harold and Joan Lance now, because Lucille Miller will probably spend ten years at Frontera. Don Turner waived his original request for the death penalty (it was generally agreed that he had demanded it only, in Edward Foley's words, "to get anybody with the slightest trace of human kindness in their veins off the jury"), and settled for life imprisonment with the possibility of parole. Lucille Miller does not like it at Frontera, and has had trouble adjusting. "She's going to have to learn humility," Turner says. "She's going to have to use her ability to charm, to manipulate."

The new house is empty now, the house on the street with the sign that says

> Private Road
> Bella Vista
> Dead End

The Millers never did get it landscaped, and weeds grow up around the fieldstone siding. The television aerial has toppled on the roof, and a trash can is stuffed with the debris of family life: a cheap suitcase, a child's game called "Lie Detector." There is a sign on what would have been the lawn, and the sign reads "ESTATE SALE." Edward Foley is trying to get Lucille Miller's case appealed, but there have been delays. "A trial always comes down to a matter of sympathy," Foley says wearily now. "I couldn't create sympathy for her." Everyone is a little weary now, weary and resigned, everyone except Sandy Slagle, whose bitterness is still raw. She lives in an apartment near the medical school in Loma Linda, and studies reports of the case in *True Police Cases* and *Official Detective Stories*. "I'd much rather we not talk about the Hayton business too much," she tells visitors, and she keeps a tape recorder running. "I'd rather talk about Lucille and what a wonderful person she is and how her rights were violated." Harold Lance does not talk to visitors at all. "We don't want to give away what we can sell," he explains pleasantly; an attempt was made to sell Lucille Miller's personal story to *Life,* but *Life* did not want to buy it. In the district attorney's offices they are prosecuting other murders now, and do not see why the Miller trial attracted so much attention. "It wasn't a very interesting murder as murders go," Don Turner says laconically. Elaine Hayton's death is no longer under investigation. "We know everything we want to know," Turner says.

Arthwell Hayton's office is directly below Edward Foley's. Some people around San Bernardino say that Arthwell Hayton suffered; others say that he did not suffer at all. Perhaps he did not, for time past is not believed to have any bearing upon time present or future, out in the golden land where every day the world is born anew. In any case, on October 17, 1965, Arthwell Hayton married again, married his children's pretty governess, Wenche Berg, at a service in the Chapel of the Roses at a retirement village near Riverside. Later the newlyweds were feted at a reception for seventy-five in the dining room of Rose Garden Village. The bridegroom was in black tie, with a white carnation in his buttonhole. The bride wore a long white *peau de soie* dress and carried a shower bouquet of sweetheart roses with stephanotis streamers. A coronet of seed pearls held her illusion veil.

HOW DO YOU RESPOND?

1. Throughout Didion's essay, she parades details before us—people, places, a culture, a time in history. What is Didion *saying* about her

dreamers? What effect does place have on these people in the golden land?

2. Didion writes, ". . . Banyan is where it happened." Can you find an antecedent, a referent, for *it*? How does Didion's use of this pronoun affect the reader?

3. Compare and contrast Didion's focus on an individual with the treatment of individuals in the essays of Momaday, Kazin, and Selzer.

WILLIAM FAULKNER

> *William Faulkner (1897–1967) was one of the most inventive and courageous prose writers of this century. After decades of incomprehension, readers slowly learned not to be afraid of his sentences' convolutions and involutions and began to hear an irresistible and obsessive prose—a prose dedicated to remembering, to digging over the complexities of the past—both the personal and family past, and the regional and national past. His vision of life is emphatically tragic, but he is never merely bleak; he gives us a rich and resonant music that carries with it an indefeasible human energy.* The Sound and the Fury, The Bear, *and* Absalom, Absalom *offer good ways of getting to know Faulkner's writing.*

A ROSE FOR EMILY

I

When Miss Emily Grierson died, our whole town went to her funeral: the men through a sort of respectful affection for a fallen monument, the women mostly out of curiosity to see the inside of her house, which no one save an old manservant—a combined gardener and cook—had seen in at least ten years.

It was a big, squarish frame house that had once been white, decorated with cupolas and spires and scrolled balconies in the heavily lightsome style of the seventies, set on what had once been our most select street. But garages and cotton gins had encroached and obliterated even the august names of that neighborhood; only Miss Emily's house was left, lifting its stubborn and coquettish decay above the cotton wagons and the gasoline pumps—an eyesore among eyesores. And now Miss Emily had gone to join the representatives of those august names where they lay in the cedar-bemused cemetery among the ranked and anonymous graves of Union and Confederate soldiers who fell at the battle of Jefferson.

Alive, Miss Emily had been a tradition, a duty, and a care; a sort of hereditary obligation upon the town, dating from that day in 1894 when Colonel Sartoris, the mayor—he who fathered the edict that no Negro woman should appear on the streets without an apron—remitted her taxes, the dispensation dating from the death of her father on into perpetuity. Not that Miss Emily would have accepted charity. Colonel Sartoris invented an involved tale to the effect that Miss Emily's father had loaned money to the town, which the town, as a matter of business, preferred this way of repaying. Only a man of Colonel Sartoris' generation and thought could have invented it, and only a woman could have believed it.

When the next generation, with its more modern ideas, became mayors and aldermen, this arrangement created some little dissatisfaction. On the first of the year they mailed her a tax notice. February came, and there was no reply. They wrote her a formal letter, asking her to call at the sheriff's office at her convenience. A week later the mayor wrote her himself, offering to call or to send his car for her, and received in reply a note on paper of an archaic shape, in a thin, flowing calligraphy in faded ink, to the effect that she no longer went out at all. The tax notice was also enclosed, without comment.

They called a special meeting of the Board of Aldermen. A deputation waited upon her, knocked at the door through which no visitor had passed since she ceased giving china-painting lessons eight or ten years earlier. They were admitted by the old Negro into a dim hall from which a staircase mounted into still more shadow. It smelled of dust and disuse—a close, dank smell. The Negro led them into the parlor. It was furnished in heavy, leather-covered furniture. When the Negro opened the blinds of one window, a faint dust rose sluggishly about their thighs, spinning with slow motes in the single sun-ray. On a tarnished gilt easel before the fireplace stood a crayon portrait of Miss Emily's father.

They rose when she entered—a small, fat woman in black, with a thin gold chain descending to her waist and vanishing into her belt, leaning on an ebony cane with a tarnished gold head. Her skeleton was small and spare; perhaps that was why what would have been merely plumpness in another was obesity in her. She looked bloated, like a body long submerged in motionless water, and of that pallid hue. Her eyes, lost in the fatty ridges of her face, looked like two small pieces of coal pressed into a lump of dough as they moved from one face to another while the visitors stated their errand.

She did not ask them to sit. She just stood in the door and listened quietly until the spokesman came to a stumbling halt. Then they could hear the invisible watch ticking at the end of the gold chain.

Her voice was dry and cold. "I have no taxes in Jefferson. Colonel Sartoris explained it to me. Perhaps one of you can gain access to the city records and satisfy yourselves."

"But we have. We are the city authorities, Miss Emily. Didn't you get a notice from the sheriff, signed by him?"

"I received a paper, yes," Miss Emily said. "Perhaps he considers himself the sheriff. . . . I have no taxes in Jefferson."

"But there is nothing on the books to show that, you see. We must go by the—"

"See Colonel Sartoris. I have no taxes in Jefferson."

"But, Miss Emily—"

"See Colonel Sartoris." (Colonel Sartoris had been dead almost ten years.) "I have no taxes in Jefferson. Tobe!" The Negro appeared. "Show these gentlemen out."

II

So she vanquished them, horse and foot, just as she had vanquished their fathers thirty years before about the smell. That was two years after her father's death and a short time after her sweetheart—the one we believed would marry her—had deserted her. After her father's death she went out very little; after her sweetheart went away, people hardly saw her at all. A few of the ladies had the temerity to call, but were not received, and the only sign of life about the place was the Negro man—a young man then—going in and out with a market basket.

"Just as if a man—any man—could keep a kitchen properly," the ladies said; so they were not surprised when the smell developed. It was another link between the gross, teeming world and the high and mighty Griersons.

A neighbor, a woman, complained to the mayor, Judge Stevens, eighty years old.

"But what will you have me do about it, madam?" he said.

"Why, send her word to stop it," the woman said. "Isn't there a law?"

"I'm sure that won't be necessary," Judge Stevens said. "It's probably just a snake or a rat that nigger of hers killed in the yard. I'll speak to him about it."

The next day he received two more complaints, one from a man who came in diffident deprecation. "We really must do something about it, Judge. I'd be the last one in the world to bother Miss Emily, but we've got to do something." That night the Board of Aldermen met—three gray-beards and one younger man, a member of the rising generation.

"It's simple enough," he said. "Send her word to have her place cleaned up. Give her a certain time to do it in, and if she don't . . ."

"Dammit, sir," Judge Stevens said, "will you accuse a lady to her face of smelling bad?"

So the next night, after midnight, four men crossed Miss Emily's lawn and slunk about the house like burglars, sniffing along the base of the brickwork and at the cellar openings while one of them performed a regular sowing motion with his hand out of a sack slung from his shoulder. They broke open the cellar door and sprinkled lime there, and in all the out-buildings. As they recrossed the lawn, a window that had been dark was lighted and Miss Emily sat in it, the light behind her, and her upright torso motionless as that of an idol. They crept quietly across the lawn and into the shadow of the locusts that lined the street. After a week or two the smell went away.

That was when people had begun to feel really sorry for her. People in our town remembering how old lady Wyatt, her great-aunt, had gone completely crazy at last, believed that the Griersons held themselves a little too high for what they really were. None of the young men were quite good enough for Miss Emily and such. We had long thought of them as a tableau; Miss Emily a slender figure in white in the background, her father a spraddled silhouette in the foreground, his back to her and clutching a horsewhip, the two of them framed by the back-flung front door. So when she got to be thirty and was still single, we were not pleased exactly, but vindicated; even with insanity in the family she wouldn't have turned down all of her chances if they had really materialized.

When her father died, it got about that the house was all that was left to her; and in a way, people were glad. At last they could pity Miss Emily. Being left alone, and a pauper, she had become humanized. Now she too would know the old thrill and the old despair of a penny more or less.

The day after his death all the ladies prepared to call at the house and offer condolence and aid, as is our custom. Miss Emily met them at the door, dressed as usual and with no trace of grief on her face. She told them that her father was not dead. She did that for three days, with the ministers calling on her, and the doctors, trying to persuade her to let them dispose of the body. Just as they were about to resort to law and force, she broke down, and they buried her father quickly.

We did not say she was crazy then. We believed she had to do that. We remembered all the young men her father had driven away, and we knew that with nothing left, she would have to cling to that which had robbed her, as people will.

III

She was sick for a long time. When we saw her again, her hair was cut short, making her look like a girl, with a vague resemblance to those angels in colored church windows—sort of tragic and serene.

The town had just let the contracts for paving the sidewalks, and in the summer after her father's death they began to work. The construction company came with niggers and mules and machinery, and a foreman named Homer Barron, a Yankee—a big, dark, ready man with a big voice and eyes lighter than his face. The little boys would follow in groups to hear him cuss the niggers, and the niggers singing in time to the rise and fall of picks. Pretty soon he knew everybody in town. Whenever you heard a lot of laughing anywhere about the square, Homer Barron would be in the center of the group. Presently we began to see him and Miss Emily on Sunday afternoons driving in the yellow-wheeled buggy and the matched team of bays from the livery stable.

At first we were glad that Miss Emily would have an interest, because the ladies all said, "Of course a Grierson would not think seriously of a Northerner, a day laborer." But there were still others, older people, who said that even grief could not cause a real lady to forget *noblesse oblige*—without calling it *noblesse oblige*. They just said, "Poor Emily. Her kinsfolk should come to her." She had some kin in Alabama; but years ago her father had fallen out with them over the estate of old lady Wyatt, the crazy woman, and there was no communication between the two families. They had not even been represented at the funeral.

And as soon as the old people said, "Poor Emily," the whispering began. "Do you suppose it's really so?" they said to one another. "Of course it is. What else could . . ." This behind their hands, rustling of craned silk and satin behind jalousies closed upon the sun of Sunday afternoon as the thin, swift clop-clop-clop of the matched team passed: "Poor Emily."

She carried her head high enough—even when we believed that she was fallen. It was as if she demanded more than ever the recognition of her dignity as the last Grierson; as if it had wanted that touch of earthiness to reaffirm her imperviousness. Like when she bought the rat poison, the arsenic. That was over a year after they had begun to say "Poor Emily," and while the two female cousins were visiting her.

"I want some poison," she said to the druggist. She was over thirty then, still a slight woman, though thinner than usual, with cold haughty black eyes in a face the flesh of which was strained across the temples and about the eyesockets as you imagine a lighthouse-keeper's face ought to look. "I want some poison," she said.

"Yes, Miss Emily. What kind? For rats and such? I'd recom—"

"I want the best you have. I don't care what kind."

The druggist named several. "They'll kill anything up to an elephant. But what you want is—"

"Arsenic," Miss Emily said. "Is that a good one?"

"Is . . . arsenic? Yes ma'am. But what you want—"

"I want arsenic."

The druggist looked down at her. She looked back at him, erect, her face like a strained flag. "Why, of course," the druggist said. "If that's what you want. But the law requires you to tell what you are going to use it for."

Miss Emily just stared at him, her head tilted back in order to look him eye for eye, until he looked away and went and got the arsenic and wrapped it up. The Negro delivery boy brought her the package; the druggist didn't come back. When she opened the package at home there was written on the box, under the skull and bones: "For rats."

IV

So the next day we all said, "She will kill herself"; and we said it would be the best thing. When she had first begun to be seen with Homer Barron, we had said, "She will marry him." Then we said, "She will persuade him yet," because Homer himself had remarked—he liked men, and it was known that he drank with the younger men in the Elk's Club—that he was not a marrying man. Later we said, "Poor Emily," behind the jalousies as they passed on Sunday afternoon in the glittering buggy, Miss Emily with her head high and Homer Barron with his hat cocked and a cigar in his teeth, reins and whip in a yellow glove.

Then some of the ladies began to say that it was a disgrace to the town and a bad example to the young people. The men did not want to interfere, but at last the ladies forced the Baptist minister—Miss Emily's people were Episcopal—to call upon her. He would never divulge what happened during that interview, but he refused to go back again. The next Sunday they again drove about the streets, and the following day the minister's wife wrote to Miss Emily's relations in Alabama.

So she had blood-kin under her roof again and we sat back to watch developments. At first nothing happened. Then we were sure that they were to be married. We learned that Miss Emily had been to the jeweler's and ordered a man's toilet set in silver, with the letters H. B. on each piece. Two days later we learned that she had bought a complete outfit of men's clothing, including a nightshirt, and we said, "They are married." We were really glad. We were glad because the two female cousins were even more Grierson than Miss Emily had ever been.

So we were surprised when Homer Barron—the streets had been finished some time since—was gone. We were a little disappointed that there was not a public blowing-off, but we believed that he had gone on to prepare for Miss Emily's coming, or to give a chance to get rid of the cousins. (By that time it was a cabal, and we were all Miss Emily's allies to help circumvent the cousins.) Sure enough, after another week they departed. And, as we had expected all along, within three days Homer Barron was back in town. A neighbor saw the Negro man admit him at the kitchen door at dusk one evening.

And that was the last we saw of Homer Barron. And of Miss Emily for some time. The Negro man went in and out with the market basket, but the front door remained closed. Now and then we would see her at a window for a moment, as the men did that night when they sprinkled the lime, but for almost six months she did not appear on the streets. Then we knew that this was to be expected too; as if that quality of her father which had thwarted her woman's life so many times had been too virulent and too furious to die.

When we next saw Miss Emily, she had grown fat and her hair was turning gray. During the next few years it grew grayer and grayer until it attained an even pepper-and-salt iron-gray, when it ceased turning. Up to the day of her death at seventy-four it was still that vigorous iron-gray, like the hair of an active man.

From that time on her front door remained closed, save for a period of six or seven years, when she was about forty, during which she gave lessons in china-painting. She fitted up a studio in one of the downstairs rooms, where the daughters and granddaughters of Colonel Sartoris' contemporaries were sent to her with the same regularity and in the same spirit that they were sent on Sundays with a twenty-five cent piece for the collection plate. Meanwhile her taxes had been remitted.

Then the newer generation became the backbone and the spirit of the town, and the painting pupils grew up and fell away and did not send their children to her with boxes of color and tedious brushes and pictures cut from the ladies' magazines. The front door closed upon the last one and remained closed for good. When the town got free postal delivery Miss Emily alone refused to let them fasten the metal numbers above her door and attach a mailbox to it. She would not listen to them.

Daily, monthly, yearly we watched the Negro grow grayer and more stooped, going in and out with the market basket. Each December we sent her a tax notice, which would be returned by the post office a week later, unclaimed. Now and then we would see her in one of the downstairs windows—she had evidently shut up the top floor of the house—like the carven torso of an idol in a niche, looking or not looking at us, we could never tell which. Thus she passed from generation to generation—dear, inescapable, impervious, tranquil, and perverse.

And so she died. Fell ill in the house filled with dust and shadows, with only a doddering Negro man to wait on her. We did not even know she was sick; we had long since given up trying to get any information from the Negro. He talked to no one, probably not even to her, for his voice had grown harsh and rusty, as if from disuse.

She died in one of the downstairs rooms, in a heavy walnut bed with a curtain, her gray head propped on a pillow yellow and moldy with age and lack of sunlight.

V

The Negro met the first of the ladies at the front door and let them in, with their hushed, sibilant voices and their quick, curious glances, and then he disappeared. He walked right through the house and out the back and was not seen again.

The two female cousins came at once. They held the funeral on the second day, with the town coming to look at Miss Emily beneath a mass of bought flowers, with the crayon face of her father musing profoundly above the bier and the ladies sibilant and macabre; and the very old men—some in their brushed Confederate uniforms—on the porch and the lawn, talking of Miss Emily as if she had been a contemporary of theirs, believing that they had danced with her and courted her perhaps, confusing time with its mathematical progression, as the old do, to whom all the past is not a diminishing road, but, instead, a huge meadow which no winter ever quite touches, divided from them now by the narrow bottleneck of the most recent decade of years.

Already we knew that there was one room in the region above stairs which no one had seen in forty years, and which would have to be forced. They waited until Miss Emily was decently in the ground before they opened it.

The violence of breaking down the door seemed to fill this room with pervading dust. A thin, acrid pall as of the tomb seemed to lie everywhere upon this room decked and furnished as for a bridal: upon the valance curtains of faded rose color, upon the rose-shaded lights, upon the dressing table, upon the delicate array of crystal and the man's toilet things backed with tarnished silver, silver so tarnished that the monogram was obscured. Among them lay a collar and tie, as if they had just been removed, which, lifted, left upon the surface a pale crescent in the dust. Upon a chair hung the suit, carefully folded; beneath it the two mute shoes and the discarded socks.

The man himself lay in the bed.

For a long while we just stood there, looking down at the profound and fleshless grin. The body had apparently once lain in the attitude of an embrace, but now the long sleep that outlasts love, that conquers even the grimace of love, had cuckolded him. What was left of him, rotted beneath what was left of the nightshirt, had become inextricable from the bed in which he lay; and upon him and upon the pillow beside him lay that even coating of the patient and biding dust.

Then we noticed that in the second pillow was the indentation of a head. One of us lifted something from it, and leaning forward, that faint and invisible dust dry and acrid in the nostrils, we saw a long strand of iron-gray hair.

How Do You Respond?

1. Emily Grierson has little money and few allies, but she is presented as a person of considerable power. Wherein does her power reside? How does she express it?

2. Faulkner does not offer explicit evaluative statements about Emily; rather, he offers details for us to interpret. From Faulkner's description, write an explicit evaluation of Emily's character.

3. The last phrase in the story is resonant with implications. How has Faulkner prepared us for it?

FOCUS ON YOUR READING

1. Compare Kazin, Momaday, and Didion. How would you characterize the forms they use in their writings? How do they work with description? Do you notice narratives? Contrasts? Discuss how they blend forms; how narrative is not divorced from description, and so on.

2. How would you characterize David Bird's point of view, his attitudes toward the homeless people in Grand Central Station? How would you characterize Selzer's attitude towards Kooch? The narrator's attitude toward Emily in "A Rose for Emily?" Didion's point of view toward Lucille Miller and the other "dreamers" in "Some Dreamers of the Golden Dream"?

3. How does Kazin take us on a journey through the kitchen of his childhood. What do his eyes focus on? How does Momaday take us to Rainy Mountain? Didion to California? Observe closely how these writers realize—"make real"—a scene, a person, a situation. When are their word-cameras still, when are they moving?

4. David Bird begins his profile with a description of Madeline; Barbara Meyer begins with a bald statement: "Stitch Drewniany died Sunday." Notice how each writer begins to describe a person. Compare and characterize the beginnings in these writings about people.

FOCUS ON YOUR WRITING

1. Write a "snapshot" description of a person or place, in which you reveal a clear, definite point of view toward your subject. You may do so explicitly—writing evaluative statements—or you may do so implicitly—selecting details that reveal your point of view.

2. Write a "moving picture" of a place, in which you take a reader along with you as you move into and through a new place. Reveal your attitude toward the place, explicitly or implicitly or both.

3. Follow the example of the passages about the smoking car (p. 215), and write two brief pieces where you use the same set of facts and represent them from two differing points of view.

4. Write a reflective piece, following the pattern of Selzer's "The Masked Marvel's Last Toehold" and Barbara Meyer's "Death Gives Life to Fond Memories," using a present situation to evoke the past.

5. Write about the place where you grew up. In what ways has it affected your values, your ways of looking at things? Keep in mind the use of particular details in Kazin's essay. He says, for instance, that the kitchen was the center of his household. Did your home hold such a center?

CHAPTER 7

❖ ❖

"A Horse Is a Graminivorous Quadruped"

DEFINING

"When I use a word," says Humpty Dumpty in *Alice in Wonderland*, "it means just what I choose it to mean—neither more nor less." And he goes on to define the word *glory* as a "nice knockdown argument." In a sense, Humpty Dumpty is right: we do use words to mean what we choose, for words take on meaning as we *use* them. Take a page from a dictionary and run down a few of the entries:

horoscope	horrific
horrendous	horror
horrent	hors d'oeuvre
horrible	horse

If you *already* know, through your own experience, about horoscopes, this dictionary definition will make sense to you:

> *horoscope*—a diagram of the heavens, showing the relative positions of planets and the signs of the zodiac, for use in calculating births, foretelling events in a person's life, etc.
>
> *Random House Dictionary*

Someone totally unfamiliar with horoscopes would probably be perplexed: how can the events in one's life be foretold through a diagram of the heavens? If you already know through your own experience about *horse*, then the following definition will probably bring *horse* into focus: "a large, strong animal with four legs, solid hoofs, and a flowing mane and tail, long ago domesticated for drawing or carrying loads, carrying riders, etc."

In his novel *Hard Times*, Charles Dickens presents a schoolmaster, Mr. Gradgrind, who is interested only in Facts:

> Teach these boys and girls nothing but Facts. Facts alone are wanted in life. Plant nothing else and root out everything else. You can only form the minds of reasoning animals upon Facts: nothing else will ever be of any service to them.

"Give me a definition of a horse," he demands of "girl number twenty," whose family trains and rides horses in a circus. But she cannot; she stammers and stutters and cannot define a horse. Her teacher cries out: "Girl number twenty possessed of no facts, in reference to one of the commonest of animals! Some boy's definition of a horse. Bitzer, yours." And Bitzer replies:

> Quadruped. Graminivorous. Forty teeth, namely, twenty-four grinders, four eyeteeth, and twelve incisive. Sheds coat in the spring; in marshy countries, sheds hoofs, too. Hoofs hard, but requiring to be shod with iron. Age known by marks in mouth.

Mr. Gradgrind turns: "Now girl number twenty . . . you know what a horse is."

Do *you*? If you had never seen a horse, would Bitzer's "definition" help? Would you be able to recognize a black stallion with a long, flowing mane as a horse? Perhaps you could, if you could get close enough to examine the teeth—according to Bitzer.

Defining—whether we define things concrete like a horse or a table or a house, or things abstract like love or freedom or trust or truth—engages all of our skills as thinkers. We spend our lives trying to understand what things are. Defining calls on all the forms of thought we can muster.

Dictionary—or lexical—definitions take us only so far. They define by *putting an object into a class* where it belongs and by *specifying distinguishing characteristics*.

A horse	is	an animal	*class*
		with four legs	
		with solid hoofs	
		with a long flowing	*distinguishing*
		mane and tail long	*characteristics*
		ago domesticated	
		for carrying loads	
		or riders, etc.	

The definition captures the *general* characteristics of horse. To further define horses, we may *classify* them:

wild horses   racing horses   show horses   ceremonial horses
work horses   riding horses   military horses

We may *compare* horses with donkeys, to mules, to ponies. We may describe the *procedure* of breeding or training horses. We may give *examples* of horses; we may *tell stories* about horses; we may *describe* particular horses: the Arabian horse, for example, with its small, neat ears, its large eyes, its wide nostrils, its high tail carriage. Description focuses on the unique, on the individual, on the particular; definition sees things in general.

When you write, you often need to define your terms, to make clear what you mean. What is democracy, freedom, communism, happiness, or success? Your notions of "success" will not necessarily be mine. I don't know what you mean by success until you stop to define, to explain, to exemplify, to show.

A definition may be only a small part of what you are writing: for example, you may offer a definition of *success* as part of a discussion of movie stars. Or *success* may *be* the subject of your work: you may explore what success means to the American middle class, or what success is in the eyes of the contemporary college student, or what success means as an aspect of the American Dream. Simone de Beauvoir takes the word *woman* as the subject of her book, *The Second Sex*: she examines the word through history, through culture, through myths, and through study of the woman's life today. In the following passage, which opens her book, she lines up synonyms—words of similar meaning—to define woman. *Woman*, says de Beauvoir, is *womb*, is *ovary*, is *female*. She then explores the word *female* by looking at its connotations—the ideas and feelings that are commonly associated with a word.

> Woman? Very simple, say the fanciers of simple formulas: she is a womb, an ovary; she is a female—this word is sufficient to define her. In the mouth of a man the epithet female has the sound of an insult, yet he is not ashamed of his animal nature; on the contrary, he is proud if someone says of him: "He is a male!" The term "female" is derogatory not because it emphasizes woman's animality, but because it imprisons her in her sex; and if this sex seems to man to be contemptible and inimical even in harmless dumb animals, it is evidently because of the uneasy hostility stirred up in him by woman. Nevertheless he wishes to find in biology a justification for this sentiment. The word *female* brings up in his mind a saraband of imagery—a vast, round ovum engulfs and castrates the agile spermatozoon; the monstrous and swollen termite queen rules over the enslaved males; the female praying mantis and the spider, satiated with love, crush and devour their partners; the bitch in heat runs through the alleys, trailing behind her a wake of depraved odors; the she-monkey presents her posterior immodestly and then steals away with hypocritical coquetry; and the most superb wild beasts—the tigress, the lioness, the panther—bed down slavishly under the imperial embrace of the male. Females sluggish, eager, artful, stupid, callous, lustful, ferocious, abased—man projects them all at once upon woman. And the fact is that she is a female. But if we are willing to stop thinking in platitudes, two questions are immediately posed: what does the female denote in the animal kingdom? And what particular kind of female is manifest in woman?

Knowing *facts*, we must tell Mr. Gradgrind, is not enough. To define, we may call upon a dictionary to find the denotative meaning, which is the most general, the most inclusive way of explaining a word. Words, however, hold a multiplicity of meanings, depending on how they are used and on who uses them.

In his *Devil's Dictionary*, Ambrose Bierce follows in Humpty Dumpty's footsteps: he uses a word to mean just what he chooses it to mean. Here are some samples:

> *admiration, n.* Our polite recognition of another's resemblance to ourselves.
>
> *bore, n.* A person who talks when you wish him to listen.
>
> *childhood, n.* The period of human life intermediate between the idiocy of infancy and the folly of youth—two removes from the sin of manhood and three from the remorse of age.
>
> *congratulation, n.* The civility of envy.
>
> *education, n.* That which discloses to the wise and disguises from the foolish their lack of understanding.
>
> *ghost, n.* The outward and visible sign of an inward fear.
>
> *habit, n.* A shackle for the free.
>
> *historian, n.* A broad-gauge gossip.
>
> *hope, n.* Desire and expectation rolled into one.
>
> *love, n.* A temporary insanity curable by marriage or by removal of the patient from the influences under which he incurred the disorder. This disease, like *caries* and many other ailments, is prevalent only among civilized races living under artificial conditions; barbarous nations breathing pure air and eating simple food enjoy immunity from its ravages. It is sometimes fatal, but more frequently to the physician than to the patient.

In one of the selections in this chapter, Leo Rosten defines a Yiddish word, *bubeleh,* which has found its way into English. In "Fun. Oh, Boy. Fun. You Could Die From It," Suzanne Britt Jordan examines the meanings of fun, arguing that we have become trapped into thinking life must be a continuous good time. Fun, she says, is a "rare jewel," a "mystery." "It cannot be caught like a virus."

Russell Baker in "American Fat" accuses Americans of avoiding "lean, plain words that cut to the bone." He draws from the language of politics and of the media to illustrate what he calls "American fat," which is language with "thick, greasy syllables" that come "lumbering down upon some poor threadbare sentence like a sack of iron on a swayback horse." Robin Lakoff also talks about talk—arguing that women are taught to speak so pleasantly, daintily, nonaggressively, that they are crippled when they go out into the world.

E. B. White examines the word *freedom* in the context of America before the Second World War. He describes himself as a man who "believes in freedom with the same burning delight, the same faith, the same intense abandon that attended its birth on this continent more than a century and a half ago." He wants to define freedom, as he knows it, as a profound contrast to the fascism sweeping Europe and apparently seducing some Americans.

Claude Brown offers example after example of "Soul Language," which he calls the vocal history of the black people. The word *nigger* he says is lexically defined as just another word for Negro or black man, yet *nigger*, he says, is perhaps the most "soulful" word in the world.

Kurt Vonnegut, Jr., in his story, "Harrison Bergeron," explores the meaning of an idea and an American ideal, that all men are created equal, by showing how a *literal* interpretation can result in a most extreme situation—where all people are *equalized*.

❖ ❖ ───────────────────────────────────────

AS YOU READ

Lexical Definitions

Writers—as do all of us—work to explain their terms. They certainly rely on the lexical (dictionary) definition, which gives both the common and rare meanings; the etymology, the origins of a word; and often synonymns, words that are similar in meaning. Indeed, dictionary definitions can be particularly informative to writers as they review the variety of meanings for a complex word like, say, *culture*. If you look up *culture* in a dictionary, you will find a range of definition, from "that which is excellent in the arts, manners, etc.," to "the sum total of ways of living built up by a group of human beings and transmitted from one generation to another." (*Random House Dictionary*: Unabridged Edition)

Stipulative Definitions

But the dictionary will not offer a complete list of meanings of a word, nor should we expect it to. Often, in scholarly or technical writing, words must be used for specialized purposes. They are given "stipulative" meanings; the writer stipulates what the word will mean in this paper; the meaning is restricted to serve this express purpose. It sometimes happens that this stipulative meaning may become common usage and, in fact, find its way into the dictionary. Margaret Mead cites an example in Ruth Benedict's famous work, *Patterns of Culture*:

> When Ruth Benedict began her work in anthropology in 1921, the term "culture," as we use it today for the systematic body of learned behavior which is transmitted from parents to children, was part of the vocabulary of a small and technical group of professional anthropologists. That today the modern world is on such easy terms with the concept of culture, that the words "in our culture" slip from the lips of educated men and women almost as effortlessly as do the phrases that refer to period and to place, is in very great part due to this book.

Benedict's stipulative usage of the word *culture* thus helped to determine the way we use the word today.

Extended Definition

An entire volume, like *Patterns of Culture*, may be devoted to an exploration of a single word. Through illustrations, contrasts, comparisons, narration; through analyses of cause and effect relationships, a writer may, fundamentally, be defining a term. In such cases, the whole book can be seen as an extended definition: what is culture; what is success; what is art. As you read, notice how writers define their terms. Do not be satisfied with a writer who offers a "Webster says—"; and in your own writing, use as many sources, as many forms, as you need to make your meaning clear to your readers.

AS YOU WRITE

Generating Material

Often the best initial source for generating definitions of terms is your own experience, your own memories, your own associations that you bring to the words. Suppose you want to define a commonly used but complex word like *love* or *truth* or *sadness* or *fun* or *snow*. In your journal, write down as quickly as you can associations that come to you. The word *snow* might evoke:

ice crystals	flakes	soft
intricately patterned	cold	melts
white	winter	frozen water vapor
accidents	bad driving	children playing

Now, turning to a dictionary to see how the word is defined, you recognize other familiar meanings:

- white spots on a television screen
- slang for cocaine or heroin
- to cover, obstruct

You also find compound words: snowball, snow-blind, snowbound, snowdrift, snowdrop, snowfall, snow job, snowman. Further, you may recall a particularly severe snowstorm, where hundreds of motorists were stranded, where some froze to death in their cars; you might remember back to childhood when a snowstorm closed the schools, and you sledded and skied and built snow-men.

Reading Your Writing

Suddenly, with the aid of a dictionary, your own memories, and your own associations, you have material on *snow*. If you were asked to write an essay on the topic, you now have a range of options. You can define the term lexically, calling upon several dictionary definitions. You can stipulate what snow means to you: you do not mean the slush that snow turns into after several days. Snow, for you, is the fresh-fallen white. Snow, for you, is the covering of winter. Or snow, for you, means a serious problem affecting motorists, storeowners, and schoolchildren, for when it snows in your part of the world, everything is disrupted.

Shaping Your Writing

In defining, as in any other writing, you want your audience to understand your point of view toward your subject. Your particular angle of vision is the key to your defining of a term, whether it is a complex term like *culture* or *socialism* or *nationalism*, where you must stipulate the meanings, or whether it is an everyday, but often equally complex phenomenon, like *snow* or *rain* or *tree*. As you use lexical and stipulative definitions as part of your writing, or as you write extensively about a term, keep in mind that your audience can always look it up in the dictionary. What they expect from you is *your* version, *your* reading of the term.

LEO ROSTEN

> *Leo Rosten (born 1908) is one of the most fertile of the twentieth century American humorists; as a result of teaching English in night school, he wrote his classic,* The Education of Hyman Kaplan, *an exploration of the hazards of trying to speak English as a second language and one of the funniest books in the language. Most of his readers are equally grateful for his amazing collection,* The Joys of Yiddish, *from which the following is taken.*

BUBELEH/BOBELEH

Pronounced *BUB-eh-leh,* using the *u* of "put," not of "tub"; rhymes with "hood a la." From Russian/Hebrew. In Hebrew, *buba* means "little doll." But the Yiddish *bube* and *bubeleh* seem independent of the Hebrew, say the experts.

Grandmother; the affectionate diminutive, really: "little grandma." (Baba, which means midwife or grandmother in Russian and other Slavic tongues, was often used in addressing any old woman, whether one's grandmother or not.)

Bubeleh, a term of endearment, is widely used for "darling," "dear child," "honey," "sweetheart."

A husband and wife may call each other *bubeleh.* Jewish mothers call both female and male babies *bubeleh.* This carries the expectation that the child in the crib will one day be a grandparent. It also honors the memory of the mother's mother: in calling a baby "little grandmother," a mother is addressing the child in the way the child will in time address its grandmother—and its child.

Bubeleh has come into vast popularity in recent years—via television. On all the night "talk" shows, the garrulous comedians, actors, actresses try to display warm, outgoing, loving natures, in fact all the obligatory coziness of show business, by greeting each other with kisses, embraces, cheek pattings—and generous doses of "bubeleh." Thus: "How are you, *bubeleh?*" or "I just loved your last picture, *bubeleh!*" or even, "*Bubeleh*, baby, where have you been?"

What struck me during the birth and vehement barrage of *bubelehs* among emphatically Anglo-Saxon, Italian, Greek, and Negro entertainers, was the fact that no one seemed to think it necessary to explain what *bubeleh* meant. I often wonder what residents of Idaho or Mississippi think those crazy people in New York or Hollywood are talking about.

❖ ❖

A Jewish mother sent her son off to his first day in school with the customary pride and precautionary advice: "So, *bubeleh*, you'll be a good boy and obey the teacher? And you won't make noise, *bubeleh*, and you'll be very polite and play nice with the other children. And when it's time to come home, you'll button up warm, so you won't catch cold, *bubeleh*. And you'll be careful crossing the street and come right home . . ." etc. etc.

Off went the little boy.

When he returned that afternoon, his mother hugged him and kissed him and exclaimed, "So did you like school, *bubeleh*? You made new friends? You *learned* something?"

"Yeah," said the boy. "I learned that my name is Irving."

How Do You Respond?

1. Rosten gives a lexical (dictionary) definition of *bubeleh*: "a term of endearment, widely used for 'darling,' 'dear child,' 'honey,' 'sweetheart.'" How else does Rosten define the word?

2. Find a word from your own childhood that, like *bubeleh*, is rich

SUZANNE BRITT JORDAN

> *Go out at night and look up at the stars. You will discover an odd fact. The Pleiades are a cluster of stars that are almost invisible when you stare directly at them, looking for them. But turn your gaze slightly to one side, and you will see them. Fun, like happiness, is rather like the Pleiades. Try to set it up, and it will escape—as Suzanne Britt Jordan discovered. Jordan writes from Raleigh, North Carolina, where she teaches at North Carolina State University.*

FUN. OH, BOY. FUN. YOU COULD DIE FROM IT.

Fun is hard to have.

Fun is a rare jewel.

Somewhere along the line people got the modern idea that fun was there for the asking, that people deserved fun, that if we didn't have a little fun every day we would turn into (sakes alive!), Puritans.

"Was it fun?" became the question that overshadowed all other questions: good questions like: Was it moral? Was it kind? Was it honest? Was it beneficial? Was it generous? Was it necessary? And (my favorite) was it selfless?

When pleasure got to be the main thing, the fun fetish was sure to follow. Everything was supposed to be fun. If it wasn't fun, then by Jove, we were going to make it fun, or else.

Think of all the things that got the reputation of being fun. Family outings were supposed to be fun. Sex was supposed to be fun. Education was supposed to be fun. Work was supposed to be fun. Walt Disney was supposed to be fun. Church was supposed to be fun. Staying fit was supposed to be fun.

Just to make sure that everybody knew how much fun we were having, we put happy faces on flunking test papers, dirty bumpers, sticky refrigerator doors, bathroom mirrors.

If a kid, looking at his very happy parents traipsing through that very happy Disney World, said, "This ain't no fun, ma," his ma's heart sank. She wondered where she had gone wrong. Everybody told her what fun family outings to Disney World would be. Golly gee, what was the matter?

Fun got to be such a big thing that everybody started to look for more and more thrilling ways to supply it. One way was to step up the level of danger or licentiousness or alcohol or drug consumption so that you could be sure that, no matter what, you would manage to have a little fun.

Television commercials brought a lot of fun and fun-loving folks into the picture. Everything that people in those commercials did looked like fun: taking Polaroid snapshots, swilling beer, buying insurance, mopping the floor, bowling, taking aspirin. We all wished, I'm sure, that we could have half as much fun as those rough-and-ready guys around the locker room, flicking each other with towels and pouring champagne. The more commercials people watched, the more they wondered when the fun would start in their own lives. It was pretty depressing.

Big occasions were supposed to be fun. Christmas, Thanksgiving and Easter were obviously supposed to be fun. Your wedding day was supposed to be fun. Your wedding night was supposed to be a whole lot of fun. Your honeymoon was supposed to be the epitome of fundom. And so we ended up going through every Big Event we ever celebrated, waiting for the fun to start.

It occurred to me, while I was sitting around waiting for the fun to start, that not much is, and that I should tell you just in case you're worried about your fun capacity.

I don't mean to put a damper on things. I just mean we ought to treat fun reverently. It is a mystery. It cannot be caught like a virus. It cannot be trapped like an animal. The god of mirth is paying us back for all those years of thinking fun was everywhere by refusing to come to our party. I don't want to blaspheme fun anymore. When fun comes in on little dancing feet, you probably won't be expecting it. In fact, I bet it comes when you're doing your duty, your job, or your work. It may even come on a Tuesday.

I remember one day, long ago, on which I had an especially good time. Pam Davis and I walked to the College Village drug store one Saturday morning to buy some candy. We were about 12 years old (fun ages). She got her Bit-O-Honey. I got my malted milk balls, chocolate stars, Chunkys, and a small bag of M&M's. We started back to her house. I was going to spend the night. We had the whole day to look forward to. We had plenty of candy. It was a long way to Pam's house but every time we got weary Pam would put her hand over her eyes, scan the horizon like a sailor and say, "Oughta reach home by nightfall," at which point the two of us would laugh until we thought we couldn't stand it another minute. Then after we got calm, she'd say it again. You should have been there. It was the kind of day and friendship and occasion that made me deeply regret that I had to grow up.

It was fun.

How Do You Respond?

1. Suzanne Britt Jordan offers a series of examples to show that people are obsessed by having fun. Can you capture in a definition what *she* means by having fun?

2. Discuss how your idea of *fun* compares with Jordan's. How would you define *fun?*

3. Jordan says, ". . . Fun. You Could Die From It." In the previous chapter, Didion wrote about some people who may have. Compare Jordan's and Didion's view of how the popular ideas, the myths, of fun, success, and happiness put pressure on individuals to measure up, to conform.

RUSSELL BAKER

> *Russell Baker (born 1925) is one of the most consistently entertaining American humorists. No one is safe when he is around, for he sees everything irreverently. He is characteristically unimpressed by his own writing, and describes his style as merely "casual": others came to speak of him as a humorist, and after a time, he says, he had no choice but to believe them. In matters of style in writing, his ideals seem close to those of another, very different, journalist—George Orwell. In other words, keep your sentences short and try to keep your language close to Anglo-Saxon. Baker would rather "use words" than "utilize a lexicon"! If you wish to read more, try* Baker's Dozen *and* Poor Russell's Almanac.

AMERICAN FAT

Americans don't like plain talk anymore. Nowadays they like fat talk. Show them a lean, plain word that cuts to the bone and watch them lard it with thick greasy syllables front and back until it wheezes and gasps for breath as it comes lumbering down upon some poor threadbare sentence like a sack of iron on a swayback horse.

"Facilitate" is typical of the case. A generation ago only sissies and bureaucrats would have said "facilitate" in public. Nowadays we are a nation of "facilitate" utterers.

"Facilitate" is nothing more than a gout-ridden, overstuffed "ease." Why has "ease" fallen into disuse among us? It is a lovely little bright snake of a word which comes hissing quietly off the tongue and carries us on, without fuss and French horns, to the object which is being eased.

This is English at its very best. Easing is not one of the great events of life; it does not call for Beethoven; it is not an idea to get drunk on, to wallow in, to encase in multiple oleaginous syllabification until it becomes a pompous ass of a word like "facilitate."

A radio announcer was interviewing a doctor the other day. The doctor worked in a hospital in which he apparently—one never really hears more than 3 percent of anything said on radio—controlled the destinies of many social misfits. The announcer asked the purpose of his work.

The doctor said it was "to facilitate the reentry into society as functioning members"—the mind's Automatic Dither Cutoff went to work at this stage, and the rest of the doctor's answer was lost, but it was too late. Seeds of gloom had been planted.

The doctor's passion for fat English had told too much. One shuddered for the patients at his hospital—"institutional complex," he probably called it—for it must be a dreadful thing to find oneself at the mercy of a man whose tongue drips the fatty greases of "facilitate." He doubtless, almost surely, says "utilize" too, when he means "use," and "implement" when he means "do."

Getting his patients out of the hospital and back home has become for this doctor "the reentry into society," a technological chore of the sort performed in outer space. Having facilitated their reentry into society, he will be able to greet them as "functioning members."

How dreadful it must be, caged up and antisocial in a beautifully sterilized container for misfits, for a patient to find himself at the mercy of men whose English is fat, who see him as an exercise in engineering and who are determined to turn him into "a functioning member."

Peace, doctors! Of course it is merely a manner of speaking, although the "merely" may not be quite so mere as it sounds. We are what we think, and very often we think what we say rather than what we say we think.

Long words, fat talk—they may tell us something about ourselves. Has the passion for fat in the language increased as self-confidence has waned? We associate plain talk with the age of national confidence. It is the stranger telling the black hat, "When you call me that, smile." It is the campaign of 1948 when a President of the United States could open a speech by saying, "My name's Truman, I'm President of the United States, and I'm trying to keep my job."

Since then campaign talk has become fatter and more pompous, as though we need sounds that seem weighty to conceal a thinness of the spirit from which they emanate. But politicians are not our corrupters here; we are all in love with the fat sound.

There is the radio disk jockey who cannot bring himself to say that the temperature at the studio is "now" forty-five degrees but must fatten it up, extend it, make more of it, score it for kettle drums, by declaring that the temperature at the studio is "currently" forty-five degrees, and often, carried into illiteracy in his passion for fat talk, "presently" forty-five degrees.

Newspapers seem to be the father and mother of fat. The bombing is never the stark, dramatic "intense," but always the drawled, overweight "intensive." Presidents are rarely allowed to "say" the weather is improving; the papers have them "declare" it, "state" it, "issue a challenge for the Weather Bureau to deny" it.

Why do we like our words so fat but our women so skinny?

How Do You Respond?

1. In his essay, Russell Baker sharply criticizes "American Fat"; how does he define this term? Can you find examples of lexical, stipulative, and extended definitions in his discussion?

2. What do you think of the language you hear about you—from the government, on newscasts? Collect examples of "fat talk" to share with the class.

3. Find examples of "fat talk" from the government and translate them into lean talk.

ROBIN LAKOFF

> *Professor of Linguistics at the University of California, Berkeley, Robin Lakoff (born 1942) studies women and their use of language so that, out of knowledge, women can see what they are doing and change the ways they subordinate themselves to others. "If we are aware of what we're doing, why we're doing it, and the effects our actions have on ourselves and everyone else," she says, "we will have the power to change." She hopes that her work "will be one small first step in the direction of a wider option of life styles, for men and women."*

YOU ARE WHAT YOU SAY

"Women's language" is that pleasant (dainty?), euphemistic, never-aggressive way of talking we learned as little girls. Cultural bias was built into the language we were allowed to speak, the subjects we were allowed to speak about, and the ways we were spoken of. Having learned our linguistic lesson well, we go out in the world, only to discover that we are communicative cripples—dammed if we do, and dammed if we don't.

If we refuse to talk "like a lady," we are ridiculed and criticized for being unfeminine. ("She thinks like a man" is, at best, a left-handed compliment.) If we do learn all the fuzzy-headed, unassertive language of our sex, we are ridiculed for being unable to think clearly, unable to take part in a serious discussion, and therefore unfit to hold a position of power.

It doesn't take much of this for a woman to begin feeling she deserves such treatment because of inadequacies in her own intelligence and education.

"Women's language" shows up in all levels of English. For example, women are encouraged and allowed to make far more precise discriminations in naming colors than men do. Words like *mauve, beige, ecru, acquamarine, lavender,* and so on, are unremarkable in a woman's active vocabulary, but largely absent from that of most men. I know of no evidence suggesting that women actually see a wider range of colors than men do. It is simply that fine discriminations of this sort are relevant to women's vocabularies, but not to men's; to men, who control most of the interesting affairs of the world, such distinctions are trivial—irrelevant.

In the area of syntax, we find similar gender-related peculiarities of speech. There is one construction, in particular, that women use conversationally far more than men: the tag-question. A tag is midway between an outright statement and a yes-no question; it is less assertive than the former, but more confident than the latter.

A *flat statement* indicates confidence in the speaker's knowledge and is fairly certain to be believed; a question indicates a lack of knowledge on some point and implies that the gap in the speaker's knowledge can and will be remedied by an answer. For example, if, at a Little League game, I have had my glasses off, I can legitimately ask someone else: "Was the player out at third?" A *tag question*, being intermediate between statement and question, is used when the speaker is stating a claim, but lacks full confidence in the truth of that claim. So if I say, "Is Joan here?" I will probably not be surprised if my respondent answers "no"; but if I say, "Joan is here, isn't she?" instead, chances are I am already biased in favor of a positive answer, wanting only confirmation. I still want a response, but I have enough knowledge (or think I have) to predict that response. A tag question, then, might be thought of as a statement that doesn't demand to be believed by anyone but the speaker, a way of giving leeway, of not forcing the addressee to go along with the views of the speaker.

Another common use of the tag-question is in small talk when the speaker is trying to elicit conversation: "Sure is hot here, isn't it?"

But in discussing personal feelings or opinions, only the speaker normally has any way of knowing the correct answer. Sentences such as "I have a headache, don't I?" are clearly ridiculous. But there are other examples where it is the speaker's opinions, rather than perceptions, for which corroboration is sought, as in "The situation in Southeast Asia is terrible, isn't it?"

While there are, of course, other possible interpretations of a sentence like this, one possibility is that the speaker has a particular answer in mind—"yes" or "no"—but is reluctant to state it baldly. This sort of tag question is much more apt to be used by women than by men in conversation. Why is this the case?

The tag question allows a speaker to avoid commitment, and

thereby avoid conflict with the addressee. The problem is that, by so doing, speakers may also give the impression of not really being sure of themselves, or looking to the addressee for confirmation of their views. This uncertainty is reinforced in more subliminal ways, too. There is a peculiar sentence intonation-pattern, used almost exclusively by women, as far as I know, which changes a declarative answer into a question. The effect of using the rising inflection typical of a yes-no question is to imply that the speaker is seeking confirmation, even though the speaker is clearly the only one who has the requisite information, which is why the question was put to her in the first place:

(Q) When will dinner be ready?
(A) Oh . . . around six o'clock . . . ?

It is as though the second speaker were saying, "Six o'clock—if that's okay with you, if you agree." The person being addressed is put in the position of having to provide confirmation. One likely consequence of this sort of speech-pattern in a woman is that, often unbeknownst to herself, the speaker builds a reputation of tentativeness, and others will refrain from taking her seriously or trusting her with any real responsibilities since she "can't make up her mind," and "isn't sure of herself."

Such idiosyncrasies may explain why women's language sounds much more "polite" than men's. It is polite to leave a decision open, not impose your mind, or views, or claims, on anyone else. So a tag-question is a kind of polite statement, in that it does not force agreement or belief on the addressee. In the same way a request is a polite command, in that it does not force obedience on the addressee, but rather suggests something to be done as a favor to the speaker. A clearly stated order implies a threat of certain consequences if it is not followed, and—even more impolite—implies that the speaker is in a superior position and able to enforce the order. By couching wishes in the form of a request, on the other hand, a speaker implies that if the request is not carried out, only the speaker will suffer; noncompliance cannot harm the addressee. So the decision is really up to the addressee. The distinction becomes clear in these examples:

Close the door.
Please close the door.
Will you close the door?

Will you please close the door?
Won't you close the door?

In the same ways as words and speech patterns used *by* women undermine her image, those used to *describe* women make matters even worse. Often a word may be used of both men and women (and perhaps of things as well); but when it is applied to women, it assumes a special meaning that, by implication rather than outright assertion, is derogatory to women as a group.

The use of euphemisms has this effect. A euphemism is a substitute for a word that has acquired a bad connotation by association with something unpleasant or embarrassing. But almost as soon as the new word comes into common usage, it takes on the same old bad connotations, since feelings about the things or people referred to are not altered by a change of name: thus new euphemisms must be constantly found.

There is one euphemism for *woman* still very much alive. The word, of course, is *lady*. *Lady* has a masculine counterpart, namely *gentleman*, occasionally shortened to *gent*. But for some reason *lady* is very much commoner than *gent(leman)*. The decision to use *lady* rather than *woman*, or vice versa, may considerably alter the sense of a sentence, as the following examples show:

(a) A woman (lady) I know is a dean at Berkeley.

(b) A woman (lady) I know makes amazing things out of shoelaces and old boxes.

The use of *lady* in (a) imparts a frivolous, or nonserious, tone to the sentence: the matter under discussion is not one of great moment. Similarly, in (b), using *lady* here would suggest that the speaker considered the "amazing things" not to be serious art, but merely a hobby or an aberration. If *woman* is used, she might be a serious sculptor. To say *lady doctor* is very condescending, since no one ever says *gentleman doctor* or even *man doctor*. For example, mention in the San Francisco *Chronicle* of January 31, 1972, of Madalyn Murray O'Hair as the *lady atheist* reduces her position to that of scatterbrained eccentric. Even *woman atheist* is scarcely defensible: sex is irrelevant to her philosophical position.

Many women argue that, on the other hand, *lady* carries with it overtones recalling the age of chivalry: conferring exalted stature on the person so referred to. This makes the term seem polite at first, but we must also remember that these implications are perilous: they suggest that a "lady" is helpless, and cannot do things by herself.

Lady can also be used to imply frivolousness, as in titles of organizations. Those that have a serious purpose (not merely that of enabling "the ladies" to spend time with one another) cannot use the word lady in their titles, but less serious ones may. Compare the Ladies' Auxiliary of a men's group, or the Thursday Evening Ladies' Browning and Garden Society with Ladies' Liberation or Ladies' Strike for Peace. What is curious about this split is that lady is in origin a euphemism—a substitute that puts a better face on something people find uncomfortable—for woman. What kind of euphemism is it that subtly denigrates the people to whom it refers? Perhaps lady functions as a euphemism for woman because it does not contain the sexual implications present in woman; it is not "embarrassing" in that way. If this is so, we may expect that, in the future, lady will replace woman as the primary word for the human female, since woman will have become too blatantly sexual. That this distinction is already made in some contexts at least is shown in the following examples, where you can try replacing woman with lady.

(a) She's only twelve, but she's already a woman.
(b) After ten years in jail, Harry wanted to find a woman.
(c) She's my woman, see, so don't mess around with her.

Another common substitute for woman is girl. One seldom hears a man past the age of adolescence referred to as a boy, save in expressions like "going out with the boys," which are meant to suggest an air of adolescent frivolity and irresponsibility. But women of all ages are "girls": one can have a man—not a boy—Friday, but only a girl—never a woman or even a lady—Friday; women have girlfriends, but men do not—in a nonsexual sense—have boyfriends. It may be that this use of girl is euphemistic in the same way the use of lady is; in stressing the idea of immaturity, it removes the sexual connotations lurking in woman. Girl brings to mind irresponsibility; you don't send a girl to do a woman's errand (or even, for that matter, a boy's errand). She is a person who is both too immature and too far from real life to be entrusted with responsibilities or with decisions of any serious or important nature.

Now let's take a pair of words which, in terms of the possible relationships in an earlier society, were simple male-female equivalents, analogous to bull: cow. Suppose we find that, for independent reasons, society has changed in such a way that the original meanings now are irrelevant. Yet the words have not been discarded, but have acquired new meanings, metaphorically related to their original senses. But suppose these new metaphorical uses are no longer parallel to each other. By seeing where the parallelism breaks down, we discover something about the different roles played by men and women in this culture. One good example of such a divergence through time is found in the pair, *master: mistress*. Once used with reference to one's power over servants, these words have become unusable today in their original master-servant sense as the relationship has become less prevalent in our society. But the words are still common.

Unless used with reference to animals, *master* now generally refers to a man who has acquired consummate ability in some field, normally nonsexual. But its feminine counterpart cannot be used this way. It is practically restricted to its sexual sense of "paramour." We start out with two terms, both roughly paraphrasable as "one who has power over another." But the masculine form, once one person is no longer able to have absolute power over another, becomes usable metaphorically in the sense of "having power over *something*." *Master* requires as its object only the name of some activity, something inanimate and abstract. But *mistress* requires a masculine noun in the possessive to precede it. One cannot say: "Rhonda is a mistress." One must be *someone's* mistress. A man is defined by what he does, a woman by her sexuality, that is, in terms of one particular aspect of her relationship to men. It is one thing to be an *old master* like Hans Holbein, and another to be an *old mistress*. The same is true of the words *spinster* and *bachelor*—gender words for "one who is not married." The resemblance ends with the definition. While *bachelor* is a neuter term often used as a compliment, *spinster* normally is used pejoratively, with connotations of prissiness, fussiness, and so on. To be a bachelor implies that one has the choice of marrying or not, and this is what makes the idea of a bachelor existence attractive, in the popular literature. He has been pursued and has successfully eluded his pursuers. But a spinster is one who has not been pursued, or at least not seriously. She is old, unwanted goods. The metaphorical connotations of *bachelor* generally suggest sexual freedom; of *spinster*, puritanism or celibacy.

These examples could be multiplied. It is generally considered a *faux pas*, in society, to congratulate a woman on her engagement, while it is correct to congratulate her fiancé. Why is this? The reason seems to be that it is impolite to remind people of things that may be uncomfortable to them. To congratulate a woman on her engagement is really to say, "Thank goodness! You had a close call!" For the man, on the other hand, there was no such danger. His choosing to marry is viewed as a good thing, but not something essential.

The linguistic double standard holds throughout the life of the relationship. After marriage, bachelor and spinster become man and wife, not man and woman. The woman whose husband dies remains "John's widow"; John, however, is never "Mary's widower."

Finally, why is it that salesclerks and others are so quick to call women customers "dear," "honey," and other terms of endearment they really have no business using? A male customer would never put up with it. But women, like children, are supposed to enjoy these endearments, rather than being offended by them.

In more ways than one, it's time to speak up.

How Do You Respond?

1. Reread Robin Lakoff's first sentence. Are you meant to take it seriously? Where do you find the first indication in the text of how you are supposed to understand "pleasant (dainty?)"? How *are* you to understand these words?

2. In your experience, do women use the kinds of language Lakoff points to? Lakoff wrote in the 70s. Discuss how you think things have changed.

3. Is unconscious prejudice in everyday language a problem only to women? Discuss examples of assumptions embedded in language that are detrimental to other groups.

E. B. WHITE

> *The United States has grown until New England is quite a small corner of the whole. Yet the New England town meeting is still the forum where important issues are discussed and clarified, raising the level of debate for the entire country. E. B. White, with his plain words and strongly held beliefs, writes from that old Yankee tradition.*

FREEDOM

I have often noticed on my trips up to the city that people have recut their clothes to follow the fashion. On my last trip, however, it seemed to me that people had remodeled their ideas too—taken in their convictions a little at the waist, shortened the sleeves of their resolve, and fitted themselves out in a new intellectual ensemble copied from a smart design out of the very latest page of history. It seemed to me they had strung along with Paris a little too long.

I confess to a disturbed stomach. I feel sick when I find anyone adjusting his mind to the new tyranny which is succeeding abroad. Because of its fundamental strictures, fascism does not seem to me to admit of any compromise or any rationalization, and I resent the patronizing air of persons who find in my plain belief in freedom a sign of immaturity. If it is boyish to believe that a human being should live free, then I'll gladly arrest my development and let the rest of the world grow up.

I shall report some of the strange remarks I heard in New York. One man told me that he thought perhaps the Nazi ideal was a sounder ideal than our constitutional system "because have you ever noticed what fine alert young faces the young German soldiers have in the newsreel?" He added: "Our American youngsters spend all their time at the movies—they're a mess." That was his summation of the case, his interpretation of the new Europe. Such a remark leaves me pale and shaken. If it represents the peak of our intelligence, then the steady march of despotism will not receive any considerable setback at our shores.

Another man informed me that our democratic notion of popular government was decadent and not worth bothering about—"because England is really rotten and the industrial towns there are a disgrace." That was the only reason he gave for the hopelessness of democracy; and he seemed mightily pleased with himself, as though he were more familiar than most with the anatomy of decadence, and had detected subtler aspects of the situation than were discernible to the rest of us.

Another man assured me that anyone who took *any* kind of government seriously was a gullible fool. You could be sure, he said, that there is nothing but corruption "because of the way Clemenceau acted at Versailles." He said it didn't make any difference really about this war. It was just another war. Having relieved himself of this majestic bit of reasoning, he subsided.

Another individual, discovering signs of zeal creeping into my blood, berated me for having lost my detachment, my pure skeptical point of view. He announced that he wasn't going to be swept away by all this nonsense, but would prefer to remain in the role of innocent bystander, which he said was the duty of any intelligent person. (I noticed, however, that he phoned later to qualify his remark, as though he had lost some of his innocence in the cab on the way home.)

Those are just a few samples of the sort of talk that seemed to be going round—talk which was full of defeatism and disillusion and sometimes of a too studied innocence. Men are not merely annihilating themselves at a great rate these days, but they are telling one another enormous lies, grandiose fibs. Such remarks as I heard are fearfully disturbing in their cumulative effect. They are more destructive than dive bombers and mine fields, for they challenge not merely one's immediate position but one's main defenses. They seemed to me to issue either from persons who could never have really come to grips with freedom, so as to understand her, or from renegades. Where I expected to find indignation, I found paralysis, or a sort of dim acquiescence, as in a child who is dully swallowing a distasteful pill. I was advised of the growing anti-Jewish sentiment by a man who seemed to be watching the phenomenon of intolerance not through tears of shame but with a clear intellectual gaze, as through a well-ground lens.

The least a man can do at such a time is to declare himself and tell where he stands. I believe in freedom with the same burning delight, the same faith, the same intense abandon which attended its birth on this continent more than a century and a half ago. I am writing my declaration rapidly, much as though I were shaving to catch a train. Events abroad give a man a feeling of being pressed for time. Actually I do not believe I am pressed for time, and I apologize to the reader for a false impression that may be created. I just want to tell, before I get slowed down, that I am in love with freedom and that it is an affair of long standing and that it is a fine state to be in, and that I am deeply suspicious of people who are beginning to adjust to fascism and dictators merely because they are succeeding in war. From such adaptable natures a smell rises. I pinch my nose.

For as long as I can remember I have had a sense of living somewhat freely in a natural world. I don't mean I enjoyed freedom of action, but my existence seemed to have the quality of free-ness. I traveled with secret papers pertaining to a divine conspiracy. Intuitively I've always been aware of the vitally important pact which a man has with himself, to be all things to himself, and to be identified with all things, to stand self-reliant, taking advantage of his haphazard connection with a planet, riding his luck, and following his bent with the tenacity of a hound. My first and greatest love affair was with this thing we call freedom, this lady of infinite allure, this dangerous and beautiful and sublime being who restores and supplies us all.

It began with the haunting intimation (which I presume every child receives) of his mystical inner life; of God in man; of nature publishing herself through the "I." This elusive sensation is moving and memorable. It comes early in life; a boy, we'll say, sitting on the front steps on a summer night, thinking of nothing in particular, suddenly hearing as with a new perception and as though for the first time the pulsing sound of crickets, overwhelmed with the novel sense of identification with the natural company of insects and grass and night, conscious of a faint answering cry to the universal perplexing question: "What is 'I'?" Or a little girl, returning from the grave of a pet bird leaning with her elbows on the windowsill, inhaling the unfamiliar draught of death, suddenly seeing herself as part of the complete story. Or to an older youth, encountering for the first time a great teacher who by some chance word or mood awakens something and the youth beginning to breathe as an individual and conscious of strength in his vitals. I think the sensation must develop in many men as a feeling of identity with God—an eruption of the spirit caused by allergies and the sense of divine existence as distinct from mere animal existence. This is the beginning of the affair with freedom.

But a man's free condition is of two parts: the instinctive freeness he experiences as an animal dweller on a planet, and the practical liberties he enjoys as a privileged member of human society. The latter is, of the two, more generally understood, more widely admired, more violently challenged and discussed. It is the practical and apparent side of freedom. The United States, almost alone today, offers the liberties and the privileges and the tools of freedom. In this land the citizens are still invited to write their plays and books, to paint their pictures, to meet for discussion, to dissent as well as to agree, to mount soapboxes in the public square, to enjoy education in all subjects without censorship, to hold court and judge one another, to compose music, to talk politics with their neighbors without wondering whether the secret police are listening, to exchange ideas as well as goods, to kid the government when it needs kidding, and to read real news of real events instead of phony news manufactured by a paid agent of the state. This is a fact and should give every person pause.

To be free, in a planetary sense, is to feel that you belong to earth. To be free, in a social sense, is to feel at home in a democratic framework. In Adolph Hitler, although he is a freely flowering individual, we do not detect either type of sensibility. From reading his book I gather that his feeling for earth is not a sense of communion but a driving urge to prevail. His feeling for men is not that they co-exist, but that they are capable of being arranged and standardized by a superior intellect—that their existence suggests not a fulfillment of their personalities but a submersion of their personalities in the common racial destiny. His very great absorption in the destiny of the German people somehow loses some of its effect when you discover, from his writings, in what vast contempt he holds *all* people. "I learned," he wrote, ". . . to gain an insight into the unbelievably primitive opinions and arguments of the people." To him the ordinary man is a primitive, capable only of being used and led. He speaks continually of people as sheep, halfwits, and impudent fools—the same people from whom he asks the utmost in loyalty, and to whom he promises the ultimate in prizes.

Here in America, where our society is based on belief in the individual, not contempt for him, the free principle of life has a chance of surviving. I believe that it must and will survive. To understand freedom is an accomplishment which all men may acquire who set their minds in that direction; and to love freedom is a tendency which many Americans are born with. To live in the same room with freedom, or in the same hemisphere, is still a profoundly shaking experience for me.

One of the earliest truths (and to him most valuable) that the author of *Mein Kampf* discovered was that it is not the written word, but the spoken word, which in heated moments moves great masses of people to noble or ignoble action. The written word, unlike the spoken word, is something which every person examines privately and judges calmly by his own intellectual standards, not by what the man standing next to him thinks. "I know," wrote Hitler, "that one is able to win people far more by the spoken than by the written word. . . ." Later he adds contemptuously: "For let it be said to all knights of the pen and to all the political dandies, especially of today: the greatest changes in this world have never yet been brought about by a goose quill! No, the pen has always been reserved to motivate these changes theoretically."

Luckily I am not out to change the world—that's being done for me, and at a great clip. But I know that the free spirit of man is persistent in nature; it recurs, and has never successfully been wiped out, by fire or flood. I set down the above remarks merely (in the words of Mr. Hitler) to motivate that spirit, theoretically. Being myself a knight of the goose quill, I am under no misapprehension about "winning people"; but I am inordinately proud these days of the quill, for it has shown itself, historically, to be the hypodermic which inoculates men and keeps the germ of freedom always in circulation, so that there are individuals in every time in every land who are the carriers, the Typhoid Mary's, capable of infecting others by mere contact and example. These persons are feared by every tyrant—who shows his fear by burning the books and destroying the individuals. A writer goes about his task today with the extra satisfaction which comes from knowing that he will be the first to have his head lopped off—even before the political dandies. In my own case this is a double satisfaction, for if freedom were denied me by force of earthly circumstance, I am the same as dead and would infinitely prefer to go into fascism without my head than with it, having no use for it any more and not wishing to be saddled with so heavy an encumbrance.

How Do You Respond?

1. What is the relationship between White's talk about fashions in clothes and his point about freedom? How does he move from clothes to freedom?
2. Notice the phrase, "But a man's free condition . . ." in the middle of the essay; what is the force of the word *but*?
3. How does White explain what he means, now, by *freedom*? The essay was written in 1940. Discuss its relevance, if any, for today.

CLAUDE BROWN

> *Claude Brown (born 1937) is best known for his book,* Manchild in the Promised Land. *Street-wise at an early age, he worked at a variety of jobs. Generalizing from the truths that he has discovered for himself, he insists that in his writing, he has moved "away from fear, toward challenges, toward the positive anger that I think every young man should have."*

THE LANGUAGE OF SOUL

Perhaps the most soulful word in the world is *nigger*. Despite its very definite fundamental meaning (the Negro man), and disregarding the deprecatory connotation of the term, *nigger* has a multiplicity of nuances when used by soul people. Dictionaries define the term as being synonymous with Negro, and they generally point out that it is regarded as a vulgar expression. Nevertheless, to those of chitlins-and-neck-bones background the word *nigger* is neither a synonym for Negro nor an obscene expression.

Nigger has virtually as many shades of meaning in Colored English as the demonstrative pronoun *that,* prior to application to a noun. To some Americans of African ancestry (I avoid using the term *Negro* whenever feasible, for fear of offending the Brothers X, a pressure group to be reckoned with), *nigger* seems preferable to *Negro* and has a unique kind of sentiment attached to it. This is exemplified in the frequent—and perhaps even excessive—usage of the term to denote either fondness or hostility.

It is probable that numerous transitional niggers and even established ex-soul brothers can—with pangs of nostalgia—reflect upon a day in the lollipop epoch of lives when an adorable lady named Mama bemoaned her spouse's fastidiousness with the strictly secular utterance: "Lord, how can one nigger be so hard to please?" Others are likely to recall a time when that drastically lovable colored woman, who was forever wiping our noses and darning our clothing, bellowed in a moment of exasperation: "Nigger, you gonna be the death o' me." And some of the brethren who have had the precarious fortune to be raised up, wised up, thrown up, or simply left alone to get up as best they could, on one of the nation's South Streets or Lenox Avenues, might remember having affectionately referred to a best friend as "My nigger."

The vast majority of "back-door Americans" are apt to agree with Webster—a nigger is simply a Negro or black man. But the really profound contemporary thinkers of this distinguished ethnic group—Dick Gregory, Redd Foxx, Moms Mabley, Slappy White, etc.—are likely to differ with Mr. Webster and define *nigger* as "something else"—a soulful "something else." The major difference between the nigger and the Negro, who have many traits in common, is that the nigger is the more soulful.

Certain foods, customs, and artistic expressions are associated almost solely with *nigger*: collard greens, neck bones, hog maws, black-eyed peas, pigs' feet, etc. A nigger has no desire to conceal or disavow any of these favorite dishes or restrain other behavioral practices such as bobbing his head, patting his feet to funky jazz, and shouting and jumping in church. This is not to be construed to say that all niggers eat chitlins and shout in church, nor that only niggers eat the aforementioned dishes and exhibit this type of behavior. It is to say, however, that the soulful usage of the term *nigger* implies all of the foregoing and considerably more.

The Language of Soul—or, as it might also be called, Spoken Soul or Colored English—is simply an honest vocal portrayal of black America. The roots of it are more than three hundred years old.

Before the Civil War there were numerous restrictions placed on the speech of slaves. The newly arrived Africans had the problem of learning to speak a new language, but also there were inhibitions placed on the topics of the slaves' conversation by slave masters and overseers. The slaves made up songs to inform one another of, say, the underground railroads' activity. When they sang "Steal Away," they were planning to steal away to the North, not to heaven. Slaves who dared to speak of rebellion or even freedom usually were severely punished. Consequently, Negro slaves were compelled to create a semi-clandestine vernacular in the way that the criminal underworld has historically created words to confound law-enforcement agents. It is said that numerous Negro spirituals were inspired by the hardships of slavery, and that what later became songs were initally moanings and coded cotton-field lyrics. To hear these songs sung today by a talented soul brother or sister or by a group is to be reminded of an historical spiritual bond that cannot be satisfactorily described by the mere spoken word.

The American Negro, for virtually all of his history, has constituted a vastly disproportionate number of the country's illiterates. Illiteracy has a way of showing itself in all attempts at vocal expression by the uneducated. With the aid of colloquialisms, malapropisms, battered and fractured grammar, and a considerable amount of creativity, Colored English, the sound of soul, evolved.

The progress has been cyclical. Often terms that have been discarded from the soul people's vocabulary for one reason or another are reaccepted years later, but usually with completely different meaning. In the Thirties and Forties *stuff* was used to mean "vagina." In the middle Fifties it was revived and used to refer to heroin. Why certain expressions are thus reactivated is practically an indeterminable question. But it is not difficult to see why certain terms are dropped from the soul language. Whenever a soul term becomes popular with whites, it is common practice for the soul folks to relinquish it. The reasoning is that "if white people can use it, it isn't hip enough for me." To many soul brothers there is just no such creature as a genuinely hip white person. And there is nothing more detrimental to anything hip than to have it fall into the square hands of the hopelessly unhip.

White Americans wrecked the expression "something else." It was bad enough that they couldn't say "sump'n else" but they weren't even able to get out "somethin' else." They had to go around saying *something else* with perfect or nearly perfect enunciation. The white folks invariably fail to perceive the soul sound in soulful terms. They get hung up in diction and grammar, and when they vocalize the expression it's no longer a soulful thing. In fact, it can be asserted that spoken soul is more of a sound than a language. It generally possesses a pronounced lyrical quality which is frequently incompatible to any music other than that ceaseless and relentlessly driving rhythm that flows from poignantly spent lives. Spoken soul has a way of coming out metered without the intention of the speaker to invoke it. There are specific phonetic traits. To the soulless ear the vast majority of these sounds are dismissed as incorrect usage of the English language and, not infrequently, as speech impediments. To those so blessed as to have had bestowed upon them at birth the lifetime gift of soul, these are the most communicative and meaningful sounds ever to fall upon human ears; the familiar "mah" instead of "my," "gonna" for "going to," "yo" for "your." *Ain't* is pronounced "ain' "; *bread* and *bed*, "bray-ud" and "bay-ud"; *baby* is never "bay-bee" but "bay-buh"; Sammy Davis Jr. is not "Sammee" but a kind of "Sam-eh"; the same goes for "Eddeh" Jefferson. No matter how many "man's" you put into your talk, it isn't soulful unless the word has the proper plaintive, nasal "maee-yun."

Spoken soul is distinguished from slang primarily by the fact that the former lends itself easily to conventional English, and the latter is diametrically opposed to adaptations within the realm of conventional English. *Police* (pronounced PO-lice) is a soul term, whereas *The Man* is merely slang for the same thing. Negroes seldom adopt slang terms from the white world and when they do the terms are usually given a different meaning. Such was the case with the term *bag*. White racketeers used it in the Thirties to refer to the graft that was paid to the police. For the past five years soul people have used it when referring to a person's vocation, hobby, fancy, etc. And once the appropriate term is given the treatment (soul vocalization), it becomes soulful.

However, borrowings from spoken soul by white men's slang—particularly teen-age slang—are plentiful. Perhaps because soul is probably the most graphic language of modern times, everybody who is excluded from Soulville wants to usurp it, ignoring the formidable fettering to the soul folks that has brought the language about. Consider *uptight, strung-out, cop, boss, kill 'em,* all now widely used outside Soulville. Soul people never question the origin of a slang term; they either dig it and make it a part of their vocabulary or don't and forget it. The expression *uptight,* which meant being in financial straits, appeared on the soul scene in the general vicinity of 1953. Junkies were very fond of the word and used it literally to describe what was a perpetual condition with them. The word was pictorial and pointed; therefore it caught on quickly in Soulville across the country. In the early Sixties when *uptight* was on the move, a younger generation of soul people in the black urban communities along the Eastern Seaboard regenerated it with a new meaning: "everything is cool, under control, going my way." At present the term has the former meaning for the older generation and the latter construction for those under thirty years of age.

It is difficult to ascertain if the term *strung-out* was coined by junkies or just applied to them and accepted without protest. Like the term *uptight* in its initial interpretation, *strung out* aptly described the constant plight of the junkie. *Strung-out* had a connotation of hopeless finality about it. *Uptight* implied a temporary situation and lacked the overwhelming despair of *strung out.* The term *cop* (meaning "to get") is an abbreviation of the word *copulation.* *Cop,* as originally used by soulful teen-agers in the early Fifties, was deciphered to mean sexual coition, nothing more. By 1955 *cop* was being uttered throughout national Soulville as a synonym for the verb *to get,* especially in reference to illegal purchases, drugs, pot, hot goods, pistols, etc. ("Man, where can I cop now?") But by 1955 the meaning was all-encompassing. Anything that could be obtained could be "copped."

The word *boss,* denoting something extraordinarily good or great, was a redefined term that had been popular in Soulville during the Forties and Fifties as a complimentary remark from one soul brother to another. Later it was replaced by several terms such as *groovy, tough, beautiful* and, most recently, *out of sight.* This last expression is an outgrowth of the former term *way out,* the meaning of which was equivocal. *Way out* had an ad hoc hickish ring to it which made it intolerably unsoulful and consequently it was soon replaced by *out of sight*, which is also likely to experience a relatively brief period of popular usage. *Out of sight* is better than *way out*, but it has some of the same negative, childish taint of its predecessor.

The expression, *kill 'em*, has neither a violent nor a malicious interpretation. It means "good luck," "give 'em hell," or "I'm pulling for you," and originated in Harlem from six to nine years ago.

There are certain classic soul terms which, no matter how often borrowed, remain in the canon and are reactivated every so often, just as standard jazz tunes are continuously experiencing renaissances. Among the classical expressions are: *solid, cool, jive* (generally as a noun), *stuff, thing, swing* (or *swinging*), *pimp, dirt, freak, heat, larceny, busted, okee doke, piece, sheet* (a jail record), *squat, square, stash, lay, sting, mire, gone, smooth, joint, blow, play, shot,* and there are many more.

Soul language can be heard in practically all communities throughout the country, but for pure, undiluted spoken soul one must go to Soul Street. There are several. Soul is located at Seventh and "T" in Washington, D.C.; on One Two Five Street in New York City; on Springfield Avenue in Newark; on South Street in Philadelphia; on Tremont Street in Boston; on Forty-seventh Street in Chicago; on Fillmore in San Francisco; and dozens of similar locations in dozens of other cities.

As increasingly more Negroes desert Soulville for honorary membership in the Establishment clique, they experience a metamorphosis, the repercussions of which have a marked influence on the young and impressionable citizens of Soulville. The expatriates of Soulville are often greatly admired by the youth of Soulville, who emulate the behavior of such expatriates as Nancy Wilson, Ella Fitzgerald, Eartha Kitt, Lena Horne, Diahann Carroll, Billy Daniels, or Leslie Uggams. The result—more often than not—is a trend away from spoken soul among the young soul folks. This abandonment of the soul language is facilitated by the fact that more Negro youngsters than ever are acquiring college educations (which, incidentally, is not the best treatment for the continued good health and growth of soul); integration and television, too, are contributing significantly to the gradual demise of spoken soul.

Perhaps colleges in America should commence to teach a course in spoken soul. It could be entitled "The Vocal History of Black America," or simply "Spoken Soul." Undoubtedly there would be no difficulty finding teachers. There are literally thousands of these experts throughout the country whose talents lie idle while they await the call to duty.

Meanwhile the picture looks dark for soul. The two extremities in the Negro spectrum—the conservative and the militant—are both trying diligently to relinquish and repudiate whatever vestige they may still possess of soul. The semi-Negro—the soul brother intent on gaining admission to the Establishment even on an honorary basis—is anxiously embracing and assuming conventional English. The other extremity, the Ultra-Blacks, are frantically adopting everything from a Western version of Islam that would shock the Caliph right out of his snugly fitting shintiyan to anything that vaguely hints of that big, bountiful black bitch lying in the arms of the Indian and Atlantic Oceans and crowned by the majestic Mediterranean Sea. Whatever the Ultra-Black is after, it's anything but soulful.

How Do You Respond?

1. Claude Brown immediately rejects the lexical definition of *nigger* as a synonym for *Negro*. Why?

2. Would you call Brown's definition stipulative or extended or both? Why? How *does* he define the term? How does he feel about the word?

3. Rosten discusses how a Jewish term spread far beyond its original community; Brown details the similar wanderings of Soul talk. Are you surprised to learn the origin of any of these words? Discuss current popular terms and their origins.

KURT VONNEGUT, JR.

> *Kurt Vonnegut, Jr. (born 1922) is a prolific novelist and short-story writer who for some time was mistaken for a science-fiction writer. Slowly we realized that the science was an incidental ingredient and that his great themes are twentieth century extensions of the great traditions of the nineteenth century: our place in the natural order and the precariousness of sanity, civilization, political and social justice, and humanism. But his themes do not account for the effect, the experience, of reading him: he is a wizard of a storyteller, with a dazzling flair for providing all those sublime pleasures that we turn to fiction for. If you want to explore further, try* Slaughterhouse Five *and* Cat's Cradle.

HARRISON BERGERON

The year was 2081, and everybody was finally equal. They weren't only equal before God and the law. They were equal every which way. Nobody was smarter than anybody else. Nobody was better looking than anybody else. Nobody was stronger or quicker than anybody else. All this equality was due to the 211th, 212th, and 213th Amendments to the Constitution, and to the unceasing vigilance of agents of the United States Handicapper General.

Some things about living still weren't quite right, though. April, for instance, still drove people crazy by not being springtime. And it was in that clammy month that the H-G men took George and Hazel Bergeron's fourteen-year-old son, Harrison, away.

It was tragic all right, but George and Hazel couldn't think about it very hard. Hazel had a perfectly average intelligence, which meant she couldn't think about anything except in short bursts. And George, while his intelligence was way above normal, had a little mental handicap radio in his ear. He was required by law to wear it at all times. It was tuned to a government transmitter. Every twenty seconds or so, the transmitter would send out some sharp noise to keep people like George from taking unfair advantage of their brains.

George and Hazel were watching television. There were tears on

Hazel's cheeks, but she'd forgotten for the moment what they were about.

On the television screen were ballerinas.

A buzzer sounded in George's head. His thoughts fled in panic, like bandits from a burglar alarm.

"That was a real pretty dance, that dance they just did," said Hazel.

"Huh?" said George.

"That dance—it was nice," said Hazel.

"Yup," said George. He tried to think a little about the ballerinas. They weren't really very good—no better than anybody else would have been anyway. They were burdened with sash-weights and bags of birdshot, and their faces were masked, so that no one, seeing a free and graceful gesture or a pretty face, would feel like something the cat drug in. George was toying with the vague notion that maybe dancers shouldn't be handicapped. But he didn't get very far with it before another noise in his ear radio scattered his thoughts.

George winced. So did two out of the eight ballerinas.

Hazel saw him wince. Having no mental handicap herself, she had to ask George what the latest sound had been.

"Sounded like somebody hitting a milk bottle with a ball peen hammer." said George.

"I'd think it would be real interesting, hearing all the different sounds," said Hazel, a little envious. "All the things they think up."

"Um," said George.

"Only, if I was Handicapper General, you know what I would do?" said Hazel. Hazel, as a matter of fact, bore a strong resemblance to the Handicapper General, a woman named Diana Moon Glampers. "If I was Diana Moon Glampers," said Hazel, "I'd have chimes on Sunday—just chimes. Kind of in honor of religion."

"I could think, if it was just chimes," said George.

"Well—maybe make 'em real loud," said Hazel. "I think I'd make a good Handicapper General."

"Good as anybody else," said George.

"Who knows better'n I do what normal is?" said Hazel.

"Right," said George. He began to think glimmeringly about his abnormal son who was now in jail, about Harrison, but a twenty-one-gun salute in his head stopped that.

"Boy!" said Hazel, "that was a doozy, wasn't it?"

It was such a doozy that George was white and trembling, and tears stood on the rims of his red eyes. Two of the eight ballerinas had collapsed to the studio floor, were holding their temples.

"All of a sudden you look so tired," said Hazel. "Why don't you stretch out on the sofa, so's you can rest your handicap bag on the pillows, honeybunch." She was referring to the forty-seven pounds of birdshot in a canvas bag, which was padlocked around George's neck. "Go on and rest the bag for a little while," she said. "I don't care if you're not equal to me for a while."

George weighed the bag with his hands. "I don't mind it," he said. "I don't notice it any more. It's just a part of me."

"You been so tired lately—kind of wore out," said Hazel. "If there was just some way we could make a little hole in the bottom of the bag, and just take out a few of them lead balls. Just a few."

"Two years in prison and two thousand dollars fine for every ball I took out," said George. "I don't call that a bargain."

"If you could just take a few out when you came home from work," said Hazel. "I mean—you don't compete with anybody around here. You just set around."

"If I tried to get away with it," said George, "then other people'd get away with it—and pretty soon we'd be right back to the dark ages again, with everybody competing against everybody else. You wouldn't like that, would you?"

"I'd hate it," said Hazel.

"There you are," said George. "The minute people start cheating on laws, what do you think happens to society?"

If Hazel hadn't been able to come up with an answer to this question, George couldn't have supplied one. A siren was going off in his head.

"Reckon it'd fall all apart," said Hazel.

"What would?" said George blankly.

"Society," said Hazel uncertainly. "Wasn't that what you just said?"

"Who knows?" said George.

The television program was suddenly interrupted for a news bulletin. It wasn't clear at first as to what the bulletin was about, since the announcer, like all announcers, had a serious speech impediment. For about half a minute, and in a state of high excitement, the announcer tried to say, "Ladies and gentlemen—"

He finally gave up, handed the bulletin to a ballerina to read.

"That's all right—" Hazel said of the announcer, "he tried. That's the big thing. He tried to do the best he could with what God gave him. He should get a nice raise for trying so hard."

"Ladies and gentlemen—" said the ballerina, reading the bulletin. She must have been extraordinarily beautiful, because the mask she wore was hideous. And it was easy to see that she was the strongest and most graceful of all the dancers, for her handicap bags were as big as those worn by two-hundred-pound men.

And she had to apologize at once for her voice, which was a very unfair voice for a woman to use. Her voice was a warm, luminous, timeless melody. "Excuse me—" she said, and she began again, making her voice absolutely uncompetitive.

"Harrison Bergeron, age fourteen," she said in a grackle squawk, "has just escaped from jail, where he was held on suspicion of plotting to overthrow the government. He is a genius and an athlete, is under-handicapped, and should be regarded as extremely dangerous."

A police photograph of Harrison Bergeron was flashed on the screen—upside down, then sideways, upside down again, then right side up. The picture showed the full length of Harrison against a background calibrated in feet and inches. He was exactly seven feet tall.

The rest of Harrison's appearance was Halloween and hardware. Nobody had ever borne heavier handicaps. He had outgrown hindrances faster than the H-G men could think them up. Instead of a little ear radio for a mental handicap, he wore a tremendous pair of earphones, and spectacles with thick wavy lenses. The spectacles were intended to make him not only half blind, but to give him whanging headaches besides.

Scrap metal was hung all over him. Ordinarily, there was a certain symmetry, a military neatness to the handicaps issued to strong people, but Harrison looked like a walking junkyard. In the race of life, Harrison carried three hundred pounds.

And to offset his good looks, the H-G men required that he wear at all times a red rubber ball for a nose, keep his eyebrows shaved off, and cover his even white teeth with black caps at snaggle-tooth random.

"If you see this boy," said the ballerina, "do not—I repeat, do not—try to reason with him."

There was the shriek of a door being torn from its hinges.

Screams and barking cries of consternation came from the television set. The photograph of Harrison Bergeron on the screen jumped again and again, as though dancing to the tune of an earthquake.

George Bergeron correctly identified the earthquake, and well he might have—for many was the time his own home had danced to the same crashing tune. "My God—" said George, "that must be Harrison!"

The realization was blasted from his mind instantly by the sound of an automobile collision in his head.

When George could open his eyes again, the photograph of Harrison was gone. A living, breathing Harrison filled the screen.

Clanking, clownish, and huge, Harrison stood in the center of the studio. The knob of the uprooted studio door was still in his hand. Ballerinas, technicians, musicians, and announcers cowered on their knees before him, expecting to die.

"I am the Emperor!" cried Harrison. "Do you hear? I am the Emperor! Everybody must do what I say at once!" He stamped his foot and the studio shook.

"Even as I stand here—" he bellowed, "crippled, hobbled, sickened—I am a greater ruler than any man who ever lived! Now watch me become what I *can* become!"

Harrison tore the straps of his handicap harness like wet tissue paper, tore straps guaranteed to support five thousand pounds.

Harrison's scrap-iron handicaps crashed to the floor.

Harrison thrust his thumbs under the bar of the padlock that secured his head harness. The bar snapped like celery. Harrison smashed his headphones and spectacles against the wall.

He flung away his rubber-ball nose, revealed a man that would have awed Thor, the god of thunder.

"I shall now select my Empress!" he said, looking down on the cowering people. "Let the first woman who dares rise to her feet claim her mate and her throne!"

A moment passed, and then a ballerina arose, swaying like a willow.

Harrison plucked the mental handicap from her ear, snapped off her physical handicaps with marvellous delicacy. Last of all, he removed her mask.

She was blindingly beautiful.

"Now—" said Harrison, taking her hand, "shall we show the people the meaning of the word dance? Music!" he commanded.

The musicians scrambled back into their chairs, and Harrison stripped them of their handicaps, too. "Play your best," he told them, "and I'll make you barons and dukes and earls."

The music began. It was normal at first—cheap, silly, false. But Harrison snatched two musicians from their chairs, waved them like batons as he sang the music as he wanted it played. He slammed them back into their chairs.

The music began again and was much improved.

Harrison and his Empress merely listened to the music for a while— listened gravely, as though synchronizing their heartbeats with it.

They shifted their weights to their toes.

Harrison placed his big hands on the girl's tiny waist, letting her sense the weightlessness that would soon be hers.

And then, in an explosion of joy and grace, into the air they sprang!

Not only were the laws of the land abandoned, but the law of gravity and the laws of motion as well.

They reeled, whirled, swiveled, flounced, capered, gamboled, and spun.

They leaped like deer on the moon.

The studio ceiling was thirty feet high, but each leap brought the dancers nearer to it.

It became their obvious intention to kiss the ceiling.

They kissed it.

And then, neutralizing gravity with love and pure will, they remained suspended in air inches below the ceiling, and they kissed each other for a long, long time.

It was then that Diana Moon Glampers, the Handicapper General, came into the studio with a double-barreled ten-gauge shotgun. She fired twice and the Emperor and the Empress were dead before they hit the floor.

Diana Moon Glampers loaded the gun again. She aimed it at the musicians and told them they had ten seconds to get their handicaps back on.

It was then that the Bergerons' television tube burned out.

Hazel turned to comment about the blackout to George. But George had gone out into the kitchen for a can of beer.

George came back in with the beer, paused while a handicap signal shook him up. And then he sat down again. "You been crying?" he said to Hazel.

"Yup," she said.

"What about?" he said.

"I forget." she said. "Something real sad on television."

"What was it?" he said.

"It's all kind of mixed up in my mind," said Hazel.

"Forget sad things," said George.

"I always do," said Hazel.

"That's my girl," said George. He winced. There was the sound of a riveting gun in his head.

"Gee—I could tell that one was a doozy," said Hazel.

"You can say that again," said George.

"Gee—" said Hazel, "I could tell that one was a doozy."

How Do You Respond?

1. At the beginning of his story, Vonnegut tells us, "everybody was finally equal." What does he mean by *equality*?

2. What politics is he playing with—conservative, liberal, reactionary, anarchist? Is the story far-fetched? Do you think that Vonnegut carries the idea too far?

3. Can you point to situations in contemporary society that are absurd attempts to equalize the citizenry? What is the utopian idea behind these attempts? How has it gone wrong? How could it go right?

FOCUS ON YOUR READING

1. Look to the remarks on three kinds of definition on p. 277–78. How do Rosten, White, and Jordan define their terms? When do they rely upon the stipulative? How do they make the terms *bubeleh, fun,* and *freedom* mean what they want them to? Look up the lexical definitions of *freedom* and *fun*. Do these definitions shed additional light on these writers' definitions? If so, how so?

2. Writers' points of view shape the way they define terms. How

do you characterize Baker's point of view toward "American Fat"? What do you think of his question, "Why do we like our words so fat but our women so skinny?" Is this so? Is this a chauvinistic remark? What does he mean by "*our* women"? How might Lakoff respond to Baker's remark?

3. The writers in this chapter look at the language from several different points of view: Russell Baker looks at language in the political arena and in the media; Robin Lakoff looks at the sociology and semantics of language; and Claude Brown looks at language as tradition and culture. How do these writers define their terms? How do they explain what they mean? What similarities and differences do you notice in their ways of defining?

FOCUS ON YOUR WRITING

1. Define a concrete word—*table, typewriter, soap, snow,* or the like—by placing it into a general class and then offering distinguishing characteristics. Then put flesh on your definition by providing stipulative and extended definitions, by providing examples, descriptions, contrasts.

2. Define an abstract word—*love, truth, freedom, success, fun*—again, by offering first a lexical definition, and then, perhaps, by rejecting it (as Claude Brown does), showing what *you* mean by the word.

3. We have said that defining relies on the general; description focuses on the particular. Define a tree, a dog, a cat, any natural object. Now *describe* the same object.

4. Write an essay on language as it reflects a particular group that you know well, or that you would like to research: women's language, men's language, corporate language, non-standard English, etc. Define and characterize through examples, descriptions, narratives—whatever you need to represent the language as you hear it.

CHAPTER 8

❖❖

"Okay, So Give Me an Example"

EXEMPLIFYING

"Mr. McGregor, how is he?" you ask an old friend from your hometown.

"In his old age," she says, "he has become quite eccentric."

"How so?" you want to know.

"Some days he walks into town in his robe and slippers in the middle of winter. It doesn't matter if it's 12 degrees, and there he is, with a navy beret on his head and a briefcase in his hand. He will stop at the post office to ask if there's any mail for Tim Crockett. He gives himself new names: Tim Crockett. Davy Jones. Nathan Silverblatt. Other times he stops in front of the Five and Ten, stands facing the big window, and with a stick held high in one hand, acts as if he's conducting an orchestra. Do you remember him when he taught us in tenth grade? He was the best math teacher around. He'd make you understand, for the first time, about isosceles triangles. I'll never forget how he used to stand in front of the room and, quick, put a number on the board, cover it, and yell, 'Simon, what number do I have under my hand?'"

Here, in the process of *exemplifying*—of showing what we mean through examples—we see the play between the concrete and the abstract, between the general and the specific. The friend says that

Mr. McGregor has become eccentric, but until she offers examples of Mr. McGregor's behavior, you don't know what she means. Through examples of his actions, his dress, you come to know "how so," how it is that Mr. McGregor is acting eccentrically. The examples add up, in the speaker's mind, to a generalization about Mr. McGregor. In the same way, the memories about Mr. McGregor as a math teacher make specific the speaker's claim that he was the "best math teacher around."

When we exemplify, we offer evidence, we present cases—for examples, for instances—to support our generalizations. The cases may be generalized narratives. In contrast to the "once" of a story, generalized narratives are repeated actions or little stories that are rolled together: *some days* he walks into town. . . . This is not an action that occured once, not an event that happened only one day, but rather actions that recur, that can be bundled up into examples. *Repeatedly,* Mr. McGregor would trick his students by covering up a number behind his back on the blackboard, to see if they were paying attention. Actions that repeat themselves form examples, and from examples, we draw abstractions, we generalize.

E. B. White, in the following passage from *One Man's Meat*, generalizes about two of his actions, "setting pictures straight" and "squaring rugs up with the room," and suggest that these two behaviors reflect his need for an "ultimate symmetry"; he wants his world to be ordered, organized, straight:

> This life I lead, setting pictures straight, squaring rugs up with the room—it suggests an ultimate symmetry toward which I strive and strain. Yet I doubt that I am any nearer my goal than I was last year, or ten years ago, even granted that this untidy world is ready for any such orderliness. Going rapidly through the hall, on an errand of doubtful import to God and country, I pause suddenly, like an ant in its tracks, and with the toe of my sneaker shift the corner of the little rug two inches in a southerly direction, so that the edge runs parallel with the floor seams. Healed by this simple geometry, I continue my journey. The act, I can only conclude, satisfies something fundamental in me; and if, fifteen minutes later on my way back, I find that the rug is again out of line, I repeat the performance with no surprise and no temper. Long ago I accepted the fact of

a rug's delinquency; it has been a pitched battle and the end is not in sight. At least one of my ancestors died lunging out of bed at the enemy, and it is more than likely that I shall fall at last, truing up a mediocre mat.

Intellectually, I am ready to admit that there is no special virtue in an accurate alignment of inanimate objects, that a picture hanging cockeyed on the wall and a rug askew are conceivably as effective as they would be straight; but in practice I can't go it. If it is my nature to adjust the stance of a watercolor rather than enjoy its substance, then that's the whole of it, and I'm lucky to get even the dubious enjoyment that I occasionally experience from coming upon it and finding it square.

The other day something or other started me thinking about these rugs and pictures (ordinarily I carry on the war absentmindedly), and by reconstructing a twelve-hour period, I figured out that I had straightened a certain rug four times, another twice, a picture once—a total of seven adjustments. I believe this to be par for my private course. Seven times three hundred and sixty-five is two thousand five hundred and fifty-five, which I think I can give as a fair estimate of my yearly penance.

FROM "REMOVAL"

When we exemplify, we offer particulars, we present evidence for our generalizations. "If you don't behave," says the teacher, "I shall make an example of you. . . ." The child is punished in front of other children so that he and the others will learn that "bad" behavior is punished. In Dick Gregory's story, "Shame," we find a teacher placing Gregory from time to time "in the idiot's seat," where all the children will see him as a "troublemaker." This action has recurred. He has been put into the idiot's seat many times. Gregory uses these recurring events to show how things were, and he used a "once," an event of one day, to offer a little story, an anecdote, as a way of presenting his case:

the "once"   It was on Thursday. I was sitting in the back of the room, in a seat with a chalk circle drawn around it. The idiot's seat, the troublemaker's seat.

generalized narrative, telling how things "were"

The teacher thought I was stupid. Couldn't spell. Couldn't read, couldn't do arithmetic. Just stupid. Teachers were never interested in finding out that you couldn't concentrate because you were so hungry, because you hadn't had any breakfast. All you could think about was noontime, would it ever come? Maybe you could sneak into the cloakroom and steal a bit of some kid's lunch out of a coat pocket. A bite of something. Paste. You can't really make a meal out of paste, or put it on bread for a sandwich, but sometimes I'd scoop a few spoonfuls out of the paste jar in the back of the room. Pregnant people get strange tastes. I was pregnant with poverty. Pregnant with dirt and pregnant with smells that made people turn away, pregnant with cold and pregnant with shoes that were never bought for me, pregnant with five other people in my bed and no Daddy in the next room, and pregnant with hunger. Paste doesn't taste too bad when you're hungry.

The teacher thought I was a troublemaker. All she saw from the front of the room was a little black boy who squirmed in his idiot's seat and made noises and poked the kids around him. I guess she couldn't see a kid who made noises because he wanted someone to know he was there.

FROM *Nigger: An Autobiography*

Gregory here calls upon his powers as a storyteller, his skill in describing the scene, his searching after causes, to show that the event, the punishment, did not fit the crime. The teacher saw him as a troublemaker because he squirmed about in his seat. Gregory couldn't sit still because he was hungry.

When we exemplify, when we present a case, we call upon various forms of thought to make our case come alive, to allow our audience to experience what we experienced. Examples take form as generalized narratives, as anecdotes, as descriptions, as listings, as small bits of information, as statistics. In "Names," Mary Mc-

Carthy offers a long list of names to render vivid her notion that "Names had a great importance for us in the convent":

> Anna Lyons, Mary Louise Lyons, Mary von Phul, Emile von Phul, Eugenia McCellan, Marjorie McPhail, Marie-Louise L'Abbé, Mary Danz, Julia Dodge, Mary Fordyce Blake, Janet Preston—these were the names (I can still tell them over like a rosary) of some of the older girls in the convent: the Virtues and the Graces.

McCarthy offers us this litany of names to generalize further: "All these names reflected the still-pioneer character of the Pacific Northwest."

In the first of the following selections, William Safire offers one example after another to give us a closetful of "Mondegreens," the name he gives to those peculiar mistaken hearings that cause some of us to translate "I pledge allegiance to the flag" as something like "I led the Pigeons to the Flag." Note how he classifies these mishearings to find a suitable way of generalizing about them.

Susan Page in "All About Pigeons" explores the problem of pigeons overpopulating American cities by telling us about pigeon lovers and pigeon haters. She presents numbers of examples, using anecdotes, like this one:

> There was this old couple in their seventies, maybe, sitting next to me, and they were feeding a flock of pigeons. I didn't think anything about it; I thought it was kind of nice. The old man was slowly throwing out bread crumbs, until he almost had this pigeon eating out of his hand. Then—bam! He grabbed the bird, strangled it, and threw it into a bag his wife was holding. Then he got up happily and strolled away.

Page offers "statistics" to show the various ways city governments have attempted to banish pigeons: "Cincinnati poisoned an estimated 15,000 pigeons last winter in a railroad yard, where the general public did not notice the bodies."

Ira Berkow puts a generalization about Joe Louis right up front in his title: "Louis Had Style In and Out of the Ring," and he then offers examples out of Louis's life as a boxer and as a man to show that he had "style." David Marcus in "An Older Brother Lets Go" piles on examples to let us see his brother as he had seen him while they were growing up; he lists brief examples that present his case: "I recalled his earlier rites of passage: his first writing lesson (I was the instructor), the first time he skated, swam, drove, shaved, dated, danced. I remember the party at which he first drank alcohol and the squeaks his voice made when it was changing." Marcus could have written another essay, "The First Time My Brother Drank Alcohol"; here in "An Older Brother," this incident is part of a list where the writer generalizes about his brother's venturing into new experiences.

Ring Lardner in his story, "Mr. and Mrs. Fix-it," offers one example after another of two so-called friends who interfere relentlessly in the narrator's life. "I never in my life seen anybody as crazy to run other people's business," the narrator tells us. "Honest to heavens, it's a wonder they let us brush our own teeth." Throughout, we see a play, an interaction, between the examples and the generalizations the narrator offers:

generalization	Thayer is what you might call a all-around handy man.
specific examples	He can mimic pretty near all the birds and beasts and fishes, he can yodel, he can play a ocarina, or he can recite Kipling or Robert H. Service, or he can do card tricks, and strike a light with no matches, and tie all the different knots. And besides that, he can make a complete radio outfit and set it up, and take pictures as good as the best professional photographers and a whole lot better. He collects autographs. And he never had a sick day in his life.

The examples add up to the generalization that Thayer is "a all-around handy man."

Russell Baker in "Summer Beyond Wish" takes us into a summer of his childhood when he felt satisfied with life even though, by today's standards, he had a lot to wish for. We wonder, right away, how there could be a summer "beyond wish," and Baker tells us— through a variety of examples, of generalized narrative, of anecdote, of description, of comparison. In the same way, Mary McCarthy uses a multiplicity of forms to tell us of the place of "Names" in her childhood.

❖ ❖ ───────────────────────────────

AS YOU READ

The Concrete

Examples take a number of *concrete* forms: They are facts, statistics, cases, instances, samples. They are the particular event, the *once* of narrative. They are recurring events represented by generalized narratives—which are signalled by words like *usually, ordinarily, generally*—pointing to the way things usually were or the way things usually are. They are the scientist's "data," the particulars of a study or an experiment. The instance, the case, the sample, the number is there to explain, to clarify, to support an abstraction or generalization.

The Abstract

As you read, keep in mind that the abstract needs the concrete, and the concrete needs the abstract. When writers offer examples, they are always examples of *something*. And within the example, even in something as seemingly static as a number, is the evaluative, the implication that this number means something. *500 people died over the weekend in automobile accidents.* That fact points to a number of evaluative statements and questions: these deaths are to be lamented. But *this* number: is the number more or less than we have come to expect? We want to know how the writer interprets the example, what he *abstracts* from it, and ultimately, how he interprets it, what it *means* to *him*.

The Fit Between Abstract and Concrete

Keep in mind, as well, that the concrete and the abstract must fit together. When we are presented with a generalization, "Women are generally paid less than men when they perform the same jobs," we say, "Okay, so give me an example." Examples brought in, say, about secretaries' or nurses' salaries, we say, won't do, for these professions are generally dominated by women. We want suitable comparisons: women lawyers and doctors being paid less than male lawyers and doctors when they perform the same functions. We scrutinize the example, and we generally want more than one case before we are satisfied.

AS YOU WRITE

Generating Material

Perhaps one of the most productive ways of working with examples is to begin with an abstraction, a generalization, an *evaluative* statement. You may take a well-known saying—"A penny saved is a penny earned" or "The early bird catches the worm" and exemplify through a variety of examples. Or you may take a statement about something close to you—"My father is a wise man"—and then fish through your sea of memories to pull out concrete examples that bring the generalization to life. You may remember how your father (or some other person who helped to raise you) valued time spent in peaceful, quiet, deliberative activities: reading, playing the piano, planting tomatoes. You recall particular *instances*, the *once's*, and the generalized narratives. You offer sayings of his that helped you get through hard times; you remember the patience he showed when you were ill as a child, the nights he stayed up with you. The collection of memories grow. You might now want to *define* wisdom; you might want to *contrast* your subject with other such subjects you know; you might want to *describe* the way he talks to people, how his ego does not interfere with his interest in others. This set of examples may not fit the person you have in mind, but you can insert another group of qualities and use the same pattern in your writing.

Reading Your Writing

When you begin with an evaluative statement, you may find that the examples, the concrete details, are pointing in another direction. You may find that you're writing not about your father's wisdom but rather about his patience. Or you may be talking about both qualities, wisdom and patience. You begin to tailor the evaluative statements to fit the examples. Or you go back and *select* those examples that fit your definition of wisdom and exclude others not pertinent. Keep in mind that the relationship between the concrete and the abstract must be evident. You'll need to adjust one to fit the other.

Shaping Your Writing

The generalization, the abstraction, what we have been calling the evaluative, is what reveals your point of view. As you write, keep the evaluative—my father is a patient man—in mind and up front, so that your reader knows why it is you're using these examples. Select examples that are relevant. Use as many cases, instances, samples as you need to support your assertions. Use concrete details to make your examples vivid, sharp, memorable. Keep your readers in mind, remembering that they do not know what you know and, therefore, need full, detailed examples.

WILLIAM SAFIRE

> *Ever since H. L. Mencken published his great book,* The American Language, *every generation has produced two or three writers with a passionate and inexhaustible interest in how we use our language. Of contemporary "lexiphiles," one of the most attentive and attention-worthy is William Safire (born 1929), who contributes a weekly column to the* New York Times Sunday Magazine. *Many of his weekly columns are collected in* On Language.

"I LED THE PIGEONS TO THE FLAG"

The most saluted man in America is Richard Stans. Legions of schoolchildren place their hands over their hearts to pledge allegiance to the flag, "and to the republic for Richard Stans."

With all due patriotic fervor, the same kids salute "one nation, under guard." Some begin with "I pledge a legion to the flag," others with "I led the pigeons to the flag."

This is not a new phenomenon. When they come to "one nation, indivisible," this generation is as likely to say, "One naked individual" as a previous generation was to murmur, "One nation in a dirigible," or, "One nation and a vegetable."

"The Stars Bangled Banner" is a great source for these creative mishearings: "the Donzerly light," "oh, the ramrods we washed," "grapefruit through the night" that our flag was still there.

Then there is the good Mrs. Shirley Murphy of the 23d Psalm: "Shirley, good Mrs. Murphy, shall follow me all the days of my life." (Surely, goodness and mercy would not lead us into Penn Station.)

We all hear the same sounds. But until we are directed by the written word to the intended meaning, we may give free rein to our imagination to invent our own meanings. (*Free rein* has to do with letting horses run; some people are changing the metaphor to government, spelling it "free reign.") Children make sounds fit the sense in their own heads. In "God Bless America," the misheard line "Through the night with a light from a bulb" makes more practical sense than "a light from above." Writes David Thomas of Maine: "In Sunday school I used to sing part of a hymn, 'I will follow Henry Joyce.' Who Henry Joyce was didn't concern me—I was following him at the top of my lungs. When I learned to read, I found the words were 'I will follow and rejoice.'"

Sometimes that awakening never takes place. "To all intents and purposes," a nice old phrase, is sometimes spoken as—and written as—"for all intensive purposes." With the onset of adulthood, correction should not be taken for granted—or "taken for granite." In the song "Lucy in the Sky with Diamonds" (its title subliminally plugging LSD), the phrase "the girl with kaleidoscope eyes" came across to one grandmother as "the girl with colitis goes by."

What is this mistaken hearing called? In a query in this space recently, I remembered that I had called bandleader Guy Lombardo "Guylum Bardo," and asked for other examples of "false homonyms." That was a slight misnomer; homonyms are words pronounced the same, but with different meanings. Along with the other examples sent in—crooner Victor Moan, actress Sophie Aloran, musician "Big Spider" Beck, pro-football back Frank O'Harris, novelist Gorvey Doll—came instruction from linguists too mentionable to numerate. In each category, childlike translation can lead to semantic change.

(1) The Guylum Bardo syndrome—the simple misdivision of

"Okay, So Give Me an Example" 325

words—is called *metanalysis*. Many of the words we use correctly today are mistaken divisions of the past: a "napron" in Middle English became an "apron"—the *n* slid over to the left; an "ekename" of six centuries ago became a "nickname"—the *n* slid to the right.

In a future century, some of today's metanalyses (for "wrong cuttings") may become accepted English. An exorbitant charge is called "a nominal egg," perhaps committed by a "next-store neighbor"; some runners, poised at the starting line, hear, "On your market— set—go!" Millions of children consider the letter of the alphabet between *k* and *p* to be "ellemeno." Meteorologists on television who speak of "a patchy fog" do not realize that many creative viewers take that to be "Apache fog," which comes in on little cat feet to scalp the unsettled settler. Affiants seeking official witness go to a land called "Notar Republic," and Danny Boy, hero of "The Londonderry Air," casts a backward glance at what is often thought of as "The London Derrière." Future historians may wonder why chicken-hearted journalists coveted "the Pullet Surprise."

(2) The "José, can you see?" syndrome—the transmutation of words when they pass through different cultures or languages—is known to linguists as the *Law of Hobson-Jobson*. British soldiers in India heard the Mohammedan cry *"Ya-Hasan, ya-Husain!"* and called it "hobson-jobson." Noel Perrin at Dartmouth College reports that American soldiers in Japan transmuted a popular Japanese song, *"Shi-i-na-na Yaru,"* into "She Ain't Got No Yo-Yo." Similarly, *"O Tannenbaum"* is sometimes rendered "Oh, atom bomb."

(3) Semantic change can come from *malapropisms*, named after Mrs. Malaprop, a character in *The Rivals*, a 1775 play by Richard Sheridan. More people than you suspect read and pronounce *misled* as "mizzled," and the verb *to misle* will one day challenge *to mislead*. Others hum what they call "the bronze lullaby," though it must spin Brahms in his grave. One fascinating malapropism is "to hold in escarole," which combines the escrow function with the slang metaphor of money as lettuce.

(4) *Folk etymology* is the term for the creation of new words by mistake or misunderstanding or mispronunciation. "Tawdry," for example, came from Saint Audrey's, a place where cheap merchandise was sold. In today's language, "harebrained" is often giddily and irresponsibly misspelled "hairbrained," perhaps on the notion that the hair is near the brain.

The slurred *and* is one of the prolific changers of phrases. When "hard and fast" is spoken quickly, it becomes "hard 'n' fast," which sometimes gets transformed to "harden-fast rules." In the same way, the old "whole kit 'n' caboodle" is occasionally written as "kitten caboodle," a good name for a satchel in which to carry a cat. ("Up and atom!" is not a member of this group; it belongs with those Christmas carolers singing, "Oh, atom bomb.")

Lest you think that such mistakes can never permanently implant themselves in the language, consider "spit 'n' image." One longtime meaning of *spit* is "perfect likeness"—a child can be the very spit of his father. But some writers have mistaken the first two words in the phrase to mean "spitting," or ejection from the mouth, and prissily added the mistaken g to the sound of "spitt'n'." Novelist Paul Theroux entitled a chapter of *Picture Palace* "A Spitting Image." From such a respected writer, one expectorates more.

What all-inclusive term can we use to encompass the changes that our brains make in the intended meaning of what we hear? Linguists suggest "homophone," "unwitting paronomasia," and "agnominatio," but those terms sound like fancified dirty words to me.

I prefer "mondegreen." This is a word coined in a 1954 *Harper's Magazine* article, "The Death of Lady Mondegren" by Sylvia Wright, which reported on the doings of "Gladly, the cross-eyed bear" (the way many children hear "Gladly the Cross I'd bear"), and other sound-alikes. Miss Wright recalled a Scottish ballad, "The Bonny Earl of Murray" from Thomas Percy's "Reliques of Ancient English Poetry," which sounded to her like this:

> Ye Highlands and ye Lowlands,
> Oh, where hae ye been?
> They hae slain the Earl Amurray,
> And Lady Mondegreen.

She envisioned the bonny Earl holding the beautiful Lady Mondegreen's hand, both bleeding profusely, but faithful unto death. "By now," Miss Wright wrote, "several of you more alert readers are jumping up and down in your impatience to interrupt and point out that, according to the poem, after they killed the Earl of Murray, they 'laid him on the green.' I know about this, but I won't give in to it. Leaving him to die all alone without even anyone to hold his hand—I won't have it."

Thanks to responsive readers, I have a column on sound defects and a whole closetful of mondegreens. But a nuff is a nuff.

How Do You Respond?

1. Do Safire's renditions of mishearings make you think of any experiences of your own? Think of misheard prayers, hymns, public statements, especially ones heard in childhood. Write down such mishearings that are part of your history.
2. At what point does Safire begin to offer generalizations to bring order to his examples? Before that point, what generalizations have you as a reader begun to formulate?
3. Safire offers some technical names—metanalysis, malapropisms—for his sound defects. What does this categorizing contribute to his essay? You may want to look up Sylvia Wright's *Harper's* article in your library. How does her treatment of this subject differ from Safire's?

SUSAN PAGE

> Susan Page was born in Wichita, Kansas, which she describes as a city with "no pigeon problem at all." Even if, as you read these words, you are not at all interested in pigeons, you will probably discover that when people like Susan Page turn their attention to a subject, whatever it may be, it gets to be interesting.

ALL ABOUT PIGEONS

An elderly woman, her ash-blond wig slightly askew and showing tufts of thin gray hair, shuffles slowly to a park bench and sits down heavily. She reaches into a shopping bag, pulls out a handful of grain, and scatters it expertly on the sidewalk. "Hello, Gwendalyn; hello, Jacob," she coos softly to two of the two-dozen-odd pigeons that gather quickly around her feet, pecking the sidewalk anxiously. "Did you think I had forgotten you?"

Since her husband died in 1967, Mrs. Evelyn Johns Schaffer has been coming to the park nearly every day, and for more than three years she has fed the pigeons that crowd around her bench. Gwendalyn, a plump, blue-gray bird with an iridescent green neck and a perky jaunt, and Jacob, a striking brown and white pigeon with an intricate feather pattern on his slightly arched back, are her favorites. At first Mrs. Schaffer brought dry bread crumbs for them, but soon she was taking part of her $120-month Social Security check and buying fifty-pound sacks of feed grain. "I used to sit down there and watch the children," she says, nodding toward a playing field nearby, "but now the pigeons keep me so busy, I just don't have the time. I sit here and feed Jacob and the rest, and watch them, and before I know it, it's time to go home."

Grass is rare in most cities, and wide-open spaces are about as easy to find as clean air. Rats, cockroaches, and dogs are signs of a world of nature among the cars and concrete, but it is the pigeon—swooping gracefully between skyscrapers, bobbing proudly down the avenue, or gossiping on a ledge—that is the ubiquitous sign of nature, the one living being besides humans that nearly every big-city dweller sees every day. "There's nothing prettier than a flock of pigeons in the city," declares Encil E. Rains, administrative vice president of the New York ASPCA and an ardent pigeon-defender. "What they contribute psychologically! I don't think man can live in an area without animals, and I can't think of anything that gives an old duffer or biddy as much pleasure as feeding the pigeons."

There are those, however, who are pigeon-haters. Indeed, some people would like to see Gwendalyn, Jacob, and their friends and relations shot, poisoned, gassed, or run out of town. Pigeons are "death carriers," says Fran Lee, the explosive president of Children Before Dogs, more widely known as the "Scoop-the-Poop Lady" because of her campaign against dog dirt on New York sidewalks. "There's pigeon poop on the streets, in the water, on the park benches, in the children's sandboxes, everywhere! Pigeons are dirty, dirty, dirty animals, they carry disease, and every single one of them should be taken away. I don't know where they should be taken, and I don't much care. I don't know why people treasure pigeons. It's just incredible!"

Mrs. Lee's campaign against pigeons is echoed by a number of scientists, doctors, and public health officials who know what pigeons do to a city. Of course, there are almost 300 different kinds of pigeons, and some present no health problems at all. There are show pigeons like the Tumbler and the Tippler, for example, which turn somersaults in the air. The Fantail has a wide, beautiful tail, and the Pouter has a grossly inflated chest that makes it look as if it had just swallowed a balloon. Homing and racing pigeons are bred, trained, and protected by pigeon-fanciers who belong to clubs and disdainfully refer to street pigeons as "diggs." It is the "diggs," roaming bands of street pigeons clustered in cities, that present the public health problems. Their droppings not only coat statues (making them disintegrate) and park benches (making them useless) but also contaminate food sold by sidewalk vendors and markets. Pigeons attract fleas, bugs, ticks, mites, and rats, all of which bring their own health problems. Pigeon dropppings can dry, crumble, become airborne, and be inhaled by humans, transmitting diseases such as a type of meningitis, histoplasmosis, and ornithosis. Some of these diseases can cause respiratory problems, some can cause permanent brain damage, and some can result in death. In New York City alone, a few people die each year from cryptococcus meningitis, an inflammation of the membrane covering the spinal cord and brain, usually traceable to pigeons.

Pigeons, which are native to Europe and parts of Asia and Africa, are now found everywhere except the Arctic, Antarctic, and a few oceanic islands. In the early cultures of the Near East, the pigeon was a sacred bird, associated with the Syrian goddess Astarte. In classical Greece the pigeon was sacred to Aphrodite, and later in Rome pigeons were associated with Venus.

Pigeons also have traditionally served utilitarian purposes. Throughout the Middle East homing pigeons were used to carry messages, and pigeons have been used in warfare from Rome's conquest of Gaul until World War II. Egyptian writings dating from 3000 B.C. report the domestication of pigeons for food; last year in the United States more than a million pounds of specially bred and raised pigeons, called "squab," were sold for food. In medieval England, the lord of the manor reserved the right to let his pigeons forage over the fields that he leased to tenants. The pigeons ate seeds and grains from newly planted fields, and gave landlords a meat supply at little expense. The government regulated the construction of pigeon houses, or dovecotes, and prescribed the method of disposing of droppings to conserve their niter, needed to manufacture gunpowder. Government-appointed inspectors enforced regulations, and collectors gathered the manure. At one time there were more than 20,000 dovecotes in England.

Street pigeons aren't usually eaten today, although the New York State law against killing pigeons exempts killing for food. Some of the city's impoverished do eat street pigeons even though they are not recommended by doctors or gourmets. A now-successful New York writer recalls that when he first came to the city in 1958 with $20 in his pocket, he stayed in an SRO hotel on 114th Street while looking for a job. "One sunny afternoon I was sitting on the benches on Broadway, and, man, was I hungry," he says. "There was this old couple in their seventies, maybe, sitting next to me, and they were feeding a flock of pigeons. I didn't think anything about it; I thought it was kind of nice. The old man was slowly throwing out bread crumbs, until he almost had this pigeon eating out of his hand. Then—bam! He grabbed the bird, strangled it, and threw it into a bag his wife was holding. Then they got up happily and strolled away."

Pigeons are sociable, live in communities, and mate for life. But the courting that precedes the mating can be tough, since the sex of pigeons is difficult to identify on sight, even for other pigeons. Females are sometimes smaller, quieter, and duller in coloring, but not always. A courting male pigeon will coo, dance, and spread and scrape his tail rather anxiously in front of a prospective partner. If the prospect turns out to be male, a fight follows. A hen lays two eggs six or seven times a year for her entire ten-to-fifteen-year lifespan, although reproduction tapers off after the first eight to ten years. About 70 percent of the baby pigeons survive, an incredible rate when one figures that if there were 10,000 young female pigeons in a city, and each one raised ten young a year, there would be 100,000 new pigeons in the city in one year. More pigeons are born, survive, and reproduce in our cities than the natural environment can handle, partly because of the availability of "unnatural" food sources, like garbage and handouts from people.

Pigeons do have some natural enemies, of course, including owls and hawks. In the 1950s a few peregrine falcons nested in the Palisades across the Hudson from New York. They would swoop down in the Wall Street area to grab startled pigeons in their talons and devour them. But the falcons seem to have disappeared, though a more common city enemy of the pigeon—the rat—is thriving. Rats will sneak up on a sluggish pigeon, grab it by the throat, kill it, and eat it. Usually they are only brave enough to attack baby pigeons, because an adult pigeon, which can weigh one pound or more, will chase away a rat. Some pigeons are killed by cars, and occasionally there are pigeon epidemics; the birds are susceptible to bacterial, fungal, viral, and parasitic diseases. Most city pigeons, however, simply die of old age.

Pigeons and their human friends have proved remarkably resourceful in evading nearly all the controls, from birth-control pellets to carbide shells to pigeon apartment complexes, that pigeon-haters have devised. One of New York's leading museums once put large black rubber owls on its wide ledges to discourage the large number of pigeons that roosted there. Within the day the pigeons had gotten over their fear of owls and were back, perched on the owls' heads. A few years ago San Francisco put a sticky coating on the ledges of some public buildings, but the pigeons got used to the goop and came back to roost. The city then tried trapping, using electric owls, and periodically exploding carbide shells outside a city building, hoping the noise would scare the pigeons away. It did, but not for long, and the program was abandoned. More frequent explosions probably would have distressed the humans in the area more than the birds. Philadelphia tried a feed that makes pigeons vomit, and then, they hoped, go away. A New York firm claimed it had a feed that made a pigeon's nervous system send "danger signals" to the other members of its flock.

Montbéliard, France, had a distinctively French plan: the town put out alcohol-soaked bread crumbs in the hope of getting its pigeons so drunk that they could easily be picked up and carted away. The pigeons apparently didn't like alcohol and wouldn't touch the crumbs, but it probably wouldn't have done much good, anyway. Paris tried shipping thousands of pigeons out of town on special trucks, but the birds made it back before the trucks did.

West Berlin was tougher. In 1962, workmen spread poisoned bread crumbs throughout the city to kill its pigeons. Pigeon-lovers had been tipped off about the program, however, and they simply followed the workmen, sweeping up the crumbs. Another city with a similar plan was thwarted when pigeon-defenders grossly overfed pigeons the day before a poisoning program was to begin, so the pigeons were too full to eat any of the poisoned crumbs. Akron, Ohio, was sneakier. In the early 1950s, the city spread out poisoned corn in the evening, when the downtown streets were deserted. They whisked the pigeon bodies up and out of sight early in the morning, while most of the residents were still asleep. Similarly, Cincinnati poisoned an estimated 15,000 pigeons last winter in a railroad yard, where the general public did not notice the bodies. A Southwestern city put out bait soaked in anesthetic, then collected the unconscious pigeons and fed them to zoo animals. Buffalo, Indianapolis, and Cleveland at various times hired teams of sharpshooters to pick off the pigeons.

A kinder control was used in Karlsruhe, Germany. The city built pigeon apartment towers in centrally located open areas. The towers provided cubes for nine pairs of birds each, with roosting and feeding facilities nearby. The back walls of the apartments were removable, for cleaning and so each pigeon egg could be pricked with a thin needle, preventing its hatching. (If the egg was simply removed, the bird would lay another.) But the excess pigeon population had to be killed, and the program was obviously expensive.

The cheapest way to deal with pigeons was demonstrated by Bayonne, New Jersey, when it passed a law forbidding "unlicensed" pigeons from flying over the city. Mobile, Alabama, tried a similar approach; there it is illegal for pigeons to eat pebbles from flat roofs. Few arrests have been reported.

Paris tried trapping with airborne nets launched from crossbows. In the early 1960s Munich tried to resettle 200,000 pigeons in rural areas. Lisbon used hawks at its airport to keep the runways free of pigeons and starlings. London tried spraying some pigeon-infested buildings with a jellylike substance that dried to a slippery crust, but the pigeons got used to the unsteady perch, and the buildings were left with a useless slippery crust and just as many birds as before. Venice, where the pigeons have abounded in St. Mark's Square for more than 700 years, recently embarked on an ambitious if slow control program. Each day 300 to 500 pigeons are netted and packed away into the country, and the practice is to continue for years. Authorities hope then to crossbreed a healthy new race of pigeons that will live in modern pigeon coops set up in nearby gardens and will be trained to commute to the Square for the tourists each day.

New York's most notable experiment occurred several years ago, when the city and the ASPCA jointly sponsored a birth-control program for pigeons. Grain soaked in contraceptive, now marketed by the G. D. Searle Company in Chicago, was scattered for a few selected flocks, and head counts were carefully kept. The contraceptive worked for about eight months, but the results were generally disappointing. Costs ran more than a dollar per pigeon per year, and without a citywide program, the pigeon population could not be expected to drop much. "Anyway," one participant observed, "you miss a coupla months and boom, you've got a bunch of pregnant pigeons again."

Pigeon, Michigan (population 1,174), has no street pigeons at all, although a wild pigeon is occasionally seen. On the other hand, Victor Bartkowski, supervisor of the Buffalo Department of Pest and Vermin Control, estimates that there is at least one and maybe two pigeons for each of the city's 465,000 people. His seven-man department traps or shoots about 30,000 pigeons each year, just to keep the number manageable. The city's control program was perhaps the first in the nation, dating to 1948. "Before that you couldn't even walk down Main Street for the pigeons." Bartkowski recalls. New York City, 450 miles to the southeast, has five million street pigeons, according to Thomas J. Dalton, a now retired public health inspector who worked on pigeon control for fifteen years. "Other cities are just as bad," Dalton says shaking his head. "Philadelphia, Baltimore, Milwaukee—they've all got problems like New York." And European cities? "They're deluged."

Dalton may be the king of pigeon control. He has been New York City's only Special Pigeon Consultant. From 1964 to 1972, he got rid of about 40 percent of its five million pigeons, he says, although the population has grown again since his retirement. Others call his figures inflated—after all, he is claiming the death of two million pigeons—but no one denies that he made significant inroads in the pigeon population. Things weren't easy for New York pigeons and their feeders when Dalton was at work.

Part of his vehemence may be personal. Dalton's asthma was aggravated by a lung disease he probably caught from the infected pigeons he worked with. Now he is in and out of hospitals for tests and treatment. His voice is rasping, and he often uses a respirator that stands nearby his chair in his Staten Island home. In addition, after the pigeon program started he discovered that he was allergic to pigeon feathers.

In 1949, after twenty-two years in the Navy, Dalton became a public health inspector for New York City. He was assigned to dog bites and gas inspections, then worked on ragweed control for a year. But he found he was allergic to ragweed, and when the department needed a volunteer for a special research project, he stepped forward.

Dr. Maxwell L. Littman, senior research scientist of the Health Department, got a $500,000 grant in 1957 to study pigeons and disease. Dalton agreed to collect pigeon droppings and run laboratory test two days a week. Gradually he became more and more involved in pigeon control, until finally he was working as a full-time Pigeon Control Consultant.

The program evolved when, as he collected droppings specimens, Dalton was approached by building owners who wanted to know how to control the pigeons in their area. So Dalton wrote a small pamphlet called "Let's Control Pigeons," which used simple words and drawings to explain the diseases that street pigeons may carry and to suggest ways to protect buildings from pigeons, such as fencing off probable roosting and nesting corners with screens and spikes. One newspaper commentator praised the pamphlet as being to pigeon control what Machiavelli's *The Prince* was to politics.

Dalton had some problems during his tenure. Some policemen refused to enforce laws against pigeon-feeding, he complains. "They say you take some old lady in for feeding the pigeons, and you're leaving some young squirt there to go unmolested. Which is wrong. You can get the old ladies for littering and if you know your business, you can get them for creating a nuisance." Dalton assisted in prosecuting fourteen cases, twelve of which ended in convictions. One elderly woman was fined after she was arrested for feeding pigeons each day at a particular spot, even after she had been warned to stop. In court she denied feeding the pigeons. She was feeding her sister, she said, who had been reincarnated in the form of a pigeon.

If cities don't start comprehensive programs of pigeon control soon, Dalton warns, "We're going to have lung diseases; we're going to have cryptococcus meningitis; we're going to have problems with mites; and we're not even going to be able to diagnose them properly because they're so similar to the symptoms of other diseases."

In New York each year, an estimated twenty people contact cryptococcus meningitis from pigeons and a few die from it. Dalton is convinced that the pigeon's high normal body temperature, 107 degrees, makes its intestine work as a kind of incubator for the disease while allowing the pigeon to escape its effects. Others think the disease develops in the rich culture of the already excreted droppings. Although cryptococcus meningitis is the most serious disease pigeons can transmit to man, it is not the only one. Others include:

Histoplasmosis, caught in the same way as cryptococcosis, and usually a mild respiratory ailment that resembles a cold. In a Kansas study, children living in buildings on which pigeons roosted were found to have a histoplasmosis infection rate three times that of children living in quarters without pigeons.

Encephalitis, or "sleeping sickness," a virus infection of the nervous system that is usually transmitted from birds to man via mosquitoes.

Salmonellosis, a bacterial food poisoning, found in about 2 percent of all pigeon droppings and a threat to outdoor markets and vendors.

Pigeon ornithosis, a usually mild virus, transmitted to humans through infected pigeon droppings and sometimes by human carriers.

Not everybody considers pigeons a serious health problem, however. Most public health experts don't worry about reasonably healthy people who have no special contact with pigeons or their droppings. But people who are especially susceptible to disease, or children who handle street pigeons and then don't wash their hands properly, risk illness. Also endangered are people who scrape droppings off a windowsill or patio. The dried droppings crumble and saturate the air. Professionals always spray the dried droppings with a liquid chemical before scraping to prevent crumbling.

One of the people who do not worry much about the threat of pigeons is the man who replaced Dalton as head of New York's pigeon control. William Powers is really more concerned about the supervision of pet shops and the control of stray dogs, two areas he also works in. "Three deaths a year from cryptococcus meningitis in a population of eight million just isn't a major health problem," he says. "We get eighteen hundred people killed here every year from carrying pistols." Other authorities point out that the diseases pigeons transmit are also carried by ducks, chickens, and other birds.

Dalton and Powers do not have kind words for one another. Dalton believes that his retirement, the pigeon-control program has deteriorated. And Powers thinks Dalton is a fanatic. "Mr. Dalton goes on the aspect of 'these vicious wild little beasties,' " says Powers, a tall, middle-aged man. "He's very adamant about it, very excited about it. Well, the pigeons are a fact of life; it's not a religion with me. We take a low priority on this, and this bothers Mr. Dalton. We have rat bites, and they are politically oriented. Pigeons, they're not too politically oriented."

In fact, in New York the laws protecting pigeons from people are stronger than the laws protecting people from pigeons. The state conservation law designed to protect banded carrier pigeons prohibits the killing of pigeons in cities unless the pigeons are injured or diseased or are required for food. All the city can do is declare the pigeons in a specific area or building a nuisance, then issue a trapping permit. A private company can then be hired to catch the pigeons and take them to the ASPCA, and the ASPCA supposedly takes them to the country and releases them. But it doesn't work that way in practice. First of all, there is an active black market in trapped street pigeons. The birds often are taken south and used for skeet-shooting instead of clay "pigeon" targets. And even if the trapped pigeons make it to the ASPCA, they aren't safe. The society simply gasses them to death, and justifies the killings under the law that allows the ASPCA to kill stray dogs. Meanwhile, the ASPCA also provides hospital facilities for several injured pigeons each month. These pigeons, which may have broken wings or other infirmities, are nursed back to health and set free, perhaps to be trapped and gassed to death later in the same building.

The Audubon Society, traditional protector of birdlife, has no such split feelings about pigeons. It scarcely recognizes the pigeon as a bird, and the prospect of a wholesale extermination of the pigeon population does not particularly alarm it. "The Audubon Society is neither for nor against pigeon control, though we do step in when the control may endanger other native birds, as in the case of scattering poison grain," says Richard Plunkett, assistant to the biologist of the Audubon Society.

Plunkett is one of those who say that controls of any kind can never do any good, anyway. "There are no cheap means, nor even any expensive means, that would be effective to combat the pigeons," Plunkett says. "There's no way to kill all of them. Trapping can't go far enough. There's no effective poison. You could get natural control on the pigeon population if you cut down on their unnatural food sources, like garbage and people feeding them. But the people simply are not ready for real pigeon control."

Mrs. Evelyn Jones Schaffer couldn't agree more. The mention of pigeon control angers and upsets her. "It's ridiculous!" she says fervently. "The pigeons are healthy. Just look at them! It's the people who are sick." When the afternoon becomes cool and her shopping bag is empty, Mrs. Schaffer turns it over and shakes out the last few grains. Then she gets to her feet and starts away. "Goodbye now, Gwendalyn," she says, as, head bobbing, the pigeon follows her for a few steps. "Goodbye. And don't worry, I'll be back tomorrow."

How Do You Respond?

1. Go through Susan Page's text and note the generalizations—pigeons have enemies, pigeons are useful, pigeons spread disease. List her generalizations. Are they interesting? Discuss how Page appeals to her readers.

2. Discuss Page's use of examples. Do you see a pattern to them? How does she make them interesting?

3. How do Page's thumbnail character studies—of Evelyn Schaffer, Thomas Dalton, etc.—contribute to the effect of her piece? Are these examples? Of what?

IRA BERKOW

> *A prolific sportswriter, Ira Berkow (born 1940) writes about a variety of sports—from boxing to baseball. Author of sports columns for the* New York Times *and several books, including* Oscar Robertson: The Golden Year *(with Walt Frazier);* Rockin' Steady, *and* Beyond the Dream, *he is a member of Baseball Writers of America.*

LOUIS HAD STYLE IN AND OUT OF THE RING:
An Appreciation

On a cold night in January 1970, three men rode in a cab to Grand Central Terminal, where they would board a train for Rochester. They happened to be going to the same awards dinner. In the back were a baseball player and a sports reporter. In the front seat was Joe Louis, the former heavy-weight champion, who stared straight ahead as the lurid city lights flashed on his broad face. He listened to the baseball player making cracks about the young cab driver, who had long hair, which was not yet the vogue among athletes.

The ballplayer said something about "hippies" and "sissies," and then about the unusual music playing on the portable radio on the front seat. Louis said nothing.

"Hey," the ballplayer finally said to the cabbie, "turn that damn hippie music off."

"That's Greek music," Louis said quietly, speaking for the first time. There was a silence except for the music.

"Oh," the ballplayer said.

Joe Louis made his point as deftly, simply and thoroughly as he had when dispatching opponents in the ring.

Louis died Sunday morning, one month short of his sixth-seventh birthday. His death, like his life, moved many people.

It was his style as much as his prowess that established Louis as one of the more important figures of his time. "I kept my nose clean," he once said. "And I had to be a gentleman. If I cut the fool, I'd have let my people down."

Blacks in America had few heroes to look up to in the 1930s—in some parts of the United States, blacks still had to get off the streets when the sun went down—and when Joe Louis won the heavy-weight championship of the world by knocking out James J. Braddock June 22, 1937, there was rejoicing. "For one night, in all the darktowns of America, the blackman was king," wrote Alistair Cooke.

Walt Frazier, the former Knick basketball star, remembers meeting Louis for the first time. They sat at the coffee shop in Caesars Palace in Las Vegas, where Louis worked as a greeter.

"I had formed an impression of him, from all that I had heard all my life about him," said Frazier. "I was kind of nervous. But he stuck out his hand and said, 'Hiya, Clyde,' like he had known me all his life. Gave me a warm feeling."

Frazier asked him about being a black athlete in the 1930s and 1940s. Louis casually told of not being allowed in some hotels. He told, too, of being in New Orleans when he saw a car hit a black man, of how ambulances from white hospitals wouldn't pick up the man.

In time, though, Louis would be admitted to some of those hotels, and he was instrumental in breaking down other racial barriers.

"It's hard for me to relate to his experiences, because I was too young to remember," Frazier said. "But Joe was a pioneer, like Jackie Robinson. He helped the black man to be proud of himself, He was someone we always looked up to."

"Black athletes have it so good today. We're reaping what he paved the way for. We should have given him a percentage of our pay."

Louis said it was Robinson who "was my hero."

"Jackie didn't bite his tongue for nothing. I just don't have the guts, you might call it, to say what he says. And I don't talk as good either, that's for sure. But you need a lot of different types to make the world better."

Louis retired as an undefeated champion in 1949. But in 1950 he decided to try a comeback. Ezzard Charles was the champion.

"I didn't want the fight," Charles would say later. "Joe was my boyhood idol. But my manager, Ray Arcel, said that if I wanted everyone to consider me the champ I'd have to fight Joe. I signed, but I wasn't happy about it."

Charles dominated the fight. "About the eighth or ninth round," Charles said, "Joe began to falter. I started dreaming, 'Could this be the great Joe Louis?' I wanted to win, but I didn't want to knock him out." Charles won on a fifteen-round decision.

Louis could look back, though, at a remarkable career: He was knocked out by Max Schmeling—Hitler's Aryan hope—then came back to knock him out in the first round; he was losing to Billy Conn after twelve rounds and then knocked him out in the thirteenth. He was also honored by his country. Once, President Franklin D. Roosevelt invited him to the White House for a visit. Roosevelt squeezed the muscle of his arm. "This is the kind of muscle we need to win a war," Roosevelt said.

"When the President squeezed my arm," Louis once recalled, "it hurt. He had strong hands from using his wheelchair."

Another time, he was asked his biggest thrill. "I was able to pay for my sister to go to Howard University," said Louis, who was the son of an Alabama sharecropper and had only a sixth-grade education. "My mother and me went down to Washington for the graduation. The three of us walked across the campus. That was the biggest thrill of my life."

In 1942, at a New York boxing writers dinner, former Mayor James J. Walker made a presentation to Louis and, in his flamboyant, sentimental style, said, "Joe Louis, you laid a rose on Abraham Lincoln's grave."

One night in 1968 Louis was again honored by the New York reporters, for his "long and meritorious service" to boxing. He was to receive the James J. Walker Award. Now Louis rose and accepted the plaque. "Thank you for voting me this James J. Walker Award," he said, in the hushed hall at the Waldorf Astoria. "I think it is a great thing. I remember when he said that I laid a rose on Lincoln's grave. I didn't know what he meant then. But I knew he was trying to make me feel good. I thought about it later on, and I understood what it was about. Thank you."

How Do You Respond?

1. Do you find a clear statement of what Berkow means by Joe Louis's style? How does Berkow convey his sense of Louis's style?

2. Reread Louis's own words as reported by Berkow. Characterize the spirit they reveal.

3. Write a short piece characterizing a friend or family member by examples of their actions.

DAVID MARCUS

> David Marcus is pleased to be the youngest writer in this collection. A recent graduate of Brown University (1982), where he was president of his senior class, Marcus has been writing for years: keeping a journal, trying his hand at articles drawn from his daily life, as we see in "An Older Brother Lets Go." "My friends accuse me of exploiting everything," he says, "and I guess I do." "As a writer," he says, "you must begin to build a track record," and so he has, having published articles in the New York Times, the Brown Daily Herald, and Newsday. He is on his way with a job as feature writer for the Miami Herald.

AN OLDER BROTHER LETS GO

There had been harbingers for months, but I had ignored them. Then one morning late in August, the mail included a bulky envelope with a Vermont postmark and a college seal. He tore it open, nervously reading aloud the names of a roommate and a dormitory. I realized that the time had arrived; I was finally losing my little brother.

He spent the remaining week dashing to send-off parties, filling an address book, buying skis and sweaters, gathering property loaned to old high school friends. At night, flopped on his bed with the phone cord snaking through a jumble of stereo components, duffel bags, and half-packed cartons, he moped. I shared his excitement and his sadness, as I had on so many occasions.

The most palpable anchor to my childhood, a proud, rambunctious, sharp-witted seventeen-year old, was being pried up and away. While his gaze swept the horizon—college, law school, career—mine turned back. I recalled his earlier rites of passage: his first writing lesson (I was the instructor), the first time he skated, swam, drove, shaved, dated, danced. I remembered the party at which he first drank alcohol and the squeaks his voice made when it was changing.

To be an older sibling is to play confidant, counselor, protector, preacher, role model, friend, and, at times, foe. Every new situation requires an ad-libbed, hit-or-miss performance. Parents, at least, have books to guide them. There is no Dr. Spock for big brothers and sisters.

Through the years I held on to only one cardinal rule: a big brother should listen. I memorized the names of his teachers, teammates, girlfriends, bosses. I knew which musicians he worshipped, which TV programs were "bad" (good). And the lingo! Adult observers found our chatter unintelligible; gradually the family car evolved into "the bomber"; parents became "rents"; goodbye turned to "later."

Brotherhood was rewarding. I relished our late-night bull sessions, held a few times each week. Hours after the "rents" had fallen asleep, my brother crept into my room to trade jokes, recount the day's events, and compare gossip. I will miss those whispered exchanges. We'll see each other on vacations and we can stay in touch by phone, of course. But our relationship will never be the same. He no longer needs me to pave the way, for he has entered "the wilderness period of his life" and is "hacking his way through the jungles of experience," in Thomas Wolfe's words.

"I've gotta get away from here. This joint is boring," he announced while examining his new skis. "Looks like I'll be doing some *bad* jumping, huh?" We had built a jump on a neighborhood golf course during a blizzard several winters ago. He was a reckless novice, small for his age, using my hand-down skis. Soon the three years between us were forgotten; we were equals. Long after dusk we trudged home to discuss our Olympic future over popcorn and hot chocolate. In those days we were an inseparable pair: challenging peers to basketball games, pooling our allowances for a calculator, pitting our parents against each other to achieve our ends.

A memorial service for our grandmother brought us as close as brothers can be. I was delivering the eulogy when, from the back row, an aunt, always hard of hearing, began a running commentary. Intended for the woman sitting next to her, the remarks were audible to everyone. After completing my speech, I darted to the men's room, where my brother joined me. For five minutes we laughed uncontrollably at the incident and cried over our first taste of death.

During recent years the strains of adolescence, the physical proximity, the shared interests and possessions spurred arguments and fist fights. In many instances we vowed never again to acknowledge one another. But somehow we reconciled every time.

On the morning of his departure, I yearn to ask my brother for an evaluation. In all my years at school I received report cards; on finishing a seventeen-year task I think I deserve compliments or critiques. I also muse about recognition; others are addressed as Ph.D., M.D., D.D.S, and so forth. Haven't I earned a B.B.—big brother—degree?

"Do me a favor, Dave. Remind the rents to send CARE packages." He is loading his belongings into a station wagon. Although I am bursting with parting advice, warnings and reassurances, I remain speechless. Together we inspect his empty, eerie, bedroom, then shut the door on his boyhood.

When we meet again at Thanksgiving he will have turned eighteen, voted in a presidential election and adjusted to a new home. Yet I still refer to him as my "little" brother. In my mind he remains the undersized fourteen-year-old standing beside me in the bathroom of a funeral parlor. We are imitating our aunt, laughing, sobbing, splashing water at each other, drying tear-streaked faces with reams of paper towels, adjusting our ties, regaining composure.

In reality he is a college freshman with a scraggly mustache, awkwardly stooping to kiss his parents. He shakes my hand, then hugs me firmly and quickly. I understand the message; it is my report card. He looks at me with the cocky, confident face of the newly independent. "Later," he says.

How Do You Respond?

1. List the generalizations from Marcus's piece. How important are they to the effect of the piece? How does Marcus make vivid the relationship between himself and his brother?

2. Marcus names himself in the piece; what is the name of his younger brother? What does his handling of this detail imply about his purpose in writing?

3. How does Marcus move through time? Where does he begin? Where does he end? How does the placement in time affect the working of the essay?

RING LARDNER

> Stories—even those that we call fiction—often grow out of real life. Ring Lardner (1885–1933) drew his characters, Mr. and Mrs. Fix-it from close friends who, when they learned of the publication of the story, didn't speak to Lardner for a week. But they forgave him almost too quickly and, according to Lardner, were right up to their old tricks again, "dictating where we shall buy our shirts, how to discipline our kiddies, what road to take South, what to order for breakfast, when to bathe in what kind of bath salts, and even how often to visit the chiropodist."

MR. AND MRS. FIX-IT

They're certainly a live bunch in this town. We ain't only been here three days and had calls already from people representin' four different organizations—the Chamber of Commerce, Kiwanis, and I forget who else. They wanted to know if we was comfortable and did we like the town and is they anything they can do for us and what to be sure and see.

And they all asked how we happened to come here instead of goin' somewheres else. I guess they keep a record of everybody's reasons for comin' so as they can get a line on what features tourists is most attracted by. Then they play up them features in next year's booster advertisin'.

Well, I told them we was perfectly comfortable and we like the town fine and they's nothin' nobody can do for us right now and we'll be sure and see all the things we ought to see. But when they asked me how did we happen to come here, I said it was just a kind of a accident, because the real reason makes too long a story.

My wife has been kiddin' me about my friends ever since we was married. She says that judgin' by the ones I've introduced her to, they ain't nobody in the world got a rummier bunch of friends than me. I'll admit that the most of them ain't, well, what you might call hot; they're different somehow than when I first hung around with them. They seem to be lost without a brass rail to rest their dogs on. But of course they're old friends and I can't give 'em the air.

We have 'em to the house for dinner every little w'ile, they and their wives, and what my missus objects to is because they don't none of them play bridge or mah jong or do cross-word puzzles or sing or dance or even talk, but jest set there and wait for somebody to pour 'em a fresh drink.

As I say, my wife kids me about 'em and they ain't really nothin' I can offer in their defense. That don't mean, though, that the shoe is all on one foot. Because w'ile the majority of her friends may not be quite as dumb as mine, just the same they's a few she's picked out who I'd of had to be under the ether to allow anybody to introduce 'em to me in the first place.

Like the Crandalls, for instance. Mrs. Crandall come from my wife's home town and they didn't hardly know each other there, but they met again in a store in Chi and it went from bad to worse till finally Ada asked the dame and her husband to the house.

Well, the husband turns out to be the fella that win the war, w'ile it seems that Mrs. Crandall was in Atlantic City once and some movin' picture company was makin' a picture there and they took a scene of what was supposed to be society people walkin' up and down the Boardwalk and Mrs. Crandall was in the picture and people that seen it when it come out, they all said that from the way she screened, why if she wanted to go into the business, she could make Gloria Swanson look like Mrs. Gump.

Now it ain't only took me a few words to tell you these things, but when the Crandalls tells their story themselves, they don't hardly get started by midnight and no chance of them goin' home till they're through even when you drop 'em a hint that they're springin' it on you for the hundred and twelfth time.

That's the Crandalls, and another of the wife's friends is the Thayers. Thayer is what you might call a all-around handy man. He can mimic pretty near all the birds and beasts and fishes, he can yodel, he can play a ocarina, or he can recite Kipling or Robert H. Service, or he can do card tricks, and strike a light without no matches, and tie all the different knots.

And besides that, he can make a complete radio outfit and set it up, and take pictures as good as the best professional photographers and a whole lot better. He collects autographs. And he never had a sick day in his life.

Mrs. Thayer gets a headache playin' bridge, so it's mah jong or rhum when she's around. She used to be a teacher of elocution and she still gives readin's if you coax her, or if you don't, and her hair is such a awful nuisance that she would get it cut in a minute only all her friends tells her it would be criminal to spoil that head of hair. And when she talks to her husband, she always talks baby talk, maybe because somebody has told her that she'd be single if he wasn't childish.

And then Ada has got still another pal, a dame named Peggy Flood who is hospital mad and ain't happy unless she is just goin' under the knife or just been there. She's had everything removed that the doctors knew the name of and now they're probin' her for new giblets.

Well, I wouldn't mind if they cut her up into alphabet soup if they'd only do such a good job of it that they couldn't put her together again, but she always comes through O.K. and she spends the intermissions at our place, describin' what all they done or what they're plannin' to do next.

But the cat's nightgown is Tom Stevens and his wife. There's the team that wins the Olympics! And they're Ada's team, not mine.

Ada met Belle Stevens on the elevated. Ada was invited to a party out on the North Side and didn't know exactly where to get off and Mrs. Stevens seen her talkin' to the guard and horned in and asked her what was it she wanted to know and Ada told her, and Mrs. Stevens said she was goin' to get off the same station Ada wanted to get off, so they got off together.

Mrs. Stevens insisted on goin' right along to the address where Ada was goin' because she said Ada was bound to get lost if she wasn't familiar with the neighborhood.

Well, Ada thought it was mighty nice of her to do so much for a stranger. Mrs. Stevens said she was glad to because she didn't know what would of happened to her lots of times if strangers hadn't been nice and helped her out.

She asked Ada where she lived and Ada told her on the South Side and Mrs. Stevens said she was sure we'd like it better on the North Side if we'd leave her pick out a place for us, so Ada told her we had a year's lease that we had just signed and couldn't break it, so then Mrs. Stevens said her husband had studied law and he claimed they wasn't no lease that you couldn't break and some evening she would bring him out to call on us and he'd tell us how to break our lease.

Well, Ada had to say sure, come on out, though we was perfectly satisfied with our apartment and didn't no more want to break the lease than each other's jaw. Maybe not as much. Anyway, the very next night, they showed up, Belle and Tom, and when they'd gone, I give 'em the nickname—Mr. and Mrs. Fix-It.

After the introductions, Stevens made some remarks about what a cozy little place we had and then he asked if I would mind tellin' what rent we paid. So I told him a hundred and a quarter a month. So he said, of course, that was too much and no wonder we wanted to break the lease. Then I said we was satisfied and didn't want to break it and he said I must be kiddin' and if I would show him the lease he would see what loopholes they was in it.

Well, the lease was right there in a drawer in the table, but I told him it was in my safety deposit box at the bank. I ain't got no safety deposit box and no more use for one than Judge Landis has for the deef and dumb alphabet.

Stevens said the lease was probably just a regular lease and if it was, they wouldn't be no trouble gettin' out of it, and meanw'ile him and his wife would see if they couldn't find us a place in the same buildin' with them.

And he was pretty sure they could even if the owner had to give some other tenant the air, because he, the owner, would do anything in the world for Stevens.

So I said yes, but suppose we want to stay where we are. So he said I looked like a man with better judgment than that and if I would just leave everything to him he would fix it so's we could move within a month. I kind of laughed and thought that would be the end of it.

He wanted to see the whole apartment so I showed him around and when we come to the bathroom he noticed my safety razor on the shelf. He said, "So you use one of them things," and I said, "Yes," and he asked me how I liked it, and I said I liked it fine and he said that must be because I hadn't never used a regular razor.

He said a regular razor was the only thing to use if a man wanted to look good. So I asked him if he used a regular razor and he said he did, so I said, "Well, if you look good, I don't want to."

But that didn't stop him and he said if I would meet him downtown the next day he would take me to the place where he bought all his razors and help me pick some out for myself. I told him I was goin' to be tied up, so just to give me the name and address of the place and I would drop in there when I had time.

But, no, that wouldn't do; he'd have to go along with me and introduce me to the proprietor because the proprietor was a great pal of his and would do anything in the world for him, and if the proprietor vouched for the razors, I could be sure I was gettin' the best razors money could buy. I told him again that I was goin' to be tied up and I managed to get him on some other subject.

Meanw'ile, Mrs. Stevens wanted to know where Ada had bought the dress she was wearin' and how much had it cost and Ada told her and Mrs. Stevens said it was a crime. She would meet Ada downtown tomorrow morning and take her to the shop where she bought her clothes and help her choose some dresses that really was dresses.

So Ada told her she didn't have no money to spend on dresses right then, and besides, the shop Mrs. Stevens mentioned was too high priced. But it seems the dame that run the shop was just like a sister to Mrs. Stevens and give her and her friends a big reduction and not only that, but they wasn't no hurry about payin'.

Well, Ada thanked her just the same, but didn't need nothin' new just at present; maybe later on she would take advantage of Mrs. Stevens's kind offer. Yes, but right now they was some models in stock that would be just beautiful on Ada and they might be gone later on. They was nothin' for it but Ada had to make a date with her; she wasn't obliged to buy nothin', but it would be silly not to go and look at the stuff that was in the joint and get acquainted with the dame that run it.

Well, Ada kept the date and bought three dresses she didn't want and they's only of one them she's had the nerve to wear. They cost her a hundred dollars a smash and I'd hate to think what the price would of been if Mrs. Stevens and the owner of the shop wasn't so much like sisters.

I was sure I hadn't made no date with Stevens, but just the same he called me up the next night to ask why I hadn't met him. And a couple of days later I got three new razors in the mail along with a bill and a note from the store sayin' that these was three specially fine razors that had been picked out for me by Thomas J. Stevens.

I don't know yet why I paid for the razors and kept 'em. I ain't used 'em and never intended to. Though I've tempted a few times to test their edge on Stevens's neck.

That same week, Mrs. Stevens called up and asked us to spend Sunday with them and when we got out there, the owner of the buildin' is there, too. And Stevens has told him that I was goin' to give up my apartment on the South Side and wanted him to show me what he had.

I thought this was a little too strong and I said Stevens must of misunderstood, that I hadn't no fault to find with the place I was in and wasn't plannin' to move, not for a year anyway. You can bet this didn't make no hit with the guy, who was just there on Stevens's say-so that I was a prospective tenant.

Well, it was only about two months ago that this cute little couple come into our life, but I'll bet we seen 'em twenty times at least. They was always invitin' us to their place or invitin' themselves to our place and Ada is one of these here kind of people that just can't say no. Which may be why I and her is married.

Anyway, it begin to seem like us and the Stevenses was livin' together and all one family, with them at the head of it. I never in my life seen anybody as crazy to run other people's business. Honest to heavens, it's a wonder they let us brush our own teeth!

Ada made the remark one night that she wished the ski jumper who was doin' our cookin' would get married and quit so's she wouldn't have to can her. Mrs. Stevens was there and asked Ada if she should try and get her a new cook, but Ada says no, the poor gal might have trouble findin' another job and she felt sorry for her.

Just the same, the next afternoon a Jap come to the apartment and said he was ready to go to work and Mrs. Stevens had sent him. Ada had to tell him the place was already filled.

Another night, Ada complained that her feet was tired. Belle said her feet used to get tired, too, till a friend of hers recommended a chiropodist and she went to him and he done her so much good that she made a regular appointment with him for once every month and paid him a flat sum and no matter how much runnin' around she done, her dogs hadn't fretted her once since this cornhusker started tendin' to 'em.

She wanted to call up the guy at his home right then and there and make a date for Ada and the only way Ada could stop her was by promisin' to go and see him the next time her feet hurt. After that, whenever the two gals met, Belle's first question was "How is your feet?" and the answer was always "Fine, thanks."

Well, I'm quite a football fan and Ada likes to go, too, when it's a big game and lots of excitement. So we decided we'd see the Illinois-Chicago game and have a look at this "Red" Grange. I warned Ada to not say nothin' about it to Tom and Belle as I felt like we was entitled to a day off.

But it happened that they was goin' to be a game at Evanston that day and the Stevenses invited us to see that one with them. So we used the other game as a alibi. And when Tom asked me later on if I'd boughten my tickets yet, instead of sayin' yes, I told him the truth and said no.

So then he said:

"I'm glad you ain't, because I and Belle has made up our mind that the Chicago game is the one we ought to see. And we'll all go together. And don't bother about tickets because I can get better ones than you can as Stagg and I is just like that."

So I left it to him to get the tickets and we might as well of set on the Adams Street bridge. I said to Stevens, I said:

"If these is the seats Mr. Stagg digs up for his old pals, I suppose he leads strangers twenty or thirty miles out in the country and blindfolds 'em and ties 'em to a tree."

Now of course it was the bunk about he and Stagg bein' so close. He may of been introduced to him once, but he ain't the kind of a guy that Stagg would go around holdin' hands with. Just the same, most of the people he bragged about knowin', why it turned out that he really did know 'em; yes, and stood ace high with 'em too.

Like, for instance, I got pinched for speedin' one night and they give me a ticket to show up in the Speeders' court and I told Stevens about and he says, "Just forget it! I'll call up the judge and have it wiped off the book. He's a mighty good fella and a personal friend of mine."

Well, I didn't want to take no chances so I phoned Stevens the day before I was supposed to appear in court, and I asked him if he'd talked to the judge. He said he had and I asked him if he was sure. So he said, "If you don't believe me, call up the judge yourself." And he give me the judge's number. Sure enough, Stevens had fixed it and when I thanked the judge for his trouble, he said it was a pleasure to do somethin' for a friend of Tom Stevens's.

Now, I know it's silly to not appreciate favors like that and not warm up to people that's always tryin' to help you along, but still a person don't relish bein' treated like they was half-witted and couldn't button their shirt alone. Tom and Belle meant all right, but I and Ada got kind of tired of havin' fault found with everything that belonged to us and everything we done or tried to do.

Beside our apartment bein' no good and our clothes terrible, we learned that my dentist didn't know a bridge from a mustache cup, and the cigarettes I smoked didn't have no taste to them, and the man that bobbed Ada's hair must of been mad at her, and neither of us would ever know what it was to live till we owned a wire-haired fox terrier.

And we found out that the liquor I'd been drinkin' and enjoyin' was a mixture of bath salts and assorted paints, and the car we'd paid seventeen hundred smackers for wasn't nowheres near as much of a car as one that Tom could of got for us for eight hundred on account of knowin' a brother-in-law of a fella that used to go to school with the president of the company's nephew, and that if Ada would take up aesthetic dancin' under a dame Belle knew about, why she'd never have no more trouble with her tonsils.

Nothin' we had or nothin' we talked about gettin' or doin' was worth a damn unless it was recommended or suggested by the Stevenses.

Well, I done a pretty good business this fall and I and Ada had always planned to spend a winter in the South, so one night we figured it out that this was the year we could spare the money and the time and if we didn't go this year we never would. So the next thing was where should we go, and we finally decided on Miami. And we said we wouldn't mention nothin' about it to Tom and Belle till the day we was goin'. We'd pretend we was doin' it out of a clear sky.

But a secret is just as safe with Ada as a police dog tethered with dental floss. It wasn't more than a day or two after we'd had our talk when Tom and Belle sprang the news that they was leavin' for California right after New Year's. And why didn't we go with them.

Well, I didn't say nothin' and Ada said it sounded grand, but it was impossible. Then Stevens said if it was a question of money, to not let that bother us as he would loan it to me and I could pay it back whenever I felt like it. That was more than Ada could stand, so she says we wasn't as poor as people seemed to think and the reason we couldn't go to California was because we was goin' to Miami.

This was such a surprise that it almost struck 'em dumb at first and all Tom could think of to say was that he'd been to Miami himself and it was too crowded and he'd lay off it if he was us. But the next time we seen 'em they had our trip all arranged.

First, Tom asked me what road we was goin' on and I told him the Big Four. So he asked if we had our reservations and I told him yes.

"Well," he said, "we'll get rid of 'em and I'll fix you up on the C.& E.I. The general passenger agent is a friend of mine and they ain't nothin' he won't do for my friends. He'll see that you're treated right and that you get there in good shape."

So I said:

"I don't want to put you to all that trouble, and besides I don't know nobody connected with the Big Four well enough for them to resent me travelin' on their lines, and as for gettin' there in good shape, even if I have a secret enemy or two on the Big Four, I don't believe they'd endanger the lives of the other passengers just to see that I didn't get there in good shape."

But Stevens insisted on takin' my tickets and sellin' 'em back to the Big Four and gettin' me fixed on the C.& E.I. The berths we'd had on the Big Four was Lower 9 and Lower 10. The berths Tom got us on the C.& E.I. was Lower 7 and Lower 8, which he said was better. I suppose he figured that the nearer you are to the middle of the car, the less chance there is of bein' woke up if your car gets in another train's way.

He wanted to know, too, if I'd made any reservations at a hotel. I showed him a wire I had from the Royal Palm in reply to a wire I'd sent 'em.

"Yes," he says, "but you don't want to stop at the Royal Palm. You wire and tell 'em to cancel that and I'll make arrangements for you at the Flamingo, over at the Beach. Charley Krom, the manager there, was born and raised in the same town I was. He'll take great care of you if he knows you're a friend of mine."

So I asked him if all the guests at the Flamingo was friends of his, and he said of course not; what did I mean?

"Well," I said, "I was just thinkin' that if they ain't, Mr. Krom probably makes life pretty miserable for 'em. What does he do, have the phone girl ring 'em up at all hours of the night, and hide their mail, and shut off their hot water, and put cracker crumbs in their beds?"

That didn't mean nothin' to Stevens and he went right ahead and switched me from one hotel to the other.

While Tom was reorganizin' my program and tellin' me what to eat in Florida, and what bait to use for barracuda and carp, and what time to go bathin' and which foot to stick in the water first, why Belle was makin' Ada return all the stuff she had boughten to wear down there and buy other stuff that Belle picked out for her at joints where Belle was so well known that they only soaked her twice as much as a stranger. She had Ada almost crazy, but I told her to never mind; in just a few more days we'd be where they couldn't get at us.

I suppose you're wonderin' why didn't we quarrel with 'em and break loose from 'em and tell 'em to leave us alone. You'd know why if you knew them. Nothin' we could do would convince 'em that we didn't want their advice and help. And nothin' we could say was a insult.

Well, the night before we was due to leave Chi, the phone rang and I answered it. It was Tom.

"I've got a surprise for you," he says. "I and Belle has give up the California idear. We're goin' to Miami instead, and on account of me knowin' the boys down at the C.& E.I., I've landed a drawin' room on the same train you're takin'. How is that for news?"

"Great!" I said, and I went back and broke it to Ada. For a minute I thought she was goin' to faint. And all night long she moaned and groaned and had hysterics.

So that's how we happened to come to Biloxi.

How Do You Respond?

1. How would you describe the tone of Lardner's narrator? Does he hold your attention throughout? How does he vary the examples he gives of his friends' traits?

2. Are you satisfied with the narrator's explanation of why he and his wife allow the Stevens to interfere in their lives? Can you tell about anybody who complains endlessly about a situation but does nothing effective to remedy it?

3. Are you surprised by the ending? Write a brief piece by one of the Stevens about the narrator and his wife.

RUSSELL BAKER

> *For one reader's experience of reading this passage, see p. 7.*

SUMMER BEYOND WISH

A long time ago I lived in a crossroads village of northern Virginia and during its summer enjoyed innocence and never knew boredom, although nothing of consequence happened there.

Seven houses of varying lack of distinction constituted the community. A dirt road meandered off toward the mountain where a bootleg still supplied whiskey to the men of the countryside, and another dirt road ran down to the creek. My cousin Kenneth and I would sit on the bank and fish with earthworms. One day we killed a copperhead which was basking on a rock nearby. That was unusual.

The heat of summer was mellow and produced sweet scents which lay in the air so damp and rich you could almost taste them. Mornings smelled of purple wisteria, afternoons of the wild roses which tumbled over stone fences and evenings of honeysuckle.

Even by standards of that time it was a primitive place. There was no electricity. Roads were unpaved. In our house there was no plumbing. The routine of summer days was shaped by these deficiencies. Lacking electric lights, one went early to bed and rose while the dew was still in the grass. Kerosene lamps were cleaned and polished in an early-morning hubbub of women, and children were sent to the spring for fresh water.

This afforded a chance to see whether the crayfish population had multiplied. Later, a trip to the outhouse would afford a chance to daydream in the Sears, Roebuck catalog, mostly about shotguns and bicycles.

With no electricity, radio was not available for pacifying the young. One or two people did have radios that operated on mail order batteries about the size of a present-day car battery, but these were not for children, though occasionally you might be invited in to hear "Amos 'n' Andy."

All I remember about "Amos 'n' Andy" at that time is that it was strange hearing voices come out of furniture. Much later I was advised that listening to "Amos n' Andy" was racist and was grateful that I hadn't heard much.

In the summer no pleasures were to be had indoors. Everything of delight occurred in the world outside. In the flowers there were hummingbirds to be seen, tiny wings fluttering so fast that the birds seemed to have no wings at all.

In the heat of midafternoon the women would draw the blinds, spread blankets on the floor for coolness, and nap, while in the fields the cattle herded together in the shade of spreading trees to escape the sun. Afternoons were absolutely still, yet filled with sounds.

Bees buzzed in the clover. Far away over the fields the chug of an ancient steam-powered threshing machine could be faintly heard. Birds rustled under the tin of the porch roof.

Rising dust along the road from the mountains signaled an approaching event. A car was coming. "Car's coming," someone would say. People emerged from houses. The approaching dust was studied. Guesses were hazarded about whom it might contain.

Then—a big moment in the day—the car would cruise past.

"Who was it?"

"I didn't get a good look."

"It looked like Packy Painter to me."

"Couldn't have been Packy. Wasn't his car."

The stillness resettled itself as gently as the dust, and you could wander past the henhouse and watch a hen settle herself to perform the mystery of laying an egg. For livelier adventure there was the field that contained the bull. There, one could test his courage by seeing how far he dared venture before running back through the fence.

The men drifted back with the falling sun, steaming with heat and fatigue, and washed in tin basins with water hauled in buckets from the spring. I knew a few of their secrets, such as who kept his whiskey hidden in a Mason jar behind the lime barrel, and what they were really doing when they excused themselves from the kitchen and stepped out into the orchard and stayed out there laughing too hard.

I also knew what the women felt about it, though not what they thought. Even then I could see that matters between women and men could become very difficult and, sometimes, so difficult that they spoiled the air of summer.

At sunset people sat on the porches. As dusk deepened, the lightning bugs came out to be caught and bottled. As twilight edged into night, a bat swooped across the road. I was not afraid of bats then, although I feared ghosts, which made the approach of bedtime in a room where even the kerosene lamp would quickly be doused seem terrifying.

I was even more afraid of toads and specifically of the toad which lived under the porch steps and which everyone assured me would, if touched, give me warts. One night I was allowed to stay up until the stars were in full command of the sky. A woman of great age was dying in the village and it was considered fit to let the children stay abroad into the night. As four of us sat there we saw a shooting star and someone said, "Make a wish."

I did not know what that meant. I didn't know anything to wish for.

How Do You Respond?

1. How does Baker distinguish the usual from the unusual? How does his "usual" strike you?

2. How would you characterize Baker's tone? Where is the tension in the piece? What is he contrasting?

3. In Chapter 1 of this book, one reader's responses to Baker's piece are noted. How do your responses differ—or agree?

MARY McCARTHY

> *"These memories of mine have been collected slowly over a period of years," says Mary McCarthy (born 1912). What happens, we might ask, when the autobiographer cannot remember? McCarthy answers, "Many a time, in the course of doing these memoirs, I have wished that I were writing fiction. The temptation to invent has been very strong where recollection is hazy and I remember the substance of an event but not the details—the color of a dress, the pattern of a carpet, the placing of a picture." Invent one must, pulling out of the past what one remembers and filling in what has been forgotten. Part of McCarthy's problem was that she was orphaned at six, so that the chain of family recollections had been broken. But she persisted and wrote the remarkable* Memories of a Catholic Childhood, *from which "Names" is taken, as well as a host of essays and novels such as* The Group, Birds of America, Vietnam, *and* The Writing on the Wall.

NAMES

Ann Lyons, Mary Louise Lyons, Mary von Phul, Emilie von Phul, Eugenia McLellan, Marjorie McPhail, Marie-Louise L'Abbé, Mary Danz, Julia Dodge, Mary Fordyce Blake, Janet Preston—these were the names (I can still tell them over like a rosary) of some of the older girls in the convent: the Virtues and Graces. The virtuous ones wore wide blue or green moire good-conduct ribbons, bandoleer-style, across their blue serge uniforms; the beautiful ones wore rouge and and powder or at least were reputed to do so. Our class, the eighth grade, wore pink ribbons (I never got one myself) and had names like Patricia ("Pat") Sullivan, Eileen Donohoe, and Joan Kane. We were inelegant even in this respect; the best name we could show, among us, was Phyllis ("Phil") Chatham, who boasted that her father's name, Ralph, was pronounced "Rafe" as in England.

Names had a great importance for us in the convent, and foreign names, French, German, or plain English (which, to us, were foreign because of their Protestant sound), bloomed like prize roses among a collection of spuds. Irish names were too common in the school to have any prestige either as surnames (Gallagher, Sheehan, Finn, Sullivan, McCarthy) or as Christian names (Kathleen, Eileen). Anything exotic had value: an "olive" complexion, for example. The pet girl of the convent was a fragile Jewish girl named Susie Lowenstein, who had pale red-gold hair and an exquisite retroussé nose, which, if we had had it, might have been called "pug." We liked her name too and the name of a child in the primary grades: Abbie Stuart Baillargeon. My favorite name, on the whole, though, was Emilie von Phul (pronounced "Pool"); her older sister, recently graduated, was called Celeste. Another name that appealed to me was Genevieve Albers, Saint Genevieve being the patron saint of Paris who turned back Attila from the gates of the city.

All these names reflected the still-pioneer character of the Pacific Northwest. I had never heard their like in the parochial school in Minneapolis, where "foreign" extraction, in any case, was something to be ashamed of, the whole drive being toward Americanization of first name and surname alike. The exceptions to this were the Irish, who could vaunt such names as Catherine O'Dea and the name of my second cousin, Mary Catherine Anne Rose Violet McCarthy, while an unfortunate German boy named Manfred was made to suffer for his. But that was Minneapolis. In Seattle, and especially in the convent of the Ladies of the Sacred Heart, foreign names suggested not immigration but emigration—distinguished exile. Minneapolis was a granary; Seattle was a port, which had attracted a veritable Foreign Legion of adventurers—soldiers of fortune, younger sons, gamblers, traders, drawn by the fortunes to be made in virgin timber and shipping and by the Alaska Gold Rush. Wars and revolutions had sent the defeated out to Puget Sound, to start a new life; the latest had been the Russian Revolution, which had shipped us, via Harbin, a Russian colony, complete with restaurant, on Queen Anne Hill. The English names in the convent, when they did not testify to direct English origin, as in the case of "Rafe" Chatham, had come to us from the South and represented a kind of internal exile; such girls as Mary Fordyce Blake and Mary McQueen Street (a class ahead of me; her sister was named Francesca) bore their double-barreled first names like titles of aristocracy from the ante-bellum South. Not all girls, by any means, were Catholic; some of the very prettiest ones—Julia Dodge and Janet Preston, if I remember rightly—were Protestants. The nuns had taught us to behave with special courtesy to these strangers in our midst, and the whole effect was of some superior hostel for refugees of all the lost causes of the past hundred years. Money could not count for much in such an atmosphere; the fathers and grandfathers of many of our "best" girls were ruined men.

Names, often, were freakish in the Pacific Northwest, particularly girls' names. In the Episcopal boarding school I went to later, in Tacoma, there was a girl called De Vere Utter, and there was a girl called Rocena and another called Hermoine. Was Rocena a mistake for Rowena and Hermoine for Hermione? And was Vere, as we called her, Lady Clara Vere de Vere? Probably. You do not hear names like those often, in any case, east of the Cascade Mountains; they belong to the frontier, where books and libraries were few and memory seems to have been oral, as in the time of Homer.

Names have more significance for Catholics than they do for other people; Christian names are chosen for the spiritual qualities of the saints they are taken from; Protestants used to name their children out of the Old Testament and now they name them out of novels and plays, whose heroes and heroines are perhaps the new patron saints of a secular age. But with Catholics it is different. The saint a child is named for is supposed to serve, literally, as a model or pattern to imitate; your name is your fortune and it tells you what you are or must be. Catholic children ponder their names for a mystic meaning, like birthstones; my own, I learned, besides belonging to the Virgin and Saint Mary of Egypt, originally meant "bitter" or "star of the sea." My second name, Therese, could dedicate me either to Saint Theresa or to the saint called the Little Flower, Soeur Thérèse of Lisieux, on whom God was supposed to have descended in the form of a shower of roses. At Confirmation, I had added a third name (for Catholics then rename themselves, as most nuns do, yet another time, when they take orders); on the advice of a nun, I had taken "Clementina," after Saint Clement, an early pope—a step I soon regretted on account of "My Darling Clementine" and her number nine shoes. By the time I was in the convent, I would no longer tell anyone what my Confirmation name was. The name I had nearly picked was "Agnes," after a little Roman virgin martyr, always shown with a lamb, because of her purity. But Agnes would have been just as bad, I recognized in Forest Ridge Convent—not only because of the possibility of "Aggie," but because it was subtly, indefinably *wrong,* in itself. Agnes would have made me look like an ass.

The fear of appearing ridiculous first entered my life, as a governing motive, during my second year in the convent. Up to then, a desire for prominence had decided many of my actions and, in fact, still persisted. But in the eighth grade, I became aware of mockery and perceived that I could not seek prominence without attracting laughter. Other people could, but I couldn't. This laughter was proceeding, not from my classmates, but from the girls of the class just above me, in particular from two boon companions, Elinor Heffernan and Mary Harty, a clownish pair—oddly assorted in size and shape, as teams of clowns generally are, one short, plump, and baby-faced, the other tall, lean, and owlish—who entertained the high-school department by calling attention to the oddities of the younger girls. Nearly every school has such a pair of satirists, whose marks are generally low and who are tolerated just because of their laziness and non-conformity; one of them (in this case, Mary Harty, the plump one) usually appears to be half asleep. Because of their low standing, their indifference to appearances, the sad state of their uniforms, their clowning is taken to be harmless, which, on the whole, it is, the object being not to wound but to divert; such girls are bored in school. We in the eighth grade sat directly in front of the two wits in study hall, so that they had us under close observation; yet at first I was not afraid of them, wanting, if anything, to identify myself with their laughter, to be initiated into the joke. One of their specialties was giving people nicknames, and it was considered an honor to be the first in the eighth grade to be let in by Elinor and Mary on their latest invention. This often happened to me; they would tell me, on the playground, and I would tell the others. As their intermediary, I felt myself almost their friend and it did not occur to me that I might be next on their list.

I had achieved prominence not long before by publicly losing my faith and regaining it at the end of a retreat. I believe Elinor and Mary questioned me about this on the playground, during recess, and listened with serious, respectful faces while I told them about my conversations with the Jesuits. Those serious faces ought to have been an omen, but if the two girls used what I had revealed to make fun of me, it must have been behind my back. I never heard any more of it, and yet just at this time I began to feel something, like a cold breath on the nape of my neck, that made me wonder whether the new position I had won for myself in the convent was as secure as I imagined. I would turn around in study hall and find the two girls looking at me with speculation in their eyes.

It was just at this time, too, that I found myself in a perfectly absurd situation, a very private one, which made me live, from month to month, in horror of discovery. I had waked up one morning, in my convent room, to find a few small spots of blood on my sheet; I had somehow scratched a trifling cut on one of my legs and opened it during the night. I wondered what to do about this, for the nuns were fussy about bedmaking, as they were about our white collars and cuffs, and if we had an inspection those spots might count against me. It was best, I decided, to ask the nun on dormitory duty, tall, stout Mother Slattery, for a clean bottom sheet, even though she might scold me for having scratched my leg in my sleep and order me to cut my toenails. You never know what you might be blamed for. But Mother Slattery, when she bustled in to look at the sheet, did not scold me at all; indeed, she hardly seemed to be listening as I explained to her about the cut. She told me to sit down; she would be back in a minute. "You can be excused from athletics today," she added, closing the door. As I waited, I considered this remark, which seemed to me strangely munificent, in view of the unimportance of the cut. In a moment, she returned, but without the sheet. Instead, she produced out of her big pocket a sort of cloth girdle and a peculiar flannel object which I first took to be a bandage, and I began to protest that I did not need or want a bandage; all I needed was a bottom sheet. "The sheet can wait," said Mother Slattery, succinctly, handing me two large safety pins. It was the pins that abruptly enlightened me; I saw Mother Slattery's mistake, even as she was instructing me as to how this flannel article, which I now understood to be a sanitary napkin, was to be put on.

"Oh, no, Mother," I said, feeling somewhat embarrassed. "You don't understand. It's just a little cut, on my leg." But Mother, again, was not listening; she appeared to have grown deaf, as the nuns had a habit of doing when what you were saying did not fit in with their ideas. And now that I knew what was in her mind, I was conscious of a funny constraint; I did not feel it proper to name a natural process, in so many words, to a nun. It was like trying not to think of their going to the bathroom or trying not to see the straggling iron-grey hair coming out of their coifs (the common notion that they shaved their heads was false). But when I offered to do so and unfastened my black stocking, she only glanced at my leg, cursorily. "That's only a scratch, dear," she said. "Now hurry up and put this on or you'll be late for chapel. Have you any pain?" "No, no, Mother!" I cried. "You don't understand!" "Yes, yes, I understand," she replied soothingly, "and you will too, a little later. Mother Superior will tell you about it some time during the morning. There's nothing to be afraid of. You have become a woman."

"I know all about that," I persisted. "Mother, please listen. I just cut my leg. On the athletic field. Yesterday afternoon." But the more excited I grew, the more soothing, and yet firm, Mother Slattery became. There seemed to be nothing for it but to give up and do as I was bid. I was in the grip of a higher authority, which almost had the power to persuade me that it was right and I was wrong. But of course I was not wrong; that would have been too good to be true. While Mother Slattery waited, just outside my door, I miserably donned the equipment she had given me, for there was no place to hide it, on account of drawer inspection. She led me down the hall to where there was a chute and explained how I was to dispose of the flannel thing, by dropping it down the chute into the laundry. (The convent arrangements were very old-fashioned, dating back, no doubt, to the days of Louis Philippe.)

The Mother Superior, Madame MacIllvra, was a sensible woman, and all through my early morning classes, I was on pins and needles, chafing for the promised interview with her which I trusted would clear things up. "*Ma Mère*," I would begin, "Mother Slattery thinks . . ." Then I would tell her about the cut and the athletic field. But precisely the same impasse confronted me when I was summoned to her office at recess-time. *I* talked about my cut, and *she* talked about becoming a woman. It was rather like a round, in which she was singing "Scotland's burning, Scotland's burning," and I was singing "Pour on water, pour on water." Neither of us could hear the other, or, rather, I could hear her, but she could not hear me. Owing to our different positions in the convent, she was free to interrupt me, whereas I was expected to remain silent until she had finished speaking. When I kept breaking in, she hushed me, gently, and took me on her lap. Exactly like Mother Slattery, she attributed all my references to the cut to a blind fear of this new, unexpected reality that had supposedly entered my life. Many young girls, she reassured me, were frightened if they had not been prepared. "And you, Mary, have lost your dear mother, who could have made this easier for you." Rocked on Madame MacIllvra's lap, I felt paralysis overtake me and I lay, mutely listening, against her bosom, my face being tickled by her white, starched, fluted wimple, while she explained to me how babies were born, all of which I had heard before.

There was no use fighting the convent. I had to pretend to have become a woman, just as, not long before, I had had to pretend to get my faith back—for the sake of peace. This pretense was decidedly awkward. For fear of being found out by the lay sisters downstairs in the laundry (no doubt an imaginary contingency, but the convent was so very thorough), I reopened the cut on my leg, so as to draw a little blood to stain the napkins, which were issued me regularly, not only on this occasion, but every twenty-eight days thereafter. Eventually, I abandoned this bloodletting, for fear of lockjaw, and trusted to fate. Yet I was in awful dread of detection; my only hope, as I saw it, was either to be released from the convent or to become a woman in reality, which might take a year, at least, since I was only twelve. Getting out of athletics once a month was not sufficient compensation for the farce I was going through. It was not my fault; they had forced me into it; nevertheless, it was I who would look silly—worse than silly; half mad—if the truth ever came to light.

I was burdened with this guilt and shame when the nickname finally found me out. "Found me out," in a general sense, for no one ever did learn the particular secret I bore about with me, pinned to the linen band. "We've got a name for you," Elinor and Mary called out to me, one day on the playground. "What is it?" I asked, half hoping, half fearing, since not all their sobriquets were unfavorable. "Cye," they answered, looking at each other and laughing. " 'Si'?" I repeated, supposing that it was based on Simple Simon. Did they regard me as a hick? "C.Y.E.," they elucidated, spelling it out in chorus. "The letters stand for something. Can you guess?" I could not and I cannot now. The closest I could come to it in the convent was "Clean Your Ears." Perhaps that was it, though in later life I have wondered whether it did not stand, simply, for "Clever

Young Egg" or "Champion Young Eccentric." But in the convent I was certain that it stood for something horrible, something even worse than dirty ears (as far as I knew, my ears were clean), something I could never guess because it represented some aspect of myself that the world could see and I couldn't, like a sign pinned on my back. Everyone in the convent must have known what the letters stood for, but no one would tell me. Elinor and Mary had made them promise. It was like halitosis; not even my best friend, my deskmate, Louise, would tell me, no matter how much I pleaded. Yet everyone assured me that it was "very good," that is, very apt. And it made everyone laugh.

This name reduced all my pretensions and solidified my sense of *wrongness*. Just as I felt I was beginning to belong to the convent, it turned me into an outsider, since I was the only pupil who was not in the know. I liked the convent, but it did not like me, as people say of certain foods that disagree with them. By this, I do not mean that I was actively unpopular, either with the pupils or with the nuns. The Mother Superior cried when I left and predicted that I would be a novelist, which surprised me. And I had finally made friends; even Emilie von Phul smiled upon me softly out of her bright blue eyes from the far end of the study hall. It was just that I did not fit into the convent pattern; the simplest thing I did, like asking for a clean sheet, entrapped me in consequences that I never could have predicted. I was not bad; I did not consciously break the rules; and yet I could never, not even for a week, get a pink ribbon, and this was something I could not understand, because I was trying as hard as I could. It was the same case as with the hated name; the nuns, evidently, saw something about me that was invisible to me.

The oddest part was all that pretending. There I was, a walking mass of lies, pretending to be a Catholic and going to confession while really I had lost my faith, and pretending to have monthly periods by cutting myself with nail scissors; yet all this had come about without my volition and even contrary to it. But the basest pretense I was driven to was the acceptance of the nickname. Yet what else could I do? In the convent, I could not live it down. To all those girls, I had become "Cye McCarthy." That was who I was. That was how I had to identify myself when telephoning my friends during vacations to ask them to the movies: "Hello, this is Cye." I loathed myself when I said it, and yet I succumbed to the name totally, making myself over into a sort of hearty to go with it—the kind of girl I hated. "Cye" was my new patron saint. This false personality stuck to me, like the name, when I entered public high school, the next fall, as a freshman, having finally persuaded my grandparents to take me out of the convent, although they could never get to the bottom of my reasons, since as I admitted, the nuns were kind, and I had made many nice new friends. What I wanted was a fresh start, a chance to begin life over again, but the first thing I heard in the corridors of the public high school was that name called out to me, like the warmest of welcomes: "Hi, there, Si!" That was the way they thought it was spelled. But this time I was resolute. After the first weeks, I dropped the hearties who called me "Si" and I never heard it again. I got my own name back and sloughed off Clementina and even Therese—the names that did not seem to me any more to be mine but to have been imposed on me by others. And I preferred to think that Mary meant "bitter" rather than "star of the sea."

How Do You Respond?

1. Mary McCarthy varies her text by dividing her topic into subgroups: names and social status, names and ethnicity, etc. How many sub-categories can you distinguish? How does she relate the categories?

2. How does the incident of the blood on the sheet fit into an essay on names? How does the incident of the nickname bestowed by the two clowns follow in the structure of the essay from the misunderstanding with the nuns?

3. McCarthy says that "Names have more significance for Catholics than they do for other people." Do you agree? What does she mean by "more significance"? Is this the meaning you got at first reading?

FOCUS ON YOUR READING

1. Notice how William Safire attempts to classify various kinds of *mishearing*. Safire tries for a term to cover a variety of examples: an "all-inclusive" term to "encompass all the changes . . . our brains make in the intended meaning of what we hear." Ira Berkow adds up his observations about Joe Louis to say that Louis had "style." Where else in the selections in this chapter do you observe writers generalizing from examples?

2. What kinds of example do writers use to present a case? What kinds of example does Susan Page offer in "All About Pigeons"? How does narrative show up in the essay? How does she *use* facts, statistics, numbers? What kinds of example does Marcus use?

3. How do contrasts—showing things as they were; showing or implying things as they are or might be—underly the Marcus and Baker pieces? How many examples revolve around the writers' seeing a situation, a person, in a contrastive fashion?

4. Susan Page presents two sides of an argument about pigeons, showing why pigeons are extolled by some and opposed by others. How do the examples she offers support each side? Would you call the argument balanced? Does she seem to favor one side over the other? If so, how do the examples work to support that side? Do you find selections in the chapter where a writer is arguing for or against a particular view, situation, idea?

FOCUS ON YOUR WRITING

1. Using the form of Marcus's essay as a guide, write your own account of letting go: a parent lets go; an older sister lets go; a child lets go; a teacher lets go; a student lets go.

2. Using the form of Berkow's essay, provide examples—narratives, descriptions, contrasts, "facts"—to show that a person has "style," or "charisma," or "class," etc. Define your notions of this characteristic word. Jot down in your journal what *you* mean by "style."

3. Do some research on a common problem as Page did (cigarette smoking, air pollution, the vast number of throw-away products that deplete natural resources) and present an argument—pro or con—about the issue.

4. What effects have names had in your life? Have you been understood or misunderstood because of your particular name? Does your name have a family history? Do you know of situations where people have been profoundly affected by what they are called? If you can write about names and naming, do so.

5. Baker implicitly contrasts the way things were when he was a child and the way things are now. He is saying, in a sense, that many of us had much more than he did as a child but were still unsatisfied. Do you agree? Write an essay in which you explore the question of being satisfied, being contented; how do material possessions and "ease" of life fit in?

CHAPTER 9

❖ ❖

"Jack Sprat Could Eat No Fat"

COMPARING AND CONTRASTING

> Jack Sprat could eat no fat,
> His wife could eat no lean,
> And so between the two of them
> They licked the platter clean.

When we look at this nursery rhyme, we see Jack Sprat *in contrast* to his wife. We might say that here we have a simple contrast: Jack could eat no fat; his wife could eat no lean. But there is more to the story than this, for when we contrast—point up differences— we also *compare*. Underlying the differences between Jack and his wife are similarities: we are talking about two *people eating*, and we are talking, most likely, about their eating meat. "Fat" and "lean" are generally connected with a roast or a steak or a lamb chop. Thus, on the basis of a common ground, two people eating meat, we point out differences—how they go about eating meat differently.

The psychologist George Kelly regards this process of seeing similarities and differences as one of our most fundamental ways of thinking. He would say that the elements in this simple tale—Jack, his wife, and their eating—make up a *construct*. A construct is a relationship in which at least two elements are similar and, at the same time, contrast with a third. There must be at least three elements in the construct, but there may be many more.

Let's say that you're comparing two dogs. They are alike, first of all, in that they are both dogs. Kelly would say that two elements of the construct are alike. You might observe that they are similar in other particular ways: they both eat meat, they both have fur, teeth, tails, etc. But they are unlike, as well, in even more particular ways: one eats large bones while the other cannot; one has long hair, the other short; and so on. Kelly believes that we perceive the world around us by observing similarities *and* differences.

If you think for a moment of the world around you, of things buzzing and booming about—noises, cars, smells, music, storms, people talking, working, sleeping, eating, fighting, laughing—and ask how we make sense of it all, Kelly would answer that, primarily, we do two things:

> we create beginnings and endings
> we see similarities and differences

Beginnings and endings are transformed into narratives, into stories we shape out of the buzzing, booming mass. Similarities and differences are transformed into comparisons and contrasts. We perform these acts all the time; they merge, one with the other. If I tell you a story—say, about a crime I witnessed the other day, a purse-snatching in the middle of Chicago—then you *relate* to my telling of the incident by calling up your own experience, and perhaps offering a similar story: you saw a purse-snatching some time ago. Or you see the act of purse-snatching as part of a common ground that you may call "crime in the cities," and relate a different event: you relate an incident about a rash of unexplained fires in a business district. Your incident may be different from mine, but the ground on which we stand is similar.

When we compare and contrast, then, we stand on common ground: there must be similar elements to compare, and there must be similar elements, as well, to contrast.

In the following passage from his autobiography, *The Words*, Jean Paul Sartre shows differences between his grandmother and grandfather by drawing points of contrast on the common ground of their interest in books and reading. Once the common ground is established as a basis for comparison, he can show differences in the ways his grandparents approach books and reading. In the grandfather's study, books were everywhere; in the grandmother's room, there were never more than two at a time, borrowed from a library. The grandfather, apparently, read as part of his life's work. The grandmother read "feminine" novels for pleasure:

> I began my life as I shall no doubt end it: amidst books. In my grandfather's study there were books everywhere. It was forbidden to dust them, except once a year, before the beginning of the October term. Though I did not yet know how to read, I already revered those standing stones; upright or leaning over, close together like bricks on the book-shelves or spaced out nobly in lanes of menhirs. I felt that our family's prosperity depended on them. They all looked alike. I disported myself in a tiny sanctuary, surrounded by ancient, heavy-set monuments which had seen me into the world, which would see me out of it, and whose permanence guaranteed me a future as calm as the past. I would touch them secretly to honor my hands with their dust, but I did not quite know what to do with them, and I was a daily witness of ceremonies whose meaning escaped me: my grandfather—who was usually so clumsy that my grandmother buttoned his gloves for him—handled those cultural objects with the dexterity of an officiant. Hundreds of times I saw him get up from his chair with an absent-minded look, walk around his table, cross the room in two strides, take down a volume without hesitating, without giving himself time to choose, leaf through it with a combined movement of his thumb and forefinger as he walked back to his chair, then, as soon as he was seated, open it sharply "to the right page," making it creak like a shoe. At times, I would draw near to observe those boxes which slit open like oysters, and I would see the nudity of their inner organs, pale, fusty leaves, slightly bloated, covered with black veinlets, which drank ink and smelled of mushrooms.
>
> In my grandmother's room, the books lay on their sides. She borrowed them from a circulating library, and I never saw more than two at a time. Those baubles reminded me of New Year goodies because their supple, glistening leaves seemed to have been cut from glossy paper. White, bright, almost new, they served as pretext for mild mysteries. Every Friday, my grandmother would get dressed to go out and would say: "I'm going to return *them*." When she got back, after removing her black

"Jack Sprat Could Eat No Fat" 371

> hat and her veil, she would take *them* from her muff, and I would wonder, mystified: "Are they the same ones?" She would "cover" them carefully, then, after choosing one of them, would settle down near the window in her easy-chair, put on her spectacles, sigh with bliss and weariness, and lower her eyelids with a subtle voluptuous smile that I have since seen on the lips of La Gioconda. My mother would remain silent and bid me do likewise. I would think of Mass, death, sleep; I would be filled with a holy stillness. From time to time, Louise would chuckle; she would call over her daughter, point to a line, and the two women would exchange a look of complicity. Nevertheless, I did not care for those two distinguished volumes. They were intruders, and my grandfather did not hide the fact that they were the object of a minor cult, exclusively feminine. On Sundays, having nothing better to do, he would enter his wife's room and stand in front of her without finding anything to say. Everyone would look at him. He would drum on the windowpane, then, not knowing what else to do, would turn to Louise and take her novel from her hands. "Charles!" she would cry furiously, "you're going to lose my place!" He would start reading, with raised eyebrows. Suddenly his forefinger would strike the volume: "I don't get it!" "But how do you expect to?" my grandmother would say. "You open to the middle!" He would end by tossing the book on the table and would leave, shrugging his shoulders.

When you draw a contrast, as Sartre does, your options for structuring a piece are two. First, you may say all, or mostly all, that you want to say about A—in this case, the grandfather—and then all, or mostly all, that you want to say about B—the grandmother. At the end of the passage, you may bring A and B together, as Sartre does when his grandfather confronts his wife and the way she reads.

Second, you may bring A and B into contrast in the same passage: My grandfather kept his books in bookcases around the room; my grandmother kept her books—only two at a time—lying on a table. My grandfather read primarily for work; my grandmother read for pleasure. A and B will be contrasted *throughout* the piece of writing. In the following passage, the poet Ted Hughes weaves together the similarities he sees between "capturing animals" and writing poems. He tells us right away that we may not think these two activities have much in common, but he is convinced, the more he thinks about it, that the "two interests have been one interest." Thus he begins with what we might imagine are strikingly different acts and shows us how they resemble each other, beneath the surface differences.

> There are all sorts of ways of capturing animals and birds and fish. I spent most of my time, up to the age of fifteen or so, trying out many of these ways and when my enthusiasm began to wane, as it did gradually, I started to write poems.
>
> You might not think that these two interests, capturing animals and writing poems, have much in common. But the more I think back the more sure I am that with me the two interests have been one interest. My pursuit of mice at threshing time when I was a boy, snatching them from under the sheaves as the sheaves were lifted away out of the stack and popping them into my pocket till I had thirty or forty crawling around in the lining of my coat, that and my present pursuit of poems seem to me to be different stages of the same fever. In a way, I suppose, I think of poems as a sort of animal. They have their own life, like animals, by which I mean that they seem quite separate from any person, even from their author, and nothing can be added to them or taken away without maiming and perhaps even killing them. And they have a certain wisdom. They know something special . . . something perhaps which we are very curious to learn. Maybe my concern has been to capture not animals particularly and not poems, but simply things which have a vivid life of their own, outside mine . . . my interest in animals began when I began.
>
> *Poetry in the Making*

Comparing and contrasting may form the structure of a piece of writing. You may be comparing and contrasting women and men athletes, or you may be writing about a time in history as it compares and contrasts to another period, or you may be writing about the similarities and differences between Picasso and Monet, or about living in the country and living in the city. These large concerns will form an entire essay or an entire book. Or you may be using comparisons and contrasts within a story or within a descriptive piece or within an argument. When the time arises for you to point out differences and similarities, you will do so, because it is one of the primary ways in which you have learned to make meaning.

One of the most striking ways to point out similarities is through *metaphor*. In a metaphor, similarity is implied. When a writer says, "Geoffrey is a lion," for example, she compares Geoffrey and lions. She may mean that Geoffrey is fierce and powerful or that he carries himself gracefully, imperially, like a lion, or that he growls. From the context that the writer provides, the reader fills in the gaps and makes connections. Metaphor often makes those connections vivid. Sartre says, for example, that his grandfather opened a book "to the right page, making it creak like a shoe." Sartre would observe those "boxes which slit open like oysters." Hughes's comparison of poems and animals is metaphoric. Poems and animals both have their own life, he says, for they are "quite separate from any person, even from their author, and nothing can be added or taken away without maiming and perhaps even killing them."

In the selections in this chapter, writers use various forms to point up differences and show similarities between people, between cultures, between periods of history. In "Wartime in Korea," Don Bauer places the Korean War and the Vietnam War side by side as he examines two incidents that he thinks have "something in common." Bauer offers us this abstraction—a generalization—that he then supports with details about the two incidents. Russell Baker takes two abstract words—*school* and *education*—and examines the process of schooling in America. One can "go through" school without getting an education. Baker doesn't tell us much about his views of becoming educated; we have to fill in the blanks. He thus presents one side of the contrast and invites us to complete the picture.

Nora Ephron takes us to her old school, Wellesley, for a class reunion, where she observes what has changed and what has stayed the same between 1962 and 1972. During the decade, the place of women in society was hotly debated, and Ephron, as reporter and as woman, examines the effects of the woman's movement on the all-girls' college. Joe McGinniss in a chapter from *Going to Extremes*, a study of Alaska, draws a stark contrast of person and of place, as he visits an Eskimo village and describes the struggle of an Eskimo woman who has worked in the "outside world" and can no longer fit into her native culture.

Flannery O'Connor in her short story, "Everything That Rises

Must Converge," also takes us into a setting where old values are seen in stark contrast to a changing world, and where a woman cannot cope with those changes. Elisabeth Kübler-Ross begins "The Fear of Death" with an anecdote of a farmer's death in Switzerland and used this event to explore the differences between one society in which death is accepted as a natural part of life and another in which people do all they can to protect themselves from the experience. Loren Eiseley in "The Long Loneliness" looks at human beings as solitary creatures in the universe, comparing and contrasting them with the dolphin. How are we different, and how are we the same? he asks, and concludes that it is the human ability to change our environment and our ability to write that set us off from all other creatures.

❖ ❖ ────────────────────────────────

AS YOU READ

Figure/Ground

Contrasts rest on similarities, and similarities underlie contrasts. We might say that similarities are the ground on which the contrast, the figure, stands. Similarities and differences underlie much of our thinking. In a narrative, for example, the *once*—the unusual, the extraordinary, the "figure"—is seen against the usual—the ordinary, the "ground." (See Chapter 3 on Narrative.) When we describe a person, a place, a situation, we often pick out the unusual, the remarkable, the striking, but we place the unusual against the usual: what stands out in that person is his flaming red hair; in most other ways, he is similar, he blends in with the crowd. When we *define*, we first present the representative features, and then we note the distinguishing features—the similarities first and then the differences. As you read, think about comparing and contrasting as fundamental ways of perceiving and shaping what we experience around us.

Past/Present

Comparisons and contrasts often bring into play the *then* and *now*, the way things were and the way things are now. Our appreciation of a tree in spring is intensified by our memory of the same tree in winter. That is the way it was; this is the way it is now. In "Reunion," Nora Ephron offers a fine example of the present in contrast to the past: this is the way college is now; that is the way it used to be. Keep in mind as you read, this basic move that often shapes a work. The relationship between things as they were and things as they are.

AS YOU WRITE

Generating Material

Because comparing and contrasting are fundamental ways of organizing experience, practice writing these fundamental ways of seeing and thinking. Take the ordinary, the daily, and explore similarities and differences—the way you used to be, the way you are now; the way a relationship used to be, the way it is now—relying on that shift from past to present. You might recall particular turning points, incidents that effected a change in you or in a relationship. Thus, within comparison and contrast, you narrate, you describe, you search for causes and anticipate effects.

Write in your journal about some of these shifts:

> the child/the adult
> innocence/experience
> gain/loss
> spring/winter
> summer/fall
> youth/age

In the same way, look around you, thinking about things as they are and their differences and similarities: raw/cooked; night/day; breakfast/dinner. Think about your hands for a moment: they are similar in many ways, but what you do with your right hand may be different from what you are able do with your left. Can you find a provocative contrast there?

Reading Your Writing

One of the traps writers may fall into when they write about comparisons and contrasts is the simple listing:

> A is like B in this way.
> A is not like B in that way.
> A is like B in this way . . .

As you read the various jottings you've made in your journal, look for patterns. Look for ways of bundling the *concrete* examples you have listed. Look for ways of putting things together. Think about whether your focus is on differences or on similarities. Think about a change from past to present. Have you been noting more similarities than differences between then and now? If so, then probably your emphasis will be on what *hasn't* changed.

Shaping Your Writing

In contrasting and comparing, as in any other kind of writing, the *evaluative*—the way you see things, the way you interpret, the answer to that question "so what"—should shape your writing. If you are working with many examples, it's a good idea to put your evaluative statements up front so that the reader knows where you are going. In the case of comparison and contrast, your statement may encompass both similarities and differences:

> Although many years have passed, and, on the surface, things look different, they're still very much the same.

The writer here will likely talk of change, but the emphasis will be on what has not changed. Conversely, the sentence may read:

> Although many years have passed and, on the surface, things don't seem to have changed, they have.

Here, we expect the emphasis to be on what has changed. (For a further discussion of shaping your writing, see page 373 above.)

DON BAUER

> *Don Bauer left Korea in 1953 with the rank of Private First Class, but he has obviously not left Korea and its war behind, as we see in this article that he submitted to the* New York Times. *Bauer now works as a credit manager for a steel production firm in Akron, Ohio.*

WARTIME IN KOREA

I hadn't thought much about "Willie" (I just can't recall his real name) in the last twenty-eight years. He wasn't, after all, much of an influence in my life. I hardly knew him. But something about the court martial of Pfc. Robert R. Garwood, the Marine convicted of collaborating with the enemy and assaulting a fellow prisoner while a captive in Vietnam, got me thinking about him again.

I think they have something in common.

Combat terrorized Willie. His fear—alive and immobilizing—was contagious. The terrible isolation of a remote listening post there in Korea was frightening enough under any circumstances, but if Willie was around it became pure hell. He heard threatening sounds, he squirmed and fidgeted and saw shadowy forms. The sound of his labored breathing echoed through the darkness like a loud stage whisper, saying: "Here we are—over here."

Willie was not your ideal combat infantryman.

He finally gave it up—said that he couldn't take it anymore—and refused to do what he had been told to do: participate in the assault of a particularly nasty hill named Outpost Kelly.

"No way," Willie said. He'd been there before, and he wasn't going back. In spite of a direct order from the company commander, he wouldn't make the trek up the dangerous slopes of O.P. Kelly. Two other men also refused to join in the attack, but the C.O. convinced them that the U.S. Army would do them more harm than the Chinese could if they persisted in their mutiny.

One of them died in the mud that day.

I didn't make the assault because I was given the safe but uncomfortable job of guarding Willie until someone came to take him to the rear. We talked and smoked. I was embarrassed. It didn't seem right to be guarding another G.I., but I was glad that I wasn't charging up O.P. Kelly with the rest of my platoon.

They came for him, slapped on the handcuffs, and took him away. We heard that he got a year and a D.D.—that's a year in Leavenworth and a dishonorable discharge.

I wondered who was better off, Willie or the guy who changed his mind and died for it.

But it's a cruel world and Willie couldn't hack it. He was a coward—a skinny nineteen-year-old coward. And I pretty much forgot about him.

They say you can't cross the same river twice because you've changed and so has the river. I don't know about the river, but I had certainly changed by the time I read about Garwood. His fear, his anguish, and his mistakes—crimes if you prefer—seemed more understandable than they would have when I guarded Willie in that stinking Korean bunker.

From this side of the river, as I pondered Garwood's ordeal, I questioned how much more I could have taken before I did what Willie did. I wondered what it could have taken to break me as Pfc. Robert Garwood had been broken.

And I wondered what had happened to Willie after they took him from my care. Did the rear-echelon people, who had never known the shriek of an incoming round, hassle him for being a coward? How did the cons treat him? Willie wasn't an armed robber or second-story man. He wasn't even a shoplifter. Thieves rank high in the criminal hierarchy but how do they rank a guy whose only crime is fear? Was the terror of prison more tolerable than the terror of combat?

Something about both cases—Willie's and Garwood's—is out of whack. Sure, it would be nice if none of the young men sent into combat broke under its strain. Most of them didn't break. And I wouldn't want to see a tickertape parade for those who did, the Willies and the Garwoods: no press conferences or award ceremonies, no yellow ribbons.

But no jails either.

I remember a few men who cracked up. When the earth around them exploded, so did their brains. They screamed, trembled, and cried until they were pulled off line and sent to an aid station. Battle fatigue it was called. They went home and got psychiatric treatment. They were given honorable discharges. They joined the V.F.W., and are now making the final payments on homes purchased with G.I. loans.

Willie didn't qualify for a G.I. loan. Neither does Garwood. Maybe none of us did.

How Do You Respond?

1. How many contrasts can you find in Bauer's essay? What is the larger, overall comparison that he makes?
2. How does it affect your reading to know that Bauer is not a professional writer, not one who makes a living at serving up regular helpings of prose?
3. Discuss a situation you have been in where some have been daring (or have done what was expected) and others have been hesitant—crossing a river, climbing a cliff, playing soccer or football, playing "I dare you" as a child. How are the brave and the cowardly related in a group of people?

RUSSELL BAKER

>   *In "School and Education," Russell Baker raises the question of what it means to be educated and, like John Holt, insists that the schools are not doing a very good job at "education." For additional biographical information on Baker, see page 285.*

SCHOOL VS. EDUCATION

By the age of six the average child will have completed the basic American education and be ready to enter school. If the child has been attentive in these pre-school years, he or she will already have mastered many skills.

From television, the child will have learned how to pick a lock, commit a fairly elaborate bank holdup, prevent wetness all day long, get the laundry twice as white, and kill people with a variety of sophisticated armaments.

From watching his parents, the child, in many cases, will already know how to smoke, how much soda to mix with whiskey, what kind of language to use when angry, and how to violate the speed laws without being caught.

At this point, the child is ready for the second stage of education, which occurs in school. There, a variety of lessons may be learned in the very first days.

The teacher may illustrate the economic importance of belonging to a strong union by closing down the school before the child arrives. Fathers and mothers may demonstrate to the child the social cohesion that can be built on shared hatred by demonstrating their dislike for children whose pigmentation displeases them. In the latter event, the child may receive visual instruction in techniques of stoning buses, cracking skulls with a nightstick, and subduing mobs with tear gas. Formal education has begun.

During formal education, the child learns that life is for testing. This stage lasts twelve years, a period during which the child learns that success comes from telling testers what they want to hear.

Early in this stage, the child learns that he is either dumb or smart. If the teacher puts intelligent demands upon the child, the child learns he is smart. If the teacher expects little of the child, the child learns he is dumb and soon quits bothering to tell the testers what they want to hear.

At this point, education becomes more subtle. The child taught by school that he is dumb observes that neither he, she, nor any of the many children who are even dumber, ever fails to be promoted to the next grade. From this, the child learns that while everybody talks a lot about the virtue of being smart, there is very little incentive to stop being dumb.

What is the point of school, besides attendance? the child wonders. As the end of the first formal stage of education approaches, school answers this question. The point is to equip the child to enter college.

Children who have been taught they are smart have no difficulty. They have been happily telling testers what they want to hear for twelve years. Being artists at telling testers what they want to hear, they are admitted to college joyously, where they promptly learn that they are the hope of America.

Children whose education has been limited to adjusting themselves to their schools' low estimates of them are admitted to less joyous colleges which, in some cases, may teach them to read.

At this stage of education, a fresh question arises for everyone. If the point of lower education was to get into college, what is the point of college? The answer is soon learned. The point of college is to prepare the student—no longer a child now—to get into graduate school. In college, the student learns that it is no longer enough simply to tell the testers what they want to hear. Many are tested for graduate school; few are admitted.

Those excluded may be denied valuable certificates to prosper in medicine, at the bar, in the corporate boardroom. The student learns that the race is to the cunning and often, alas, to the unprincipled.

Thus, the student learns the importance of destroying competitors and emerges richly prepared to play his role in the great simmering melodrama of American life.

Afterward, the former student's destiny fulfilled, his life rich with Oriental carpets, rare porcelain, and full bank accounts, he may one day find himself with the leisure and the inclination to open a book with a curious mind, and start to become educated.

How Do You Respond?

1. What is the large, overarching contrast in Baker's essay? What precisely is he contrasting?

2. How does Baker exemplify his views toward school? Toward education?

3. Baker's tone is heavily ironic. What positive values is he actually upholding? How realistic do you think is the hope he expresses in his last sentence?

NORA EPHRON

> Nora Ephron (born 1941) began writing a column about women for Esquire *magazine in 1972. The column, she says, "was my idea, and I wanted to do it for a couple of specific, self-indulgent reasons and one general reason. Self-indulgent specifics first: I needed an excuse to go to my tenth reunion at Wellesley College. . . ." Her "one general reason" was to take a look at American women—the changes they were going through, the changes she herself was going through. For the past decade, Ephron has written poignantly, persuasively, and humorously about women and popular culture in her essays for* Esquire, New York *magazine,* McCalls, Cosmopolitan, *and in her books,* Wallflower at the Orgy, Crazy Salad, *and* Scribble, Scribble.

REUNION

A boy and a girl are taking a shower together in the bathroom. How to explain the significance of it? It is a Friday night in June, the first night of the tenth reunion of the Class of 1962 of Wellesley College, and a member of my class has just returned from the bathroom with the news. A boy and a girl are taking a shower together. No one can believe it. Ten years and look at the changes. Ten years ago, we were allowed men in the rooms on Sunday afternoons only, on the condition the door be left fourteen inches ajar. One Sunday during my freshman year, a girl in my dormitory went into her room with a date and not only closed the door but put a sock on it. (The sock—I feel silly remembering nonsense like this, but I do—was a Wellesley signal meaning "Do Not Disturb.") Three hours later, she and the boy emerged and she was wearing a different outfit. No one could believe it. We were that young. Today boys on exchange programs from MIT and Dartmouth live alongside the girls, the dormitory doors lock, and some of the women in my class—as you can see from the following excerpt from one letter to our tenth-reunion record book—have been through some changes themselves:

"In the past five years I have (1) had two children and two abortions, (2) moved seriously into politics, working up to more responsible positions on bigger campaigns, (3) surrendered myself to what I finally acknowledged was my lifework—the women's revolution, (4) left my husband and children to seek my fortune and on the way (5) fallen desperately, madly, totally in love with a beautiful man and am sharing a life with him in Cambridge near Harvard Square where we're completely incredibly happy doing the work we love and having amazing life adventures."

I went back to my reunion at Wellesley to write about it. I'm doing a column, that's why I'm going, I said to New York friends who were amazed that I would want anything to do with such an event. I want to see what happened, I said—to my class, to the college. (I didn't say that I wanted my class and the college to see what had happened to me, but that of course was part of it, too.) A few years ago, Wellesley went through a long reappraisal before rejecting coeducation and reaffirming its commitment to educating women; that interested me. Also, I wondered how my class, almost half of which has two or more children, was dealing with what was happening to women today. On Friday evening, when my classmate and I arrived at the dormitory that was our class headquarters, we bumped into two Wellesley juniors. One of them asked straight off if we wanted to see their women's liberation bulletin board. They took us down the corridor to a cork board full of clippings, told us of their battle to have a full-time gynecologist on campus, and suddenly it became important for us to let them know we were not what they thought. We were not those alumnae who came back to Wellesley because it was the best time of their lives; we were not those cardigan-sweatered, Lilly Pulitzered matrons or Junior League members or League of Women Voters volunteers; we were not about to be baited by their bulletin board. We're not Them. I didn't come to reunion because I wanted to. I'm here to write about it. Understand?

Wellesley College has probably the most beautiful campus in the country, more lush and gorgeous than any place I have ever seen. In June, the dogwood and azalea are in bloom around Lake Waban, the ivy spurts new growth onto the collegiate Gothic buildings, the huge maples are obscenely loaded with shade. So idyllic, in the literal sense—an idyll before a rude awakening. There was Wellesley, we were told, and then, later, there would be the real world. The real world was different. "Where, oh where are the staid alumnae?" goes a song Wellesley girls sing, and they answer, "They've gone out from their dreams and theories. Lost, lost in the wide, wide world." At Wellesley we would be allowed to dream and theorize. We would be taken seriously. It would not always be so.

Probably the most insidious influence on the students ten years ago was the one exerted by the class deans. They were a group of elderly spinsters who believed that the only valuable role for Wellesley graduates was to go on to the only life the deans knew anything about—graduate school, scholarship, teaching. There was no value at all placed on achievement in the so-called real world. Success of that sort was suspect; worse than that, it was unserious. Better to be a housewife, my dear, and to take one's place in the community. *Keep a hand in.* This policy was not just implicit but was actually articulated. During my junior year, in a romantic episode that still embarrasses me, I became engaged to a humorless young man whose primary attraction was that he was fourth in his class at Harvard Law School. I went to see my class dean about transferring to Barnard for my senior year before being married. "Let me give you some advice," she told me. "You have worked so hard at Wellesley. When you marry, take a year off. Devote yourself to your husband and your marriage." I was incredulous. To begin with, I had not worked hard at Wellesley—anyone with my transcript in front of her ought to have been able to see that. But far more important, I had always intended to work after college; my mother was a career woman who had successfully indoctrinated me and my sisters that to be a housewife was to be nothing. Take a year off being a wife? Doing what? I carried the incident around with me for years, repeating it from time to time as positive proof that Wellesley wanted its graduates to be merely housewives. Then, one day, I met a woman who had graduated ten years before me. She had never wanted anything but to be married and have children; she, too, had gone to see this dean before leaving Wellesley and marrying. "Let me give you some advice," the dean told her. "Don't have children right away. Take a year to work." And so I saw. What Wellesley wanted was for us to avoid the extremes, to be instead that thing in the middle. Neither a rabid careerist nor a frantic mamma. That thing in the middle: a trustee. "Life is not all dirty diapers and runny noses," writes Susan Connard Chenoweth in the class record. "I do make it into the real world every week to present a puppet show on ecology called *Give a Hoot, Don't Pollute.*" The deans would be proud of Susan. She is on her way. A doer of good works. An example to the community. Above all, a Samaritan.

I never went near the Wellesley College chapel in my four years there, but I am still amazed at the amount of Christian charity that school stuck us all with, a kind of glazed politeness in the face of boredom and stupidity. Tolerance, in the worst sense of the word. Wellesley was not alone in encouraging this for its students, but it always seemed so sad that a school that could have done so much for women put so much energy into the one area women should be educated out of. How marvelous it would have been to go to a women's college that encouraged impoliteness, that rewarded aggression, that encouraged argument. Women by the time they are eighteen are so damaged, so beaten down, so tyrannized out of behaving in all the wonderful outspoken ways unfortunately characterized as masculine; a college committed to them has to take on the burden of repair—of remedial education, really. I'm not just talking about vocational guidance and placement bureaus (which are far more important than anyone at these schools believes) but also about the need to force young women to define themselves before they abdicate the task and become defined by their husbands. *What do you think? What is your opinion?* No one ever asked. We all graduated from Wellesley able to describe everything we had studied—Baroque painting, Hindemith, Jacksonian democracy, Yeats—yet we were never asked what we thought of any of it. *Do you like it? Do you think it is good? Do you know that even if it is good you do not have to like it?* During reunion weekend, at the Saturday-night class supper, we were subjected to an hour of dance by a fourth-rate Boston theatre ensemble which specializes in eighth-rate Grotowski crossed with the worst of *Marat/Sade.* Grunts. Moans. Jumping about imitating lambs. It was absolutely awful. The next day, a classmate with the improbable name of Muffy Kleinfeld asked me what I thought of it. "What did *you* think of it?" I replied. "Well," she said, "I thought their movements were quite expressive and forceful, but I'm not exactly sure what they were trying to do dramatically." *But what did you think of it?*

I am probably babbling a bit here, but I feel a real anger toward Wellesley for blowing it, for being so damned irrelevant. Like many women involved with the movement, I have come full circle in recent years: I used to think that anything exclusively for women (women's pages, women's colleges, women's novels) was a bad idea. Now I am all in favor of it. But when Wellesley decided to remain a women's college, it seemed so pointless to me. Why remain a school for women unless you are prepared to deal with the problems women have in today's society? Why bother? If you are simply going to run a classy liberal-arts college in New England, an ivory tower for $3,900 a year, why not let the men in?

Wellesley *has* changed. Some of the changes are superficial: sex in the dorms, juicy as it is, probably has more to do with the fact that it is 1972 than with real change. On the other hand, there are changes that are almost fundamental. The spinster deans are mostly gone. There is a new president, and she has actually been married. Twice. Many of the hangovers from an earlier era—when Wellesley was totally a school for the rich as opposed to now, when it is only partially so—have been eliminated: sit-down dinners with maids and students waiting on tables; Tree Day, a spring rite complete with tree maidens and tree plantings; the freshman-class banner hunt. Hoop rolling goes on, but this year a feminist senior won and promptly denounced the rite as trivial and sexist. Bible is no longer required. More seniors are applying to law school. "They are not as polite as you were," says history professor Edward Gulick, which sounds promising. Yet another teacher tells me that the students today are more like us than like the class of 1970. The graduation procession is an endless troupe of look-alikes, cookie-cutter perfect faces with long straight hair parted in the middle. Still, there are at least three times as many black faces among them as there were in my time.

And there is the graduation speaker, Eleanor Holmes Norton, a black who is New York City Commissioner of Human Rights. Ten years ago, our speaker was Santha Rama Rau, who bored us mightily with a low-keyed speech on the need to put friendship above love of country. The contrast is quite extraordinary: Norton, an outspoken feminist and mesmerizing public speaker, raises her fist to the class as she speaks. "The question has been asked," she says, "'What is a woman?' A woman is a person who makes choices. A woman is a dreamer. A woman is a planner. A woman is a maker, and a mother. A woman is a person who makes choices. A woman builds bridges. A woman makes children and makes cars. A woman writes poetry and songs. A woman is a person who makes choices. You cannot even simply become a mother anymore. You must *choose* motherhood. Will you choose change? Can you become its vanguard?" It is a moving speech, full of comparisons between women today and the young blacks of the 1960s; midway through, a Madras-jacketed father, absolutely furious, storms down the aisle, collars his graduating daughter, and drags her off to tell her what he thinks of it. She returns a few minutes later to join her class in a standing ovation.

As for my class, two things are immediately apparent. The housewives, who are openly elated at being sprung from the responsibility of children for a weekend, are nonetheless very defensive about women's liberation and wary of those of us who have made other choices. In the class record book, the most common expression is "women's lib notwithstanding," as in this from Janet Barton Mostafa: "I'm thrilled to find, women's lib to the contrary notwithstanding, that motherhood is a pretty joyful experience. Shakespeare will have to wait in the wings a year or two." *You cannot even simply become a mother anymore. You must choose motherhood.* "I steeled myself against coming," one of the housewives said at reunion. "I was sure I was going to have to defend myself." Neither she nor any other housewife will have to defend herself this trip; we are all far too polite. Still, it is interesting that the housewives—not the working mothers or the single or divorced women—are self-conscious. Which brings me to the second trend: the number of women at reunion who are not just divorced but proudly divorced, wearing their new independence as a kind of badge. I cannot imagine that previous Wellesley reunions attracted any divorced women at all.

On Saturday afternoon, our class meets formally. The meeting is conducted by the outgoing class president, B. J. Diener, the developer of Breck One Dandruff Shampoo. She has brought each of us a bottle of the stuff, a gesture some of the class think is in poor taste. I think it is sweet. B. J. is saying that the college ought to do more for its alumnae—hold symposia around the country, provide reading lists on selected subjects, run correspondence courses for graduate school credits. I find myself involved in debate about the wisdom of all this—I hadn't meant to get involved, but here I am, with my hand up, about to say that it sounds suspiciously like suburban clubwomen. As it happens, I am sitting in the back with a small group of fellow troublemakers, and we all end up waving our hands and speaking out. "It seems to me," says one, "that all this is in the same spirit of elitism we've tried to get away from since leaving Wellesley." Says another: "Where is the leadership of Wellesley when it comes to graduate-school quotas for women? If Wellesley is going to stand out and be a special place for women, it should be standing up and making a loud noise about it." One thing leads to another, and the Class of 1962 ends up passing a unanimous resolution urging the college to take a position of leadership in the women's movement. It seems a stunning and miraculous victory, and so, giddy, we push on to yet another controversial topic. That morning, graduation exercises had been leafleted by a campus group urging Wellesley to sell its stocks in companies manufacturing products for war; we think the class should support them. President Diener thinks this is a terrible idea, and she musters all her Harvard Business School expertise to suggest instead that we ask the college to vote its shares against company management. Hands are up all over the room. "The whole purpose of Wellesley's investment is to make money," says one woman, "and I for one don't care if they want to invest it in whorehouses." The motion to urge the college to sell its war stocks is defeated 30–8. The eight of us leave together, flushed with the partial success of our troublemaking, and suddenly I feel depressed and silly. We had come back to make a little trouble but, like the senior who won hoop rolling and denounced it, we all tend toward tiny little rebellions, harmless nips at the system. We will never make any real trouble. Wellesley helped see to that.

And the nonsense. My God, the nonsense. At reunion, most of the students are gone and classes are over for the year. All that remains is a huge pile of tradition. Singing on the chapel steps. Fruit punch and tea in the afternoon. Class cheers and class songs. On Sunday morning, the last day of a hopelessly over-scheduled weekend, the reunion classes parade down to the alumnae meeting. Each class carries a felt banner and each woman wears a white dress decorated with some kind of costume insignia, also in class colors. My class is holding plastic umbrellas trimmed with huge bouquets of plastic violets and purple ribbons. The class of 1957 is waving green feather dusters. Nineteen thirty-two is wearing what look like strawberry shortcakes but turn out to be huge red crowns;

1937 is in chefs' hats and aprons with signs reading, "'37 is alive and cooking!" I am standing on the side, defiant in my non-umbrellaness, as the Class of 1952 comes down the path with red backpacks strapped on; in the midst of them I see a woman I know, a book editor, who is marching with her class but is not wearing a backpack. I start to laugh, because it seems clear to me that we both think we are somehow set apart from all this—she because she is not wearing anything on her back, I because I am taking notes. We are both wrong, of course.

I can pretend that I have come back to Wellesley only because I want to write about it, but I am really here because I still care, I still care about this Mickey Mouse institution; I am foolish enough to think that someday it will do something important for women. That I care at all, that I am here at all, makes me one of Them. I am not exactly dumb—but we are all dumb. This college is about as meaningful to the educational process in America as a perfume factory is to the national economy. And all of us care, which makes us all idiots for wasting a minute thinking about the place.

How Do You Respond?

1. Ephron's essay builds on a large contrast between *then* and *now*. List in the opposing columns the way things were and the way things are now. Do you see an overall theme in these changes?

2. What contrasts do you see between 1972, when Ephron wrote, and today?

3. Ephron's essay comes down to a final contrast, a self-contradiction. Discuss the dilemma she presents in contrasting the fact of caring and the futility of caring.

JOE McGINNISS

> Author of The Selling of the President, Heroes, and Going to Extremes, Joe McGinniss (born 1942) set off for Alaska, the last frontier. He lived there for two years, traveling across the state, stopping along the way to talk and listen—to Eskimos, to oilworkers at Prudhoe Bay, to teachers, to those who "choose" to live in this place. "Alaska," says McGinniss, "was, clearly, a place one would have to choose. Not a place one just happened to stumble across." The village, in the following selection, is one of those places on this last of the American frontiers.

THE VILLAGE

The town of Bethel sits where the Kuskokwim River—a river which flows for eight hundred miles—begins to widen and to empty into Kuskokwim Bay. This is in the southwestern part of Alaska, about five hundred roadless miles, and three mountain ranges, west of Anchorage. It is good fishing country, and unparalleled for the hunting of waterfowl, but it is not much to look at either from the air or from the ground; either from a distance or up close.

The population of Bethel is about 3,000, making it approximately the same size as Barrow and Nome. It is as run-down as Barrow but without the distinction of being in the Artic. And it was founded by missionaries, not by gold seekers, and thus is lacking in the lusty traditions of Nome.

Bethel is, in fact, the only town in Alaska with a Hebrew name. Chosen by the Moravian missionaries who arrived there in the late nineteenth century, to find an Eskimo village called Mumtrekhologamute. Life was difficult enough without that, so they changed the name to Bethel, after a passage in Genesis, wherein "God said unto Jacob, arise and go up to Bethel, and dwell there . . ." which seemed to indicate, to anyone who had spent time in Bethel, Alaska, that Jacob was not, after all, one of God's chosen people.

It is, in short, a shabby, dreary town, in flat, dull, river delta country—a part of Alaska that might as well be Kansas, except for the summer mosquitoes and winter cold.

Bethel is, however, the administrative, commercial, and transportation hub for the dozens of Eskimo villages that are scattered across western Alaska like pieces of birdseed thrown in a yard. The little places that the Moravians did not get to, and that retain, therefore, the Eskimo names that no white man—with the possible exception of Duncan Pryde—can properly pronounce: Kongigamak, Kwigillingok, Kvigatluk.

It was in one such village, a Russian Orthodox Eskimo village with a population of only 200, that Olive Cook had lived for the first eighteen years of her life. Until she had written to the senator's office, and he had found her a job in the Department of the Interior, and she had gone off to Washington, D.C.

In the village, Olive Cook had not given much thought to what sort of place Washington, D.C., would actually be. Just that it would not be the village was enough. In the village, in the summer, fishing was the main occupation. Catching salmon and whitefish, then drying the fish, and smoking them, and putting away enough to ensure that there would be food for the winter. In the winter, in the village, there seeemed to be no occupation at all. Just endless miles of snow, and endless days of empty sterile, bitter cold and, worst of all, from Olive Cook's point of view, isolation.

She was of that generation of Eskimo—the first such generation—for whom the ancient tasks, the centuries of culture and tradition, had lost their meaning. The white man and his technology, and the Eskimo's new awareness of the outside world, had put the primitive society under a pressure that it seemed unlikely to survive. And it was the teen-agers and young adults—like Olive Cook—who were feeling the pressure most acutely. For them, the village of their birth was no longer, necessarily, the place where they would have to spend the rest of their lives.

Olive Cook had been to Bethel frequently. She had once even traveled to Anchorage, and had seen there a way of life involving automobiles and movie theaters and restaurants. A way of life that enabled people to heat their homes simply by turning a dial; that permitted them to consume food which they had not had to kill themselves; and that gave them money, apparently, for doing no more than sitting in a warm building all day, playing with pieces of paper, and talking to each other on the telephone.

Olive Cook, by the time she was eighteen, was sick of the village. Sick of fish, sick of snow, sick of seeing the same thirty or forty wooden shacks every day and the same two hundred people every week. And sick, most of all, of sleeping, as she had done since her infancy, in the same room as her parents: the bedroom half of the two-room wooden shack on the riverbank in which she and her parents and her two younger brothers and her younger sister had always lived.

Nothing in Olive Cook's experience, however, or in her education or in her genetic heritage, had prepared her to cope with Washington, D.C., in July. The temperature was 96 degrees and the humidity was over 90 percent. The temperature remained in the 90s for most of her first month in the city, a factor which—in combination with homesickness, culture shock, and the responsibility of working for the first time at a job with fixed hours, in surroundings that were totally alien to all she'd ever known—brought her to the edge of nervous breakdown.

She was aware, for the first time in her life, that she was a member of a racial minority. And, in Washington, seemingly a minority of one. She did not fit in with whites and she did not fit in with blacks, and there was not what one could call any Eskimo social network in the city.

She was an attractive young woman, but in Washington, as one of the thousands of attractive young women with government jobs, Olive Cook inspired few second glances.

To make matters worse, her job—a low-level clerical position for which she was inadequately trained—proved to be less than rewarding. What she did for most of the day was to sit at her desk and wonder what was going on all around her.

And what she did for most of her nights was either to go back to her cramped, unattractive apartment, and wonder why she had ever wanted to leave the village, or, more frequently, to go out to a party, where, due to her nervousness and her inexperience and her feelings of isolation and insecurity, she would drink too much too quickly, or, if the opportunity presented itself, smoke so much dope that, temporarily, she would no longer care where she was.

Except for eating salad, there was little about Washington that she enjoyed. And while the salads were marvelous—for eighteen years she had lived in a place where the nearest thing to fresh greens had been packages of Doublemint gum—all the lettuce in Washington was not enough to overcome the sense of loss and confusion she felt.

The village had always seemed so stifling, so confining, and the life she would lead were she to stay there had seemed as barren and bleak as the frozen winter tundra which began outside her family's kitchen window and stretched on, unchanging, for hundreds of miles.

Yet as empty as Eskimo life had once seemed, it had become clear to Olive Cook that the ways of her people were almost infinitely more rewarding than the existence that was available to a single Eskimo girl from a small, backward village who had made the mistake of moving to Washington, D.C.

At least that seemed clear some of the time. At other times Olive Cook felt that there was nowhere she belonged. And nowhere she would ever belong. That she would not be able to go home again. But that neither would she be able to remain in the white man's world.

There were times—in fact, it may have been most of the time—that Olive Cook felt she would always be lost and confused. That she—and many others of her generation—had been cut loose forever from the moorings of Eskimo life and were doomed to drift endlessly on seas that they would never come to know.

By December, Olive Cook had decided that she needed to go back to the village for a while. To go home for Christmas. Not so much for the white man's Christmas of December 25, but for the Russian Orthodox Christmas festival—the Slavic—which was celebrated for a full week in early January. Her village was one in which the Russian Orthodox religion—which had been brought to the region two centuries earlier by the first white men to travel there—had endured. And where the week of the Slavic celebration was considered to be at once the most festive and the most solemn time of the year.

It would be, for Olive Cook, an opportunity to try to come to some sort of terms with herself. With her Eskimo heritage. And with whatever it was that she intended to do with her life.

She arranged for a two-week vacation and flew home. Through Chicago, to Anchorage, and then to Bethel; and then on a Delaire Flying Service charter flight—in a single-engine plane that landed on skis instead of wheels—to the village.

After she had been back for a few days, I called her on the village telephone. There was only one phone for the village—in the home of a man named Yeako Slim. It was a business. He would come fetch you if you received an incoming call, but on outgoing calls he took a commission.

I called one Sunday afternoon in January when it was 30 degrees below zero and dark in the village. I asked to speak to Olive Cook. The connection was not terribly good. Yeako Slim said something which I did not understand. Then, apparently, he went to get her.

It was a ten-minute walk from Yeako Slim's shack to the shack, at the south end of the village, where the Cook family lived. And then Olive had to put on her parka and her boots. Altogether, it took her more than twenty minutes to get to the phone.

She told me, as she had first told me in Washington, on the October night when I had met her, that it would be okay if I came to visit for the Slavic. I said I would fly out the next day.

Bethel was an hour and twenty minutes from Anchorage. The Wien terminal was a big wooden shack. There was a large, pushy crowd waiting for the plane, a mixture of Eskimos and whites. Waiting to board the plane and fly out of Bethel and back to the twentieth century.

In Alaska, the airplane does not just cover distance. It is also a time machine. You get on in Anchorage, an aggressive, if tacky, late-twentieth-century American city, and get off, eighty minutes later, not just five hundred miles away, but also fifty years back in time. No plumbing, only occasional electricity, and with the few streets of the town not yet paved.

The Wien terminal was a couple of miles outside of town. The Delaire Flying Service was right in the middle of the town, in a small wooden shack on the bank of the river. The river, of course, was frozen and covered with snow. The Kuskokwim is a big river by the time it reaches Bethel, maybe half a mile wide. The Delaire plane was a single-engine six-seater which used skis in the winter and pontoons in the summer. The fare to the village was thirty-two dollars but that could be divided among however many people happened to be making a given trip. I was lucky. There were three Eskimo women already waiting for a flight. That made it only eight dollars apiece. There was no schedule. We would go when the pilot turned up, and when the plane was in shape, and when they could fit this trip in among the shuttles back and forth to other villages. In the small Eskimo villages of Alaska, you call for the airplane the way, in a city, you call a cab.

It was a clear and windless day, with the temperature 20 below zero. By now, I had grown used to such temperatures. The sun glowed orange to the west. The village was at the same latitude, with the same amount of winter daylight, as Anchorage. Which was about the only thing that the village and Anchorage had in common.

The plane landed smoothly, on skis, on the river that served as the main street of the village.

In the distance, I saw a figure walking slowly up the river. A bulky figure, in a parka, maybe about a hundred yards away. The figure waved an arm. I waved back. This was Olive Cook, I assumed. She had heard the plane—in the village, you could not help but hear the plane—and had come out to see if I was on it. I picked up my duffel bag by one end, and, dragging the other end through the snow, I headed toward her.

"Hey, you crazy guy, you really nuts, you know that? I never thought you would come. How long you staying anyway? It's very crowded here for the Slavic. I think you just be in the way." Then she laughed. A bit hysterically, I thought.

"Look at that bag. What you got in there? You got presents for me, I sure hope. I don't know where you going to put a big bag like that. We don't have no extra space in our house. When you going back? When you tell that pilot to come for you? Oh boy, you crazy guy, I don't know what you are doing here."

We walked down the river to her house. Most of the village had been built on the east bank of the river. The Cook family, and one or two others, lived on the west bank, so in summer to pick up their mail, or to use the telephone, or simply to go out and visit, they would have to cross the river in a boat. In winter, of course, it made no difference. The river was like a six-lane highway right through town.

The house was an unpainted wooden shack. Olive pushed open the door and we stepped inside, accompanied by billows of steam.

"Take off your boots, you!" This was Olive's mother. Glaring at me, and pointing to a pile of boots by the door. In my socks, I stepped into the room that served as kitchen, living room, and dining room, and as bedroom for Olive's younger brothers and her cousin.

The room contained a wood-burning stove, a big table, and a couch that folded out to be a bed. There was a basin to wash in. Water was obtained by melting ice. There was a small storage closet, separated from the kitchen by a curtain. At the rear of the storage closet there was a bucket. This bucket was the Cook family's toilet. Every couple of days, they dumped it outside and started again. In spring, when breakup came—when the snow melted and the ground thawed and the river started flowing—the winter's waste pile would gradually disappear. As would all the other waste piles around the village.

There was a second, smaller room. With a bed in one corner for the parents, a bunk bed next to it, a bunk bed at the other end, and a cot pushed up against a wall. Normally, five people slept in this room. The parents, Olive, her sister, who was fourteen years old, and a male relative who lived with the family much of the time.

Olive's father was sitting cross-legged by the stove, working intently with a knife. A bald and bloody carcass lay beside him. He looked up, nodded once, went back to work.

"What's the matter?" Olive said. "You never seen anybody skin a fox?"

There was fur, blood, gristle, and bones all over the floor. Olive's father worked silently, with head bowed. He was a short man, of medium build, with a crew cut. Her mother was taller, lighter in color, less Asiatic looking.

"Hey, what do you think?" her mother said. "This is some kind of hotel? What you come here for with that big bag?"

"It's not so big."

"Yeah, where you think we gonna put it? We don't have no space in here."

"Hey, goddamm you," Olive said. "I sure hope you brought us some vegetables."

But no, I had not brought vegetables. I should have. I had thought of buying vegetables and fruit in Anchorage. But then I had been in a rush to catch my plane.

Olive's father put down his knife, wiped his bloody hands on his pants, and sat down at the table to eat lunch. Olive's mother put a bowl in front of me. She filled it with a light brown, pasty substance. There was a plate of pilot bread—thick, flat crackers—to go with it.

"I hope you like moose soup." Olive said. "That's all we eat here in the winter."

Actually this was not quite true. That night, for dinner, following an afternoon during which Olive took me on a walking tour of the village, there was moose stew. The difference was, moose stew had gristly joints of moose in it, while the soup was just moose-flavored gruel.

As soon as the evening meal was over, Olive's father went back to the floor, where, now that he was finished skinning fox, he had started to build a blackfish trap.

Blackfish were oily little fish that swam all winter long in the river that flowed through the village. To catch them, you lowered the trap into the water through a hole in the ice, and pulled it out the next day. The trap was made of freshly cut wood, which was peeled, cut into strips, and then woven together to make a basket. A cone was placed over the open end. The fish would swim into the basket but then would be unable to get out.

It was a painstaking, intricate process, but Olive's father worked quickly, with total concentration, his sharp knife flashing, his stubby, worn fingers handling the wood the way a professional blackjack dealer handles cards.

The children had disappeared right after dinner into the other room of the house. Olive was helping her mother wash some clothes. They had an old-fashioned washtub, with a wringer that had to be cranked by hand.

By 9 P.M. Olive's father had almost finished the trap. Just two or three more strips to weave into place. His breathing was steady and rhythmic. He sat with head bowed, legs crossed, nothing moving but the masterful hands. To watch him work was to see not just the heart of a separate culture, but, it seemed, the essence of a dying age.

All over Alaska, Eskimos were giving up, moving to the cities, signing on for govenment aid. Taking jobs on the pipeline, or staying home and cashing welfare checks. Some, the more adaptable, had begun going to school to learn white men's trades: real estate, construction, and other forms of profitable entrepreneurship.

But here, in the village, was Al Cook. A survivor. Impervious to the assaults of time and progress upon the sacred traditions of his people.

His expression had not changed; he had not uttered a sound for more than an hour. The blackfish trap had come to seem an extension of himself. Then, suddenly, Olive's eight-year-old brother ran in from the back room.

"Papa, Papa!" the boy shouted. "Hurry up! Hurry up! 'Six Million Dollar Man' on TV!"

Al Cook dropped his knife. He tossed the almost completed blackfish trap aside. He jumped to his feet, his face animated for the first time all day. Grinning and chattering and rubbing his hands in anticipation, he hurried toward the other room, following his son.

"Oh boy," he said. "Hurry up." Motioning for me to accompany him. "'Six Million Dollar Man' on TV."

Television was new. This was its first winter in the village, which had been chosen as part of a pilot project. Ostensibly, to see if the introduction of television would improve the quality of Eskimo life. Although some considered it a not so subtle form of genocide.

For the villagers, television was the biggest innovation since the airplane. Even bigger, in a way, since the airplane affected the lives of a comparatively small percentage of the population, whereas television influenced every life.

No more were ancient stories told late into the night. No more the quiet visits, the dances, the little games. Now, not even a blackfish trap was more important than a program as exciting as "The Six Million Dollar Man."

For the first time in history, the Eskimo had been given an opportunity to live vicariously. And he had seized it and was clinging to it for dear life. No matter that very few of the viewers could understand the dialogue—the English spoken was too quick, and the accent, to the Eskimo ear, was too foreign—the picture alone was enough. After centuries of staring into the flickering fire through the night, the village people could now stare at electronic images that flickered in a variety of adventurous ways.

It was television, I soon discovered, even more than the celebration of the Slavic, around which the life of the village seemed to revolve. There was only one channel—from Bethel. It broadcast a mixture of commercial and educational programs. The children watched "Sesame Street" each afternoon. Little Eskimo kids coming off the tundra and sitting three feet from the screen. Learning to count from one to ten in Spanish. Gone was the symbolism of the raven and the bear. The new gods were Big Bird, and Bert and Ernie.

It did not matter what program was on. After centuries of changeless frozen winter, where the only thing that moved for miles around was the snow when the wind happened to blow, it was now possible to turn one switch and this magic machine would bring a seemingly infinite variety of hallucinatory images before your eyes. It was almost a form of peyote.

"Starsky and Hutch." "Charlie's Angels." "Mister Rogers." The residents of the village loved them all. One afternoon, the entire Cook family sat transfixed for half an hour watching "Book Beat" as Robert Cromie directed questions at Saul Bellow.

I slept on the folding couch in the front room. The eight-year-old was next to me. His cousin slept next to him. A younger brother slept on the floor. Olive's parents got up at 6 A.M. Her father went outside and attached a sled to their snow machine. Her mother made coffee, then went to help with the sled.

"Where are they off to at this time of day?" I asked Olive.

"To Bethel."

"To Bethel? By snow machine? But that must be fifty miles away."

"Yeah, so what? Otherwise, how we gonna get our food for the Slavic? You think we can phone up and they deliver?"

Most of the food the Cook family ate was obtained by hunting or fishing. They caught fish in the summer and smoke-dried what they did not eat. In the fall, they froze the fish they caught. They also shot ducks and geese, and at least one moose every year. For incidental foods, there was a small store in the village, which had its goods delivered by charter flight from Bethel, after a Wien flight from Anchorage, and after a longer cargo flight, or shipment by barge or truck, from somewhere outside of Alaska. It was all this lugging around that made a can of string beans cost $2.50.

For the Slavic, however, the village store was not enough. For the Slavic, and maybe one or two other times during the winter, Olive's parents would travel all the way to Bethel by snow machine to do their shopping. Then all the way home the same day. This could be done only in winter, of course. In summer, there was no way to reach Bethel on the ground.

When the sled was attached, Olive's parents came back inside. They ate crackers with jam and drank coffee. Then they told their children what the chores were for the day. I gave Olive's mother some money for the food, in place of the vegetables I did not bring from Anchorage. She thanked me, they put on their parkas, and they were gone.

"How much did you give her?" Olive asked.

"Thirty dollars."

"Yeah, why don't you give her more, you rich white man? You come out here and eat all our food and take up all our space with your goddamn duffel bag, I trip over it every time I go in to take a piss. Why are you here? Didn't you know I was just drunk and stoned when I invited you?"

I shrugged. This seemed just Olive's way of saying good morning. I spread some butter and jam on a piece of pilot bread for my breakfast. Kool-Aid was the only thing to drink. The little kids drank Kool-Aid all the time, and chewed gum constantly, and told their mother to be sure to bring back the Sugar Pops. I think they saw commercials for sugared breakfast cereals on TV.

"Now what are you going to do, goddamn you? I got to do the wash. I am not here just to entertain you. Why don't you go play with the kids, that's all you are good for. Go on, don't bother me, I don't have no time for you. I got to be nice to you yesterday just because my mother and my father are around, but today they are gone and I wish that you were gone, too."

Then, inexplicably, she broke into a grin and leaned close to me and squeezed my arm and said, "Hey, don't worry. I just get a little upset, that is all. I'm only fooling. It's okay. You stay here as long as you want."

She did another load of wash, she mopped the floors, refusing my offers to help, and she tried to make a spaghetti sauce that afternoon, to show her parents the kind of food she ate in Washington. The sauce was doing well, too, until she decided that, having no meatballs, she should instead add little pieces of moose.

That night, there was a basketball game against a team from a nearby village to the north. The game was played in the school gymnasium. The gymnasium had a low roof, and the baskets were only nine feet high, but, otherwise, basketball was basketball, anywhere in the world.

Olive and I sat in the second row of folding wooden bleachers. The bleachers were only half filled. Another sign of the impact of television. Before TV, it had been standing room only for every game.

It was apparent from the start that the village team was outclassed. The opponents were bigger, stronger, faster, and had a guard who hit twenty-foot jump shots. The score, at the end of the first quarter, was 28–16.

Between quarters, the village players seemed embroiled in hot debate. There was much waving of arms, and voices were raised. Then, while some of the players sat back down on the bench in disgust, two members of the team walked over to where Olive and I were sitting.

"You play basketball?"

"A little bit. Long time ago."

The two players were about five feet six inches tall. No one on either team was more than three inches taller. I was over six three in bare feet.

"You play now. For us."

"No, I couldn't do that. I mean, look . . . I don't even have any sneakers."

"You play in socks."

"No, I think I'll just—"

"Goddamn you!" Olive shouted. "You play!"

So I played. For the whole second quarter and for part of the third. Until finally the village players had to admit that I was not such a great white hope after all. At least not in socks.

I scored four points. I got three or four rebounds. I committed a couple of fouls. And I slipped and fell about a dozen times on the highly waxed floor.

I might not have helped the village team, but I did prove to be a favorite with the crowd. They didn't react when I scored, but each time I slipped they gave me a standing ovation.

Midway through the third quarter time was called. The village team now trailed by twenty points. There was another heated discussion among my teammates. In their own language. A decision was reached and announced: "Okay, you, now go sit down." I was replaced by a kid five foot two.

The Slavic began the next day. It did not seem a very structured affair. Village leaders would carry a prayer wheel and incense into a home, followed by whoever was participating at any given time. As many people as possible would crowd into the house, and then, for twenty minutes or half an hour, they would chant prayers and sing ancient Russian hymns. When the singing was over, food would be served. And that was the problem. The praying and the singing were not so bad: exotic enough to be interesting for a while, and kind of stirring, really, when you realized how closely in touch these people still were with the days when the only white men in Alaska were the Russians.

But after the singing came the food. Sometimes there would be moose soup. Sometimes fermented seal meat, which was worse. But always as a staple, there was something called Eskimo ice cream. This was either seal oil or Crisco, whipped to a batter-like consistency, and laced heavily with a particularly noxious and bitter type of berry.

Unfortunately, you were expected to eat it. To pass a bowl back unfinished would have been considered not merely rude but, under the circumstances, almost blasphemous. And this stuff was served at every house.

At each house, also, the children were given bags full of candy. For three days, no one under the age of fourteen in the village ate anything else. And no matter how much they ate, their reserve supply seemed to increase. They would have candy enough, by the conclusion of the Slavic, to last them until freeze-up again the next fall. That they would have any teeth left was a doubtful proposition.

It was by far the most awesome, revolting, and chilling orgy of sugar consumption I'd ever seen. No Halloween, no Easter Sunday, no Christmas vacation in even the most permissive or uncaring American household could have begun to approach what Slavic meant to Eskimo children in western Alaska. And the parents did not seem bothered by it in the least. It was history, tradition; this was the way it had always been done. Not even a recent warning from the Russian Orthodox bishop, based in Sitka, that sugar consumption during the Slavic should be curtailed had any effect. No wonder that by the time he reached puberty, the average Eskimo child had fewer teeth in his mouth than a Boston Bruins defenseman.

Over the next twenty-four hours it became obvious that Olive Cook did truly regret having invited me to the Slavic. She had never expected that I would come, she was deeply embarrassed by my presence—I was, other than the schoolteacher, the only white person in the village—and she would feel immense relief when I departed. In addition to that, I couldn't take any more Eskimo ice cream.

I walked over to Yeako Slim's house and phoned the flying service in Bethel. They said they would send out a plane the next morning. I paid Yeako Slim a dollar for the call. There was a sign on the wall which said: PLEASE TRY TO AVOID SCRIBBLING ON TELEPHONE LOGS. SHOW SOME RESPECT. If you made a call, you marked down where you called and how long you talked. Then, every once in a while Yeako Slim would make you pay. It was like owing money at the grocery store.

It was cloudy in the village that day, and the temperature was up close to zero. The Cook family was busy, preparing for the arrival of the Slavic procession at their house. In the afternoon I took a long walk across a frozen lake.

The village ended right in the Cook's backyard. From there you could go seventy-five miles west and, in winter, not see another living thing. The seventy-five miles would bring you to the western edge of Alaska. The edge of the continent once again. The Bering Sea, and Russia beyond it. You could go a hundred miles north and not see another living thing. Until you hit the frozen Yukon River at a place called Pilot Station. This was the Yukon, which had started in Canada, a thousand miles to the east, now almost at the end of its run.

And from the village, in no matter what direction you went, you would have to cover pretty near a hundred miles before you came to any land that rose more than one hundred feet above sea level. Most of the people in the village had never been that far from their homes.

In the evening, in the Cooks' house, all was ready for the celebration of the Slavic. The children were dressed in their finest clothes. Their hair was combed, their faces washed. Olive's mother and father had finished the cleaning and the preparation of the food. There was no more to do but to wait for the procession to arrive.

The eight-year-old went out to see how much longer it might be. He came back saying two more houses, and then ours. That meant maybe an hour, maybe two. The family crowded into the bedroom and turned on the TV. The program was a public television production of "Macbeth." The little boy thought it superb. Lots of sword fights. Olive's father felt it was not quite as good as "The Six Million Dollar Man," Macbeth, of course, not being bionic.

"Macbeth" was followed by a special: "Christmas from Disneyland." A one-hour program which had been broadcast across the rest of America three weeks before. Disney characters singing Christmas carols; Mickey Mouse riding in a sleigh. Glittery decorations strung from palm trees.

The entire Cook family was ecstatic. They had heard about this place called Disneyland, and now here it was, right in their home, for them to see.

I don't know if it was Anita Bryant who was the hostess, but someone like that. It was classic Disney, "Silver Bells," "Frosty the Snowman," "Rudolph the Red-nosed Reindeer." In the village they had real reindeer practically outside their back door, but this was better. This was TV.

A chorus of children dressed as snowballs was standing in front of a phony cathedral, singing "Santa Claus Is Coming to Town," when, very softly, in the bacground, the first faint sounds of the approaching Slavic procession could be heard.

The worshippers had left the last house on the other side of the river, and now were walking slowly across, spinning the prayer wheel, waving the incense, singing the ancient Russian processional hymn. Fifty or sixty people, keeping a centuries-old tradition alive.

They crossed the river and started up the path toward the front door. The singing was coming now in rich, mellow tones through the frigid night air.

Olive's mother got up and turned off the television. Disneyland vanished. The Slavic procession arrived, as it had been arriving among these people for two hundred years.

Olive jumped to her feet and angrily threw a dish towel against a wall. "This goddamn Slavic ruins everything," she yelled. "You can't even watch real Christmas on TV."

In the morning, when I left, Olive came with me, even though there were three days left of Slavic. Her decision was sudden: she packed in a hurry, laughing and crying, as the pilot waited impatiently by the plane. For a couple of days, she said, she'd stay in Bethel, where there were people she wanted to see. Then she would go to Anchorage, where she wanted to spend a few days being drunk. Eventually, she would go back to Washington, to the Department of the Interior to try again; but this time with less enthusiasm than despair.

How Do You Respond?

1. What does McGinniss contrast in his essay? What methods does he use to present the contrasts to the reader?

2. One contrast concerns individuals—differences between people in different places and in different times. How does he make these contrasts vivid and specific?

3. McGinniss discusses Olive but never indicates what she is like until he begins to quote her directly. He refers to her abusive style of speech only once, but never evaluates or explains her attitude toward him. Were you surprised when Olive first spoke? How do you explain her way of talking? How do you accept it? Why?

FLANNERY O'CONNOR

> *Critics speak of "Flannery O'Connor country," the American South where O'Connor was born (1925) and died (1964). Her writings reflect her firm rootings in her native South. "Ours is a real Bible belt," she once said. "We have a sense of the absolute . . . a sense of Moses' face as he pulverized the idols . . . a sense of time, place, and eternity joined." A distinguished novelist and short story writer, O'Connor is known best for her fiction,* Wise Blood, A Good Man is Hard to Find, The Violent Bear It Away—*and for her love of raising peacocks.*

EVERYTHING THAT RISES MUST CONVERGE

Her doctor had told Julian's mother that she must lose twenty pounds on account of her blood pressure, so on Wednesday nights Julian had to take her downtown on the bus for a reducing class at the Y. The reducing class was designed for working girls over fifty, who weighed from 165 to 200 pounds. His mother was one of the slimmer ones, but she said ladies did not tell their age or weight. She would not ride the buses by herself at night since they had been integrated, and because the reducing class was one of her few pleasures, necessary for her health, and *free*, she said Julian could at least put himself out to take her, considering all she did for him. Julian did not like to consider all she did for him, but every Wednesday night he braced himself and took her.

She was almost ready to go, standing before the hall mirror, putting on her hat, while he, his hands behind him, appeared pinned to the door frame, waiting like Saint Sebastian for the arrows to begin piercing him. The hat was new and had cost her seven dollars and a half. She kept saying. "Maybe I shouldn't have paid that for it. No, I shouldn't have. I'll take it off and return it tomorrow. I shouldn't have bought it."

Julian raised his eyes to heaven. "Yes, you should have bought it," he said. "Put it on and let's go." It was a hideous hat. A purple velvet flap came down on one side of it and stood up on the other; the rest of it was green and looked like a cushion with the stuffing

"Jack Sprat Could Eat No Fat" 407

out. He decided it was less comical than jaunty and pathetic. Everything that gave her pleasure was small and depressed him.

She lifted the hat one more time and set it down slowly on top of her head. Two wings of gray hair protruded on either side of her florid face, but her eyes, sky-blue, were as innocent and untouched by experience as they must have been when she was ten. Were it not that she was a widow who had struggled fiercely to feed and clothe and put him through school and who was supporting him still, "until he got on his feet," she might have been a little girl that he had to take to town.

"It's all right, it's all right," he said. "Let's go." He opened the door himself and started down the walk to get her going. The sky was a dying violet and the houses stood out darkly against it, bulbous liver-colored monstrosities of a uniform ugliness though no two were alike. Since this had been a fashionable neighborhood forty years ago, his mother persisted in thinking they did well to have an apartment in it. Each house had a narrow collar of dirt around it in which sat, usually, a grubby child. Julian walked with his hands in his pockets, his head down and thrust forward and his eyes glazed with the determination to make himself completely numb during the time he would be sacrificed to her pleasure.

The door closed and he turned to find the dumpy figure, surmounted by the atrocious hat, coming toward him. "Well," she said, "you only live once and paying a little more for it, I at least won't meet myself coming and going."

"Some day I'll start making money," Julian said gloomily—he knew he never would—"and you can have one of those jokes whenever you take the fit." But first they would move. He visualized a place where the nearest neighbors would be three miles away on either side.

"I think you're doing fine," she said, drawing on her gloves. "You've only been out of school a year. Rome wasn't built in a day."

She was one of the few members of the Y reducing class who arrived in hat and gloves and who had a son who had been to college. "It takes time," she said "and the world is in such a mess. This hat looked better on me than any of the others, though when she brought it out I said, 'Take that thing back. I wouldn't have it on my head,' and she said, 'Now wait till you see it on,' and then she put it on me, I said, 'We-ull,' and she said, 'If you ask me, that

hat does something for you and you do something for the hat, and besides,' she said, 'with that hat, you won't meet yourself coming and going.' "

Julian thought he could have stood his lot better if she had been selfish, if she had been an old hag who drank and screamed at him. He walked along, saturated in depression, as if in the midst of his martyrdom he had lost his faith. Catching sight of his long, hopeless, irritated face, she stopped suddenly with a grief-stricken look, and pulled back on his arm. "Wait on me," she said. "I'm going to the house and take this thing off and tomorrow I'm going to return it. I was out of my head. I can pay the gas bill with that seven-fifty."

He caught her arm in a vicious grip. "You are not going to take it back," he said. "I like it."

"Well," she said, "I don't think I ought . . ."

"Shut up and enjoy it," he muttered, more depressed than ever.

"With the world in the mess it's in," she said, "it's a wonder we can enjoy anything. I tell you, the bottom rail is on the top."

Julian sighed.

"Of course," she said, "if you know who you are, you can go anywhere." She said this every time he took her to the reducing class. "Most of them in it are not our kind of people," she said, "but I can be gracious to anybody. I know who I am."

"They don't give a damn for your graciousness," Julian said savagely. "Knowing who you are is good for one generation only. You haven't the foggiest idea where you stand now or who you are."

She stopped and allowed her eyes to flash at him. "I most certainly do know who I am," she said, "and if you don't know who you are, I'm ashamed of you."

"Oh hell," Julian said.

"Your great-grandfather was a former governor of this state," she said. "Your grandfather was a prosperous landowner. Your grandmother was a Godhigh."

"Will you look around you," he said tensely, "and see where you are now?" and he swept his arm jerkily out to indicate the neighborhood, which the growing darkness at least made less dingy.

"You remain what you are," she said. "Your great-grandfather had a plantation and two hundred slaves."

"There are no more slaves," he said irritably.

"They were better off when they were," she said. He groaned to see that she was off on that topic. She rolled onto it every few days like a train on an open track. He knew every stop, every junction, every swamp along the way, and knew the exact point at which her conclusion would roll majestically into the station: "It's ridiculous. It's simply not realistic. They should rise, yes, but on their own side of the fence."

"Let's skip it," Julian said.

"The ones I feel sorry for," she said, "are the ones that are half white. They're tragic."

"Will you skip it?"

"Suppose we were half white. We would certainly have mixed feelings."

"I have mixed feelings now," he groaned.

"Well let's talk about something pleasant," she said. "I remember going to Grandpa's when I was a little girl. Then the house had double stairways that went up to what was really the second floor—all the cooking was done on the first. I used to like to stay down in the kitchen on account of the way the walls smelled. I would sit with my nose pressed against the plaster and take deep breaths. Actually the place belonged to the Godhighs but your grandfather Chestny paid the mortgage and saved it for them. They were in reduced circumstances." she said, "but reduced or not, they never forgot who they were."

"Doubtless that decayed mansion reminded them," Julian muttered. He never spoke of it without contempt or thought of it without longing. He had seen it once when he was a child before it had been sold. The double stairways had rotted and been torn down. Negroes were living in it. But it remained in his mind as his mother had known it. It appeared in his dreams regularly. He would stand on the wide porch, listening to the rustle of oak leaves, then wander through the high-ceilinged hall into the parlor that opened onto it and gaze at the worn rugs and faded draperies. It occurred to him that it was he, not she, who could have appreciated it. He preferred its threadbare elegance to anything he could name and it was because of it that all the neighborhoods they had lived in had been a torment to him—whereas she had hardly known the difference. She called her insensitivity "being adjustable."

"And I remember the old darky who was my nurse, Caroline.

There was no better person in the world. I've always had a great respect for my colored friends," she said. "I'd do anything in the world for them and they'd . . ."

"Will you for God's sake get off that subject?" Julian said. When he got on a bus by himself, he made it a point to sit down beside a Negro, in reparation as it were for his mother's sins.

"You're mighty touchy tonight," she said. "Do you feel all right?"

"Yes I feel all right," he said. "Now lay off."

She pursed her lips. "Well, you certainly are in a vile humor," she observed. "I just won't speak to you at all."

They had reached the bus stop. There was no bus in sight and Julian, his hands still jammed in his pockets and his head thrust forward, scowled down the empty street. The frustration of having to wait on the bus as well as ride on it began to creep up his neck like a hot hand. The presence of his mother was borne in upon him as she gave a pained sigh. He looked at her bleakly. She was holding herself very erect under the preposterous hat, wearing it like a banner of her imaginary dignity. There was in him an evil urge to break her spirit. He suddenly unloosened his tie and pulled it off and put it in his pocket.

She stiffened. "Why must you look like *that* when you take me to town?" she said. "Why must you deliberately embarrass me?"

"If you'll never learn where you are," he said, "you can at least learn where I am."

"You look like a—thug," she said.

"Then I must be one," he murmured.

"I'll just go home," she said. "I will not bother you. If you can't do a little thing like that for me . . ."

Rolling his eyes upward, he put his tie back on. "Restored to my class," he muttered. He thrust his face toward her and hissed, "True culture is in the mind, the *mind,*" he said, and tapped his head, "the mind."

"It's in the heart," she said, "and in how you do things and how you do things is because of who you *are.*"

"Nobody in the damn bus cares who you are."

"I care who I am," she said icily.

The lighted bus appeared on top of the next hill and as it approached, they moved out into the street to meet it. He put his hand under her elbow and hoisted her up on the creaking step. She entered with a little smile, as if she were going into a drawing room where everyone had been waiting for her. While he put in the tokens, she sat down on one of the broad front seats for three which faced the aisle. A thin woman with protruding teeth and long yellow hair was sitting on the end of it. His mother moved up beside her and left room for Julian beside herself. He sat down and looked at the floor across the aisle where a pair of thin feet in red and white canvas sandals were planted.

His mother immediately began a general conversation meant to attract anyone who felt like talking. "Can it get any hotter?" she said and removed from her purse a folding fan, black with a Japanese scene on it, which she began to flutter before her.

"I reckon it might could," the woman with the protruding teeth said, "but I know for a fact my apartment couldn't get no hotter."

"It must get the afternoon sun," his mother said. She sat forward and looked up and down the bus. It was half filled. Everybody was white. "I see we have the bus to ourselves," she said. Julian cringed.

"For a change," said the woman across the aisle, the owner of the red and white canvas sandals. "I come on one the other day and they were thick as fleas—up front and all through."

"The world is in a mess everywhere," his mother said. "I don't know how we've let it get in this fix."

"What gets my goat is all those boys from good families stealing automobile tires," the woman with the protruding teeth said. "I told my boy, I said you may not be rich but you been raised right and if I ever catch you in any such mess, they can send you on to the reformatory. Be exactly where you belong."

"Training tells," his mother said. "Is your boy in high school?"

"Ninth grade," the woman said.

"My son just finished college last year. He wants to write but he's selling typewriters until he gets started," his mother said.

The woman leaned forward and peered at Julian. He threw her such a malevolent look that she subsided against the seat. On the floor across the aisle there was an abandoned newspaper. He got up and got it and opened it out in front of him. His mother discreetly continued the conversation in a lower tone but the woman across the aisle said in a loud voice, "Well that's nice. Selling typewriters is close to writing. He can go right from one to the other."

"I tell him," his mother said, "that Rome wasn't built in a day."

Behind the newspaper Julian was withdrawing into the inner compartment of his mind where he spent most of his time. This was a kind of mental bubble in which he established himself when he could not bear to be a part of what was going on around him. From it he could see out and judge but in it he was safe from any kind of penetration from without. It was the only place where he felt free of the general idiocy of his fellows. His mother had never entered it but from it he could see her with absolute clarity.

The old lady was clever enough and he thought that if she had started from any of the right premises, more might have been expected of her. She lived according to the laws of her own fantasy world, outside of which he had never seen her set foot. The law of it was to sacrifice herself for him after she had first created the necessity to do so by making a mess of things. If he had permitted her sacrifices, it was only because her lack of foresight had made them necessary. All her life had been a struggle to act like a Chestny without the Chestny goods, and to give him everything she thought a Chestny ought to have; but since, said she, it was fun to struggle, why complain? And when you had won, as she had won, what fun to look back on the hard times! He could not forgive her that she had enjoyed the struggle and that she thought *she* had won.

What she meant when she said she had won was that she had brought him up successfully and had sent him to college and that he had turned out so well—good looking (her teeth had gone unfilled so that his could be straightened), intelligent (he realized he was too intelligent to be a success), and with a future ahead of him (there was of course no future ahead of him). She excused his gloominess on the grounds that he was still growing up and his radical ideas on his lack of practical experience. She said he didn't yet know a thing about "life," that he hadn't even entered the real world—when already he was as disenchanted with it as a man of fifty.

The further irony of all this was that in spite of her, he had turned out so well. In spite of going to only a third-rate college, he had, on his own initiative, come out with a first-rate education; in spite of growing up dominated by a small mind, he had ended up with a large one; in spite of all her foolish views, he was free of prejudice and unafraid to face facts. Most miraculous of all, instead of being blinded by love for her as she was for him, he had cut himself emotionally free of her and could see her with complete objectivity. He was not dominated by his mother.

The bus stopped with a sudden jerk and shook him from his meditation. A woman from the back lurched forward with little steps and barely escaped falling in his newspaper as she righted herself. She got off and a large Negro got on. Julian kept his paper lowered to watch. It gave him a certain satisfaction to see injustice in daily operation. It confirmed his view that with a few exceptions there was no one worth knowing within a radius of three hundred miles. The Negro was well dressed and carried a briefcase. He looked around and then sat down on the other end of the seat where the woman with the red and white canvas sandals was sitting. He immediately unfolded a newspaper and obscured himself behind it. Julian's mother's elbow at once prodded insistently into his ribs. "Now you see why I won't ride on these buses by myself," she whispered.

The woman with the red and white canvas sandals had risen at the same time the Negro sat down and had gone further back in the bus and taken the seat of the woman who had got off. His mother leaned forward and cast her an approving look.

Julian rose, crossed the aisle, and sat down in the place of the woman with the canvas sandals. From this position, he looked serenely across at his mother. Her face had turned an angry red. He stared at her, making his eyes the eyes of a stranger. He felt his tension suddenly lift as if he had openly declared war on her.

He would have liked to get in conversation with the Negro and to talk with him about art or politics or any subject that would be above the comprehension of those around them, but the man remained entrenched behind his paper. He was either ignoring the change of seating or had never noticed it. There was no way for Julian to convey his sympathy.

His mother kept her eyes fixed reproachfully on his face. The woman with the protruding teeth was looking at him avidly as if he were a type of monster new to her.

"Do you have a light?" he asked the Negro.

Without looking away from his paper, the man reached in his pocket and handed him a packet of matches.

"Thanks," Julian said. For a moment he held the matches foolishly. A NO SMOKING sign looked down upon him from over the door. This alone would not have deterred him; he had no cigarettes. He had quit smoking some months before because he could not afford it. "Sorry," he muttered and handed back the matches. The Negro lowered the paper and gave him an annoyed look. He took the matches and raised the paper again.

His mother continued to gaze at him but she did not take advantage of his momentary discomfort. Her eyes retained their battered look. Her face seemed to be unnaturally red, as if her blood pressure had risen. Julian allowed no glimmer of sympathy to show on his face. Having got the advantage, he wanted desperately to keep it and carry it through. He would have liked to teach her a lesson that would last her a while, but there seemed no way to continue the point. The Negro refused to come out from behind his paper.

Julian folded his arms and looked stolidly before him, facing her but as if he did not see her, as if he had ceased to recognize her existence. He visualized a scene in which, the bus having reached their stop, he would remain in his seat and when she said, "Aren't you going to get off," he would look at her as at a stranger who had rashly addressed him. The corner they got off on was usually deserted, but it was well lighted and it would not hurt her to walk by herself the four blocks to the Y. He decided to wait until the time came and then decide whether or not he would let her get off herself. He would have to be at the Y at ten to bring her back, but he could leave her wondering if he was going to show up. There was no reason for her to think she could always depend on him.

He retired again into the high-ceilinged room sparsely settled with large pieces of antique furniture. His soul expanded momentarily but then he became aware of his mother across from him and the vision shriveled. He studied her coldly. Her feet in little pumps dangled like a child's and did not quite reach the floor. She was training on him an exaggerated look of reproach. He felt completely detached from her. At that moment he could with pleasure have slapped her as he would have slapped a particularly obnoxious child in his charge.

He began to imagine various unlikely ways by which he could teach her a lesson. He might make friends with some distinguished Negro professor or lawyer and bring him home to spend the evening. He would be entirely justified but her blood pressure would rise to 300. He could not push her to the extent of making her have a stroke, and moreover, he had never been successful at making any Negro friends. He had tried to strike up an acquaintance on the bus with some of the better types, with ones that looked like professors or ministers or lawyers. One morning he had sat down next to a distinguished-looking dark brown man who had answered his questions with a sonorous solemnity but who had turned out to be an undertaker. Another day he had sat down beside a cigar-smoking Negro with a diamond ring on his finger, but after a few stilted pleasantries, the Negro had rung the buzzer and risen, slipping two lottery tickets into Julian's hand as he climbed over him to leave.

He imagined his mother lying desperately ill and his being able to secure only a Negro doctor for her. He toyed with that idea for a few minutes and then dropped it for a momentary vision of himself participating as a sympathizer in a sit-in demonstration. This was possible but he did not linger with it. Instead, he approached the ultimate horror. He brought home a beautiful suspiciously Negroid woman. Prepare yourself, he said. There is nothing you can do about it. This is the woman I've chosen. She's intelligent, dignified, even good, and she's suffered and she hasn't thought it *fun*. Now persecute us, go ahead and persecute us. Drive her out of here, but remember, you're driving me too. His eyes were narrowed and through the indignation he had generated, he saw his mother across the aisle, purple-faced, shrunken to the dwarf-like proportions of her moral nature, sitting like a mummy beneath the ridiculous banner of her hat.

He was tilted out of his fantasy again as the bus stopped. The door opened with a sucking hiss and out of the dark a large, gaily dressed, sullen-looking colored woman got on with a little boy. The child, who might have been four, had on a short plaid suit and a Tyrolean hat with a blue feather in it. Julian hoped that he would sit down beside him and that the woman would push in beside his mother. He could think of no better arrangement.

As she waited for her tokens, the woman was surveying the seating possibilities—he hoped with the idea of sitting where she was least wanted. There was something familiar-looking about her but Julian could not place what it was. She was a giant of a woman. Her face was set not only to meet opposition but to seek it out. The downward tilt of her large lower lip was like a warning sign: DON'T TAMPER WITH ME. Her bulging figure was encased in a green crepe dress and her feet overflowed in red shoes. She had on a hideous hat. A purple velvet flap came down on one side of it and stood up on the other; the rest of it was green and looked like a cushion with the stuffing out. She carried a mammoth red pocketbook that bulged throughout as if it were stuffed with rocks.

To Julian's disappointment, the little boy climbed up on the empty seat beside his mother. His mother lumped all children, black and white, into the common category, "cute," and she thought little Negroes were on the whole cuter than little white children. She smiled at the little boy as he climbed on the seat.

Meanwhile the woman was bearing down upon the empty seat beside Julian. To his annoyance, she squeezed herself into it. He saw his mother's face change as the woman settled herself next to him and he realized with satisfaction that this was more objectionable to her than it was to him. Her face seemed almost gray and there was a look of dull recognition in her eyes, as if suddenly she had sickened at some awful confrontation. Julian saw that it was because she and the woman had, in a sense, swapped sons. Though his mother would not realize the symbolic significance of this, she would feel it. His amusement showed plainly on his face.

The woman next to him muttered something unintelligible to herself. He was conscious of a kind of bristling next to him, a muted growling like that of an angry cat. He could not see anything but the red pocketbook upright on the bulging green thighs. He visualized the woman as she had stood waiting for her tokens—the ponderous figure, rising from the red shoes upward over the solid hips, the mammoth bosom, the haughty face, to the green and purple hat.

His eyes widened.

The vision of the two hats, identical, broke upon him with the radiance of a brilliant sunrise. His face was suddenly lit with joy. He could not believe that Fate had thrust upon his mother such a lesson. He gave a loud chuckle so that she would look at him and see that he saw. She turned her eyes on him slowly. The blue in them seemed to have turned a bruised purple. For a moment he had an uncomfortable sense of her innocence, but it lasted only a second before principle rescued him. Justice entitled him to laugh. His grin hardened until it said to her as plainly as if he were saying aloud: Your punishment exactly fits your pettiness. This should teach you a permanent lesson.

Her eyes shifted to the woman. She seemed unable to bear looking at him and to find the woman preferable. He became conscious again of the bristling presence at his side. The woman was rumbling like a volcano about to become active. His mother's mouth began to twitch slightly at one corner. With a sinking heart, he saw incipient signs of recovery on her face and realized that this was going to strike her suddenly as funny and was going to be no lesson at all. She kept her eyes on the woman and an amused smile came over her face as if the woman were a monkey that had stolen her hat. The little Negro was looking up at her with large fascinated eyes. He had been trying to attract her attention for some time.

"Carver!" the woman said suddenly. "Come heah!"

When he saw that the spotlight was on him at last, Carver drew his feet up and turned himself toward Julian's mother and giggled.

"Carver!" the woman said. "You heah me? Come heah!"

Carver slid down from the seat but remained squatting with his back against the base of it, his head turned slyly around toward Julian's mother, who was smiling at him. The woman reached a hand across the aisle and snatched him to her. He righted himself and hung backwards on her knees, grinning at Julian's mother. "Isn't he cute?" Julian's mother said to the woman with the protruding teeth.

"I reckon he is," the woman said without conviction.

The Negress yanked him upright but he eased out of her grip and shot across the aisle and scrambled, giggling wildly, onto the seat beside his love.

"I think he likes me," Julian's mother said, and smiled at the woman. It was the smile she used when she was being particularly gracious to an inferior. Julian saw everything lost. The lesson had rolled off her like rain on a roof.

The woman stood up and yanked the little boy off the seat as if she were snatching him from contagion. Julian could feel the rage in her at having no weapon like his mother's smile. She gave the child a sharp slap across his leg. He howled once and then thrust his head into her stomach and kicked his feet against her shins. "Behave," she said vehemently.

The bus stopped and the Negro who had been reading the newspaper got off. The woman moved over and set the little boy down with a thump between herself and Julian. She held him firmly by the knee. In a moment he put his hands in front of his face and peeped at Julian's mother through his fingers.

"I see yooooooooo!" she said and put her hand in front of her face and peeped at him.

The woman slapped his hand down. "Quit yo' foolishness," she said, "before I knock the living Jesus out of you!"

Julian was thankful that the next stop was theirs. He reached up and pulled the cord. The woman reached up and pulled it at the same time. Oh my God, he thought. He had the terrible intuition that when they got off the bus together, his mother would open her purse and give the little boy a nickel. The gesture would be as natural to her as breathing. The bus stopped and the woman got up and lunged to the front, dragging the child who wished to stay on, after her. Julian and his mother got up and followed. As they neared the door, Julian tried to relieve her of her pocketbook.

"No," she murmured, "I want to give the little boy a nickel."

"No!" Julian hissed. "No!"

She smiled down at the child and opened her bag. The bus door opened and the woman picked him up by the arm and descended with him, hanging at her hip. Once in the street she set him down and shook him.

Julian's mother had to close her purse while she got down the bus step but as soon as her feet were on the ground, she opened it again and began to rummage inside. "I can't find but a penny," she whispered, "but it looks like a new one."

"Don't do it!" Julian said fiercely between his teeth. There was a streetlight on the corner and she hurried to get under it so that she could better see into her pocketbook. The woman was heading off rapidly down the street with the child hanging backward on her hand.

"Oh little boy!" Julian's mother called and took a few quick steps and caught up with them just beyond the lamppost. "Here's a bright new penny for you," and she held out the coin, which shone bronze in the dim light.

The huge woman turned and for a moment stood, her shoulders lifted and her face frozen with frustrated rage, and stared at Julian's mother. Then all at once she seemed to explode like a piece of machinery that had been given one ounce of pressure too much. Julian saw the black fist swing out with the red pocketbook. He shut his eyes and cringed as he heard the woman shout, "He don't take nobody's pennies!" When he opened his eyes, the woman was disappearing down the street with the little boy staring wide-eyed over her shoulder. Julian's mother was sitting on the sidewalk.

"I told you not to do that," Julian said angrily. "I told you not to do that!"

He stood over her for a minute, gritting his teeth. Her legs were stretched out in front of her and her hat was on her lap. He squatted down and looked her in the face. It was totally expressionless. "You got exactly what you deserved," he said. "Now get up."

He picked up her pocketbook and put what had fallen out back in it. He picked the hat up off her lap. The penny caught his eye on the sidewalk and he picked that up and let it drop before her eyes into the purse. Then he stood up and leaned over and held his hands out to pull her up. She remained immobile. He sighed. Rising above them on either side were black apartment buildings, marked with irregular rectangles of light. At the end of the block a man came out of a door and walked off in the opposite direction. "All right," he said, "suppose somebody happens by and wants to know why you're sitting on the sidewalk?"

She took the hand and, breathing hard, pulled heavily up on it and then stood for a moment, swaying slightly as if the spots of light in the darkness were circling around her. Her eyes, shadowed and confused, finally settled on his face. He did not try to conceal his irritation. "I hope this teaches you a lesson," he said. She leaned forward and her eyes raked his face. She seemed trying to determine his identity. Then, as if she found nothing familiar about him, she started off with a headlong movement in the wrong direction.

"Aren't you going on to the Y?" he asked.

"Home," she muttered.

"Well, are we walking?"

For answer she kept going. Julian followed along, his hands behind him. He saw no reason to let the lesson she had had go without backing it up with an explanation of its meaning. She might as well be made to understand what had happened to her. "Don't think that was just an uppity Negro woman," he said. "That was the whole colored race which will no longer take your condescending pennies. That was your black double. She can wear the same hat as you, and to be sure," he added gratuitously (because he thought it was funny), "it looked better on her than it did on you. What all this means," he said, "is that the old world is gone. The old manners are obsolete and your graciousness is not worth a damn." He thought bitterly of the house that had been lost for him. "You aren't who you think you are," he said.

She continued to plow ahead, paying no attention to him. Her hair had come undone on one side. She dropped her pocketbook and took no notice. He stooped and picked it up and handed it to her but she did not take it.

"You needn't act as if the world had come to an end," he said, "because it hasn't. From now on you've got to live in a new world and face a few realities for a change. Buck up," he said, "it won't kill you."

She was breathing fast.

"Let's wait on the bus," he said.

"Home," she said thickly.

"I hate to see you behave like this," he said. "Just like a child. I should be able to expect more of you." He decided to stop where he was and make her stop and wait for a bus. "I'm not going any farther," he said, stopping. "We're going on the bus."

She continued to go on as if she had not heard him. He took a few steps and caught her arm and stopped her. He looked into her face and caught his breath. He was looking into a face he had never seen before. "Tell Grandpa to come get me," she said.

He stared, stricken.

"Tell Caroline to come get me," she said.

Stunned, he let her go and she lurched forward again, walking as if one leg were shorter than the other. A tide of darkness seemed to be sweeping her from him. "Mother!" he cried. "Darling, sweetheart, wait!" Crumpling, she fell to the pavement. He dashed forward and fell at her side, crying, "Mamma, Mamma!" He turned her over. Her face was fiercely distorted. One eye, large and staring, moved slightly to the left as if it had become unmoored. The other remained fixed on him, raked his face again, found nothing and closed.

"Wait here, wait here!" he cried and jumped up and began to run for help toward a cluster of lights he saw in the distance ahead of him. "Help, help!" he shouted, but his voice was thin, scarcely a thread of sound. The lights drifted farther away the faster he ran and his feet moved numbly as if they carried him nowhere. The tide of darkness seemed to sweep him back to her, postponing from moment to moment his entry into the world of guilt and sorrow.

How Do You Respond?

1. What expectations are aroused by O'Connor's title, "Everything That Rises Must Converge?" What does the title have to do with the story?
2. How does O'Connor point up what she sees as the deep similarities between the two women?
3. How does the narrator see himself? How does the author see him? How does O'Connor use the narrator's own words to give both views?

ELISABETH KÜBLER-ROSS

> *Elisabeth Kübler-Ross (born in Zurich in 1926) did relief work in post-war Europe and practiced medicine as a country doctor in Switzerland. Her books,* On Death and Dying, Questions and Answers on Death and Dying, Death: The Final Stage, *and her many articles on death and dying for contemporary magazines do not mean that she is preoccupied with morbid concerns; on the contrary, Kübler-Ross speaks for consciousness, for a moral and ethical consciousness, that respects the individual's right—to the end—to know and choose.*

THE FEAR OF DYING

The ancient Hebrews regarded the body of a dead person as something unclean and not to be touched. The early American Indians talked about the evil spirits and shot arrows in the air to drive the spirits away. Many other cultures have rituals to take care of the "bad" dead person, and they all originate in this feeling of anger which still exists in all of us, though we dislike admitting it. The tradition of the tombstone may originate in this wish to keep the bad spirits deep down in the ground, and the pebbles that many mourners put on the grave are left-over symbols of the same wish. Though we call the firing of guns at military funerals a last salute, it is the same symbolic ritual as the Indian used when he shot his spears and arrows into the skies.

I give these examples to emphasize that man has not basically changed. Death is still a fearful, frightening happening, and fear of death is a universal fear even if we think we have mastered it on many levels.

What has changed is our way of coping and dealing with death and dying and our dying patients.

Having been raised in a country in Europe where science is not so advanced, where modern techniques have just started to find their way into medicine, and where people still live as they did in this country half a century ago, I may have had an opportunity to study a part of the evolution of mankind in a shorter period.

I remember as a child the death of a farmer. He fell from a tree and was not expected to live. He asked simply to die at home, a wish that was granted without questioning. He called his daughters into the bedroom and spoke with each one of them alone for a few minutes. He arranged his affairs quietly, though he was in great pain, and distributed his belongings and his land, none of which was to be split until his wife should follow him in death. He also asked each of his children to share in the work, duties, and tasks that he had carried on until the time of the accident. He asked his friends to visit him once more, to bid good-bye to them. Although I was a small child at the time, he did not exclude me or my siblings. We were allowed to share in the preparations of the family just as we were permitted to grieve with them until he died. When he did die, he was left at home, in his own beloved home which he had built, and among his friends and neighbors who went to take a last look at him where he lay in the midst of flowers in the place he had lived in and loved so much. In that country today there is still no make-believe slumber room, no embalming, no false makeup to pretend sleep. Only the signs of very disfiguring illnesses are covered up with bandages and only infectious cases are removed from the home before the burial.

Why do I describe such "old-fashioned" customs? I think they are an indication of our acceptance of a fatal outcome, and they help the dying patient as well as his family to accept the loss of a loved one. If a patient is allowed to terminate his life in the familiar and beloved environment, it requires less adjustment for him. His own family knows him well enough to replace a sedative with a glass of his favorite wine; or the smell of a home-cooked soup may give him the appetite to sip a few spoons of fluid which, I think, is still more enjoyable than an infusion. I will not minimize the need for sedatives and infusions and realize full well from my own experience as a country doctor that they are sometimes life-saving and often unavoidable. But I also know that patience and familiar people and foods could replace many a bottle of intravenous fluids given for the simple reason that it fulfills the physiological need without involving too many people and/or individual nursing care.

The fact that children are allowed to stay at home where a fatality has stricken and are included in the talk, discussions, and fears gives them the feeling that they are not alone in the grief and gives them the comfort of shared responsibility and shared mourning. It prepares them gradually and helps them view death as part of life, an experience which may help them grow and mature.

This is in great contrast to a society in which death is viewed as taboo, discussion of it is regarded as morbid, and children are excluded with the presumption and pretext that it would be "too much" for them. They are then sent off to relatives, often accompanied with some unconvincing lies of "Mother has gone on a long trip" or other unbelievable stories. The child senses that something is wrong, and his distrust in adults will only multiply if other relatives add new variations of the story, avoid his questions or suspicions, shower him with gifts as a meager substitute for a loss he is not permitted to deal with. Sooner or later the child will become aware of the changed family situation and, depending on the age and personality of the child, will have an unresolved grief and regard this incident as frightening, mysterious, in any case very traumatic experience with untrustworthy grownups, which he has no way to cope with.

We would think that our great emancipation, our knowledge of science and of man, has given us better ways and means to prepare ourselves and our families for this inevitable happening. Instead the days are gone when a man was allowed to die in peace and dignity in his own home.

The more we are making advancements in science, the more we seem to fear and deny the reality of death. How is this possible?

We use euphemisms, we make the dead look as if they were asleep, we ship the children off to protect them from the anxiety and turmoil around the house if the patient is fortunate enough to die at home, we don't allow children to visit their dying parents in the hospitals, we have long and controversial discussions about whether patients should be told the truth—a question that rarely arises when the dying person is tended by the family physician who has known him from delivery to death and who knows the weaknesses and strengths of each member of the family.

I think there are many reasons for this flight away from facing death calmly. One of the most important facts is that dying nowadays is more gruesome in many ways, namely, more lonely, mechanical, and dehumanized; at times it is even difficult to determine technically when the time of death has occurred.

Dying becomes lonely and impersonal because the patient is often taken out of his familiar environment and rushed to an emergency room. Whoever has been very sick and has required rest and comfort especially may recall his experience of being put on a stretcher and enduring the noise of the ambulance siren and hectic rush until the hospital gates open. Only those who have lived through this may appreciate the discomfort and cold necessity of such transportation which is only the beginning of a long ordeal—hard to endure when you are well, difficult to express in words when noise, light, bumps, and voices are all too much to put up with. It may well be that we might consider more the patient under the sheets and blankets and perhaps stop our well-meant efficiency and rush in order to hold the patient's hand, to smile, or to listen to a question. I include the trip to the hospital as the first episode in dying, as it is for many. I am putting it exaggeratedly in contrast to the sick man who is left at home—not to say that lives should not be saved if they can be saved by a hospitalization but to keep the focus on the patient's experience, his needs and his reactions.

When a patient is severely ill, he is often treated like a person with no right to an opinion. It is often someone else who makes the decision if and when and where a patient should be hospitalized. It would take so little to remember that the sick person too has feelings, has wishes and opinions, and has—most important of all—the right to be heard.

Well, our presumed patient has now reached the emergency room. He will be surrounded by busy nurses, orderlies, interns, residents, a lab technician perhaps who will take some blood, an electrocardiogram technician who takes the cardiogram. He may be moved to X-ray and he will overhear opinions of his condition and discussions and questions to members of the family. He slowly but surely is beginning to be treated like a thing. He is no longer a person. Decisions are made often without his opinion. If he tries to rebel he will be sedated and after hours of waiting and wondering whether he has the strength, he will be wheeled into the operating room or intensive treatment unit and become an object of great concern and great financial investment.

He may cry for rest, peace, and dignity, but he will get infusions, transfusions, a heart machine, or tracheotomy if necessary. He may want one single person to stop for one single minute so that he can ask one single question—but he will get a dozen people around the clock, all busily preoccupied with his heart rate, pulse, electrocardiogram or pulmonary functions, his secretions or excretions but not with him as a human being. He may wish to fight it all but it is going to be a useless fight since all this is done in the fight for his life, and if they can save his life they can consider the person afterwards. Those who consider the person first may lose precious time to save his life! At least this seems to be the rationale or justification behind all this—or is it? Is the reason for this increasingly mechanical, depersonalized approach our own defensiveness? Is this approach our own way to cope with and repress the anxieties that a terminally or critically ill patient evokes in us? Is our concentration on equipment, on blood pressure, our desperate attempt to deny the impending death which is so frightening and discomforting to us that we displace all our knowledge onto machines, since they are less close to us than the suffering face of another human being which would remind us once more of our lack of omnipotence, our own limits and failures, and last but not least perhaps our own mortality?

How Do You Respond?

1. Kübler-Ross contrasts two worlds: a world of human tradition and a world of technocratic efficiency. How does she show the difference between the two worlds?

2. Kübler-Ross also discusses cause and effect in our treatment of the dying. How does she contrast the possible explanations for our emphasis on medical technology?

3. Kübler-Ross observes, ". . . if they can save his life they can consider the person afterwards." This implies a contrast between "his life" and "the person." Discuss.

LOREN EISELEY

> *Archaeologist, anthropologist, naturalist, poet—Loren Eiseley (1907–1977) wore these many hats, but as W. H. Auden remarked, "If I have understood Eiseley rightly, the first point . . . is that in order to be a scientist, an artist, a doctor, a lawyer, or what-have-you, one has first to be a human being." The descendant of American pioneers, Eiseley began his career among the sunflower forests and high plains of Nebraska and ended at the University of Pennsylvania as Benjamin Franklin Professor of Anthropology and the History of Science. He wrote prolifically: essays for scientific journals and popular magazines, poetry, and books, of which the best known are* The Immense Journey, The Unexpected Universe, *and* The Star Thrower, *from which the following selection is taken.*

THE LONG LONELINESS

There is nothing more alone in the universe than man. He is alone because he has the intellectual capacity to know that he is separated by a vast gulf of social memory and experiment from the lives of his animal associates. He has entered into the strange world of history, of social and intellectual change, while his brothers of the field and forest remain subject to the invisible laws of biological evolution. Animals are molded by natural forces they do not comprehend. To their minds there is no past and no future. There is only the everlasting present of a single generation—its trails in the forest, its hidden pathways of the air and in the sea.

Man, by contrast, is alone with the knowledge of his history until the day of his death. When we were children we wanted to talk to animals and struggled to understand why this was impossible. Slowly we gave up the attempt as we grew up into the solitary world of human adulthood; the rabbit was left on the lawn, the dog was relegated to his kennel. Only in acts of inarticulate compassion, in rare and hidden moments of communion with nature, does man briefly escape his solitary destiny. Frequently in science fiction he dreams of worlds with creatures whose communicative power is the equivalent of his own.

It is with a feeling of startlement, therefore, and eager interest touching the lost child in every one of us, that the public has received the recent accounts of naval research upon the intelligence of one of our brother mammals—the sea-dwelling bottle-nosed porpoise or dolphin.

These small whales who left the land millions of years ago to return to the great mother element of life, the sea, are now being regarded by researchers as perhaps the most intelligent form of life on our planet next to man. Dr. John Lilly of the Communications Research Institute in the Virgin Islands reports that the brain of the porpoise is 40 percent larger than man's and is just as complex in its functional units. Amazed by the rapidity with which captive porpoises solved problems that even monkeys found difficult, Dr. Lilly is quoted as expressing the view that "man's position at the top of the hierarchy [of intelligence] begins to be questioned."

Dr. Lilly found that his captives communicated in a series of underwater whistles and that, in addition, they showed an amazing "verbalizing" ability in copying certain sounds heard in the laboratory. The experimental animal obviously hoped to elicit by this means a reproduction of the pleasurable sensations he had been made to experience under laboratory conditions. It is reported that in spite of living in a medium different from the one that man inhabits, and therefore having quite a different throat structure, one of the porpoises even uttered in a Donald-Duckish voice a short number series it had heard spoken by one of the laboratory investigators.

The import of these discoveries is tremendous and may not be adequately known for a long time. An animal from a little-explored medium, which places great barriers in the way of the psychologist, has been found to have not only a strong social organization but to show a degree of initiative in experimental communicative activity unmatched by man's closest relatives, the great apes. The porpoises reveal, moreover, a touching altruism and friendliness in their attempts to aid injured companions. Can it be, one inevitably wonders, that man is so locked in his own type of intelligence—an intelligence that is linked to a prehensile, grasping hand giving him power over his environment—that he is unable to comprehend the intellectual life of a highly endowed creature from another domain such as the sea?

Perhaps the water barrier has shut us away from a potentially communicative and jolly companion. Perhaps we have some things still to learn from the natural world around us before we turn to the far shores of space and whatever creatures may await us there. After all, the porpoise is a mammal. He shares with us an ancient way of birth and affectionate motherhood. His blood is warm, he breathes air as we do. We both bear in our bodies the remnants of a common skeleton torn asunder for divergent purposes far back in the dim dawn of mammalian life. The porpoise has been superficially streamlined like a fish.

His are not, however, the cold-blooded ways of the true fishes. Far higher on the tree of life than fishes, the dolphin's paddles are made-over paws, rather than fins. He is an ever-constant reminder of the versatility of life and its willingness to pass through strange dimensions of experience. There are environmental worlds on earth every bit as weird as what we may imagine to revolve by far-off suns. It is our superficial familiarity with this planet that inhibits our appreciation of the unknown until a porpoise, rearing from a tank to say Three-Two-Three, re-creates for us the utter wonder of childhood.

Unless we are specialists in the study of communication and its relation to intelligence, however, we are apt to oversimplify or define poorly what intelligence is, what communication and language are, and thus confuse and mystify both ourselves and others. The mysteries surrounding the behavior of the bottle-nosed porpoise, and even of man himself, are not things to be probed simply by the dissector's scalpel. They lie deeper. They involve the whole nature of the mind and its role in the universe.

We are forced to ask ourselves whether native intelligence in another form than man's might be as high as or even higher than his own, yet be marked by no such material monuments as man has placed upon the earth. At first glance we are alien to this idea, because man is particularly a creature who has turned the tables on his environment so that he is now engrossed in shaping it, rather than being shaped by it. Man expresses himself upon his environment through the use of tools. We therefore tend to equate the use of tools in a one-to-one relationship with intelligence.

The question we must now ask ourselves, however, is whether this involves an unconsciously man-centered way of looking at intelligence. Let us try for a moment to enter the dolphin's kingdom and the dolphin's body, retaining, at the same time, our human intelligence. In this imaginative act, it may be possible to divest ourselves of certain human preconceptions about our kind of intelligence and at the same time to see more clearly why mind, even advanced mind, may have manifestations other than the tools and railroad tracks and laboratories that we regard as evidence of intellect. If we are particularly adept in escaping from our own bodies, we may even learn to discount a little the kind of world of rockets and death that our type of busy human curiosity, linked to a hand noted for its ability to open assorted Pandora's boxes, has succeeded in foisting upon the world as a symbol of universal intelligence.

We have now sacrificed, in our imagination, our hands for flippers and our familiar land environment for the ocean. We will go down into the deep waters as naked of possessions as we entered life itself. We will take with us one thing alone that exists among porpoises as among men: an ingrained biological gregariousness— a sociality that in our new world will permit us to run in schools, just as early man ran in the packs that were his ancient anthropoid heritage. We will assume in the light of Dr. Lilly's researches that our native intelligence, as distinguished from our culturally transmitted habits, is very high. The waters have closed finally over us, our paws have been sacrificed for the necessary flippers with which to navigate.

The result is immediately evident and quite clear. No matter how well we communicate with our fellows through the water medium we will never build drowned empires in the coral; we will never inscribe on palace walls the victorious boasts of porpoise kings. We will know only water and the wastes of water beyond the power of man to describe. We will be secret visitors in hidden canyons beneath the mouths of torrential rivers. We will survey in innocent astonishment the flotsam that pours from the veins of continents—dead men, great serpents, giant trees—or perhaps the little toy boat of a child loosed far upstream will come floating past. Bottles with winking green lights will plunge by us into the all-embracing ooze. Meaningless appearances and disappearances will comprise our philosophies. We will hear the earth's heart ticking in its thin granitic shell. Volcanic fires will growl ominously in steam-filled crevices. Vapor, bird cries, and sea wrack will compose our memories. We will see death in many forms and, on occasion, the slow majestic fall of battleships through the green light that comes from beyond our domain.

Over all that region of wondrous beauty we will exercise no more control than the simplest mollusk. Even the octopus with flexible arms will build little shelters that we cannot imitate. Without hands we will have only the freedom to follow the untrammeled sea winds across the planet.

Perhaps if those whistling sounds that porpoises make are truly symbolic and capable of manipulation in our brains, we will wonder about the world in which we find ourselves—but it will be a world not susceptible to experiment. At best we may nuzzle in curiosity a passing shipbottom and be harpooned for our pains. Our thoughts, in other words, will be as limited as those of the first men who roved in little bands in the times before fire and the writing that was to open to man the great doorway of his past.

Man without writing cannot long retain his history in his head. His intelligence permits him to grasp some kind of succession of generations; but, without writing, the tale of the past rapidly degenerates into fumbling myth and fable. Man's greatest epic, his four long battles with the advancing ice of the great continental glaciers, has vanished from human memory without trace. Our illiterate fathers disappeared and with them, in a few scant generations, died one of the great stories of all time. This episode has nothing to do with the biological quality of a brain as between then and now. It has to do instead with a device, an invention made possible by the hand. That invention came too late in time to record eyewitness accounts of the years of the Giant Frost.

Primitives of our own species, even today, are historically shallow in their knowledge of the past. Only the poet who writes speaks his message across the millennia to other hearts. Only in writing can the cry from the great cross on Golgotha still be heard in the minds of men. The thinker of perceptive insight, even if we allow him for the moment to be a porpoise rather than a man, has only his individual glimpse of the universe until such time as he can impose that insight upon unnumbered generations. In centuries of pondering, man has come upon but one answer to this problem: speech translated into writing that passes beyond human mortality.

Writing, and later printing, is the product of our adaptable many-purposed hands. It is thus, through writing, with no increase in genetic, inborn capacity since the last ice advance, that modern man carries in his mind the intellectual triumphs of all his predecessors who were able to inscribe their thoughts for posterity.

All animals that man has reason to believe are more than usually intelligent—our relatives the great apes, the elephant, the raccoon, the wolverine, among others—are problem solvers, and in at least a small way manipulators of their environment. Save for the instinctive calls of their species, however, they cannot invent words for new situations nor get their fellows to use such words. No matter how high the individual intelligence, its private world remains a private possession locked forever within a single, perishable brain. It is this fact that finally balks our hunger to communicate even with the sensitive dog who shares our fireside.

Dr. Lilly insists, however, that the porpoises communicate in high-pitched, underwater whistles that seem to transmit their wishes and problems. The question then becomes one of ascertaining whether these sounds represent true language—in the sense of symbolic meanings, additive, learned elements—or whether they are simply the instinctive signals of a pack animal. To this there is as yet no clear answer, but the eagerness with which laboratory sounds and voices were copied by captive porpoises suggests a vocalizing ability extending perhaps to or beyond the threshold of speech.

Most of the intelligent land animals have prehensile, grasping organs for exploring their environment—hands in man and his anthropoid relatives, the sensitive inquiring trunk in the elephant. One of the surprising things about the porpoise is that his superior brain is unaccompanied by any type of manipulative organ. He has, however, a remarkable range-finding ability involving some sort of echo-sounding. Perhaps this acute sense—far more accurate than any man has been able to devise artificially—brings him greater knowledge of his watery surroundings than might at first seem possible. Human beings think of intelligence as geared to things. The hand and the tool are to us the unconscious symbols of our intellectual achievement. It is difficult for us to visualize another kind of lonely, almost disembodied intelligence floating in the wavering green fairyland of the sea—an intelligence possibly near or comparable to our own but without hands to build, to transmit knowledge by writing, or to alter by one hairsbreadth the planet's surface. Yet at the same time there are indications that this is a warm, friendly, and eager intelligence quite capable of coming to the assistance of injured companions and striving to rescue them from drowning. Porpoises left the land when mammalian brains were still small and primitive. Without the stimulus provided by agile exploring fingers, these great sea mammals have yet taken a divergent road toward intelligence of a high order. Hidden in their sleek bodies is an impressively elaborated instrument, the reason for whose appearance is a complete enigma. It is as though both man and porpoise were each part of some great eye which yearned to look both outward on eternity and inward to the sea's heart—that fertile entity so like the mind in its swarming and grotesque life.

Perhaps man has something to learn after all from fellow creatures without the ability to drive harpoons through living flesh, or poison with strontium the planetary winds. One is reminded of those watery blue vaults in which, as in some idyllic eternity, Herman Melville once saw the sperm whales nurse their young. And as Melville wrote of the sperm whale, so we might now paraphrase his words in speaking of the porpoise. "Genius in the porpoise? Has the porpoise ever written a book, spoken a speech? No, his great genius is declared in his doing nothing particular to prove it. It is declared in his pyramidical silence." If man had sacrificed his hands for flukes, the moral might run, he would still be a philosopher, but there would have been taken from him the devasting power to wreak his thought upon the body of the world. Instead he would have lived and wandered, like the porpoise, homeless across currents and winds and oceans, intelligent, but forever the lonely and curious observer of unknown wreckage falling through the blue light of eternity. This role would now be a deserved penitence for man. Perhaps such a transformation would bring him once more into that mood of childhood innocence in which he talked successfully to all things living but had no power and no urge to harm. It is worth at least a wistful thought that someday the porpoise may talk to us and we to him. It would break, perhaps, the long loneliness that has made man a frequent terror and abomination even to himself.

How Do You Respond?

1. Eiseley contrasts dolphin and human environments, speculating on their influence on intelligence. What major contrast does he find?

2. Eiseley contrasts human history before and after the ice ages. What major difference does he find? Can you think of differences that he does not mention that extend human experience?

3. Eiseley writes poetically of dolphin intelligence. He writes disparagingly of human destructiveness. What facts does he cite to support his views? Does he play fair with the evidence?

FOCUS ON YOUR READING

1. Russell Baker in "School Versus Education" says that American children do not receive an education when they go through school. He leaves us to wonder what he means by education when he says that the former student "may one day find . . . the leisure and the inclination to open a book with a curious mind, and start to become educated." Where would you go from there? How would you define "being educated"?

2. Joe McGinniss in "The Village" points up a number of contrasts between contemporary American living and living in an Eskimo village. How does he point up the differences? How do other writers in the chapter point up differences? What strategies do they use to shape their writing so that we know they are contrasting, comparing? Do they present all of one case first and then all of another? Do they weave together points about one case with points about another?

3. Contrasts involve seeing both the figure and the ground: the difference against the similarity. Don Bauer places side by side two incidents that have much in common; where is the figure, and where is the ground? Where is the figure, and where is the ground in other selections in the chapter?

4. In several of the selections—those by Ephron, O'Connor, and McGinniss—we see contrasts between old values and new ones that are replacing them. In each case, there is both gain and loss. How would you characterize the losses and gains in these pieces? How would you characterize the writers' points of view toward the losses and gains?

FOCUS ON YOUR WRITING

1. Ephron insists that colleges—particularly women's colleges—have a responsibility for encouraging women to do more than walk a balance between housewifery and career. Write about your views on this subject—on feminism and the education of women. Should *men* be educated for more than a career? What is the relation between the study of art, history, and literature and vocational skills?

2. Write about your notions of education. What does it mean to be educated? Do you agree with Baker that American schools do

not encourage one to become educated? Why? Why not? Define your terms. What do you mean by schooling? By being educated? Check the lexical meanings of *school* and *education*.

3. Kübler-Ross writes about how contemporary Americans protect themselves from the realities of death. Argue for or against the view that we need to protect ourselves from the starkness of death.

4. Compare and contrast two people you know. Follow a pattern in which you present all you can about A and then all you can about B. Now try a pattern where you weave together points about A and B. Which works better? Why?

5. Write about going back to a place—a high school, a hometown—or write about meeting an old friend or teacher. Describe the changes you observe. Have the changes occurred for the better, for the worse, or for both? Make certain that your attitude, your points of view, your evaluative statements infuse your representation.

The Public Voice

CHAPTER 10

❖ ❖

"I Have a Dream"

ARGUMENT

I have a dream that one day this nation will rise up and live out the true meaning of its creed: "We hold these truths to be self evident; that all men are created equal."

I have a dream that one day on the red hills of Georgia the sons of former slaves and the sons of former slave owners will be able to sit down together at the table of brotherhood.

I have a dream that the state of Mississippi, a desert state sweltering with the heat of injustice and oppression, will be transformed into an oasis of freedom and justice.

I have a dream that my four little children will one day live in a nation where they will not be judged by the color of their skin but by the content of their character.

I have a dream today.

These words come from Martin Luther King's speech, "I Have a Dream," delivered at the Lincoln Memorial in 1963, commemorating the one-hundredth anniversary of Lincoln's signing of the Emancipation Proclamation. Here King speaks with a public voice. He has personal concerns—he hopes for a better world for his own children. But his purpose is larger. He offers his own world view to persuade others to share it and to confirm and strengthen the commitment of those who already agree with it. He hopes that things will *change*.

When we present an argument, when we present a case, to an audience, we always imply a contrast: we see things as they are *now*, and we attempt to show how they could be *tomorrow*. This play between the present and the future is the central rhythm of argument.

King moves back and forth, between the present as it is and the future as he hopes it will be. He calls on the very structure of Lincoln's Gettysburg Address (see Chapter 5). He begins with a contrast: the promises of the past and the facts of the present. "Five score years ago," he says, "a great American, in whose symbolic shadow we stand, signed the Emancipation Proclamation." Promises of the past, however, have not been fulfilled. This is the present situation: "the Negro is still not free." King defines his terms: "One hundred years later, the life of the Negro is still sadly crippled by the manacles of segregation and the chains of discrimination." This is the present, he says, and he has "come here today" to dramatize an appalling condition.

Things must change. In all argument, the speaker or writer presents a case for one specific purpose: to effect change. Presenters of arguments want to *persuade* others to think along their lines and to take action to effect change. King wants people to move into "the palace of justice," but he urges them to do so peacefully, to meet "physical force with soul force." He presents his ideas about the future and the ways in which people should behave to effect change. In an argument, the notion of *should* is fundamental: on the one side, we say, this is the way things are; on the other side, this is the way they *should* be.

"I Have a Dream" is an eloquent model of political argument. Behind the eloquence stands King's conviction, his passion for a cause. As speaker, King states the issues involved and offers his suggestions for the future. He *describes* the present situation; he *defines* his terms; he takes us through a lesson in history so that we can size up the present in relation to the past. He invites us to see a historical process; he looks at *causes* and at *effects*. He *exemplifies*:

> There are those who are asking the devotees of civil rights, "When will you be satisfied?" We can never be satisfied as long

> as the Negro is the victim of the unspeakable horrors of police brutality. We can never be satisfied as long as our bodies, heavy with the fatigue of travel, cannot gain lodging in the motels of the highways and the hotels of the cities. We cannot be satisfied as long as the Negro's basic mobility is from a smaller ghetto to a larger one. We can never be satisfied as long as a Negro in Mississippi cannot vote and a Negro in New York believes he has nothing for which to vote.

King appeals to logic: this was the promise and now a debt must be paid for the unfulfilled promise. He appeals to emotion, particularly through the rhythms of his speech that rise to incantation: "I have a dream . . ." "I have a dream . . ." "I have a dream. . . ."

Again this play or interaction between things as they are and things as they should be, between the present and the future, is the fundamental structure of political writings and of argument. John F. Kennedy, in calling on Americans to "ask not what your country can do for you, ask what you can do for your country," points his audience toward action, toward the future. Winston Churchill, in his impassioned speeches during the Second World War, plays on that rhythm between present and future in calling on his fellow Englishmen to do their duty, to fight until the end:

- Victory at all costs, victory in spite of all terror; victory, victory however long and hard the road may be; for without victory there is no survival.
- We shall fight on the beaches, we shall fight on the landing grounds, we shall fight in the fields and in the streets, we shall never surrender.
- If we open a quarrel between the past and the present, we shall find that we have lost the future.
- In the past we have had a light which flickered, in the present we have a light which flames, and in the future there will be a light which shines over all the land and sea.

When we present a case—whether we are calling for action, as Churchill does, or whether we are trying to persuade someone to attend one college rather than another—we address our audience directly. We are aware of who they are, and we attempt to anticipate what they are thinking. If we assume a sympathetic audience—as King does—then we speak to our audience as sympathizers. If we assume an uncommitted audience or an antagonistic audience, then we must show that we recognize their point of view, their side of the argument. Always, we need to be aware of the tension between the pros and cons.

Suppose you are attempting to sell your car, a 1975 Ford LTD with power steering, power brakes, power windows, air conditioning, stereo—the works. You know quite well that the car is a gas-guzzler; to deny this fact to a prospective buyer would be foolish. You take on a "yes, but . . ." position. "*Yes*, the car does consume fuel, *but* it offers all these conveniences. . . ."

Argument depends on logic. In arguing, you must be aware of the pros and cons. In presenting an assertion, you must supply evidence, examples, descriptions, and anecdotes, as appropriate. Argument also calls on emotion. You will appeal to your audience as fellow-citizens, fellow dog-lovers, fellow pollutionists, fellow anti-pollutionists. You will call them into a fellowship of believers. Argument asks the audience to create a bond with you, to join your tribe, to become a member of your club.

Argument is like exemplifying, where you offer a general proposition and present examples. You begin by describing and defining the problem—the issue as you see it. You define your terms, showing what you mean by freedom, equality, pollution. In describing, you encourage your audience to perceive what *is*, so they can't say they didn't know. You present the situation as you see it, but anticipate their objections. You offer an interpretation of causes and anticipate effects. You move back and forth between the present and the future; if we don't change current laws about air pollution, then these will be the results. If we change, then we can hope for these effects.

Writers in the following selections present their views on a number of issues—from the politics of contemporary America to the politics of eighteenth century Ireland; from the politics of language to the benefits of running. In each selection, notice how the writer takes a case to the public and presents a public voice, a voice that, while impassioned, is not incredible; for, while passion of conviction must lie behind every argument, the speaker and writer are always after credibility: they want to be believed.

AS YOU READ

Assertions

At the center of every argument is a statement of belief, the point of the argument, an assertion that things should remain the same or that they should change:

> School boards must hold the line on teachers' salaries.
> Taxes must not be reduced.
> The elderly must become an integral part of society.
> Private citizens must be protected from prying photographers.
> Guns must be controlled by government regulations.

The presentation of an argument need not proceed to a conclusion; it may *focus* on beliefs, on the writer's saying, "This is the way I see things"; "This is the way things are"; "This is the situation, the problem." The move to the future—to the *should*—may stop short of a plan. Once convinced of the nature of the problem, we may be invited to share in coming up with a solution. Or the discussion may move on to a full plan to carry out. As you read the selections in this chapter, look for assertions, the center that all else revolves around. Observe the relationships of time: how do the past, present, and future interact? Were things "better" in the past? How are they now? What does the future promise? What, to the writer, represents the ideal state? What is normal?

Induction and Deduction

When writers work inductively, they present the situation first—through description, narratives, examples, contrasts, definitions, and so on. They *lead into* an assertion. When writers work deductively, they state up front what they believe, what they claim, and then *lead from* the assertion, offering support through examples, narratives, descriptions. As you read, observe whether an argument begins with examples and then leads to an assertion, or whether it leads from an assertion and is followed by examples.

Persuasion and Tone

In a real sense, persuasion underlies all forms of speech, all forms of writing. When we say, "It's a lovely day," or when we tell about what happened to us on the way to work, we hope to convince others to see things our way, to confirm what we do see, experience, and think. We want to be convincing, persuasive. As you read, pay attenion to the line of the argument, to the assertions and to the support, the evidence. Pay attention, as well, to the tone. Tone expresses the way writers and speakers hold their beliefs and, simultaneously, their attitudes toward their audience. Are they heckling? Dogmatic? Provoking? Patronizing? Quietly reasonable? *What* in the audience is being appealed to? In other words, the ways we hold our beliefs and the ways we attempt to persuade are two sides of the same coin. When we say, "She was persuasive," we mean that her tone, her manner, was acceptable to *us*; we approved of it, and we found her arguments plausible—they "made sense" for us. Similarly, when we accept a rule, a political belief, a way of making policy, we are saying, in effect, "we are convinced."

AS YOU WRITE

Generating Material

When you think of argument, you may recall the fights you have had with friends, sisters, brothers, or parents. You may recall childhood insults and abuses. But public argument is not this kind of exchange. Public argument depends on reasonableness, on presenting a case clearly, convincingly, even cooly. At the center of argument is an assertion of belief. It is possible in a debate to argue either side of a question, but a sincere argument will express your own beliefs, convictions, and your view of the way things should be.

Whether you are writing about a private, personal belief or about a public issue, express your own beliefs and why you believe as you do. Present the situation as you see it, stating what you see as the problem. If you offer a solution, draw up a list of pros and cons, anticipating objections your audience could raise. Write quickly in your journal about your beliefs on daily, personal matters: why you think you deserve a raise in pay; why you need a car; why you think one rock group is better than another. Write about public issues, trying to get to the core of your beliefs on nuclear pile-ups, on solar energy, on abortion, on capital punishment. What are your views? Your attitudes? Are they yours, or have you taken them over from the media or a partisan group? Try to spell them out. Supply evidence, support. Do some research.

Reading Your Writing

Observe how you have begun to present your case. Are you moving inductively or deductively—beginning with examples and then leading your audience to an assertion, or stating the problem and encapsulating a plan of action? Whom are you writing to? Are you assuming an informed, sympathetic audience? How much information on the issue does your audience need? What attitude do you take toward the issue? How urgent is the problem as you see it? If you present a plan, are the steps clearly sequenced?

Shaping Your Writing

Whether you begin inductively or deductively, your assertions should be clear, and the problem should be apparent from your presentation of it. Now, your job is to convince, to persuade. You must use all the support you can—examples, narratives, descriptions, definitions—to show your readers that you have thought through the problem and considered both sides. You must establish that your way of looking at things is reasonable, and that your audience stands to gain from agreeing with you and acting as you suggest. Keep in mind that you are working with contrasts, that you have a particular goal in mind, that your argument moves toward the future. You are arguing for a *should*: this is the way you *should* believe; this is the way things *should* be.

ART CAREY

> *In 1980, Art Carey ran in his twelfth Boston Marathon. That's the last we heard of him. He may still be running the features section of the Philadelphia* Enquirer's *Sunday Magazine.*

THE BOSTON MARATHON: PASSING OF AN AMERICAN PASTIME

Tomorrow, for about three hours, I will take part in a protest demonstration. To dramatize my grievances, I will run 26 miles 385 yards from a rural village called Hopkinton to the towering Prudential Center in downtown Boston. I will not be carrying any signs. In fact, the only thing that will distinguish me from several thousand other people who will be traveling the same route is that I won't be wearing an official number.

The purpose of the demonstration will be to lament the passing of a wonderful American pastime—running, as I knew it and think it ought to be—and there could be no better occasion for staging such a protest than America's most venerable long-distance footrace, the 84th Boston Athletic Association Marathon.

As I see it, running became imperiled about three years ago, in the thick of the Me Decade and just as the Culture of Narcissism was reaching its zenith. Suddenly, pectorally perfect Bruce Jenner and massively mesomorphic Arnold Schwarzenegger had become pop heroes, and it became chic to worry about your waistline, sagging chin, and flaccid muscles. Then, James Fixx wrote *The Complete Book of Running,* which quickly lapped all the other self-help, guru, and diet books on the bestseller lists. Overnight, it seemed, running has zoomed from weird to respectable, even fashionable. Everyone who was anyone was trotting around in 60 dollar running shoes and flashy warm-up suits from Bloomingdale's.

Some trendies, unfortunately, really got hooked. It was not enough simply to run and be run over in Central Park. To prove your mettle, you had to race, and of course, this meant that eventually, you had to run the ultimate race—the marathon—and the ultimate marathon—Boston.

Soon, what had once been a nice little neighborhood jaunt in Beantown and environs became a veritable Jock Woodstock. As the field climbed past three, then four, then five thousand runners, the race organizers, in a desperate attempt to cope with the chaos, began imposing qualifying times. Last year, any man under 40 years of age who wished to run with an official number had to have completed a certified marathon in less than three hours. Even with that restriction, though, more than 7,800 officially qualified runners showed up. This year, with the qualifying time for men under 40 lowered to a fast-stepping 2 hours 50 minutes, about 6,000 are expected to run.

I failed to qualify. Oh, I suppose I could have if I had been willing to spend a couple hours each day running 15 miles or more. But I'm too busy, and running is too monotonous to devote so much time to it. I still regard it as a hobby, something I do in my spare time for fun.

And that's the way Boston used to be—fun. When I first ran in the marathon way back in 1968 as a skinny high-school senior, there were only 900 runners at the starting line. I wound up dropping out after 17 miles; actually I nearly passed out and had to be carted into Boston in an ambulance. Still, I got a big charge out of it because the event was so joyous and the people were so colorful and bizarre.

I'll never forget this one guy, a burly Irishman who showed up at the starting line with some of his drinking buddies. His hairy beer belly was only partially covered by a Beethoven sweatshirt. He was wearing plaid Bermuda shorts that nearly touched his knees, dark, over-the-calf socks and torn-up high black sneakers. He got warmed up by downing a six-pack and belching. When the gun went off, he exploded like he was running the anchor leg of a 440-yard relay. After only about 200 yards, he suddenly pulled up short, green in the face, and anointed the curb with his breakfast.

That's what Boston was all about, I thought then and still think now. It's a chance for hams and shams, and desk-bound Walter Mittys to realize their dreams of athletic glory. For a few bucks, some stinging blisters, some aching joints—and some guts—any plumber or professor can rub shoulders with running's great and go home bragging to family and friends that, yes, he was there, he took part in the World Series of Running, the Super Bowl of Marathoning, and what's more, finished.

These days, though, the officials don't see it that way. John D. (Jock) Semple, the feisty, tough-talking Scotsman who is the assistant director of the marathon, says the unofficial runners are an execrable lot who are ruining the marathon. "I hate them," he told me. "I'd have 'em all shot if I could get my hands on 'em."

I think Semple is overloaded on carbohydrates. The people who are ruining Boston are all those lean, humorless, glaze-eyed, hard-core, semi-pro addicts who will instantly numb your senses with their tedious talk about shoes and training, and times, and diet, and running as psychic phenomenon and running as mystic experience, etc., etc., ad nauseam.

So I say let's do away with the qualifying times and official numbers. Let's give running back to the barstool jockeys, the once-around-the-block joggers, the armchair athletes and weekend hackers. Let's open up the marathon and make it the great American folk celebration and rite of spring that it ought to be.

How Do You Respond?

1. How does Carey move between the past, present, and future? What is he lamenting?
2. How were things in the past? Better? Worse? Than what? How are things now?
3. What does Carey hope for the future? What is his plan? Is it convincing, persuasive?

ELLEN GOODMAN

> Ellen Goodman's syndicated column for the Boston Globe now appears in more than 200 newspapers across the country. "To write a column," says Goodman (born 1941), "you need the egocentric confidence that your view of the world is important enough to be read, then you need the pacing of a long-distance runner to write day after day, week after week, year after year. . . ." Goodman's writings won her a Pulitzer Prize for Journalism in 1980 and have been collected in Turning Points, Close to Home, and At Large.

PROTECTION FROM THE PRYING CAMERA

Maybe it was the year-end picture roundup that finally did it. Maybe it was the double exposure to the same vivid photographs. Or perhaps it was the memory of three amateur photographers carefully standing in the cold last fall, calculating their f-stops and exposures with light meters, trying to find the best angle, pointing their cameras at a drunk in a doorway. Or maybe it was simply my nine-year-old cousin playing Candid Camera at the family gathering.

But whatever the reason, it has finally hit me. We have become a nation of Kodachrome, Nikon, Instamatic addicts. But we haven't yet developed a clear idea of the ethics of picture-taking. We haven't yet determined the parameters of privacy in a world of flash cubes and telescopic lenses.

We "take" pictures. As psychologist Stanley Milgram puts it, "A photographer takes a picture, he does not create it or borrow it." But who has given us the right to "take" those pictures and under what circumstances?

Since the camera first became portable, we have easily and repeatedly aimed it at public people. It has always been open shooting season on them. With new technology, however, those intrusions have intensified. This year, someone with a camera committed the gross indecency of shooting an unaware Greta Garbo in the nude—and *People* printed it.

This year, again, Ron Galella "took" the image of Jacqueline Onassis and sold it as if it belonged to him. This year, we have pictures of a crumpled Wayne Hays, an indiscreet Nelson Rockefeller, and two presidential candidates in every imaginable pose from the absurd to the embarrassing.

We have accepted the idea that public people are always free targets for the camera—without even a statute of limitations for Jackie or Garbo. We have also accepted the idea that a private person becomes public by being involved in a public event. The earthquake victims of Guatemala, the lynched leftists of Thailand, the terror-stricken of Ireland—their emotions and their bodies become frozen images.

The right of the public to know, to see and to be affected is considered more important than the right of the individual to mourn, or even die, in privacy.

What happens now, however, when cameras proliferate until they are as common as television sets? What happens when the image being "taken" is that of a butcher, a baker, or a derelict, rather than a public figure? Do we all lose our right to privacy simply by stepping into view?

Should we be allowed to point cameras at each other? To regard each other as objects of art? Does the photographer or the photographed own the image?

Several years ago, *Time* photographer Steve Northup, who had covered Vietnam, and Watergate, took a group of students around Cambridge shooting pictures. He quietly insisted that they ask every pizza-maker, truck driver and beautician for permission. His attitude toward private citizens was one of careful respect for the power of "exposure." In contrast to this, the average camera bug—like the average tourist—too often goes about snapping "quaint" people, along with "quaint" scenes: See the natives smile, see the natives carrying baskets of fruit, see the native children begging, see the drunk in the doorway. As Milgram wrote, "I find it hard to understand wherein the photographer has derived the right to keep for his own purposes the image of the peasant's face."

Where do we get the right to bring other people home in a canister? Where did we lose the right to control our image?

In a study that Milgram conducted last year, a full 65 percent of the people to whom his students talked in midtown Manhattan refused to have their pictures taken, refused to be photographed. I don't think they were camera shy, in the sense of being vain. Rather, they were reluctant to have their pictures "taken."

The Navahos long believed that the photographer took a piece of them away in his film. Like them, we are coming to understand the power of these frozen images. Photographs can help us to hold onto the truth of our past, to make our history and identity more real. Or they can rip something away from us as precious as the privacy which once clothed Greta Garbo.

How Do You Respond?

1. Goodman places her argument in the context of time: "It has finally hit me"—now. What is characteristic of now? What has "finally" hit her?

2. What forms of writing does Goodman use to show what hit her? Does she move inductively or deductively?

3. What does she think we should do in the future instead of what we are doing now? How do you know?

MARGARET MEAD

> Two distinguished women helped to put anthropology on the map—Ruth Benedict and Margaret Mead (1901–1978). Mead worked in various fields—family structures, mental health, ecology, and the nature of culture—and wrote a number of classic texts, Coming of Age in Samoa, The Study of Culture at a Distance, and Blackberry Winter, her autobiography. Toward the end of her life, she became passionately interested in the ways in which society uses, misuses, and abuses the elderly. "Retirement" she saw as a kind of injury—a way of saying to someone, "You are useless." She worked hard, with determination and passion, right to the end of her life.

GRANDPARENTS HAVE COPPED OUT

I would like particularly to talk about the need to develop a new style of aging in our own society. I would like to suggest that maybe we could do a little more for the older American than we are doing in the present. Everyone who is aging has a chance to develop this new style. Everyone who is working with old people can contribute to this new style.

Young people in this country have been accused of not caring for their parents the way they would have in the old country, in Puerto Rico, in the Old South, or in Italy. And this is true, but it is also true that old people in this country have been influenced by an American ideal of independence and autonomy. The most important thing in the world is to be independent. So we live alone, perhaps on the verge of starvation, in time without friends, but we are independent. This standard American style has been forced on every ethnic group in the country, although there are many groups in this country for whom the ideal is not practical. It is a poor ideal and pursuing it does a great deal of harm.

This ideal of independence also contains a tremendous amount of unselfishness. In talking to today's young mothers, I have asked them what kind of grandmothers they think they are going to be. I hear devoted, loving mothers say that when they are through raising their children, they have no intention of becoming grandmothers.

They are astonished to hear that in most of the world throughout most of its history, families have been three- or four-generation families, living under the same roof. We have over-emphasized the small family unit—father, mother, small children. We think it is wonderful if Grandma and Grandpa, if he's still alive, can live alone.

We have reached the point where we think the only thing we can do for our children is to stay out of their hair and the only thing we can do for our daughter-in-law is to see as little of her as possible. Old people's hotels, even the best run, are filled with older people who believe the only thing they can do for their children is to look cheerful when they come to visit. So in the end, older people have to devote all their energies to "not being a burden."

We are beginning to see what a tremendous price we've paid for our emphasis on independence and autonomy. We have isolated old people and we've cut off the children, the young people, from their grandparents. One of the reasons we have as bad a generation gap today as we do is that grandparents have copped out. Young people are being deprived of the thing they need most—perspective, to know why their parents behave so peculiarly and why their grandparents say the things they do.

In peasant communities where things didn't change, and where people died in the beds they were born in, grandparents taught the young what the end of life was going to be. So you looked at your mother, if you were a girl, and learned what it was like to be a bride, a young mother. Then you looked at your grandmother and you knew what it was like to be old. Children learned what it was to age and die while they were small. They were prepared for the end of life at the beginning.

It is interesting to realize that early in human society we developed a method of keeping old women alive. The human being is the only animal to have a menopause. So women do stop having babies, and if they haven't died by the time they stop, women can become quite strong and can live quite a long time. For countless centuries, old women have been around who knew things that no one else knew . . . that ten, twenty, thirty years ago there was a hurricane or a famine, and they knew what people did. And this emphasizes one of the functions of older people in a society. However, today this is a function whose usefulness is disappearing. We can be dead certain that when our grandchildren reach our age, they will not be living as we live today.

Today grandparents, old people in general, have something quite different to contribute. Their generation has seen the most change in the world, and the young today need to learn that there has been change. They need to know about their past before they can understand the present and plot the future.

Young people also need reassurance that change does not mean the end of the world, merely an end to the world as they first saw it. Older people remember that we have had periods of disorder in this country before. Some of them can remember the Time of Troubles in Ireland. Some of them remember the riots after World War I and those after World War II and they remember that we got them in hand. Because the ties between generations have been broken, young people have lost this perspective.

Normally we talk about the heartless young people who don't have room for their parents in their lives, much less in their apartments. But old people today have tremendous advantages, and these advantages make them much less dependent.

We all look so young to each other. Sometimes we kid ourselves that we look young to the young, which is nonsense. But we have our hair cut and styled in the most modern fashion, dye it in the most modern colors. It is wonderful how young your old friends look. Old people have never been cheered up in this way before.

My grandmother may have been treated with a certain respect, but she was formally dressed in a way that her grandmother had been, in a way that made her feel old. Today we dress old people in a way that makes them feel young.

On the subways, which I've been riding for fifty years, two things have happened: people have stopped giving up their seats to the old, and old people have stopped accepting seats when they are offered. "I'll stand, thank you."

What we need to do is to find a style of aging that will keep and foster this independence, but will encourage old people to be thinking of what they can do for someone else. If we are going to change the style, change the relationship between young and old, older people have to take the lead by finding ways to relate either to their own grandchildren or to someone else's.

As long as we say that youth has no need for age, young people in this country aren't interested in old people, in seeing them or listening to them, there will be an enormous number of things in our society that are not being done, but which could be done by old people.

How Do You Respond?

1. Mead contrasts the way things were, the characteristics of yesterday, and the way things are now, the characteristics of today. How were things yesterday? How are they now?
2. What does Mead propose for the future? Does she offer a specific plan? Does she convince you that things need to change?
3. How would you characterize her tone? Do you notice any signs that this is a recorded talk and not a speech read from a script?

LEWIS THOMAS

> *"The whole dear notion of one's own self—marvelous old free-willed, free-enterprising, autonomous, independent, isolated island of a self—is a myth," says Lewis Thomas (born 1913), who calls himself a "biology watcher." Neurologist, teacher, administrator, writer, Thomas contributed a monthly column to* the New England Journal of Medicine. *These "Notes of a Biology Watcher" grew into two volumes:* Lives of a Cell, *which won the National Book Award in 1974, and* Medusa and the Snail, *from which the following selection is taken.*

TO ERR IS HUMAN

Everyone must have had at least one personal experience with a computer error by this time. Bank balances are suddenly reported to have jumped from $379 into the millions, appeals for charitable contributions are mailed over and over to people with crazy-sounding names at your address, department stores send the wrong bills, utility companies write that they're turning everything off, that sort of thing. If you manage to get in touch with someone and complain, you then get instantaneously typed, guilty letters from the same computer, saying, "Our computer was in error, and an adjustment is being made in your account."

These are supposed to be the sheerest, blindest accidents. Mistakes are not believed to be part of the normal behavior of a good machine. If things go wrong, it must be a personal, human error, the result of fingering, tampering, a button getting stuck, someone hitting the wrong key. The computer, at its normal best, is infallible.

I wonder whether this can be true. After all, the whole point of computers is that they represent an extension of the human brain, vastly improved upon but nonetheless human, superhuman maybe. A good computer can think clearly and quickly enough to beat you at chess, and some of them have even been programmed to write obscure verse. They can do anything we can do, and more besides.

It is not yet known whether a computer has its own consciousness, and it would be hard to find out about this. When you walk into one of those great halls now built for the huge machines, and stand listening, it is easy to imagine that the faint, distant noises are the sound of thinking, and the turning of the spools gives them the look of wild creatures rolling their eyes in the effort to concentrate, choking with information. But real thinking, and dreaming, are other matters.

On the other hand, the evidences of something like an *unconscious,* equivalent to ours, are all around, in every mail. As extensions of the human brain, they have been constructed with the same property of error, spontaneous, uncontrolled, and rich in possibilities.

Mistakes are at the very base of human thought, embedded there, feeding the structure like root nodules. If we were not provided with the knack of being wrong, we could never get anything useful done. We think our way along by choosing between right and wrong alternatives, and the wrong choices have to be made as frequently as the right ones. We get along in life this way. We are built to make mistakes, coded for error.

We learn, as we say, by "trial and error." Why do we always say that? Why not "trial and rightness" or "trial and triumph"? The old phrase puts it that way because that is, in real life, the way it is done.

A good laboratory, like a good bank or a corporation or government, has to run like a computer. Almost everything is done flawlessly, by the book, and all the numbers add up to the predicted sums. The days go by. And then, if it is a lucky day, and a lucky laboratory, somebody makes a mistake: the wrong buffer, something in one of the blanks, a decimal misplaced in reading counts, the warm room off by a degree and a half, a mouse out of his box, or just a misreading of the day's protocol. Whatever, when the results come in, something is obviously screwed up, and then the action can begin.

The misreading is not the important error; it opens the way. The next step is the crucial one. If the investigator can bring himself to say, "But even so, look at that!" then the new finding, whatever it is, is ready for snatching. What is needed, for progress to be made, is the move based on the error.

Whenever new kinds of thinking are about to be accomplished, or new varieties of music, there has to be an argument beforehand. With two sides debating in the same mind, haranguing, there is an amiable understanding that one is right and the other wrong. Sooner or later the thing is settled, but there can be no action at all if there are not the two sides, and the argument. The hope is in the faculty of wrongness, the tendency toward error. The capacity to leap across mountains of information to land lightly on the wrong side represents the highest of human endowments.

It may be that this is a uniquely human gift, perhaps even stipulated in our genetic instructions. Other creatures do not seem to have DNA sequences for making mistakes as a routine part of daily living, certainly not for programmed error as a guide for action.

We are at our human finest, dancing with our minds, when there are more choices than two. Sometimes there are ten, even twenty different ways to go, all but one bound to be wrong, and the richness of selection in such situations can lift us onto totally new ground. This process is called exploration and is based on human fallibility. If we had only a single center in our brains, capable of responding only when a correct decision was to be made, instead of the jumble of different, credulous, easily conned clusters of neurones that provide for being flung off into blind alleys, up trees, down dead ends, out into blue sky, along wrong turnings, around bends, we could only stay the way we are today, stuck fast.

The lower animals do not have this splendid freedom. They are limited, most often, to absolute infallibility. Cats, for all their good side, never make mistakes. I have never seen a maladroit, clumsy, or blundering cat. Dogs are sometimes fallible, occasionally able to make charming minor mistakes, but they get this way by trying to mimic their masters. Fish are flawless in everything they do. Individual cells in a tissue are mindless machines, perfect in their performance, as absolutely inhuman as bees.

We should have this in mind as we become dependent on more complex computers for the arrangement of our affairs. Give the computers their heads, I say; let them go their way. If we can learn to do this, turning our heads to one side and wincing while the work proceeds, the possibilities for the future of mankind, and computerkind, are limitless. Your average good computer can make calculations in an instant which would take a lifetime of slide rules for any of us. Think of what we could gain from the near infinity of precise, machine-made miscomputation which is now so easily within our grasp. We would begin the solving of some of our hardest problems. How, for instance, should we go about organizing ourselves for social living on a planetary scale, now that we have become, as a plain fact of life, a single community? We can assume, as a working hypothesis, that all the right ways of doing this are unworkable. What we need, then, for moving ahead, is a set of wrong alternatives much longer and more interesting than the short list of mistaken courses that any of us can think up right now. We need, in fact, an infinite list, and when it is printed out we need the computer to turn on itself and select, at random, the next way to go. If it is a big enough mistake, we could find ourselves on a new level, stunned, out in the clear, ready to move again.

How Do You Respond?

1. What does Thomas assert? What tone does he use? Is he playing with us? What does he want to convince us of?

2. Does he want to diminish our belief in *human* intelligence? What attitude is he trying to counter?

3. Notice Thomas's sweeping generalizations (computers can do anything we can do, and more besides; cats never make mistakes). Are you supposed to take them literally? How do you know? *How* serious is Thomas? What about?

ROBERT PAUL SMITH

> Where Did You Go? Out. What Did You Do? Nothing *is the ingenious title of a book by Robert Paul Smith (1915–1977). Smith was an untiring supporter of kids and believed that if parents would only let them alone, they would grow up okay. Clearly, Smith had a penchant for composing memorable titles: his works include* How to Grow Up in One Piece; How to Do Nothing with Nobody; *and* The Tender Trap.

LET YOUR KIDS ALONE

When I was a kid, the way we got to play baseball was this: school was out, we ran home and hooked a handful of cookies, hollered, "I'm home, goin' out on the block," grabbed a beat-up fielder's glove, went out on the block and met a friend who had an old first baseman's mitt and a ball, went down the block a little and hollered at the kid who had the bat. So we proceeded until we had rounded up all those kids who were not chained to piano practice, making model airplanes, lying on their backs studying the ceiling, feeding their rabbits, or writing out one thousand times, "I will not put blotting paper in the inkwell." We went to the vacant lot and played a game resembling major league baseball only in that it was played with a bat and bases. It was fun.

My kid went to play soccer the other day. The way you play soccer now is this: you bring home from school a mimeographed schedule for the Saturday morning soccer league. There are six teams, named after colleges, and the schedule is so arranged that at the end of the season, by a mathematical process of permutations and combinations that would take me six weeks to figure out, every team has played every other team and every kid has shown up at the right hour the right number of times. There are always exactly eleven men on each team, the ball is regulation size, the games are played on a regulation-size field with regulation-size soccer goals, and there is a regulation-size adult to referee.

After the game, I asked my kid, "Was it fun?" "Yes," he said, but he didn't sound sure. "We lost 3–0." When I was a kid, we lost 3–0 too—and also 16–2 and 135–3 at soccer or baseball or kick-the-can—but by the time we had fought about where the strike zone was, what was out of bounds and who was offside, we could wind up winning the argument, if not the game.

Because, you see, it was *our* game. I think that my kid was playing someone else's game. I think he was playing Big Brother's game.

Big Brother, in this case, is all the parents who cannot refrain from poking their snoots into a world where they have no business to be, into the whole wonderful world of a kid, which is wonderful precisely because there are no grownups in it. In come today's parents, tramping down the underbrush, cutting down the trees, driving away the game, making the place hideous with mimeographed sheets and names and regulations. They are into everything. They refuse to let anything alone if there is a kid connected with it. They have invented a whole new modern perversion: child-watching.

There are two main groups of child-watchers. The first, which includes the PTAs and the child study leagues and the children's mental hygiene groups, watches but does not touch. These are the peepers through one-way glass, the keepers of notebooks, the givers of tests.

The second group watches *and* touches—and also coaches and uniforms and proliferates rulebooks. This group manages such things as the soccer leagues and the Little Leagues and the Cub Scouts and the Boy Scouts and the Girl Scouts and Brownies and the Sea Scouts and the Explorer Scouts and, I'd bet, the Satellite Scouts. These are the getters down on all fours, the spies in the children's world, the ones who cannot be sure whether they wish the kids to be as grownup as themselves, or wish themselves to be as childish as the kids.

All this child-watching and child-helping and child-pushing has made it tough for the kids to do anything without a complete set of instructions. Of course, once in a while they do break through the instruction barrier. This afternoon following the soccer game, my kid went off on his own business. This consisted of assembling an arrangement of batteries and resistors and what I have learned are called capacitors (not condensers), which makes five tiny neon tubes blink in a manner I can only describe as infuriating. Obviously this was fun for him. There are no plans for constructing such a machine. Indeed, it may be the first time such a machine has been built. So he built it. But he did not go outside and do the idle footling of a soccer ball which I used to do because the kid next door happened to have a soccer ball, and he did not play one-o-cat or throw a football around or even watch squirrels.

He did not do this because, although Big Brother has organized every league known to man and issued a rule book therefore, he has not yet put out a mimeographed sheet of instructions on watching squirrels. There are no books on how to be a lousy right fielder (it came to me natural), and in no book does it say that when you go to make a tackle, of course you shut your eyes and lie about it later. No doubt these books are being written.

Perhaps the finest single example of an organization that is devoted to not leaving the kids alone is the Scouts. It is not my intention to knock the Scouts as a whole. It is a well-meaning organization devoted to salutary works. I am sure that its officials are high-principled, admirable people. I merely wish to point out that the name of the organization is the *Boy* Scouts. It is for *boys*. And yet there is a small, wallet-sized card printed by the Boy Scouts of America entitled "The Scout Parent's Opportunity." Among the exhortations on this card are these:

"Be a companion to your own son." "Weave Cub Scouting into home-life pattern." "Use the program to draw the family closer." "Be with your son at all pack meetings." "Work closely with the Den Mother."

The day an organization, *any* organization, tells me how to be a companion to my son is the day I am going to take a good hard look at that organization, and if they mean it for real, I am going to prepare to mount the barricades. I find "The Scout Parent's Opportunity" a terrifying document, but it is as nothing compared to another communiqué from the same organization. This is a sheet of yellow paper headed HERE ARE THE THINGS YOU DO TO BECOME A BOBCAT.

Well, the very first thing you do to become a Bobcat is learn and take the Cub Scout promise: "I promise to DO MY BEST to do my DUTY to GOD and my COUNTRY, to be SQUARE, and to OBEY the Law of the Pack." (The capital letters are *not* mine.) Only after you have said you will OBEY the Law of the Pack do you find out what the Law the of the Pack is. The very first article of the Law is,

"The Cub Scout FOLLOWS Akela." Then you hear that "Akela means 'Good Leader'—your mother and father, your teacher, your Cubmaster, and many other people who have shown that they are the kind of people who are able and willing to help you." Follow this reasoning carefully: first you say you will do something; then you find out what it is that you have promised to do; and then you find out what the thing you have promised to do means.

Before I let my kid subscribe to this, he is going to have a little talk with OLD FATHER, who is going to HOLLER at him GOOD AND LOUD. And what OLD FATHER is going to TELL him is never sign a BLANK CHECK, and before he goes off following Akela, he better take a GOOD HARD LOOK at all these people who have shown that they are "able and willing" to help him and find out where they are able and willing to lead him TO.

Bobcats, I have news for you. I know who Akela is, and he is not all those people. He is the old leader of the wolves in Kipling's Mowgli stories, and during wolf meetings he lies quietly on the Council Rock, interpreting the law and keeping order by means of dignity and aloofness. He spends a great deal of time keeping his mouth shut and he spends absolutely no time at all down in the grass with the young cubs playing Pin the Tail on the Hartebeest or Ring Around the Cobra.

I know a father in Connecticut whose kid FOLLOWED Akela to a Den, and after several sessions the kid wanted out. He did not know how to convey this horrible intelligence to Akela, so instead he went to his father. Apparently he thought quitting the Scouts was like breaking with the Communist party, or trying to get away from George Raft and being cut down by a machine gun at the corner of Fifth and Main.

The thing that drove this boy away from the Cub Scouts grew out of the little joker in one corner of the Bobcats' contract. It is called the "Parents' O.K." and it says: "We have had an active part in our son's first Cub Scout experience—becoming a Bobcat. We have tried to see things through his eyes and not expect too much. On the other hand, we haven't been too easy. We have helped him complete all the Bobcat requirements and we are satisfied that he has done his best."

This sounds mawkish but fairly harmless. The way my friend from Connecticut tells it, it isn't harmless at all. "Your kid brings you a book called the Wolf Cub Scout Book. If, Lord help us, you're a Good Scout Dad, you read a little of the book. On page 18 is something called 'Feats of Skill,' and your kid has to do any three of them to pass. He can choose a frontward, backward and falling somersault, or playing catch with someone twenty feet away, or climbing at least twelve feet up a tree, or swimming thirty feet in shallow water, or walking a two-by-four forward, sideways and backward. Now I'm for this, so I watch my kid practice. He tries and he doesn't get anywhere near twelve feet up the tree. I say, 'No, that's about five feet. You didn't do it.' When he tries to walk backward on the two-by-four, he falls off, so I say, 'Give it a little more work.' After all, I'm the one who's got to sign a paper saying he passed the test."

I could see why my friend was concerned: when he signs contracts, he fulfills them.

"So there's this pack meeting," my friend continued, "and they start giving kids badges because they have done their feats of skill. After a while, my boy and I see this one kid from our block who we *know* can't find his bottom with both hands in the dark, and he's getting a badge because he did the feats of skill. It's 'proven.' His mother signed the pledge. My kid looks at me. Something is very fishy here, is what he is thinking. That goof climbed twelve feet up a tree? Then why can't he climb stairs very good? It didn't take my kid long to figure it out: mothers lie and scoutmasters believe them. So he quit."

"That summer my kid took a look at an island in the middle of a lake at a kind of farm he goes to. He was the littlest kid there. He swam out and back and wrote a letter home, and in the envelope was a weed from the island. I didn't have to tell him it was a feat of skill and the weed was a badge. He knew."

I suggested to my friend that he tell his kid that Akela—Mr. Kipling's Akela—would have known it, too, and so would Dan Beard, whose concern in helping found the Boy Scouts was to get kids out on their own in the country where they could learn to be independent.

I hear that things are bad in the Brownie world, too. One Boston mother complains that she was required to learn to do everything her daughter had to learn to do to become a Brownie. At what cost to her self-esteem she cannot say, she even had to learn to sing, with gestures, the "Brownie Smile Song," which includes the words, "I have something in my pocket." And what mother has in her pocket is a smile, which she takes out and puts on her face. I ask you.

A New York City mother swears that when her daughter was "invested" in the Brownies, all the mothers had to be invested too. "I went to the investiture," this mother says, "and before I knew it, I and all the other mothers were standing up in a line, reciting the Brownie oath and having badges pinned on us."

Well, what's the point? The real point is that this kind of jazz doesn't fool anyone but the parents. The kids know that any grownup who gets down on all fours and makes mudpies with them is either a spy or a fool. Not that kids don't like spending time with grown-ups, but what they want is for the grownup to take them into his world. They are familiar with the child's world, they can handle themselves there. But a grownup can take them to a new place, an exciting world of cigars and restaurants with linen napkins and automobiles and tall people. But do parents do this today? No, they are too busy being Real Dandy Scout Dads and True Blue Brownie Moms.

The Scouts, of course, are only an example. This same attitude is found everywhere that parents and children get together. Anybody who thinks that the kids don't understand what is going on is living in a dream. These kids watch their parents making spectacles of themselves, and they reach conclusions. All parents who are now, or ever have been, down on all fours should give careful thought to the conclusions that they invite their kids to reach.

It seems to me that we are doing things we do not really want to do for kids who do not really want to have them done. Perhaps the saddest proof of all is provided by the town of Proctor, Minnesota, where members of the Duluth, Missabe and Iron Range Railway Employees Association actually go out on the street to try to get kids to use their bowling alleys, golf course, ball park, football field, rifle range, skating rink, and tennis courts. No sale. The Proctor Moose Lodge offered to give away quarters to all the children of its 450 members on the Fourth of July. All the kids had to do was show up and hold out their hands. The first year only 50 kids bothered to show and the next year fewer than 25. The project was abandoned.

And when Proctor sponsored a safety contest open to all the school kids in town, only one boy entered. Naturally he won first prize, a watch, but since he already had a watch he asked for $10 instead.

For reasons of their own the kids of Proctor don't want to use the bowling alleys, don't want to walk that far for a quarter, don't care very much about safety. I suspect that the main reason is that they never asked for any of these things and would rather be left alone. What is true for the kids of Proctor is going to be true for the kids of San Francisco and Chicago and New York and Ashtabula. The thing to do, I think, is for us to stop pestering them.

To this end I have formed an organization called Modern Parents Anonymous, or MPA (not under any circumstances to be confused with a recently formed Seattle organization known as PPPTA, or Proud Papas of the Parent-Teachers Association). MPA got its start one night when four supposedly adult persons—my wife and I and another couple—were sitting in moderately comfortable chairs in our moderately well-heated, well-lighted living room. All four of us read books and magazines, we have minds to think with and an enormous world to think about. So for two hours we talked about— children.

The actions of our children seemed more sensible to me than our own. They had looked into the living room some time before, seen that grownups were in tedious conclave, said hello and good-by and left. They were not wasting their time talking about us. The moment I realized this, MPA was born.

The principal goal of MPA is to encourage parents to think and worry and talk about something other than their own offspring. I have a list of things that might be talked about: freedom, liberty, the mating habits of Eskimos, the difference between Conté crayon and charcoal, the difference between voltage and amperage, religion, Ralph De Palma, the inflation of a basketball, the principle of a two-stroke engine, money, marbles, and chalk. These intelligent areas of discourse I obtained from my kids. The care and handling of parents is not, of course, on their list. They stay away from this topic with consummate ease.

Last year I wrote a book which suggested, in the mildest possible ways, that if people remembered what a nuisance grownups were when they were kids, perhaps now that they were in turn presumably grownups they might like to get off the kids' backs. The mail has been fantastic, all in agreement, and most fantastic of all have been the communications from PTA groups asking me to come and holler at them.

I am booked for one such PTA talk in the near future, and I have a letter on the subject from the program chairman. "We need you, Mr. Smith," the letter says. "We want to stimulate our parents to think seriously about the probable risk of too many set designs for living and about the possible triumphs of unstressed, unconformist ways of growing."

Translating from the PTA-ese, I take this to mean that they want me to tell them how to leave their kids alone to grow up in peace. Well, I will go, and if I do not lose my nerve I will tell them that the way to leave kids alone is to leave them alone.

How Do You Respond?

1. What is Smith's plan for leaving kids alone? Is it implicit or explicit? How does the past work in his view of things?

2. What form of writing does Smith use to support his assertions? How would you characterize his tone?

3. Does your experience support or contradict Smith's criticisms of adult-organized activities for kids? Did you or didn't you enjoy Cub/Brownie/Scout/Campfire/Little League programs? Why? What do you think of such experience now?

JONATHAN SWIFT

> Jonathan Swift (1667–1745) was an extraordinary genius in the "Age of Reason." While the intelligentsia of Europe basked in the glories of human reason and dreams of human perfectibility, he was driven to subvert such facile optimism; and so he explored the precariousness of human reason, of civilization. In his master stroke—Gulliver's Travels—he leads us irresistibly to the conclusion that we are self-deluding apes. In his Modest Proposal, he seizes the bland and complacent manners of reasonableness in order to shock his readers into contemplating a scandalous fact: Ireland, a savagely exploited colony, had been reduced to a state of abject distress so deep that such a proposal for disposing of "surplus" mouths would in fact appear to be perfectly reasonable!

A MODEST PROPOSAL
FOR
PREVENTING THE CHILDREN OF POOR PEOPLE IN IRELAND FROM BEING A BURDEN TO THEIR PARENTS OR COUNTRY, AND FOR MAKING THEM BENEFICIAL TO THE PUBLIC

It is a melancholy object to those who walk through this great town,* or travel in the country, when they see the streets, the roads and cabin-doors crowded with beggars of the female sex, followed by three, four, or six children, all in rags, and importuning every passenger for an alms. These mothers, instead of being able to work for their honest livelihood, are forced to employ all their time in strolling, to beg sustenance for their helpless infants, who, as they grow up, either turn thieves for want of work, or leave their dear native country to fight for the Pretender in Spain, or sell themselves to the Barbadoes.

I think it is agreed by all parties that this prodigious number of children, in the arms, or on the backs, or at the heels of their mothers, and frequently of their fathers, is in the present deplorable

---

*Dublin

state of the kingdom a very great additional grievance; and therefore whoever could find out a fair, cheap, and easy method of making these children sound and useful members of the commonwealth would deserve so well of the public as to have his statue set up for a preserver of the nation.

But my intention is very far from being confined to provide only for the children of professed beggars; it is of a much greater extent, and shall take in the whole number of infants at a certain age who are born of parents in effect as little able to support them as those who demand our charity in the streets.

As to my own part, having turned my thoughts for many years upon this important subject, and maturely weighed the several schemes of other projectors, I have always found them grossly mistaken in their computation. It is true a child just dropped from its dam may be supported by her milk for a solar year with little other nourishment, at most not above the value of two shillings, which the mother may certainly get, or the value in scraps, by her lawful occupation of begging, and it is exactly at one year old that I propose to provide for them, in such a manner as, instead of being a charge upon their parents, or the parish, or wanting food and raiment for the rest of their lives, they shall, on the contrary, contribute to the feeding and partly to the clothing of many thousands.

There is likewise another great advantage in my scheme, that it will prevent those voluntary abortions, and that horrid practice of women murdering their bastard children, alas, too frequent among us, sacrificing the poor innocent babes, I doubt, more to avoid the expense than the shame, which would move tears and pity in the most savage and inhuman beast.

The number of souls in Ireland being usually reckoned one million and a half, of these I calculate there may be about two hundred thousand couples whose wives are breeders, from which number I subtract thirty thousand couples who are able to maintain their own children, although I apprehend there cannot be so many under the present distresses of the kingdom, but this being granted, there will remain an hundred and seventy thousand breeders. I again subtract fifty thousand for those women who miscarry, or whose children die by accident or disease within the year. There only remain an hundred and twenty thousand children of poor parents annually born: the question therefore is, how this number shall be reared, and provided for, which, as I have already said, under the present situation of affairs is utterly impossible by all the methods hitherto proposed, for we can neither employ them in handicraft or agriculture; we neither build houses (I mean in the country), nor cultivate land: they can very seldom pick up a livelihood by stealing until they arrive at six years old, except where they are of towardly parts, although I confess they learn the rudiments much earlier, during which time they can however be properly looked upon only as probationers, as I have been informed by a principal gentleman in the County of Cavan, who protested to me that he never knew above one or two instances under age of six, even in a part of the kingdom so renowned for the quickest proficiency in that art.

I am assured by our merchants that a boy or a girl, before twelve years old, is no saleable commodity, and even when they come to this age, they will not yield above three pounds, or three pounds and half-a-crown at most on the Exchange, which cannot turn to account either to the parents or the kingdom, the charge of nutriment and rags having been at least four times that value.

I shall now therefore humbly propose my own thoughts, which I hope will not be liable to the least objection.

I have been assured by a very knowing American of my acquaintance in London, that a young healthy child well nursed is at a year old a most delicious, nourishing, and wholesome food, whether stewed, roasted, baked, or boiled, and I make no doubt that it will equally serve in a fricassee, or a ragout.

I do therefore humbly offer it to public consideration, that of the hundred and twenty thousand children already computed, twenty thousand may be reserved for breed, whereof only one fourth part to be males, which is more than we allow to sheep, black-cattle, or swine, and my reason is that these children are seldom the fruits of marriage, a circumstance not much regarded by our savages, therefore one male will be sufficient to serve four females. That the remaining hundred thousand may at a year old be offered in sale to the persons of quality, and fortune, through the kingdom, always advising the mother to let them suck plentifully in the last month, so as to render them plump, and fat for a good table. A child will make two dishes at an entertainment for friends, and when the family dines alone, the fore or hind quarter will make a reasonable dish, and seasoned with a little pepper or salt will be very good boiled on the fourth day, especially in winter.

I have reckoned upon a medium,* that a child just born will weigh 12 pounds, and in a solar year if tolerably nursed increaseth to 28 pounds.

I grant this food will be somewhat dear, and therefore very proper for landlords, who, as they have already devoured most of the parents, seem to have the best title to the children.

Infant's flesh will be in season throughout the year, but more plentiful in March, and a little before and after, for we are told by a grave author, an eminent French physician,† that fish being a prolific diet, there are more children born in Roman Catholic countries about nine months after Lent than at any other season; therefore reckoning a year after Lent, the markets will be more glutted than usual, because the number of Popish infants is at least three to one in this kingdom, and therefore it will have one other collateral advantage by lessening the number of Papists among us.

I have already computed the charge of nursing a beggar's child (in which list I reckon all cottagers, labourers, and four-fifths of the farmers) to be about two shillings *per annum,* rags included, and I believe no gentleman would repine to give ten shillings for the carcass of a good fat child, which, as I have said, will make four dishes of excellent nutritive meat, when he hath only some particular friend or his own family to dine with him. Thus the Squire will learn to be a good landlord and grow popular among his tenants, the mother will have eight shillings net profit, and be fit for work until she produces another child.

Those who are more thrifty (as I must confess the times require) may flay the carcass; the skin of which artificially dressed, will make admirable gloves for ladies, and summer boots for fine gentlemen.

As to our city of Dublin, shambles‡ may be appointed for this purpose, in the most convenient parts of it, and butchers we may be assured will not be wanting, although I rather recommend buy-

*average
†Rabelais
‡slaughter houses

ing the children alive, and dressing them hot from the knife, as we do roasting pigs.

A very worthy person, a true lover of his country, and whose virtues I highly esteem, was lately pleased, in discoursing on this matter, to offer a refinement upon my scheme. He said that many gentlemen of this kingdom, having of late destroyed their deer, he conceived that the want of venison might be well supplied by the bodies of young lads and maidens, not exeeding fourteen years of age, nor under twelve, so great a number of both sexes in every county being now ready to starve, for want of work and service: and these to be disposed of by their parents if alive, or otherwise by their nearest relations. But with due deference to so excellent a friend, and so deserving a patriot, I cannot be altogether in his sentiments. For as to the males, my American acquaintance assured me from frequent experience that their flesh was generally tough and lean, like that of our schoolboys, by continual exercise, and their taste disagreeable, and to fatten them would not answer the charge. Then as to the females, it would, I think with humble submission, be a loss to the public, because they soon would become breeders themselves: and besides, it is not improbable that some scrupulous people might be apt to censure such a practice (although indeed very unjustly) as a little bordering upon cruelty, which I confess, hath always been with me the strongest objection against any project, however well intended.

But in order to justify my friend, he confessed that this expedient was put into his head by the famous Psalmanazar,* a native of the island Formosa, who came from thence to London, above twenty years ago, and in conversation told my friend that in his country when any young person happened to be put to death, the executioner sold the carcass to persons of quality, as a prime dainty, and that, in his time, the body of a plump girl of fifteen, who was crucified for an attempt to poison the emperor, was sold to his Imperial Majesty's Prime Minister of State, and other great Mandarins of the Court, in joints from the gibbet, at four hundred crowns. Neither indeed can I deny that if the same use were made of several plump young girls in this town who, without one single groat to their fortunes, cannot stir abroad without a chair, and appear at the

---

*A French imposter, exposed shortly before Swift wrote.

playhouse and assemblies in foreign fineries, which they never will pay for, the kingdom would not be the worse.

Some persons of a desponding spirit are in great concern about that vast number of poor people, who are aged, diseased, or maimed, and I have been desired to employ my thoughts what course may be taken to ease the nation of so grievous an encumberance. But I am not in the least pain upon that matter, because it is very well known that they are every day dying, and rotting, by cold, and famine, and filth, and vermin, as fast as can be reasonably expected. And as to the younger labourers they are now in almost as hopeful a condition. They cannot get work, and consequently pine away from want of nourishment, to a degree that if at any time they are accidentally hired to common labour, they have not strength to perform it; and thus the country and themselves are in a fair way of being soon delivered from the evils to come.

I have too long digressed, and therefore shall return to my subject. I think the advantages by the proposal which I have made are obvious and many, as well as of the highest importance.

For first, as I have already observed, it would greatly lessen the number of Papists, with whom we are yearly over-run, being the principal breeders of the nation, as well as our most dangerous enemies, and who stay at home on purpose with a design to deliver the kingdom to the Pretender, hoping to take their advantage by the absence of so many good Protestants, who have chosen rather to leave their country than stay at home and pay tithes against their conscience to an idolatrous Episcopal curate.

Secondly, the poorer tenants will have something valuable of their own, which by law may be made liable to distress, and help to pay their landlord's rent, their corn and cattle being already seized, and money a thing unknown.

Thirdly, whereas the maintenance of an hundred thousand children, from two years old, and upwards, cannot be computed at less than ten shillings a piece *per annum,* the nation's stock will be thereby increased fifty thousand pounds *per annum,* besides the profit of a new dish, introduced to the tables of all gentlemen of fortune in the kingdom, who have any refinement in taste, and the money will circulate among ourselves, the goods being entirely of our own growth and manufacture.

Fourthly, the constant breeders, besides the gain of eight shillings sterling *per annum,* by the sale of their children, will be rid of the charge of maintaining them after the first year.

Fifthly, this food would likewise bring great custom to taverns, where the vintners will certainly be so prudent as to procure the best receipts for dressing it to perfection, and consequently have their houses frequented by all the fine gentlemen, who justly value themselves upon their knowledge in good eating; and a skilful cook, who understands how to oblige his guests, will contrive to make it as expensive as they please.

Sixthly, this would be a great inducement to marriage, which all wise nations have either encouraged by rewards, or enforced by laws and penalties. It would increase the care and tenderness of mothers toward their children, when they were sure of a settlement for life, to the poor babes, provided in some sort by the public to their annual profit instead of expense. We should soon see an honest emulation among the married women, which of them could bring the fattest child to the market. Men would become as fond of their wives, during the time of their pregnancy, as they are now of their mares in foal, their cows in calf, or sows when they are ready to farrow, nor offer to beat or kick them (as it is too frequent a practice) for fear of a miscarriage.

Many other advantages might be enumerated. For instance, the addition of some thousand carcasses in our exportation of barrelled beef; the propagation of swine's flesh, and improvement in the art of making good bacon, so much wanted among us by the great destruction of pigs, too frequent at our tables, are no way comparable in taste or magnificence to a well-grown, fat yearling child, which roasted whole will make a considerable figure at a Lord Mayor's feast, or any other public entertainment. But this and many others I omit, being studious of brevity.

Supposing that one thousand families in this city would be constant customers for infants' flesh, besides others who might have it at merry meetings, particularly weddings and christenings; I compute that Dublin would take off annually about twenty thousand carcasses, and the rest of the kingdom (where probably they will be sold somewhat cheaper) the remaining eighty thousand.

I can think of no objection that will possibly be raised against this proposal, unless it should be urged that the number of people will be thereby much lessened in the kingdom. This I freely own, and it was indeed one principal design in offering it to the world. I desire the reader will observe, that I calculate my remedy for this one individual Kingdom of IRELAND, and for no other that ever was, is, or, I think, ever can be upon earth. Therefore let no man talk to me of other expedients: *Of taxing our absentees at five shillings a pound: Of using neither clothes, nor household furniture, except what is of our own growth and manufacture: Of utterly rejecting the materials and instruments that promote foreign luxury: Of curing the expensiveness of pride, vanity, idleness, and gaming in our women: Of introducing a vein of parsimony, prudence, and temperance: Of learning to love our Country, wherein we differ even from* LAPLANDERS, *and the inhabitants of* TOPINAMBOO: *Of quitting our animosities and factions, nor act any longer like the Jews, who were murdering one another at the very moment their city was taken: Of being a little cautious not to sell our country and consciences for nothing: Of teaching landlords to have at least one degree of mercy towards their tenants.* Lastly, *of putting a spirit of honesty, industry, and skill into our shopkeepers, who, if a resolution could now be taken to buy only our native goods, would immediately unite to cheat and exact upon us in the price, the measure and the goodness, nor could ever yet be brought to make one fair proposal of just dealing, though often and earnestly invited to it.*

Therefore I repeat, let no man talk to me of these and the like expedients, till he hath at least a glimpse of hope that there will ever be some hearty and sincere attempt to put them in practice.

But as to myself, having been wearied out for many years with offering vain, idle, visionary thoughts, and at length utterly despairing of success, I fortunately fell upon this proposal, which as it is wholly new, so it hath something solid and real, of no expense and little trouble, full in our own power, and whereby we can incur no danger in disobliging ENGLAND. For this kind of commodity will not bear exportation, the flesh being of too tender a consistence to admit a long continuance in salt, although perhaps I could name a country which would be glad to eat up our whole nation without it.

After all I am not so violently bent upon my own opinion as to reject any offer, proposed by wise men, which shall be found equally innocent, cheap, easy, and effectual. But before something of that kind shall be advanced in contradiction to my scheme, and offering a better, I desire the author, or authors, will be pleased maturely to consider two points. First, as things now stand, how they will be able to find food and raiment for a hundred thousand useless mouths and backs? And secondly, there being a round million of creatures in human figure, throughout this kingdom, whose whole subsistence put into a common stock would leave them in debt two millions of pounds sterling; adding those who are beggars by profession, to the bulk of farmers, cottagers, and labourers with their wives and children, who are beggars in effect; I desire those politicians who dislike my overture, and may perhaps be so bold to attempt an answer, that they will first ask the parents of these mortals whether they would not at this day think it a great happiness to have been sold for food at a year old, in the manner I prescribe, and thereby have avoided such a perpetual scene of misfortunes as they have since gone through, by the oppression of landlords, the impossibility of paying rent without money or trade, the want of common sustenance, with neither house nor clothes to cover them from the inclemencies of weather, and the most inevitable prospect of entailing the like, or greater miseries upon their breed forever.

I profess in the sincerity of my heart that I have not the least personal interest in endeavouring to promote this necessary work, having no other motive than the public good of my country, by advancing our trade, providing for infants, relieving the poor, and giving some pleasure to the rich. I have no children by which I can propose to get a single penny; the youngest being nine years old, and my wife past child-bearing.

How Do You Respond?

1. How are we to take Swift and his "Modest Proposal"? "Seriously"? Why do you think so?
2. How would you characterize his tone? Is he serious? modest? angry? ironic? reasonable? Do you find his argument convincing? Why or why not?
3. Swift states his plan, digresses, and then returns to its six main advantages. What is the effect of this restatement? What other devices does Swift use in order to convince the reader?

GEORGE ORWELL

> "Politics and the English Language" (published in 1946) is perhaps Orwell's most famous essay. In it, he weds two of his passionate interests—language and politics, and probes their interrelationships. For biographical notes on Orwell, see pages 57 and 103.

POLITICS AND THE ENGLISH LANGUAGE

Most people who bother with the matter at all would admit that the English language is in a bad way, but it is generally assumed that we cannot by conscious action do anything about it. Our civilization is decadent and our language—so the argument runs—must inevitably share in the general collapse. It follows that any struggle against the abuse of language is a sentimental archaism, like preferring candles to electric light or hansom cabs to aeroplanes. Underneath this lies the half-conscious belief that language is a natural growth and not an instrument which we shape for our own purposes.

Now, it is clear that the decline of a language must ultimately have political and economic causes: it is not due simply to the bad influence of this or that individual writer. But an effect can become a cause, reinforcing the original cause and producing the same effect in an intensified form, and so on indefinitely. A man may take to drink because he feels himself to be a failure, and then fail all the more completely because he drinks. It is rather the same thing that is happening to the English language. It becomes ugly and inaccurate because our thoughts are foolish, but the slovenliness of our language makes it easier for us to have foolish thoughts. The point is that the process is reversible. Modern English, especially written English, is full of bad habits which spread by imitation and which can be avoided if one is willing to take the necessary trouble. If one gets rid of these habits one can think more clearly, and to think clearly is a necessary first step towards political regeneration: so that the fight against bad English is not frivolous and is not the exclusive concern of professional writers. I will come back to this presently, and I hope that by that time the meaning of what I have said here will have become clearer. Meanwhile, here are five specimens of the English language as it is now habitually written.

These five passages have not been picked out because they are especially bad—I could have quoted far worse if I had chosen—but because they illustrate various of the mental vices from which we now suffer. They are a little below the average, but are fairly representative samples. I number them so that I can refer back to them when necessary:

> (1) I am not, indeed, sure whether it is not true to say that the Milton who once seemed not unlike a seventeenth-century Shelley had not become, out of an experience ever more bitter in each year, more alien *(sic)* to the founder of that Jesuit sect which nothing could induce him to tolerate.
>
> Professor Harold Laski
> (Essay in *Freedom of Expression*)

> (2) Above all, we cannot play ducks and drakes with a native battery of idioms which prescribes such egregious collocations of vocables as the Basic *put up with* for *tolerate* or *put at a loss* for *bewilder*.
>
> Professor Lancelot Hogben (*Interglossa*)

> (3) On the one side we have the free personality: by definition it is not neurotic, for it has neither conflict nor dream. Its desires, such as they are, are transparent, for they are just what institutional approval keeps in the forefront of consciousness; another institutional pattern would alter their number and intensity, there is little in them that is natural, irreducible, or culturally dangerous. But *on the other side*, the social bond itself is nothing but the mutual reflection of these self-secure integrities. Recall the definition of love. Is not this the very picture of a small academic? Where is there a place in this hall of mirrors for either personality or fraternity?
>
> Essay on psychology in *Politics* (New York)

> (4) All the "best people" from the gentlemen's clubs, and all the frantic fascist captains, united in common hatred of Socialism and bestial horror of the rising tide of the mass revolution-

ary movement, have returned to acts of provocation, to foul incendiarism, to medieval legends of poisoned wells, to legalize their own destruction of proletarian organizations, and rouse the agitated petty-bourgeoisie to chauvinistic fervor on behalf of the fight against the revolutionary way out of the crisis.

COMMUNIST PAMPHLET

(5) If a new spirit is to be infused into this old country, there is one thorny and contentious reform which must be tackled, and that is the humanization and galvanization of the B.B.C. Timidity here will bespeak canker and atrophy of the soul. The heart of Britain may be sound and of strong beat, for instance, but the British lion's roar at present is like that of Bottom in Shakespeare's *Midsummer Night's Dream*—as gentle as any sucking dove. A virile new Britain cannot continue indefinitely to be traduced in the eyes, or rather ears, of the world by the effete languors of Langham Place, brazenly masquerading as "standard English." When the Voice of Britain is heard at nine o'clock, better far and infinitely less ludicrous to hear aitches honestly dropped than the present priggish, inflated, inhibited, school-ma'amish arch braying of blameless bashful mewing maidens!

LETTER IN *Tribune*

Each of these passages has faults of its own, but, quite apart from avoidable ugliness, two qualities are common to all of them. The first is staleness of imagery; the other is lack of precision. The writer either has a meaning and cannot express it, or he inadvertently says something else, or he is almost indifferent as to whether his words mean anything or not. This mixture of vagueness and sheer incompetence is the most marked characteristic of modern English prose, and especially of any kind of political writing. As soon as certain topics are raised, the concrete melts into the abstract and no one seems able to think of turns of speech that are not hackneyed: prose consists less and less of *words* chosen for the sake of their meaning, and more and more of *phrases* tacked together like the sections of a prefabricated hen-house. I list below, with notes and examples, various of the tricks by means of which the work of prose-construction is habitually dodged:

DYING METAPHORS

A newly invented metaphor assists thought by evoking a visual image, while on the other hand a metaphor which is technically "dead" (e.g. *iron resolution*) has in effect reverted to being an ordinary word and can generally be used without loss of vividness. But in between these two classes there is a huge dump of worn-out metaphors which have lost all evocative power and are merely used because they save people the trouble of inventing phrases for themselves. Examples are: *Ring the changes on, take up the cudgels for, toe the line, ride roughshod over, stand shoulder to shoulder with, play into the hands of, no axe to grind, grist to the mill, fishing in troubled waters, on the order of the day, Achilles' heel, swan song, hotbed.* Many of these are used without knowledge of their meaning (what is a "rift," for instance?), and incompatible metaphors are frequently mixed, a sure sign that the writer is not interested in what he is saying. Some metaphors now current have been twisted out of their original meaning without those who use them even being aware of the fact. For example, *toe the line* is sometimes written *tow the line*. Another example is *the hammer and the anvil*, now always used with the implication that the anvil gets the worst of it. In real life it is always the anvil that breaks the hammer, never the other way about: a writer who stopped to think what he was saying would be aware of this, and would avoid perverting the original phrase.

OPERATORS OR VERBAL FALSE LIMBS

These save the trouble of picking out appropriate verbs and nouns, and at the same time pad each sentence with extra syllables which give it an appearance of symmetry. Characteristic phrases are *render inoperative, militate against, make contact with, be subjected to, give rise to, give grounds for, have the effect of, play a leading part (role) in, make itself felt, take effect, exhibit a tendency to, serve the purpose of,* etc., etc. The keynote is the elimination of simple verbs. Instead of being a single word, such as *break, stop, spoil, mend, kill,* a verb becomes a *phrase,* made up of a noun or adjective tacked on to some general-purpose verb such as *prove, serve, form, play, render.* In addition, the passive voice is wherever possible used in preference to the active, and noun constructions are used instead of gerunds (*by examination of* instead of *by examin-*

ing). The range of verbs is further cut down by means of the *-ize* and *de-* formations, and the banal statements are given an appearance of profundity by means of the *not un-* formation. Simple conjunctions and prepositions are replaced by such phrases as *with respect to, having regard to, the fact that, by dint of, in view of, in the interests of, on the hypothesis that;* and the ends of sentences are saved from anticlimax by such resounding commonplaces as *greatly to be desired, cannot be left out of account, a development to be expected in the near future, deserving of serious consideration, brought to a satisfactory conclusion* and so on and so forth.

PRETENTIOUS DICTION

Words like *phenomenon, element, individual* (as noun), *objective, categorical, effective, virtual, basic, primary, promote, constitute, exhibit, exploit, utilize, eliminate, liquidate,* are used to dress up simple statements and give an air of scientific impartiality to biased judgments. Adjectives like *epoch-making, epic, historic, unforgettable, triumphant, age-old, inevitable, inexorable, veritable,* are used to dignify the sordid processes of international politics, while writing that aims at glorifying war usually takes on an archaic color, its characteristic words being: *realm, throne, chariot, mailed fist, trident, sword, shield, buckler, banner, jackboot, clarion.* Foreign words and expressions such as *cul de sac, ancien régime, deus ex machina, mutatis mutandis, status quo, gleichschaltung, weltanschauung,* are used to give an air of culture and elegance. Except for the useful abbreviations *i.e., e.g.,* and *etc.,* there is no real need for any of the hundreds of foreign phrases now current in English. Bad writers, and especially scientific, political and sociological writers, are nearly always haunted by the notion that Latin or Greek words are grander than Saxon ones, and unnecessary words like *expedite, ameliorate, predict, extraneous, deracinated, clandestine, subaqueous* and hundreds of others constantly gain ground from their Anglo-Saxon opposite numbers.* The jargon peculiar to Marx-

---

*An interesting illustration of this is the way in which the English flower names which were in use till very recently are being ousted by Greek ones, *snapdragon* becoming *antirrhinum*, *forget-me-not* becoming *myosotis*, etc. It is hard to see any practical reason for this change of fashion: it is probably due to an instinctive turning-away from the more homely word and a vague feeling that the Greek is scientific.

ist writing (*hyena, hangman, cannibal, petty bourgeois, these gentry, lacquey, flunkey, mad dog, White Guard,* etc.) consists largely of words and phrases translated from Russsian, German or French; but the normal way of coining a new word is to use a Latin or Greek root with the appropriate affix and, where necessary, the *-ize* formation. It is often easier to make up words of this kind (*deregionalize, impermissible, extramarital, non-fragmentary* and so forth) than to think up the English words that will cover one's meaning. The result, in general, is an increase in slovenliness and vagueness.

MEANINGLESS WORDS

In certain kinds of writing, particularly in art criticism and literary criticism, it is normal to come across long passages which are almost completely lacking in meaning.* Words like *romantic, plastic, values, human, dead, sentimental, natural, vitality,* as used in art criticism, are strictly meaningless, in the sense that they not only do not point to any discoverable object, but are hardly ever expected to do so by the reader. When one critic writes, "The outstanding feature of Mr. Xs work is its living quality," while another writes, "The immediately striking thing about Mr. X's work is its peculiar deadness," the reader accepts this as a simple difference of opinion. If words like *black* and *white* were involved, instead of the jargon words *dead* and *living,* he would see at once that language was being used in an improper way. Many political words are similarly abused. The word *Fascism* has now no meaning except in so far as it signifies "something not desirable." The words *democracy, socialism, freedom, patriotic, realistic, justice,* have each of them several different meanings which cannot be reconciled with one another. In the case of a word like *democracy,* not only is there no agreed definition, but the attempt to make one is resisted from all sides. It is almost universally felt that when we call a country

---

*Example: "Comfort's catholicity of perception and image, strangely Whitmanesque in range, almost the exact opposite in aesthetic compulsion, continues to evoke that trembling atmospheric accumulative hinting at a cruel, an inexorably serene timelessness. . . . Wrey Gardiner scores by aiming at simple bull's-eyes with precision. Only they are not so simple, and through his contented sadness runs more than the surface bitter-sweet of resignation." (*Poetry Quarterly.*)

democratic we are praising it: consequently the defenders of every kind of régime claim that it is a democracy, and fear that they might have to stop using the word if it were tied down to any one meaning. Words of this kind are often used in a consciously dishonest way. That is, the person who uses them has his own private definition, but allows his hearer to think he means something quite different. Statements like *Marshal Pétain was a true patriot, The Soviet Press is the freest in the world, The Catholic Church is opposed to persecution,* are almost always made with intent to deceive. Other words used in variable meanings, in most cases more or less dishonestly, are: *class, totalitarian, science, progressive, reactionary, bourgeois, equality.*

Now that I have made this catalogue of swindles and perversions, let me give another example of the kind of writing that they lead to. This time it must of its nature be an imaginary one. I am going to translate a passage of good English into modern English of the worst sort. Here is a well-known verse from *Eccelesiastes:*

> I returned and saw under the sun, that the race is not to the swift, nor the battle to the strong, neither yet bread to the wise, nor yet riches to men of understanding, nor yet favour to men of skill; but time and chance happeneth to them all.

Here it is in modern English:

> Objective consideration of contemporary phenomena compels the conclusion that success or failure in competitive activities exhibits no tendency to be commensurate with innate capacity, but that a considerable element of the unpredictable must invariably be taken into account.

This is a parody, but not a very gross one. Exhibit (3), above, for instance, contains several patches of the same kind of English. It will be seen that I have not made a full translation. The beginning and ending of the sentence follow the original meaning fairly closely, but in the middle the concrete illustrations—race, battle, bread—dissolve into the vague phrase "success or failure in competitive activities." This had to be so, because no modern writer of the kind I am discussing—no one capable of using phrases like "objective consideration of contemporary phenomena"—would ever tabulate his thoughts in that precise and detailed way. The whole tendency of modern prose is away from concreteness. Now analyse these two sentences a little more closely. The first contains forty-nine words but only sixty syllables, and all its words are those of everyday life. The second contains thirty-eight words of ninety syllables: eighteen of its words are from Latin roots, and one from Greek. The first sentence contains six vivid images, and only one phrase ("time and chance") that could be called vague. The second contains not a single fresh, arresting phrase, and in spite of its ninety syllables it gives only a shortened version of the meaning contained in the first. Yet without a doubt it is the second kind of sentence that is gaining ground in modern English. I do not want to exaggerate. This kind of writing is not yet universal, and outcrops of simplicity will occur here and there in the worst-written page. Still, if you or I were told to write a few lines on the uncertainty of human fortunes, we should probably come much nearer to my imaginary sentence than to the one from Ecclesiastes.

As I have tried to show, modern writing at its worst does not consist in picking out words for the sake of their meaning and inverting images in order to make the meaning clearer. It consists in gumming together long strips of words which have already been set in order by someone else, and making the results presentable by sheer humbug. The attraction of this way of writing is that it is easy. It is easier—even quicker, once you have the habit—to say *In my opinion it is not an unjustifiable assumption that* than to say *I think*. If you use ready-made phrases, you not only don't have to hunt about for words; you also don't have to bother with the rhythms of your sentences, since these phrases are generally so arranged as to be more or less euphonious. When you are composing in a hurry—when you are dictating to a stenographer, for instance, or making a public speech—it is natural to fall into a pretentious, Latinized style. Tags like *a consideration which we should do well to bear in mind* or *a conclusion to which all of us would readily assent* will save many a sentence from coming down with a bump. By using stale metaphors, similes, and idioms, you save much mental effort, at the cost of leaving your meaning vague, not only for your reader but for yourself. This is the significance of mixed metaphors. The sole aim of a metaphor is to call up a visual image.

When these images clash—as in *The Fascist octopus has sung its swan song, the jackboot is thrown into the melting pot*—it can be taken as certain that the writer is not seeing a mental image of the objects he is naming; in other words he is not really thinking. Look again at the examples I gave at the beginning of this essay. Professor Laski (1) uses five negatives in fifty-three words. One of these is superfluous, making nonsense of the whole passage, and in addition there is the slip *alien* for *akin,* making further nonsense, and several avoidable pieces of clumsiness which increase the general vagueness. Professor Hogben (2) plays ducks and drakes with a battery which is able to write prescriptions, and, while disapproving of the everyday phrase *put up with,* is unwilling to look *egregious* up in the dictionary and see what it means; (3), if one takes an uncharitable attitude towards it, is simply meaningless: probably one could work out its intended meaning by reading the whole of the article in which it occurs. In (4), the writer knows more or less what he wants to say, but an accumulation of stale phrases chokes him, like tea leaves blocking a sink. In (5), words and meaning have almost parted company. People who write in this manner usually have a general emotional meaning—they dislike one thing and want to express solidarity with another—but they are not interested in the detail of what they are saying. A scrupulous writer, in every sentence that he writes, will ask himself at least four questions, thus: What am I trying to say? What words will express it? What image or idiom will make it clearer? Is this image fresh enough to have an effect? And he will probably ask himself two more: Could I put it more shortly? Have I said anything that is avoidably ugly? But you are not obliged to go to all this trouble. You can shirk it by simply throwing your mind open and letting the ready-made phrases come crowding in. They will construct your sentences for you—even think your thoughts for you, to a certain extent—and at need they will perform the important service of partially concealing your meaning even from yourself. It is at this point that the special connection between politics and the debasement of language becomes clear.

In our time it is broadly true that political writing is bad writing. Where it is not true, it will generally be found that the writer is some kind of rebel, expressing his private opinions and not a "party line." Orthodoxy, of whatever color, seems to demand a lifeless, imitative style. The political dialects to be found in pamphlets, leading articles, manifestos, White Papers and the speeches of undersecretaries do, of course, vary from party to party, but they are all alike in that one almost never finds in them a fresh, vivid, home-made turn of speech. When one watches some tired hack on the platform mechanically repeating the familiar phrases—*bestial atrocities, iron heel, bloodstained tyranny, free peoples of the world, stand shoulder to shoulder*—one often has a curious feeling that one is not watching a live human being but some kind of dummy: a feeling which suddenly becomes stronger at moments when the light catches the speaker's spectacles and turns them into blank discs which seem to have no eyes behind them. And this is not altogether fanciful. A speaker who uses that kind of phraseology has gone some distance towards turning himself into a machine. The appropriate noises are coming out of his larynx, but his brain is not involved as it would be if he were choosing his words for himself. If the speech he is making is one that he is accustomed to make over and over again, he may be almost unconscious of what he is saying, as one is when one utters the responses in church. And this reduced state of consciousness, if not indispensable, is at any rate favorable to political conformity.

In our time, political speech and writing are largely the defence of the indefensible. Things like the continuance of British rule in India, the Russian purges and deportations, the dropping of the atom bombs on Japan, can indeed be defended, but only by arguments which are too brutal for most people to face, and which do not square with the professed aims of political parties. Thus political language has to consist largely of euphemism, question-begging, and sheer cloudy vagueness. Defenceless villages are bombarded from the air, the inhabitants driven out into the countryside, the cattle machine-gunned, the huts set on fire with incendiary bullets: this is called *pacification*. Millions of peasants are robbed of their farms and sent trudging along the roads with no more than they can carry: this is called *transfer of population* or *rectification of frontiers*. People are imprisoned for years without trial, or shot in the back of the neck, or sent to die of scurvy in Arctic lumber camps: this is called *elimination of unreliable elements*. Such phraseology is needed if one wants to name things without calling up mental pictures of them. Consider for instance some comfortable English professor defending Russian totalitarianism. He cannot say outright, "I believe in killing off your opponents when you can get good results by doing so." Probably, therefore, he will say something like this: "While freely conceding that the Soviet régime exhibits certain features which the humanitarian may be inclined to deplore, we must, I think, agree that a certain curtailment of the right to political opposition is an unavoidable concomitant of transitional periods, and that the rigors which the Russian people have been called upon to undergo have been amply justified in the sphere of concrete achievement."

The inflated style is itself a kind of euphemism. A mass of Latin words falls upon the facts like soft snow, blurring the outlines and covering up all the details. The great enemy of clear language is insincerity. When there is a gap between one's real and one's declared aims, one turns as it were instinctively to long words and exhausted idioms, like a cuttlefish squirting out ink. In our age there is no such thing as "keeping out of politics." All issues are political issues, and politics itself is a mass of lies, evasions, folly, hatred, and schizophrenia. When the general atmosphere is bad, language must suffer. I should expect to find—this is a guess which I have not sufficient knowledge to verify—that German, Russian, and Italian languages have all deteriorated in the last ten or fifteen years, as a result of dictatorship.

But if thought corrupts language, language can also corrupt thought. A bad usage can spread by tradition and imitation, even among people who should and do know better. The debased language that I have been discussing is in some ways very convenient. Phrases like *a not unjustifiable assumption, leaves much to be desired, would serve no good purpose, a consideration which we should do well to bear in mind*, are a continuous temptation, a packet of aspirins always at one's elbow. Look back through this essay, and for certain you will find that I have again and again committed the very faults I am protesting against. By this morning's post I have received a pamphlet dealing with conditions in Germany. The author tells me that he "felt impelled" to write it. I open it at random, and here is almost the first sentence that I see: "[The Allies] have an opportunity not only of achieving a radical transformation of Germany's social and political structure in such a way as to avoid a nationalistic reaction in Germany itself, but at the same time of laying the foundations of a co-operative and unified Europe." You see, he "feels impelled" to write—feels, presumably, that he has something new to say—and yet his words, like cavalry horses answering the bugle, group themselves automatically into the familiar dreary pattern. This invasion of one's mind by ready-made phrases (*lay the foundations, achieve a radical transformation*) can only be prevented if one is constantly on guard against them, and every such phrase anaesthetizes a portion of one's brain.

I said earlier that the decadence of our language is probably curable. Those who deny this would argue, if they produced an argument at all, that language merely reflects existing social conditions, and that we cannot influence its development by any direct tinkering with words and constructions. So far as the general tone or spirit of a language goes, this may be true, but it is not true in detail. Silly words and expressions have often disappeared, not through any evolutionary process but owing to the conscious action of a minority. Two recent examples were *explore every avenue* and *leave no stone unturned,* which were killed by the jeers of a few journalists. There is a long list of flyblown metaphors which could similarly be got rid of if enough people would interest themselves in the job; and it should also be possible to laugh the *not un-* formation out of existence,* to reduce the amount of Latin and Greek in the average sentence, to drive out foreign phrases and strayed scientific words, and, in general, to make pretentiousness unfashionable. But all these are minor points. The defence of the English language implies more than this, and perhaps it is best to start by saying what it does *not* imply.

To begin with it has nothing to do with archaism, with the salvaging of obsolete words and turns of speech, or with the setting up of a "standard English" which must never be departed from. On the contrary, it is especially concerned with the scrapping of every word or idiom which has outworn its usefulness. It has nothing to do with correct grammar and syntax, which are of no importance so long as one makes one's meaning clear, or with the avoidance of Americanisms, or with having what is called a "good prose style." On the other hand it is not concerned with fake simplicity and the

---

*One can cure oneself of the *not un-* formation by memorizing this sentence: *A not unblack dog was chasing a not unsmall rabbit across a not ungreen field.*

attempt to make written English colloquial. Nor does it even imply in every case preferring the Saxon word to the Latin one, though it does imply using the fewest and shortest words that will cover one's meaning. What is above all needed is to let the meaning choose the word, and not the other way about. In prose, the worst thing one can do with words is to surrender to them. When you think of a concrete object, you think wordlessly, and then, if you want to describe the thing you have been visualizing you probably hunt about till you find the exact words that seem to fit it. When you think of something abstract you are more inclined to use words from the start, and unless you make a conscious effort to prevent it, the existing dialect will come rushing in and do the job for you, at the expense of blurring or even changing your meaning. Probably it is better to put off using words as long as possible and get one's meaning as clear as one can through pictures or sensations. Afterwards one can choose—not simply accept—the phrases that will best cover the meaning, and then switch round and decide what impression one's words are likely to make on another person. This last effort of the mind cuts out all stale or mixed images, all prefabricated phrases, needless repetitions, and humbug and vagueness generally. But one can often be in doubt about the effect of a word or a phrase, and one needs rules that one can rely on when instinct fails. I think the following rules will cover most cases:

(i) Never use a metaphor, simile or other figure of speech which you are used to seeing in print.
(ii) Never use a long word where a short one will do.
(iii) If it is possible to cut a word out, always cut it out.
(iv) Never use the passive where you can use the active.
(v) Never use a foreign phrase, a scientific word or a jargon word if you can think of an everyday English equivalent.
(vi) Break any of these rules sooner than say anything outright barbarous.

These rules sound elementary, and so they are, but they demand a deep change of attitude in anyone who has grown used to writing in the style now fashionable. One could keep all of them and still write bad English, but one could not write the kind of stuff that I quoted in those five specimens at the beginning of this article.

I have not here been considering the literary use of language, but merely language as an instrument for expressing and not for concealing or preventing thought. Stuart Chase and others have come near to claiming that all abstract words are meaningless, and have used this as a pretext for advocating a kind of political quietism. Since you don't know what Fascism is, how can you struggle against Fascism? One need not swallow such absurdities as this, but one ought to recognize that the present political chaos is connected with the decay of language, and that one can probably bring about some improvement by starting at the verbal end. If you simplify your English, you are freed from the worst follies of orthodoxy. You cannot speak any of the necessary dialects, and when you make a stupid remark its stupidity will be obvious, even to yourself. Political language—and with variations this is true of all political parties, from Conservatives to Anarchists—is designed to make lies sound truthful and murder respectable, and to give an appearance of solidity to pure wind. One cannot change this all in a moment, but one can at least change one's own habits, and from time to time one can even, if one jeers loudly enough, send some worn-out and useless phrase—some *jackboot, Achilles' heel, hotbed, melting pot, acid test, veritable inferno* or other lump of verbal refuse—into the dustbin where it belongs.

How Do You Respond?

1. Orwell claims that "an effect can become a cause, reinforcing the original cause and producing the same effect in an intensified form, and so on indefinitely." What are the causes and what are the effects: how does language affect politics, and how does politics affect language?

2. Sort out Orwell's arguments: what are his assertions? How does he support them?

3. How would you characterize his tone? Compare his approach with some present-day language critics—such as Bernstein, Newman, Safire, Simon.

EDGAR ALLAN POE

> "Father of the American short story" and "Father of the modern detective story" are two of the titles often bestowed upon Edgar Allan Poe (1809–1849). Once we read Poe's short stories, like "The Tell-Tale Heart," "The Cask of Amontillado," "The Fall of the House of Usher," and his poems, "The Raven," "Ulalume," and "Annabel Lee," we are not likely to forget the haunting melancholy, the mystery, the music of Poe's lines. He deserves to be read aloud—but not late at night.

THE TELL-TALE HEART

True!—nervous—very, very dreadfully nervous I had been and am; but why *will* you say that I am mad? The disease had sharpened my senses—not destroyed—not dulled them. Above all was the sense of hearing acute. I heard all things in the heaven and in the earth. I heard many things in hell. How, then, am I mad? Hearken! and observe how healthily—how calmly I can tell you the whole story.

It is impossible to say how first the idea entered my brain; but once conceived, it haunted me day and night. Object there was none. Passion there was none. I loved the old man. He had never wronged me. He had never given me insult. For his gold I had no desire. I think it was his eye! Yes, it was this! He had the eye of a vulture—a pale blue eye, with a film over it. Whenever it fell upon me, my blood ran cold; and so by degrees—very gradually—I made up my mind to take the life of the old man, and thus rid myself of the eye forever.

Now this is the point. You fancy me mad. Madmen know nothing. But you should have seen *me*. You should have seen how wisely I proceeded—with what caution—with what foresight—with what dissimulation I went to work! I was never kinder to the old man than during the whole week before I killed him. And every night, about midnight, I turned the latch of his door and opened it—oh so gently! And then, when I had made an opening sufficient for my head, I put in a dark lantern, all closed, closed, so that no light shone out, and then I thrust in my head. Oh, you would have laughed to see how cunningly I thrust it in! I moved it slowly—very, very slowly, so that I might not disturb the old man's sleep. It took me an hour to place my whole head within the opening so far that I could see him as he lay upon his bed. Ha!—would a madman have been so wise as this? And then, when my head was well in the room, I undid the lantern cautiously—oh, so cautiously—cautiously (for the hinges creaked)—I undid it just so much that a single thin ray fell upon the vulture eye. And this I did for seven long nights—every night just at midnight—but I found the eye always closed; and so it was impossible to do the work; for it was not the old man who vexed me, but his Evil Eye. And every morning, when the day broke, I went boldly into the chamber, and spoke courageously to him, calling him by name in a hearty tone, and inquiring how he had passed the night. So you see he would have been a very profound old man, indeed, to suspect that every night, just at twelve, I looked in upon him while he slept.

Upon the eighth night I was more than usually cautious in opening the door. A watch's minute hand moves more quickly than did mine. Never before that night, had I *felt* the extent of my own powers—of my sagacity. I could scarcely contain my feelings of triumph. To think that there I was, opening the door, little by little, and he not even to dream of my secret deeds or thoughts. I fairly chuckled at the idea; and perhaps he heard me; for he moved on the bed suddenly, as if startled. Now you may think that I drew back—but no. His room was as black as pitch with the thick darkness, (for the shutters were close fastened, through fear of robbers,) and so I knew that he could not see the opening of the door, and I kept pushing it on steadily, steadily.

I had my head in, and was about to open the lantern, when my thumb slipped upon the tin fastening, and the old man sprang up in bed, crying out—"Who's there?"

I kept quite still and said nothing. For a whole hour I did not move a muscle, and in the meantime I did not hear him lie down. He was still sitting up in bed listening;—just as I have done, night after night, hearkening to the death watches in the wall.

Presently I heard a slight groan, and I knew it was the groan of mortal terror. It was not a groan of pain or of grief—oh, no!—it was the low stifled sound that arises from the bottom of the soul when overcharged with awe. I knew the sound well. Many a night, just at midnight, when all the world slept, it has welled up from my own bosom, deepening, with its dreadful echo, the terrors that distracted me. I say I knew it well. I knew what the old man felt, and pitied him, although I chuckled at heart. I knew that he had been lying awake ever since the first slight noise, when he had turned in the bed. His fears had been ever since growing upon him. He had been trying to fancy them causeless, but could not. He had been saying to himself—"It is nothing but the wind in the chimney—it is only a mouse crossing the floor," or "it is merely a cricket which has made a single chirp." Yes, he had been trying to comfort himself with these suppositions: but he had found all in vain. *All in vain;* because Death, in approaching him had stalked with his black shadow before him, and enveloped the victim. And it was the mournful influence of the unperceived shadow that caused him to feel—although he neither saw nor heard—to *feel* the presence of my head within the room.

When I had waited a long time, very patiently, without hearing him lie down, I resolved to open a little—a very, very little crevice in the lantern. So I opened it—you cannot imagine how stealthily, stealthily—until, at length, a simple dim ray, like the thread of the spider, shot from out the crevice and fell full upon the vulture eye.

It was open—wide, wide open—and I grew furious as I gazed upon it. I saw it with perfect distinctness—all a dull blue, with a hideous veil over it that chilled the very marrow in my bones; but I could see nothing else of the old man's face or person: for I had directed the ray as if by instinct, precisely upon the damned spot.

And have I not told you that what you mistake for madness is but over acuteness of the senses?—now, I say, there came to my ears a low, dull, quick sound, such as a watch makes when enveloped in cotton. I knew *that* sound well, too. It was the beating of the old man's heart. It increased my fury, as the beating of a drum stimulates the soldier into courage.

But even yet I refrained and kept still. I scarcely breathed. I held the lantern motionless. I tried how steadily I could maintain the ray upon the eye. Meantime the hellish tattoo of the heart increased. It grew quicker and quicker, and louder and louder every instant. The old man's terror *must* have been extreme! It grew louder, I say, louder every moment!—do you mark me well? I have told you that I am nervous: so I am. And now at the dead hour of the night, amid the dreadful silence of that old house, so strange a noise as this excited me to uncontrollable terror. Yet, for some minutes longer I refrained and stood still. But the beating grew louder, louder! I thought the heart must burst. And now a new anxiety seized me—the sound would be heard by a neighbour! The old man's hour had come! With a loud yell, I threw open the lantern and leaped into the room. He shrieked once—only once. In an instant I dragged him to the floor, and pulled the heavy bed over him. I then smiled gaily, to find the deed so far done. But, for many minutes, the heart beat on with a muffled sound. This, however, did not vex me; it would not be heard through the wall. At length it ceased. The old man was dead. I removed the bed and examined the corpse. Yes, he was stone, stone dead. I placed my hand upon the heart and held it there many minutes. There was no pulsation. He was stone dead. His eye would trouble me no more.

If still you think me mad, you will think so no longer when I describe the wise precautions I took for the concealment of the body. The night waned, and I worked hastily, but in silence. First of all I dismembered the corpse. I cut off the head and the arms and legs.

I then took up three planks from the flooring of the chamber, and deposited all between the scantlings. I then replaced the boards so cleverly, so cunningly, that no human eye—not even his—could have detected any thing wrong. There was nothing to wash out—no stain of any kind—no blood-spot whatever. I had been too wary for that. A tub had caught all—ha! ha!

When I had made an end of these labors, it was four o'clock—still dark as midnight. As the bell sounded the hour, there came a knocking at the street door. I went down to open it with a light heart,—for what had I now to fear? There entered three men, who introduced themselves, with perfect suavity, as officers of the police. A shriek had been heard by a neighbour during the night; suspicion of foul play had been aroused; information had been lodged at the police office, and they (the officers) had been deputed to search the premises.

I smiled,—for *what* had I to fear? I bade the gentlemen welcome. The shriek, I said, was my own in a dream. The old man, I mentioned, was absent in the country. I took my visitors all over the house. I bade them search—search *well*. I led them, at length, to *his* chamber. I showed them his treasures, secure, undisturbed. In the enthusiasm of my confidence, I brought chairs into the room, and desired them *here* to rest from their fatigues, while I myself, in the wild audacity of my perfect triumph, placed my own seat upon the very spot beneath which reposed the corpse of the victim.

The officers were satisfied. My *manner* had convinced them. I was singularly at ease. They sat, and while I answered cheerily, they chatted of familiar things. But, ere long, I felt myself getting pale and wished them gone. My head ached, and I fancied a ringing in my ears: but still they sat and still chatted. The ringing became more distinct:—it continued and became more distinct: I talked more freely to get rid of the feeling: but it continued and gained definiteness—until, at length, I found that the noise was *not* within my ears.

No doubt I now grew *very* pale;—but I talked more fluently, and with a heightened voice. Yet the sound increased—and what could I do? It was *a low, dull, quick sound—much such a sound as a watch makes when enveloped in cotton*. I gasped for breath—and yet the officers heard it not. I talked more quickly—more vehemently; but the noise steadily increased. I arose and argued about trifles, in a high key and with violent gesticulations; but the noise steadily increased. Why *would* they not be gone? I paced the floor to and fro with heavy strides, as if excited to fury by the observations of the men—but the noise steadily increased. Oh God! what *could* I do? I foamed—I raved—I swore! I swung the chair upon which I had been sitting, and grated it upon the boards, but the noise arose over all and continually increased. It grew louder—louder—*louder!* And still the men chatted pleasantly, and smiled. Was it possible they heard not? Almighty God!—no, no! They heard!—they suspected!—they *knew!*—they were making a mockery of my horror—this I thought, and this I think. But anything was better than this agony! Anything was more tolerable than this derision! I could bear those hypocritical smiles no longer! I felt that I must scream or die! and now—again!—hark! louder! louder! louder! *louder!* "Villians!" I shrieked, "dissemble no more! I admit the deed!—tear up the planks! here, here!—it is the beating of his hideous heart!"

How Do You Respond?

1. In Poe's famous short story, the narrator is arguing with the reader. What is he or she trying to convince us of? Are we convinced? Why?
2. How would you characterize the tone of the narrator? Would the narrator agree with your characterization?
3. What does the framework of argument add to the narrative?

TONI MORRISON

> *Author of several novels*—The Bluest Eye, Sula, The Black Book, Song of Solomon—*Toni Morrison (born 1931) writes always about the same thing, she says, "which is how people relate to one another and miss it or hang onto it . . . about love and how to survive—not to make a living—but how to survive whole in a world where we are all of us, in some measure, victims of something." The following piece is adapted from her commencement address at Barnard College.*

CINDERELLA'S STEPSISTERS

Let me begin by taking you back a little. Back before the days at college. To nursery school, probably, to a once-upon-a-time time when you first heard, or read, or, I suspect, even saw "Cinderella." Because it is Cinderella that I want to talk about; because it is Cinderella who causes me a feeling of urgency. What is unsettling about that fairy tale is that it is essentially the story of a household—a world, if you please—of women gathered together and held together in order to abuse another woman. There is, of course, a rather vague absent father and a nick-of-time prince with a foot fetish. But neither has much personality. And there are the surrogate "mothers," of course (god- and step-), who contribute both to Cinderella's grief and to her release and happiness. But it is her stepsisters who interest me. How crippling it must have been for those young girls to grow up with a mother, to watch and imitate that mother, enslaving another girl.

I am curious about their fortunes after the story ends. For contrary to recent adaptations, the stepsisters were not ugly, clumsy, stupid girls with outsize feet. The Grimm collection describes them as "beautiful and fair in appearance." When we are introduced to them they are beautiful, elegant, women of status, and clearly women of power. Having watched and participated in the violent dominion of another woman, will they be any less cruel when it comes their turn to enslave other children, or even when they are required to take care of their own mother?

It is not a wholly medieval problem. It is quite a contemporary one: feminine power when directed at other women has historically been wielded in what has been described as a "masculine" manner. Soon you will be in a position to do the very same thing. Whatever your background—rich or poor—whatever the history of education in your family—five generations or one—you have taken advantage of what has been available to you at Barnard and you will therefore have both the economic and social status of the stepsisters *and* you will have their power.

I want not to *ask* you but to *tell* you not to participate in the oppression of your sisters. Mothers who abuse their children are women, and another woman, not an agency, has to be willing to stay their hands. Mothers who set fire to school buses are women, and another woman, not an agency, has to tell them to stay their hands. Women who stop the promotion of other women in careers are women, and another woman must come to the victim's aid. Social and welfare workers who humiliate their clients may be women, and other women colleagues have to deflect their anger.

I am alarmed by the violence that women do to each other: professional violence, competitive violence, emotional violence. I am alarmed by the willingness of women to enslave other women. I am alarmed by a growing absence of decency on the killing floor of professional women's worlds. You are the women who will take your place in the world where *you* can decide who shall flourish and who shall wither; you will make distinctions between the deserving poor and the undeserving poor; where you can yourself determine which life is expendable and which is indispensable. Since you will have the power to do it, you may also be persuaded that you have the right to do it. As educated women the distinction between the two is first-order business.

I am suggesting that we pay as much attention to our nurturing sensibilities as to our ambition. You are moving in the direction of freedom and the function of freedom is to free somebody else. You are moving toward self-fulfillment, and the consequences of that fulfillment should be to discover that there is something just as important as you are and that just-as-important thing may be Cinderella—or your stepsister.

In your rainbow journey toward the realization of personal goals, don't make choices based only on your security and your safety. Nothing is safe. That is not to say that anything ever was, or that anything worth achieving ever should be. Things of value seldom are. It is not safe to have a child. It is not safe to challenge the status quo. It is not safe to choose work that has not been done before. Or to do old work in a new way. There will always be someone there to stop you. But in pursuing your highest ambitions, don't let your personal safety diminish the safety of your stepsister. In wielding the power that is deservedly yours, don't permit it to enslave your stepsisters. Let your might and your power emanate from that place in you that is nurturing and caring.

Women's rights is not only an abstraction, a cause; it is also a personal affair. It is not only about "us"; it is also about me and you. Just the two of us.

How Do You Respond?

1. How does Morrison use the Cinderella tale to comment on contemporary women? What is the problem as she sees it?

2. What does Morrison believe should be done about the problem? Do you believe that there is a problem? Morrison spoke in 1979. Have things changed since then?

3. Who do you think is Morrison's audience? What assumptions does she make about her audience?

MARTIN LUTHER KING

The Nobel Peace Prize of 1964 was awarded to Martin Luther King, Jr., (1929–1968) for his contributions, as leader of the American civil rights movement, to peace and understanding among races. Four years later, he died violently by an assassin's hand in Memphis, Tennessee, where he had gone to support a strike of garbage collectors. In his many writings, his "Letter from Birmingham Jail," his Why We Can't Wait, *his speech, "I Have a Dream," given on the one hundredth anniversary of Lincoln's Gettyburg Address, King is the eloquent voice of peaceful resistance to those conditions that oppress America's minorities.*

I HAVE A DREAM

Five score years ago, a great American, in whose symbolic shadow we stand, signed the Emancipation Proclamation. This momentous decree came as a great beacon light of hope to millions of Negro slaves who had been seared in the flames of withering injustice. It came as a joyous daybreak to end the long night of captivity.

But one hundred years later, we must face the tragic fact that the Negro is still not free. One hundred years later, the life of the Negro is still sadly crippled by the manacles of segregation and the chains of discrimination. One hundred years later, the Negro lives on a lonely island of poverty in the midst of a vast ocean of material prosperity. One hundred years later, the Negro is still languishing in the corners of American society and finds himself an exile in his own land. So we have come here today to dramatize an appalling condition.

In a sense we have come to our nation's Capitol to cash a check. When the architects of our republic wrote the magnificent words of the Constitution and the Declaration of Independence, they were signing a promissory note to which every American was to fall heir. This note was a promise that all men would be guaranteed the unalienable rights of life, liberty, and the pursuit of happiness.

It is obvious today that America has defaulted on this promissory note insofar as her citizens of color are concerned. Instead of honoring this sacred obligation, America has given the Negro people a bad check; a check which has come back marked "insufficient funds." But we refuse to believe that the bank of justice is bankrupt. We refuse to believe that there are insufficient funds in the great vaults of opportunity of this nation. So we have come to cash this check—a check that will give us upon demand the riches of freedom and the security of justice. We have also come to this hallowed spot to remind America of the fierce urgency of *now*. This is no time to engage in the luxury of cooling off or to take the tranquilizing drug of gradualism. *Now* is the time to make real the promises of Democracy. *Now* is the time to rise from the dark and desolate valley of segregation to the sunlit path of racial justice. *Now* is the time to open the doors of opportunity to all of God's children. *Now* is the time to lift our nation from the quicksands of racial injustice to the solid rock of brotherhood.

It would be fatal for the nation to overlook the urgency of the moment and to underestimate the determination of the Negro. This sweltering summer of the Negro's legitimate discontent will not pass until there is an invigorating autumn of freedom and equality. 1963 is not an end, but a beginning. Those who hope that the Negro needed to blow off steam and will now be content will have a rude awakening if the nation returns to business as usual. There will be neither rest nor tranquility in America until the Negro is granted his citizenship rights. The whirlwinds of revolt will continue to shake the foundations of our nation until the bright day of justice emerges.

But there is something I must say to my people who stand on the warm threshold which leads into the palace of justice. In the process of gaining our rightful place we must not be guilty of wrongful deeds. Let us not seek to satisfy our thirst for freedom by drinking from the cup of bitterness and hatred. We must forever conduct our struggle on the high plane of dignity and discipline. We must not allow our creative protest to degenerate into physical violence. Again and again we must rise to the majestic heights of meeting physical force with soul force. The marvelous new militancy which has engulfed the Negro community must not lead us to a distrust of all white people, for many of our white brothers, as evidenced by their presence here today, have come to realize that their destiny is tied up with our destiny and their freedom is inextricably bound to our freedom. We cannot walk alone.

And as we walk, we must make the pledge that we shall march

ahead. We cannot turn back. There are those who are asking the devotees of civil rights, "When will you be satisfied?" We can never be satisfied as long as the Negro is the victim of the unspeakable horrors of police brutality. We can never be satisfied as long as our bodies, heavy with the fatigue of travel, cannot gain lodging in the motels of the highways and the hotels of the cities. We cannot be satisfied as long as the Negro's basic mobility is from a smaller ghetto to a larger one. We can never be satisfied as long as a Negro in Mississippi cannot vote and a Negro in New York believes he has nothing for which to vote. No, no, we are not satisfied, and we will not be satisfied until justice rolls down like waters and righteousness like a mighty stream.

I am not unmindful that some of you have come here out of great trials and tribulations. Some of you have come fresh from narrow jail cells. Some of you have come from areas where your quest for freedom left you battered by the storms of persecution and staggered by the winds of police brutality. You have been the veterans of creative suffering. Continue to work with the faith that unearned suffering is redemptive.

Go back to Mississippi, go back to Alabama, go back to South Carolina, go back to Georgia, go back to Louisiana, go back to the slums and ghettoes of our northern cities, knowing that somehow this situation can and will be changed. Let us not wallow in the valley of despair.

I say to you today, my friends, that in spite of the difficulties and frustrations of the moment I still have a dream. It is a dream deeply rooted in the American dream.

I have a dream that one day this nation will rise up and live out the true meaning of its creed: "We hold these truths to be self-evident; that all men are created equal."

I have a dream that one day on the red hills of Georgia the sons of former slaves and the sons of former slave-owners will be able to sit down together at the table of brotherhood.

I have a dream that the state of Mississippi, a desert state sweltering with the heat of injustice and oppression, will be transformed into an oasis of freedom and justice.

I have a dream that my four little children will one day live in a nation where they will not be judged by the color of their skin but by the content of their character.

I have a dream today.

I have a dream that the state of Alabama, whose governor's lips are presently dripping with the words of interposition and nullification, will be transformed into a situation where little black boys and black girls will be able to join hands with little white boys and white girls and walk together as sisters and brothers.

I have a dream today.

I have a dream that one day every valley shall be exalted, every hill and mountain shall be made low, the rough places will be made plain, and the crooked places will be made straight, and the glory of the Lord shall be revealed, and all flesh shall see it together.

This is our hope. This is the faith with which I return to the South. With this faith we will be able to hew out of the mountain of despair a stone of hope. With this faith we will be able to transform the jangling discords of our nation into a beautiful symphony of brotherhood. With this faith we will be able to work together, to pray together, to struggle together, to go to jail together, to stand up for freedom together, knowing that we will be free one day.

This will be the day when all of God's children will be able to sing with new meaning:

> My country, 'tis of thee
> Sweet land of liberty
>   Of thee I sing:
> Land where my fathers died,
> Land of the pilgrims' pride,
> From every mountainside
>   Let freedom ring.

And if America is to be a great nation this must become true. So let freedom ring from the prodigious hilltops of New Hampshire. Let freedom ring from the heightening Alleghenies of Pennsylvania!

Let freedom ring from the snowcapped Rockies of Colorado!

Let freedom ring from the curvaceous peaks of California!

But not only that; let freedom ring from Stone Mountain of Georgia!

Let freedom ring from every hill and molehill of Mississippi. From every mountainside, let freedom ring.

When we let freedom ring, when we let it ring from every village and every hamlet, from every state and every city, we will be able to speed up that day when all of God's children, black men and white men, Jews and Gentiles, Protestants and Catholics, will be able to join hands and sing in the words of the old Negro spiritual, "Free at last! free at last! thank God almighty, we are free at last!"

How Do You Respond?

1. King's "I Have a Dream" is a record of a delivered speech. To hear King's rhythms, cadences, and dynamics—the power of his words—read the speech aloud. What is lost, or gained, in the translation to writing?

2. What is King's argument? What does he want? To what extent does he imply or propose a program? What effect does he want to cause in his hearers?

3. Earlier in this book, E. B. White discussed the power of the spoken word to move people; in this chapter, George Orwell condemns the corruption of political language. How do you think that King's speech measures up to the standards of these stern critics?

FOCUS ON YOUR READING

1. Observe the contrast between the way the Boston Marathon used to be and the way it is now, according to Art Carey. Note how the author laments the passing of the marathon as a "great American folk celebration" and shows us what it has become. How does this essential move between the way things were and the way things are now infuse other selections in this chapter?

2. Margaret Mead insists that there are many things in our society that could be done by old people. She argues that things *should* be different. Identify the places in the selections where you see an explicit statement that things *should* be different.

3. Ellen Goodman begins "Protection from the Prying Camera" inductively, with examples of what she has observed. Does she lead to a specific assertion? A plan? Observe how Goodman and the other writers in this chapter shape their essays—whether they move inductively or deductively.

4. Notice how Orwell defines and exemplifies each of his terms in "Politics and the English Language." Observe how each of the writers in this chapter support an argument—by narrating, describing, showing causes and effects, defining, exemplifying.

FOCUS ON YOUR WRITING

1. Follow the structure of Martin Luther King's argument, "I Have a Dream," and write your own essay about a social or political situation that you would like to see changed. "I have a dream" that there will be no more war, that all men and women will be equal, that cars will be banned from the city streets.

2. Write your own version of Robert Paul Smith's "Let Your Kids Alone," either extending his argument or disputing it (Don't Let Your Kids Alone). Or take another point of view: "Kids, let your parents alone."

3. Agree or disagree with Lewis Thomas's assertion that we learn by making mistakes. Draw on your own experience in learning to drive a car or play a musical instrument or work a computer, etc.

4. Write an essay following the pattern of "The Boston Marathon: Passing of an American Pastime," showing how something small has been transformed into something large. Has there been loss or gain? Were things better the old way?

5. Write an essay where you argue for or against the elderly being a vital part of American society. You may try a satiric approach, as Swift does in "A Modest Proposal."

KEEPING YOUR JOURNAL

1. Ellen Goodman in "Protection from the Prying Camera" questions the loss of personal privacy when we are "allowed to point cameras at each other." Where do you stand on this issue? Record in your journal your perceptions of the gains and losses that result from use of the "prying camera."

2. Margaret Mead says that grandparents have "copped out" because they do not think about what they can do for the young. Is Mead right, do you think, in putting the blame on the elderly? What about the young and their inability to ask the elderly to be a part of their lives? Write in your journal about your position on this issue.

3. Lewis Thomas urges us not to worry about computers, to "give computers their heads," to "let them go their way." What does he mean by this? Is he arguing that we let computers run the world? Record your opinions in your journal.

4. Have you observed in the language all about you the dying metaphors, meaningless words, pretentious diction that Orwell discusses in "Politics and the English Language"? Reserve a place in your notebook to record words and phrases that reflect Orwell's charge that the English language is in a bad way.

THEMATIC TABLE OF CONTENTS
❖ ❖ ───────────────────────────────

1. People
2. Places
3. Nature
4. Childhood and Adolescence
5. School and Education
6. War and Politics
7. Writing and Language
8. Race and Culture
9. Sex and Feminism
10. The Individual and Society
11. Science and Technology
12. Sports and Recreation
13. Death and Dying
14. Short Stories

PEOPLE

James Thurber, "The Unicorn in the Garden," Chapter 3
Philip Slater, "A Modern Fable," Chapter 3
Maxine Hong Kingston, from "No Name Woman," Chapter 3
Pearl Rowe, "Cookies at Midnight," Chapter 3
Ernest Hemingway, "Hills Like White Elephants," Chapter 3
Richard Wright, "The Ethics of Living Jim Crow," Chapter 3
Grace Paley, "Wants," Chapter 3
Kate Chopin, "Story of an Hour," Chapter 4
Tillie Olsen, "I Stand Here Ironing," Chapter 5
David Bird, "Two Homeless Persons Adrift in Grand Central," Chapter 6
Barbara Meyer, "Death Gives Life to Fond Memories," Chapter 6
Richard Selzer, "The Masked Marvel's Last Toehold," Chapter 6
Joan Didion, "Some Dreamers of the Golden Dream," Chapter 6
William Faulkner, "A Rose for Emily," Chapter 6

Thematic Table of Contents 505

Ira Berkow, "Louis Had Style In and Out of the Ring," Chapter 8
David Marcus, "An Older Brother Lets Go," Chapter 6
Ring Lardner, "Mr. and Mrs. Fix-It," Chapter 8
Joe McGinness, "The Village," Chapter 9
Flannery O'Connor, "Everything That Rises Must Converge," Chapter 9
Don Bauer, "Wartime in Korea," Chapter 9
Edgar Allan Poe, "The Tell-Tale Heart," Chapter 10

PLACES

George Orwell, "A Hanging," Chapter 3
Alfred Kazin, "The Kitchen," Chapter 6
N. Scott Momaday, "The Way to Rainy Mountain," Chapter 6
Joan Didion, "Some Dreamers of the Golden Dream," Chapter 6
Russell Baker, "Summer Beyond Wish," Chapter 8
Joe McGinniss, "The Village," Chapter 9
Art Carey, "The Boston Marathon: Passing of an American Pastime," Chapter 10

NATURE

Dorothy Wordsworth, from *Journals*, Chapter 2
Henry David Thoreau, from *Selected Journals*, Chapter 2
Echo and Narcissus, Chapter 3
North Wind and the Sun, Chapter 3
Jean John, "The How-to of Terrariums," Chapter 4
N. Scott Momaday, "The Way to Rainy Mountain," Chapter 6
Russell Baker, "Summer Beyond Wish," Chapter 8
Loren Eiseley, "The Long Loneliness," Chapter 9
George Orwell, "Some Thoughts on the Common Toad," Chapter 4

CHILDHOOD AND ADOLESCENCE

Anne Frank, from *The Diary of a Young Girl*, Chapter 2
Maxine Hong Kingston, "No Name Woman," Chapter 3
Pearl Rowe, "Cookies at Midnight," Chapter 3
Richard Wright, "The Ethics of Living Jim Crow," Chapter 3

———————"My Library Card," Chapter 5
Tillie Olsen, "I Stand Here Ironing," Chapter 5
Selma Fraiberg, "Why Does a Baby Smile?" Chapter 5
Barbara Meyer, "Death Gives Life to Fond Memories," Chapter 6
David Marcus, "An Older Brother Lets Go," Chapter 8
Russell Baker, "Summer Beyond Wish," Chapter 8
Mary McCarthy, "Names," Chapter 8
Robert Paul Smith, "Let Your Kids Alone," Chapter 10
Ellen Willis, "Memoirs of a Non-Prom Queen," Chapter 5

WRITING AND LANGUAGE

Virginia Woolf, from "A Writer's Diary," Chapter 2
Muriel Rukeyser, "The Process of Writing a Poem," Chapter 4
Russell Baker, "American Fat," Chapter 7
Claude Brown, "Soul Language," Chapter 7
Robin Lakoff, "You Are What You Say," Chapter 7
William Safire, "I Led the Pigeons to the Flag," Chapter 8
Loren Eiseley, "The Long Loneliness," Chapter 9
George Orwell, "Politics and the English Language," Chapter 10

SCHOOL AND EDUCATION

Richard Wright, "My Library Card," Chapter 5
John Holt, "How Teachers Make Children Hate Reading," Chapter 5
Russell Baker, "School vs. Education," Chapter 9
Nora Ephron, "Reunion," Chapter 9
Robert Paul Smith, "Let Your Kids Alone," Chapter 10

WAR AND POLITICS

George Orwell, "A War-time Diary," Chapter 2
———————"A Hanging," Chapter 3
———————"Some Thoughts on the Common Toad," Chapter 4
———————"Politics and the English Language," Chapter 10
Dick Gregory, "Farewell to Food," Chapter 4
Abraham Lincoln, "The Gettysburg Address," Chapter 5

E. B. White, "Freedom," Chapter 7
Kurt Vonnegut, Jr., "Harrison Bergeron," Chapter 7
Don Bauer, "War-time in Korea," Chapter 9
Jonathan Swift, "A Modest Proposal," Chapter 10
Martin Luther King, Jr., "I Have a Dream," Chapter 10

RACE AND CULTURE

Philip Slater, "A Modern Fable," Chapter 3
Maxine Hong Kingston, "No-Name Woman," Chapter 3
Richard Wright, "The Ethics of Living Jim Crow," Chapter 3
—————"My Library Card," Chapter 5
George Orwell, "A Hanging," Chapter 3
Dick Gregory, "A Farewell to Food," Chapter 4
Tom Wolfe, "The Sexed-Up, Doped-Up, Hedonistic Heaven of the Boom-Boom '70s," Chapter 4
Alvin and Heidi Toffler, "The Changing American Family," Chapter 4
Joan Didion, "Some Dreamers of the Golden Dream," Chapter 6
William Faulkner, "A Rose for Emily," Chapter 6
Joe McGinniss, "The Village," Chapter 9
Flannery O'Connor, "Everything That Rises Must Converge," Chapter 9
Margaret Mead, "Grandparents Have Copped Out," Chapter 10
Elisabeth Kübler-Ross, "The Fear of Dying," Chapter 9

SEX AND FEMINISM

Kate Chopin, "Story of an Hour," Chapter 4
Ellen Willis, "Memoirs of a Non-Prom Queen," Chapter 5
Tillie Olsen, "I Stand Here Ironing," Chapter 5
Maxine Hong Kingston, "No-Name Woman," Chapter 3
Grace Paley, "Wants," Chapter 3
Joan Didion, "Some Dreamers of the Golden Dream," Chapter 6
Robin Lakoff, "You Are What You Say," Chapter 7
Nora Ephron, "Reunion," Chapter 9
Toni Morrison, "Cinderella's Stepsisters," Chapter 10

THE INDIVIDUAL AND SOCIETY

May Sarton, from *Journal of a Solitude*, Chapter 2
Henry David Thoreau, from *Selected Journals*, Chapter 2
Anne Frank, from *The Diary of a Young Girl*, Chapter 2
Benjamin Franklin, from the *Autobiography*, Chapter 3
Philip Slater, "A Modern Fable," Chapter 3
Richard Wright, "The Ethics of Living Jim Crow," Chapter 3
——————"My Library Card," Chapter 5
George Orwell, "A Hanging," Chapter 3
Kate Chopin, "Story of an Hour," Chapter 4
Alvin and Heidi Toffler, "The Changing American Family," Chapter 4
Tillie Olsen, "I Stand Here Ironing," Chapter 5
Ellen Willis, "Memoirs of a Non-Prom Queen," Chapter 5
David Bird, "Two Homeless Persons Adrift in Grand Central," Chapter 6
Kurt Vonnegut, Jr., "Harrison Bergeron," Chapter 7
E. B. White, "Freedom," Chapter 7
Don Bauer, "Wartime in Korea," Chapter 9
Nora Ephron, "Reunion," Chapter 9
Flannery O'Connor, "Everything That Rises Must Converge," Chapter 9
Elisabeth Kübler-Ross, "The Fear of Dying," Chapter 9
Ellen Goodman, "Protection from the Prying Camera," Chapter 10
Robert Paul Smith, "Let Your Kids Alone," Chapter 10

SCIENCE AND TECHNOLOGY

George Orwell, "Some Thoughts on the Common Toad," Chapter 4
Kurt Vonnegut, Jr., "Harrison Bergeron," Chapter 7
Loren Eiseley, "The Long Loneliness," Chapter 9
Lewis Thomas, "To Err is Human," Chapter 9
Philip Slater, "A Modern Fable," Chapter 3

SPORTS AND RECREATION

Jean John, "The How-to of Terrariums," Chapter 4
Suzanne Britt Jordan, "Fun. Oh, Boy. Fun. You Could Die From It," Chapter 7

Ira Berkow, "Louis Had Style In and Out of the Ring," Chapter 8
Richard Selzer, "The Masked Marvel's Last Toehold," Chapter 6
Russell Baker, "Summer Beyond Wish," Chapter 8
Art Carey, "The Boston Marathon: Passing of an American Pastime," Chapter 10

DEATH AND DYING

Kate Chopin, "Story of an Hour," Chapter 4
William Faulkner, "A Rose for Emily," Chapter 6
Abraham Lincoln, "The Gettysburg Address," Chapter 5
George Orwell, "A Hanging," Chapter 4
Barbara Meyer, "Death Gives Life to Fond Memories," Chapter 6
Pearl Rowe, "Cookies at Midnight," Chapter 3
Richard Selzer, "The Masked Marvel's Last Toehold," Chapter 6
N. Scott Momaday, "The Way to Rainy Mountain," Chapter 6
Elisabeth Kübler Ross, "The Fear of Dying," Chapter 9

SHORT STORIES

Ernest Hemingway, "Hills Like White Elephants," Chapter 3
Grace Paley, "Wants," Chapter 3
Kate Chopin, "Story of an Hour," Chapter 4
Tillie Olsen, "I Stand Here Ironing," Chapter 5
William Faulkner, "A Rose for Emily," Chapter 6
Kurt Vonnegut, Jr., "Harrison Bergeron," Chapter 7
Ring Lardner, "Mr. and Mrs. Fix-It," Chapter 8
Flannery O'Connor, "Everything That Rises Must Converge," Chapter 9
Edgar Allan Poe, "The Tell-Tale Heart," Chapter 10

ACKNOWLEDGMENTS

❖❖

CHAPTER 1

Seamus Heaney, "The Makings of a Music: Reflections on the Poetry of Wordsworth and Keats," (The Kenneth Allott Lectures, University of Liverpool, February 9, 1978); *Preoccupations: Selected Prose 1968–1978*, London: Faber and Faber, 1980.

Ted Hughes, *Poetry in the Making*, London: Faber and Faber, 1967.

William Stafford, *Writing the Australian Crawl: Views on the Writer's Vocation*, Ann Arbor: University of Michigan Press, 1978.

Virginia Woolf, "How Should One Read a Book?" from *The Second Common Reader;* copyright © 1932 by Harcourt Brace Jovanovich, Inc.; renewed 1960 by Leonard Woolf. Reprinted by permission of the publisher. Published in the British Commonwealth in *The Common Reader:* Second Series; reprinted by permission of the Author's Literary Estate and The Hogarth Press Ltd.

CHAPTER 2

Joan Didion, "On Keeping a Notebook," from *Slouching Towards Bethlehem;* copyright © 1966, 1968 by Joan Didion. Reprinted by permission of Farrar, Straus and Giroux, Inc.

F. Scott Fitzgerald, "Conversations and Things Overheard," from "The Note-Books," in *The Crack-Up*; copyright © 1945 by New Directions Publishing Corporation. Reprinted by permission of New Directions.

Acknowledgments

Dorothy Wordsworth, from *Journals of Dorothy Wordsworth*, edited by Mary Moorman; copyright © 1971 by the Trustees of Dove Cottage. Reprinted by permission of Oxford University Press.

May Sarton, *Journal of a Solitude*; copyright © 1973 by May Sarton. Reprinted by permission of W. W. Norton & Company.

Henry David Thoreau, from *Selected Journals of Henry David Thoreau*, The New American Library.

Virginia Woolf, from *A Writer's Diary*; copyright © 1953, 1954 by Leonard Woolf, renewed 1981 by Quentin Bell and Angelica Garnett. Reprinted by permission of Harcourt Brace Jovanovich, Inc.

Anne Frank, from *The Diary of a Young Girl*. Copyright © 1952 by Otto H. Frank. Reprinted by permission of Doubleday & Company, Inc., New York City, and of Vallentine, Mitchell & Co. Ltd., London.

George Orwell, "War-time Diaries," from *The Collected Essays, Journalism and Letters of George Orwell*, Volume 2 (My Country Right or Left, 1940–1943); copyright © 1968 by Sonia Brownell Orwell. Reprinted by permission of Harcourt Brace Jovanovich, Inc., and the estate of the late George Orwell and Martin Secker & Warburg Ltd.

CHAPTER 3

William Byrd, *The Secret Diary of William Byrd of Westover, 1709–1712*, Capricorn Books, G. P. Putnam Sons, 1963.

Joan Didion, *The White Album*, New York City: Simon and Schuster, 1979.

James Thurber, "The Unicorn in the Garden," from *Fables for Our Time*, (New York: Harper & Row). Copyright © 1940 by James Thurber; copyright © 1965 by Helen Thurber.

Benjamin Franklin, *Autobiography and Selections from His Other Writings*, Indianapolis: Bobbs-Merrill, 1952.

Philip Slater, "A Modern Fable," from *The Pursuit of Loneliness*; copyright © 1976 by Philip Slater. Reprinted by permission of Beacon Press, Boston.

Maxine Hong Kingston, "No Name Woman," from *The Woman Warrior*. Copyright © 1975, 1976 by Maxine Hong Kingston. Reprinted by permission of Alfred A. Knopf, Inc.

512 Acknowledgments

Pearl Rowe, "Cookies at Midnight," *Pittsburgh Press*, June 8, 1980; first printed in *The Los Angeles Times*.

Ernest Hemingway, "*Hills Like White Elephants*," from *Men Without Women*. Copyright © 1927 by Charles Scribner's Sons; renewed 1955 by Ernest Hemingway. Reprinted with the permission of Charles Scribner's Sons.

Richard Wright, "The Ethics of Living Jim Crow," from *Uncle Tom's Children*. Copyright © 1937 by Richard Wright; renewed 1965 by Ellen Wright. Reprinted by permission of Harper & Row, Publishers, Inc.

Grace Paley, "Wants," from *Enormous Changes at the Last Minute;* copyright © 1971, 1974 by Grace Paley. Reprinted by permission of Farrar, Straus and Giroux, Inc.

George Orwell, "A Hanging," from *Shooting an Elephant and Other Essays;* Copyright © 1945, 1946, 1949, 1950 by Sonia Brownell Orwell; renewed, 1973, 1974 by Sonia Orwell. Reprinted by permission of Harcourt Brace Jovanovich, Inc., Mrs. Sonia Brownell Orwell, the estate of the late George Orwell, and Martin Secker & Warburg, Ltd.

CHAPTER 4

Craig Claibourne, "Cheese Soufflé," from *The New York Times Cookbook*. Copyright © 1961 by Craig Claibourne. Reprinted by permission of Harper & Row, Publishers, Inc.

Kai T. Erikson, *Everything in Its Path*, New York City: Simon and Schuster, 1976.

Jean Johns, "The 'How To' of Terrariums," Mamaroneck (N.Y.) *Daily Times*, November 2, 1973.

Sam Long, "How to Sharpen a Knife," from *Scissors Sam Says Be Sharp*. Copyright © 1972 by Calvin Long. Reprinted by permission of Capra Press.

Dick Gregory, "Farewell to Food," from *Up from Nigger*. Copyright © 1976 by Dick Gregory. Reprinted with permission of Stein and Day Publishers.

Kate Chopin, "Story of an Hour." See *Complete Works of Kate Chopin*, Baton Rouge: Louisiana State University Press, 1969.

Alvin and Heidi Toffler, "The Changing American Family," from *The*

Family Weekly, March 21, 1981; copyright © 1981 by Alvin and Heidi Toffler. Reprinted by permission of Curtis Brown, Ltd.,

George Orwell, "Some Thoughts on the Common Toad," from *Shooting an Elephant and Other Essays;* Copyright © 1945, 1946, 1949, 1950 by Sonia Brownell Orwell; renewed, 1973, 1974 by Sonia Orwell. Reprinted by permission of Harcourt Brace Jovanovich, Inc., Mrs. Sonia Brownell Orwell, the estate of the late George Orwell, and Martin Secker & Warburg, Ltd.

Muriel Rukeyser, "The Process of Writing a Poem," from *The Life of Poetry*. Reprinted by permission of International Creative Management, Inc.; copyright © 1949, 1975.

CHAPTER 5

Jean L'Anselme, "Falling Bricks," from *The Ring Around the World*, Translated from the French by Michael Benedikt. Copyright, Rapp and Whiting Ltd.

Selma Fraiberg, "A Fable" from "All About Witches, Ogres, Tigers, and Mental Health," and "Why Does a Baby Smile?" from *The Magic Years*. (New York: Charles Scribner's Sons, 1959) Copyright © 1959 by Selma H. Fraiberg. Reprinted with the permission of Charles Scribner's Sons.

Tillie Olsen, "I Stand Here Ironing," from *Tell Me a Riddle*. Copyright © 1956 by Tillie Olsen. Reprinted by permission of Delacorte Press/Seymour Lawrence.

Richard Wright, "My Library Card," from *Black Boy*. Copyright 1937, 1942, 1944, 1945 by Richard Wright. Reprinted by permission of Harper & Row, Publishers, Inc.

Ellen Willis, "Memoirs of a Non-Prom Queen," from *Rolling Stone*, August 26, 1976. Reprinted by permission of Ellen Willis/Clarke Literary Agency, Inc.; copyright © 1976 by Rolling Stone.

John Holt, "How Teachers Make Children Hate Reading," from *The Underachieving School*, Pitman Publishing Corporation; first printed in *Redbook Magazine*, November 1967. Copyright © 1967 by John Holt; reprinted by permission.

Tom Wolfe, "The Sexed-Up, Doped-Up, Hedonistic Heaven of the Boom Boom '70s," *Life* Magazine, December 1979; copyright © 1979 by Tom Wolfe.

CHAPTER 6

David Byrd, "Two Homeless Persons Adrift in Grand Central," *The New York Times*, March 20, 1981. Copyright © 1981 by The New York Times Company. Reprinted by permission.

Barbara Meyer, "Death Gives Life to Fond Memories," *The New York Times*, April 20, 1980. Copyright © 1980 by The New York Times Company. Reprinted by permission.

Richard Selzer, "The Masked Marvel's Last Toehold," from *Confessions of a Knife*; copyright © 1979 by David Goldman and Janet Selzer, Trustees. Reprinted by permission of Simon & Shuster, a Division of Gulf & Western Corporation.

Alfred Kazin, "The Kitchen," from *A Walker in the City*. Copyright © 1951, 1979 by Alfred Kazin. Reprinted by permission of Harcourt Brace Jovanovich, Inc.

N. Scott Momaday, "The Way to Rainy Mountain," from *The Way to Rainy Mountain*, Albuquerque: University of New Mexico Press; copyright © 1976 by N. Scott Momaday.

Joan Didion, "Some Dreamers of the Golden Dream," from *Slouching Towards Bethlehem*; copyright © 1966, 1968 by Joan Didion. Reprinted by permission of Farrar, Straus and Giroux, Inc.

William Faulkner, "A Rose for Emily," copyright © 1930 and renewed 1958 by William Faulkner. Reprinted from *Selected Short Stories of William Faulkner*, by permission of Random House, Inc.

CHAPTER 7

Simon de Beauvoir, *The Second Sex*, edited and translated by H. M. Parshley, New York City: Alfred A. Knopf, 1953. Reprinted by permission.

Ruth Benedict, "Preface," *Patterns of Culture*, Mentor Books, 1960

Leo Rosten, "Bubeleh," from *The Joys of Yiddish*; copyright © 1968 by Leo Rosten. Reprinted by permission of McGraw-Hill Book Company.

Suzanne Britt Jordan, "Fun. Oh, Boy. Fun. You Could Die From It," *New York Times*, December 23, 1979. Copyright © 1979 by The New York Times Company. Reprinted by permission.

Russell Baker, "American Fat," from *So This Is Depravity* (New York: St. Martins Press, 1980); copyright © 1973, 1980 by Russell Baker. Reprinted by permission of the Harold Matson Company, Inc.

Robin Lakoff, "Your Are What You Say", *Ms* Magazine, July 1974. Copyright © 1974 by Robin Lakoff. Reprinted by permission.

E. B. White, "Freedom," from *One Man's Meat*. Copyright © 1940. 1968 by E. B. White. Reprinted by permission of Harper & Row, Publishers, Inc.

Claude Brown, "The Language of Soul," from *Esquire Magazine*, April 1968; copyright © 1968 by Claude Brown. Reprinted by permission of the Sterling Lord Agency, Inc.

Kurt Vonnegut, Jr., "Harrison Bergeron," from *Welcome to the Monkey House*, copyright © 1961 by Kurt Vonnegut, Jr.; reprinted by permission of Delacorte Press/Seymour Lawrence. Originally published in *The Magazine of Fantasy and Science Fiction*.

CHAPTER 8

E. B. White, "This Life I Lead," from *One Man's Meat*. Copyright © 1938, 1966 by E. B. White. Reprinted by permission of Harper & Row, Publishers, Inc.

William Safire, "I Led the Pigeons to the Flag," *New York Times*, May 22, 1979. Copyright © 1979 by The New York Times Company. Reprinted by permission.

Susan Page, "All About Pigeons," the *Atlantic Monthly*, November 1974; copyright © 1974 by The Atlantic Monthly Company, Boston 02116. Reprinted by permission.

Ira Berkow, "Louis Had Style In and Out of the Ring," *New York Times*, April 14, 1981. Copyright © 1981 by The New York Times Company. Reprinted by permission.

David Marcus, "An Older Brother Lets Go," *Brown Daily Herald* (Providence, Rhode Island), October 10, 1980. Copyright © 1980 by David Marcus.

Ring Lardner, "Mr. and Mrs. Fix-It," copyright 1925, 1953 by Ellis A. Lardner. From *Best Short Stories of Ring Lardner*, copyright © 1957 by Charles Scribner's Sons. Reprinted with permission of Charles Scribner's Sons.

Russell Baker, "Summer Beyond Wish," from *So This Is Depravity* (New York: St. Martins Press, 1980); copyright © 1973, 1980 by Russell Baker. Reprinted by permission of the Harold Matson Company, Inc.

Mary McCarthy, "Names," from *Memories of a Catholic Girlhood*. Copyright © 1957 by Mary McCarthy. Reprinted by permission of Harcourt Brace Jovanovich, Inc.

CHAPTER 9

George Kelly, *Theory of Personality: Psychology of Personal Constructs*, New York City: W. W. Norton, 1963.

Jean Paul Sartre, "Reading," from *The Words*. Translation copyright © 1964 by George Braziller, Inc.

Ted Hughes, *Poetry in the Making*, London: Faber and Faber, 1967.

Don Bauer, "Wartime in Korea," *New York Times*, March 21, 1981. Copyright © 1981 by The New York Times Company. Reprinted by permission.

Russell Baker, "School vs. Education," from *So This Is Depravity* (New York: St. Martins Press, 1980); copyright © 1973, 1980 by Russell Baker. Reprinted by permission of the Harold Matson Company, Inc.

Nora Ephron, "Reunion," from *Crazy Salad: Some Things About Women*. Copyright © 1972 by Nora Ephron. Reprinted by permission of Alfred A. Knopf, Inc.

Joe McGinniss, "The Village," from *Going to Extremes*. Copyright © 1980 by Joe McGinniss. Reprinted by arrangement with The New American Library, Inc., New York City.

Flannery O'Connor, "Everything That Rises Must Converge," from *Everything That Rises Must Converge*, copyright © 1961, 1965 by the estate of Mary Flannery O'Connor. Reprinted by permission of Farrar, Straus and Giroux, Inc.

Elisabeth Kübler-Ross, "On the Fear of Death," from *On Death and Dying*. Copyright © 1969 by Elisabeth Kübler-Ross. Reprinted with permission of Macmillan Publishing Co., Inc.

Loren Eiseley, "The Long Loneliness," from *The Star Thrower*. First printed in *The American Scholar* 30:1 (December 1960); copyright © 1978 by the Estate of Loren C. Eiseley. Reprinted by permission of Times Books, a division of Quadrangle/The New York Times Book Co., Inc.

CHAPTER 10

Gerard Manley Hopkins, "St. Winefred's Well," from *Poems of Gerard Manley Hopkins*, New York City: Oxford University Press, 1967.

Art Carey, "The Boston Marathon: Passing of an American Pastime," *The New York Times*, April 20, 1980. Copyright © 1980 by The New York Times Company. Reprinted by permission.

Ellen Goodman, "Protection From the Prying Camera," from *Close to Home*, Fawcett Crest Books. Copyright © 1979 by the Boston Globe Newspaper Company/Washington Post Writers Group. Reprinted with permission.

Margaret Mead, "Grandparents Have Copped Out," *New York Times*, June 12, 1971. Copyright © 1971 by The New York Times Company. Reprinted by permission.

Lewis Thomas, "To Err is Human," from *The Medusa and the Snail: More Notes of a Biology Watcher*. Copyright © 1976 by Lewis Thomas. Originally published in the *New England Journal of Medicine*. Reprinted by permission of Viking Penguin, Inc.

Robert Paul Smith, "Let Your Kids Alone," from *Life* Magazine, January 27, 1958; copyright © 1958. Reprinted by permission of International Creative Management.

Jonathan Swift, "A Modest Proposal." See *Jonathan Swift: A Selection of His Works*, New York City: Odyssey Press, 1965.

George Orwell, "Politics and the English Language", from *Shooting an Elephant and Other Essays*. Copyright © 1945, 1946, 1949, 1950 by Sonia Brownell Orwell; renewed, 1973, 1974 by Sonia Orwell. Reprinted by permission of Harcourt Brace Jovanovich, Inc., Mrs. Sonia Brownell Orwell, the estate of the late George Orwell, and Martin Secker & Warburg, Ltd.

Edgar Allan Poe, "The Tell-Tale Heart." See *Complete Stories and Poems of Edgar Allan Poe*, New York City: Doubleday.

Toni Morrison, "Cinderella's Stepsisters," from *Ms.* Magazine, September 1979. Copyright © 1979 by Toni Morrison.

Martin Luther King, Jr., "I Have a Dream"; Copyright © 1963 by Martin Luther King, Jr. Reprinted by permission of Joan Daves.

INDEX

❖ ❖

"Abraham and Isaac", 74–75
abstract, 70, 73, 321
Aesop, 76
"All About Pigeons" (Page), 327–37
"American Fat" (Baker), 285–87
argument, xi, 438, 441
assertion, 442
associations, 14
Autobiography (Franklin), 82–83

Baker, Russell, 7, 285, 354, 379
Bauer, Don, 377
Benedict, Ruth, 278
Berkow, Ira, 338
Bible, the, 74
Bierce, Ambrose, 275
Bird, David, 220
Blair, Eric, 103
"The Boston Marathon: Passing of an American Pastime" (Carey), 445–47

Brown, Claude, 300
"Bubeleh/Bobeleh," 280
Bullfinch's Mythology, 77
Byrd, William, 19

Carey, Art, 445
cause and effect, 153, 156, 439
change, 116, 439, 440
"The Changing American Family" (Toffler), 135–40
Chopin, Kate, 132
"Cinderella's Stepsisters" (Morrison), 494–96
Claibourne, Craig, 111–113
classifying, 274
comparing, 368, 371
Conan Doyle, Sir Arthur, 6
concrete, 70, 73, 156, 217, 321, 376
"Congratulations to a Critic" (Einstein), 21
a construct, 368
"Cookies at Midnight" (Rowe), 88–91

de Beauvoir, Simone, 274
"A Death Gives Life to Fond Memories" (Meyer), 224–26
deduction, 442
defining, xi, 273, 374, 439
definitions
    extended, 278
    lexical, 273, 277
    stipulative, 277
describing, xi, 211, 439
details, 218
The Devil's Dictionary (Bierce), 276
The Diary of a Young Girl (Frank), 20, 52–56
diaries, 18
Dickens, Charles, 213, 273
dictionary definition, 273
Didion, Joan, 18, 22, 67, 234
distinguishing characteristics, 274, 374
dying metaphor, 478

"Echo and Narcissus" (Ovid), 77–79
Einstein, Albert, 21
Eiseley, Loren, 426
Ephron, Nora, 382
Erikson, Kai T., 113
"The Ethics of Living Jim Crow" (Wright), 97–99
evaluation, xi, 72, 115, 217, 376
"Everything That Rises Must Converge" (O'Connor), 406–21
"Everything in Its Path" (Erikson), 113–14
exemplifying, 315, 320, 439
expectations, 12
extended definition, 278

fables, 70, 154
"Falling Bricks" (L'Anselme), 161–62
"Farewell to Food" (Gregory), 123–31
Faulkner, William, 260
"The Fear of Dying" (Kübler–Ross), 421–25
figure and ground, 374
Fitzgerald, F. Scott, 30
folk etymology, 325
Fraiberg, Selma, 162
Frank, Anne, 20, 52
Franklin, Benjamin, 82
"Freedom" (White), 295–300
Frost, Robert, xi, 6
"Fun. Oh, Boy. Fun. You Could Die from It" (Jordan), 282–84

generalization, 318, 320, 373
"The Gettysburg Address" (Lincoln), 174–75
Goodman, Ellen, 448
"Grandparents Have Copped Out" (Mead), 451–54
The Grasmere Journals (Wordsworth), 33–37
Great Expectations (Dickens), 213–14
Gregory, Dick, 123
ground, 374

"A Hanging" (Orwell), 13, 103–108
Hard Times (Dickens), 273

"Harrison Bergeron" (Vonnegut), 307–13
Hemingway, Ernest, 92
"Hills Like White Elephants" (Hemingway), 92–96
Hobson–Jobson, 325
Holmes, Sherlock, 6
Holt, John, 188
homophone, 326
Hopkins, Gerard Manley, 114
"How Should One Read a Book?" (Woolf), 10
"How Teachers Make Children Hate Reading" (Holt) 188–98
how-to, 111
"The 'How To' of Terrariums" (John), 118–20
"How to Sharpen Knives" (Long), 120–122
Hughes, Ted, 371

"I Have a Dream" (King), 438, 497–501
"I Led the Pigeons to the Flag" (Safire), 323–27
induction, 442
inference, 5, 158
"I Stand Here Ironing" (Olsen), 4, 166–74

James, William, 69
John, Jean, 118
Jordan, Suzanne Britt, 282
Journal of a Solitude (Sarton), 38–41
journals, 18, 21, 63
        keeping a journal, 63–65, 72, 151, 502
The Journals (Thoreau), 42–48

Kazin, Alfred, 232
Kelly, George, 368–69
King, Martin Luther, Jr. 438, 497
Kingston, Maxine Hong, 70, 85
"The Kitchen" (Kazin), 232–37
Kübler–Ross, Elisabeth, 421

Labov, William, xi
L'Anselme, Jean, 161

Lakoff, Robin, 288
"The Language of Soul" (Brown), 300–306
Lardner, Ring, 344
"Lee" (Bird), 222
"Let Your Kids Alone" (Smith), 458–65
lexical definition, 273, 277
Lincoln, Abraham, 174
"Louis Had Style In and Out of the Ring" (Berkow), 338–40
"The Long Loneliness" (Eiseley), 426–33
Long, Sam, 120

"Madeline" (Bird), 220
The Magic Years (Fraiberg), 154–55
malapropism, 325
Marcus, David, 341
"The Masked Marvel's Last Toehold" (Selzer), 227–32
McCarthy, Mary, 357
McGinniss, Joe, 390
Mead, Margaret, 451
meaningless words, 480
"Memoirs of a Non-Prom Queen" (Willis), 185–87
metanalysis, 325
metaphor, 373, 478
Meyer, Barbara, 224
"A Modern Fable" (Slater), 83–84
"A Modest Proposal" (Swift), 466–74
Momaday, N. Scott, 238
mondegreen, 326
Morrison, Toni, 494
moving picture, 213
"Mr. and Mrs. Fix-It" (Lardner), 344–53
"My Library Card" (Wright), 176–84
mythology, 153

"Names" (McCarthy), 357–65
narrative, 69, 71, 158, 318
narrative core, xi
"No Name Woman" (Kingston), 85–87

"The North Wind and the Sun" (Aesop), 76
notebooks, 18
The Note-Books (Fitzgerald), 30–33

observation, 5, 158
O'Connor, Flannery, 406
"An Older Brother Lets Go" (Marcus), 341–43
Olsen, Tillie, 4, 166
"On Keeping a Notebook" (Didion), 18, 22–29
once, 70, 317, 374
One Man's Meat (White), 316
operators (verbal false limbs), 478
ordinary/extraordinary, 71, 374
Orwell, George, 13, 20, 57, 103, 141, 475
    rules for writing, 487
overview, 113
Ovid, 77

Page, Susan, 327
Paley, Grace, 100
Patterns of Culture, 278
persuasion, 439, 443
Poe, Edgar Allan, 489
Poetry in the Making (Hughes), 372
point of view, 214, 217
"Politics and the English Language" (Orwell), 475–88
pretentious diction, 479
procedure, 110
    and narrative, 114
"The Process of Writing a Poem" (Rukeyser), 145–149
"Protection from the Prying Camera" (Goodman), 448–50

Rawnsley, Rev. Canon, 9
"Removal" (White), 316–17
"Reunion" (Ephron), 382–87
"A Rose for Emily" (Faulkner), 260–69
Rosten, Leo, 280

Rowe, Pearl, 88
Rukeyser, Muriel, 145

Safire, William, 323
Sarton, May, 20, 38
Sartre, Jean Paul, 369
"School vs. Education" (Baker), 379–81
The Second Sex (de Beauvoir), 274
"A Secret Diary" (Byrd), 19–20
selecting, 115, 215
Selzer, Richard, 227
sequencing, 115
"The Sexed-up, Doped-up, Hedonistic Heaven of the Boom-Boom 70s" (Wolfe), 199–207
Slater, Philip, 83
Smith, Robert Paul, 458
snapshot, 212
"Some Dreamers of the Golden Dream" (Didion), 218, 234–59
"Some Thoughts on the Common Toad" (Orwell), 141–44
Soufflé, Cheese (Claibourne), 111–12
so what? 73, 115
"The Speckled Band" (Conan Doyle), 6
"St. Winefred's Well" (Hopkins), 114–15
Stafford, William, 5
stipulative definition, 277
"The Story of an Hour" (Chopin), 132–34
"Summer Beyond Wish" (Baker), 7, 354–56
Swift, Jonathan, 466

tension, 71
"The Tell-Tale Heart" (Poe), 489–93
then and now, 374, 439
then what? 156
Thomas, Lewis, 454
Thoreau, Henry David, 42
Thurber, James, 80
"To Err Is Human" (Thomas), 454–57

Toffler, Alvin, 135
Toffler, Heidi, 135
tone, 443
"Two Homeless Persons Adrift in Grand Central" (Bird), 220–24

"The Unicorn in the Garden" (Thurber), 80–81

"The Village" (McGinniss), 390–405
Vonnegut, Kurt, Jr., 307

"Wants" (Paley), 100–102
War-Time Diary: 1940 (Orwell), 57–63
"Wartime in Korea" (Bauer), 377–79
The Way to Rainy Mountain (Momaday), 238–42
The White Album (Didion), 69
White, E. B., 2, 295, 316
why? 153–54, 155–56
"Why Does the Baby Smile?" (Fraiberg), 162–65
Willis, Ellen, 185
Wittgenstein, Ludwig, xi, 217
Wolfe, Tom, 199
Woolf, Virginia, 10, 48
The Words (Sartre), 370–71
Wordsworth, Dorothy, 20, 33
Wordsworth, William, xi, 8
Wright, Richard, 97, 176
A Writer's Diary (Woolf), 48–52
"Writing the Australian Crawl," 5

"You Are What You Say" (Lakoff), 288–94